DAVID ARONSON

PAINTINGS · DRAWINGS · SCULPTURE

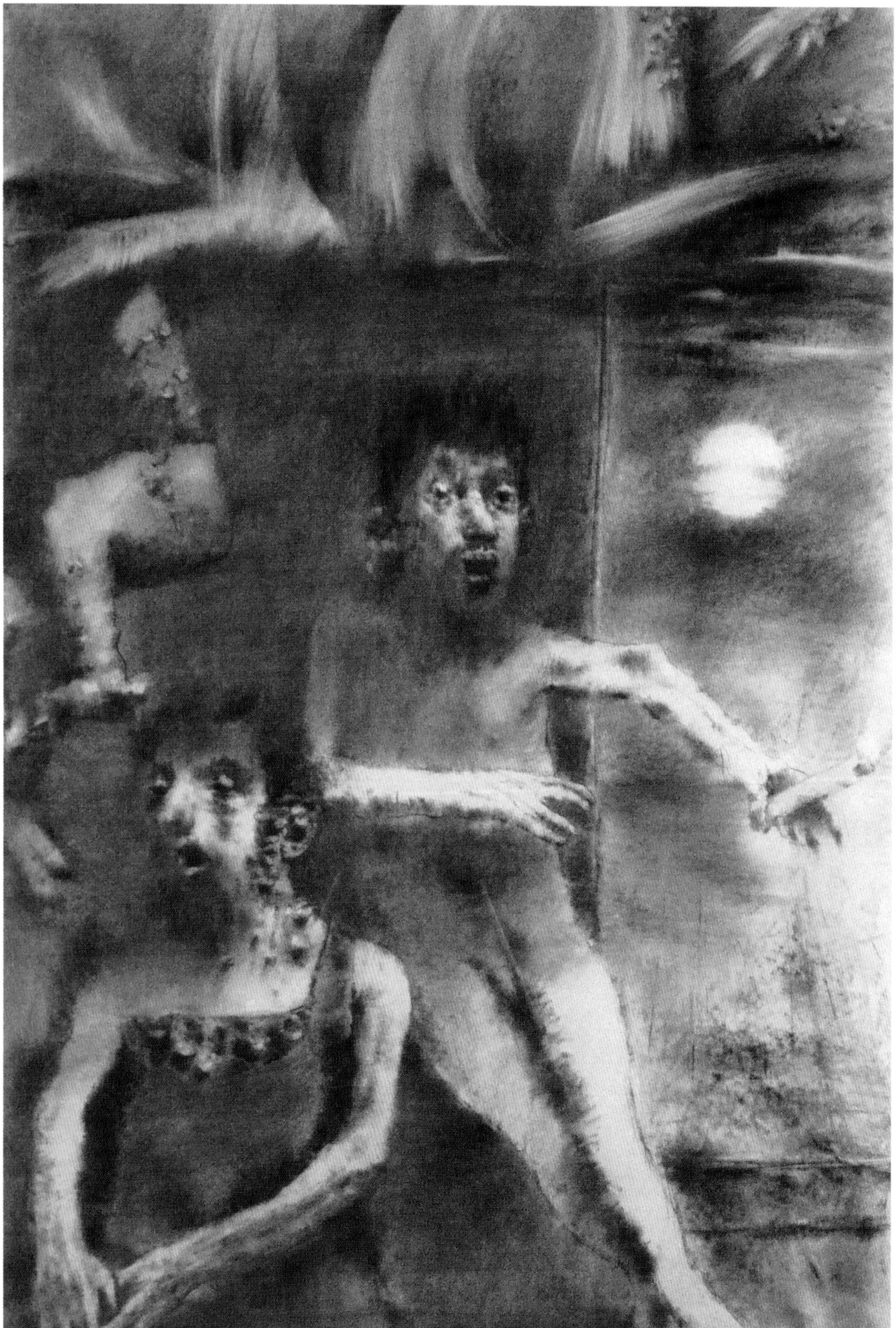

Moonworshipers, 1960
charcoal
80 x 48"
Private Collection

DAVID ARONSON

PAINTINGS · DRAWINGS · SCULPTURE

Interpretive essay by
ASHER D. BIEMANN

Reproduction of 1967 Boston University Lecture by
DAVID ARONSON

Afterward by
BERNARD H. PUCKER

PUCKER ART PUBLICATIONS · BOSTON · 2004

DAVID ARONSON

PAINTINGS • DRAWINGS • SCULPTURE

Published by Pucker Art Publications
2004

PUCKER GALLERY
171 Newbury Street
Boston, MA 02116
Tel: 617.267.9473
Fax: 617.424.9759
Email: contactus@puckergallery.com
www.puckergallery.com

DESIGNED
by Leslie Anne Feagley

EDITED
by Jeanne Vee Koles

PHOTO EDITING
by Kenneth Gray

Library of Congress Cataloging-in-Publication Data
Aronson, David, 1923- David Aronson : paintings, drawings, sculpture / with an interpretive text by Asher D. Biemann ; reproduction of 1967 Boston University lecture by David Aronson ; afterward by Bernard H. Pucker.
p. cm.
Includes bibliographical references and index.
ISBN 1-879985-12-8
1. Aronson, David, 1923---Catalogs. I. Biemann, Asher D. II. Title.

N6537.A7132A4 2004
709'.2--dc22

2004009673

Printed in China by South China Printing Company Limited

Distributed by Syracuse University Press
www.SyracuseUniversityPress.syr.edu

aronson

TABLE OF CONTENTS

To my parents
whose foresight removed their family
from the path of the oncoming Holocaust
— D.A.

To my father
Who has taught me to see, love art, and rebel
— A.D.B.

THE MAGIC REBEL:
THE WORK OF DAVID ARONSON

THE PARADOX

WE BEGIN WITH *THE PARADOX* of 1942 (Fig. 1). David Aronson was only 19 years old and a second-year student at the School of the Museum of Fine Arts, Boston, better known as the "Museum School,"[1] when he completed the painting. "I painted a picture of a group of characters passing the time in a cafe," he wrote more than two decades later. "Against the back wall arose two Gothic church windows, and on the right, serving to support one of the figure's arms, was a 2x3-inch panel upon which was hung a motley collection of jewel-like junk."[2] It was in this panel that the young artist could best demonstrate his technical skills. An assortment of randomly chosen, unrelated objects is carefully spread out before us in great detail and *trompe-l'œil* realism: Rings, gems, the dial of a phone, mechanical parts, a small drawing, buttons, a magnifying glass showing enlarged letters, and much else that cannot easily be identified. The paradox unfolds when, in an unnaturally collapsed space, the panel begins to also serve as a table, the objects oscillating between hanging by their own weight and soaring in the air. A tiny figure emerges at the bottom, reaching towards the objects; another is oddly placed beneath the panel, squeezed into the lower corner of the painting. Lured into a deceptive realism of things, our eyes are puzzled by the juxtaposition of miniature life and *nature morte,* a contrast that reduplicates itself in the "real life" characters. Like the objects in the panel, the people in the cafe seem to be placed into random relation without ever belonging together. They have come to socialize, but their recognition of each other is strangely impaired. Where intimacy emerges, as in the couple quietly holding hands, an onlooker from behind threatens their privacy; where conversation occurs, as in the couple in front, an active third listener prevents it from turning into dialogue. A woman casually leaning against the table has withdrawn from all human interaction surrounding her; but her indifference also grants her independence. We see a waiter in the background. His power to act upon the group without belonging to it sets him apart from the other characters: He becomes the ultimate bystander to the scene. It is through him that our eyes wander to the pair of Gothic windows rising in the back of the room. We have seen that Aronson later referred to them as "church windows," windows whose mere shape attaches a spiritual element to an overwhelmingly mundane representation. But unlike for the Gothic architect, whose utmost goal was to replace masonry with light, the light in Aronson's windows remains oddly subdued and mysterious, only adding to an already gloomy atmosphere. If the windows do indeed suggest sacrality, then it is a sacrality that seems displaced and called into question by the secular setting. The sacred and the profane, if such categories even apply, seem to be blended into each other, and we do not know whether the sacred has been profaned or the profane sacralized. What we see, then, is a trifold realism, the realism of things, crisp, colorful, and deceptive; the realism of the human, misshapen, introverted, and filled with a quiet anxiety; and the realism of what one might call the spiritual, opaque, veiled, and mystical. These realisms, these "seeming incompatibles and incongruities," as the artist notes,[3] are paradoxical in the usual sense of the word: They are unexpected, incomprehensible,

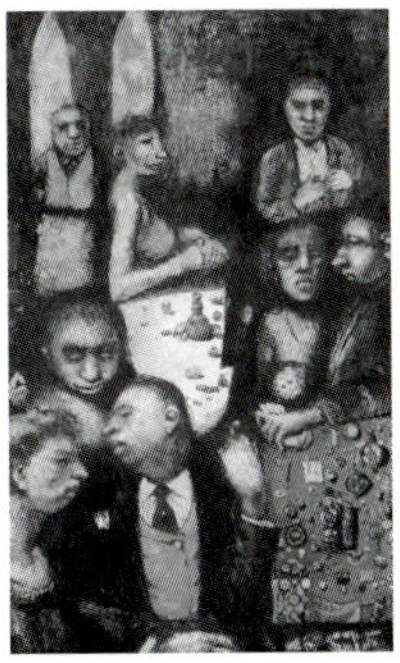

Figure 1

senseless. But they are also paradoxical in the sense of reaching beyond what the Greek word *doxa* implied to the philosophers: They reach beyond mere opinion, belief, delusion.

The Paradox may well be considered a formative painting in David Aronson's career. On a conscious level, Aronson admits, it reflected no more than a "flippant observation on society;"[4] on a hidden level, however, it touched upon streaks of alienation, religious upheaval, and a quest for the meaning of reality, all of which are recurring undercurrents in Aronson's work.

The Paradox also set the tone for the young Aronson's stylistic leanings. The meticulous illusionism of the 17th century Haarlem painters and the magic realism of William Harnett (1848-1892), Salvadore Dali (1904-1989), and Ivan Albright (1897-1983) are named as sources of inspiration.[5] One is also reminded of the work of Jack Levine (b. 1915), especially of his 1937 painting *The Feast of Pure Reason,* which mockingly aimed at the Boston upper middle class.[6] But we can most readily identify allusions to the German Expressionists and post-Expressionists of the 1920s and early 1930s. If we are to place David Aronson's work into the context of a particular school, then, it would have to be Expressionism, or more accurately, the Boston Expressionism that manifested itself in the post World War II era.[7] Boston Expressionism, as we will see, was the product of a substantial reception of European—particularly German—Expressionist art that began in the mid 1930s and extended through the late 1950s. The work of David Aronson not only belonged to this movement, but also helped shape its course.

EXPRESSIONISM IN THE GERMAN CONTEXT

Most historians agree that the term "Expressionism" emerged in the early 1910s from the German reception of the French "wild" painters *(les fauves)* associated with the circle around Henri Matisse (1869-1954).[8] In the preface to the catalogue of the 1911 Berlin Secession exhibition, the young independent painters from Paris, Georges Braque (1882-1963), Pablo Picasso (1881-1973), and Maurice de Vlaminck (1876-1958) among them, were referred to as "Expressionists."[9] "Expressionism," though anything but clearly defined, soon advanced to a diffusive vogue word among critics, labeling art, literature, music, cinema, and philosophy alike. It became synonymous with aesthetic protest, social revolution, and counter-culture in a larger sense. It described the mood of an entire generation rebelling against the repressive cultures of Imperial Germany and the Habsburg monarchy. "We want to create freedom of elbows and freedom of life *(Arm-und Lebensfreiheit)* against the well-fed forces of old," read Ernst Ludwig Kirchner's manifesto of *Die Brücke* already in 1906.[10] In the years preceding World War I, Expressionism, *Neue Kunst* (New Art), and Post-Impressionism were interchangeable terms for an art direction that reveled in the crudeness of reality, uninhibited vitality, and the renunciation of all aesthetic norm. "They know no program and no restraint," wrote Franz Marc in 1912 in the artist's almanac *Der Blaue Reiter:* "They only want to venture forward at all cost, like a stream wherein all possible and impossible is swept along, putting their trust in an all-purifying power."[11] The "wild" art, Marc continues, aimed not only at an innovation of form and style but at a "rebirth of thought" *(Neugeburt des Denkens),* at the "reawakening" of mysticism and of the "primordial elements in art." From its very beginnings, Expressionism articulated an attitude of life rather than a stylistic program. *Creating* reality rather than *representing* it, became the new credo. Despite their lack of stylistic coherence and reluctance to be subsumed under a homogeneous *nom de guerre,* the Expressionists—or those who came to be called Expressionists—shared a disdain for impressionist naturalism, rebelled against the aestheticization of reality, and the harmonization of feeling, promoting, instead, their quest for emotional truthfulness, a perception of reality that was entwined in the contradictions and absurdities of the human condition. "Expressionism is a worldview, impressionism is a fashion," the periodical *Der Sturm* (The Storm) declared.[12] When, in 1914, Paul Fechter published the first monograph on Expressionism, he characterized the movement precisely as a rebellion against materialist society, against the aestheticism of the beautiful, against bourgeois impressionism: "The decorative had to become secondary, the heightened humanity and spirituality essential."[13] Expressionism, for Fechter, who was clearly influenced by Kandinsky's famous tractate *Über das Geistige in der Kunst* (Concerning the Spiritual in Art) of 1912, meant nothing inherently new but, rather, a "becoming aware of the original meaning and emotional significance of artistic creativity as such."[14] It represented a rebirth of an "age-old metaphysical longing," a mystical "Weltgefühl" whose roots reached back to mediaeval culture and to the worldview of the Gothic. In Fechter's Germanocentric view, Expressionism signified a turning away from scientific "intellectualism" and a return to the "mysticism of the heart." "It is no longer our task to perceive, but to experience *(erleben)*," he wrote, "to climb the regions of the soul that correspond to [the feeling] that created the work of art."[15] This process of re-experiencing, of noncognitive, purely emotional consonance, established the bridge between artist and observer; not empathy, but evocation of feeling. The purer the feeling, the truer the equivalence of emotion. It was for this reason that Wassily Kandinsky marveled at the universal accessibility of primitive art, for "like ourselves, these pure artists sought to express only inner and essential feelings in their works."[16] To Kandinsky, the "awakening soul," purified of the "nightmare of materialism," was about to return to the genuineness of feeling and spirit, expressing itself in expression only, in a "form that is able to stir the senses."[17]

Such stirring of the senses characterized the early period of Expressionism, ranging from what Fechter called "intensive" (i.e. world-negating) Expressionism to "extensive" (i.e. world-affirming) Expressionism.[18] When, in 1916, Hermann Bahr, the relentless critic of culture, described the movement as a "single cry for help" *(ein einziger Notschrei)*, he captured the distress of the time and the tone that prevailed in many images: "The human being screams after his soul."[19]

In the years immediately following World War I, the first great disaster for 20th century Europe, and greater even for defeated Germany, this "cry for help" reached its climax. "We must devote our hearts and nerves to the cries of pain from the poor deceived people," Max Beckmann wrote in his "confession" in 1918. "Now is the time for us to be as close as possible to humanity."[20] Artists, writers, and intellectuals rallied around the common cause of infusing a downtrodden society and war-corrupted politics with "spirit" *(Geist)* and "deed" *(Tat)*. Kurt Hiller's "activist" program of 1917 called for a "reshaping of the world following the command of the idea."[21] In November 1918, the "Council of Spiritual Workers" *(Rat geistiger Arbeiter)* vowed to "erase slavery of any kind from the surface of the earth," demanding political and social reforms that included, among other things, the establishment of a pan-national parliament, the abolishment of all military institutions, the socialization of all land, the separation of church and state, and the freedom of sexual orientation.[22] The intellectual as proletarian, as *Arbeiter am Geist* (Worker at the Spirit) with a utopian vision of a better humanity became a common motif of the time. Max Pechstein's frontispiece to the 1919 pamphlet *An alle Künstler!* (To All Artists!) reflected a similar notion: The artist rises above a city of smokestacks, his outstretched arm reaching to unknown heights while a giant heart in his chest is consumed by wild flames. "We build into the unknown," wrote the author of *Der Geist der Utopie* in 1918, "we build into the unknown to search for the true, the real, where all that is merely factual disappears—*incipit vita nova* [let new life begin]!"[23]

The new "man of deed," lifting himself up from beneath the rubble of war, acted on behalf of what was believed to be the self-redemption of humanity. Utopia was rehabilitated. This, however, did not turn the Expressionists into idealists. On the contrary, most exponents of Expressionism, most activists of the mind, whether philosophers, poets, painters, or revolutionaries, maintained that their work represented realism of the purest kind, that it was, in fact, identical with a reality that had yet to be "realized."

It is impossible, of course, to speak of a coherent Expressionist worldview, or ideology, even within the limits of the German context. The movement saw itself too much in constant flux, spread too far across the disciplines to establish clear aesthetic and philosophical principles. It expressed a particular feeling of life in a particular time rather than formulating a specific style or idea. Thus Expressionism could attach itself to the figurative as well as to the abstract, to the mystical as well as to the rational, to emotions as well as to machines, to nationalism as well as to socialism, to the apocalyptic as well as to the utopian. It was this inner proliferation, deliberate chaotization, and above all popularization that, arguably, led to the decline of the first Expressionist era. After Kirchner and Beckmann, wrote a former apostle of Expressionism in 1920, there was nothing more than "convulsion, racket, rumpus." The young artists, Kasimir Edschmid continues, had only one thing in mind: "How can I put myself into the most twisted, spectacular, and *meschuggene* position?"[24] By 1921, Expressionism was declared "dead" or at least "dying."[25] Also dying were the hopes of the political revolutionaries of 1918/19. Their leaders had been assassinated, and the German Republic of 1920 was led by the Center Party at the exclusion of the Socialists and other liberals.

"TRANSCENDENTAL OBJECTIVITY"

Yet, at the eclipse of Expressionism, the art historian Franz Roh wrote in 1925, a "conversion" *(Bekehrung)* occurred: Instead of "phantastic dreams," our own world returned in "morning-light clarity"—"An intimately worldly, world-devout art has emerged."[26] What Roh tried to grasp was a post-Expressionist return to the "objects," the recovery of "reality in relation to its visibility." As in Expressionism, this "new realism" conceived of itself as "real" reality, but while the early Expressionists were focused on their personal emotional existence, the liberation of their own feeling, the post-Expressionists sought objectivity *(Objektnähe)* as an expression of their inner spirituality: "Not a copying, but a strict erection—creation—of objects."[27] "I do not cry," said Max Beckmann already in 1918, "I only think of the object *(Sache)*."[28] Through objectivity Beckmann could articulate an internal critique of Expressionism in decay. "From the false, sentimental mysticism of affectation we will return, I hope, to a transcendental objectivity *(transzendentale Sachlichkeit)*."[29] "Transcendental objectivity" was the paradox of the new, post-Expressionist direction. Bending the lines of "intensive" and "extensive" Expressionism, Beckmann formulated a non-materialist objectivism, a spiritual rationality, a realism that Franz Roh would later call "magic": "The mystery does not enter the world of representation but remains hidden behind it."[30] In his book *The Overcoming of Expressionism* (1927), the cultural philosopher Emil Utitz gave a similar assessment of the new movement: "The sense for the factual awakens again, but this factual has a different face than the facticity of the scientific world view. It is strangely mysterious in its undeniable corporeality, it is rational and irrational at the same time."[31]

What Beckmann, Roh, and Utitz put in philosophical terms became manifest in the 1925 exhibition *Neue Sachlichkeit* (New Objectivism)[32] in Mannheim. New Objectivism was now touted as the overcoming of an all-rebellious, hyperbolic Expressionism, a softening of the activist dissonances, a maturing, and a return to the spiritual in art, to the "true Expressionism," as Paul Westheim put it once referring to Max Beckmann.[33] In their "new desire for depersonalization,"[34] in their transcending the confines of subjectivity, the artists of New Objectivism were seen to have recaptured the humanistic spirit of "original" Expressionism. They had replaced the chaotic moralist with what Franz Roh called the "ethical homo politicus."[35] New Objectivism, then, was received as a return to the order of things as well as to the order of human life. But while the anarchy of emotion and the revolt against the political establishment seemed to have subsided, the ideals of the "wild" generation continued to exist, only in a more orderly fashion: "We seek a kind of aristocratic Bolshevism," Beckmann wrote in 1927, a society of black-tie proletarians.[36] Balance, moderation, and self-control accompanied the new world view. And the artist, the "true creator of the world," would lead the way to human freedom.

We can only mention in passing that, like Expressionism, *Neue Sachlichkeit* was at once freely hailed as the true manifestation of the German "spirit" and denounced as internationalist, in particular, Americanist, rubbish.[37] The infamous exhibition *Entartete Kunst* (Degenerate Art) of 1937 assembled over 700 pieces that were supposed to illustrate the "decay of art since 1910."

THE PARADOX AS A COMMENTARY

Here we shall return to David Aronson's painting *The Paradox*. It belongs, to be sure, to the history of what is to be considered American art, and there is no immediate biographical connection between the artist and the tangled experience of German Expressionism. Yet, it is also akin—both in subject and style—to the post-Expressionism we have encountered above. An atmospheric reference exists to the work of Otto Dix (1891-1969), George Grosz (1893-1959), and, most conspicuously, to Max Beckmann's (1884-1950) later creative period. Like many exponents of the *Neue Sachlichkeit,* Aronson chooses the café as a place of urban socialization, as a microcosmic upper city, to reveal the invisible depths of society.[38] His characters are metropolitan, members of a privileged class. They are placed in a strict compositional order that reflects their submission to social order. A stiff sterility surrounds their emotions and external appearance. Even the lovers remain *sachlich.* But their *Sachlichkeit* is not objectivity. An intense humanness emerges from their carefully heightened features, an uncouth naturalness that breaks through the cool elegance of dress. And while our eyes wander back and forth between the panel of things and the group of people, we find that objectivity has not deceived us: Things remain things and people are people, but hidden behind it all looms a mystery that cannot be unlocked.

The Paradox, then, is less an epigonous work of New Objectivism itself, than a *commentary* on it. It transcends objectivity in a way Beckmann perhaps intended when he spoke of *"transzendentale Sachlichkeit,"* an objectivism that did not objectify the mystery of reality. But it also questions the very idea of objectivism. As in the *trompe l'œil* panel, the *Sachlichkeit* of the painting is only a veil that disguises human fantasies and fears. Were we to undress the painting, so to speak, we would stare at the contorted humanity of Breughel's or Goya's universe.

KARL ZERBE AND THE MUSEUM SCHOOL

David Aronson's commentary on post-Expressionism was anything but accidental. After all, his teacher and mentor at the Boston Museum School was the German emigré painter Karl Zerbe (1903-1972), himself a descendent of German Expressionism who felt deeply influenced by Beckmann.

Born in Berlin, but growing up in Paris and Frankfurt, Zerbe briefly trained to be a chemist before becoming a student at the progressive Debschitzschule in Munich, named after Wilhelm von Debschitz (1871-1948) who, together with Hermann Obrist (1863-1927), founded the school in 1902.[39] Predating the early Bauhaus and anticipating many of its ideas, the Debschitzschule was primarily concerned with the material experience of the art work, deliberately blurring the distinctions between fine arts and applied crafts. With its strong emphasis on craftsmanship, the school encouraged its students to experiment freely with a variety of materials and techniques, rather than pursue one special medium from the start. When Karl Zerbe joined the school in 1921, its most important teachers were Joseph Eberz (1880-1942) and Karl Caspar (1879-1956), both leading figures in the German Expressionist movement.[40] Expressionism, albeit in its moderate, figurative form, would soon determine Zerbe's artistic language and, indeed, world view. Between 1924 and 1926, he became acquainted with the art of *Neue Sachlichkeit* (New Objectivism), particularly the work of Max Beckmann, George Grosz, and Otto Dix. Oskar Kokoschka (1886-1980), too, clearly influenced the young Zerbe, and it was, in fact, George Gaspari, Kokoschka's dealer in Munich, who represented Zerbe's work. Defamed by the Nationalsocialists, who would later include his work (at least one of his paintings) in the exhibition *Entartete Kunst* (Degenerate Art) of 1937, Zerbe left Germany for Boston in 1935 to first teach at the Fine Arts Guild and then become the Head of Painting at the Museum School (from 1937 to 1955), succeeding Alexandre Iacovleff (1887-1938), a Russian emigré, trained at the St. Petersburg Academy of Fine Arts. Iacovleff had directed the school between 1934 and 1937, slowly steering it away from the traditional academic values of his predecessors and introducing some of the didactic methods Zerbe would later freely adopt, such as the suspension of drawing from plaster models.[41] Within this spirit of reform, Zerbe's arrival was hailed by contemporary artists and students as a "breath of fresh air," a long overdue infusion of ideas from Europe.[42] And indeed, Zerbe's leadership soon helped radically transform the rather conservative and parochial palate that distinguished Boston from the far more progressive taste of its rival city New York.[43]

Yet, the infusion of European avant-garde ideas in Boston was not entirely the work of Karl Zerbe. As Judith Bookbinder has argued in her magisterial study on the Germanic influences in Boston Expressionism, the receptivity of Boston's cultural elite to German culture and, in fact, immigrants, reached far back into the nineteenth century and extended from its leading educational institution across the Charles River to the beginnings of the Boston Symphony Orchestra and the Museum of Fine Arts.[44] But, above all, it was the Germanic (later Busch-Reisinger) Museum at Harvard, originally founded by the German literary historian Kuno Francke in 1897 and reopened in 1921 with a grant by the St. Louis brewer Adolphus Busch, that began to function as a window to Northern European modernism in the 1930s and 1940s, showing and acquiring the very "degenerate" art Nazi Germany had forcefully excised from its culture.[45]

European modernist sources also lay at the foundation of two teachers of the older generation, Harold Zimmerman, a graduate of the Museum School and private art tutor, and Denman Ross (1853-1935), a Harvard professor emeritus and renowned theorist of chronomatics and design. Zimmerman's interest in the works of James Ensor (1860-1949), Chaim Soutine (1893-1943), Georges Rouault (1871-1958), and Paul Cézanne (1839-1903), and Ross' progressive teachings of color harmony proved to be formative to their two most influential students, Hyman Bloom (b. 1913) and Jack Levine. While Bloom, who had immigrated with his parents from Latvia in 1920, tested the limits of figurative painting and became increasingly attracted to mystical sources and Eastern philosophies, seeking the spiritual dimensions of art, Levine, a native Bostonian, maintained the role of the artist as social critic, particularly under the influence of George Grosz and the German playwright Berthold Brecht (1898-1956).[46] By the 1930s, Bloom and Levine, the latter leaving Boston in 1942 and relocating to New York after World War II, were considered the major forces behind the rise of Expressionism in Boston.

In short, by the time Karl Zerbe took over the leadership of the Museum School where he was assisted by, among others, the young David Aronson in the period between 1943 and 1954, the groundwork for a modernism specific to the Boston area had already been laid. Zerbe's role was to develop a curriculum that combined a thoroughly modernist approach to the process of painting with a conservative training in its techniques. His students were typically introduced to a range of works, including Picasso, Braque, Kokoschka, Beckmann, and the members of the German Expressionist group *Der Blaue Reiter*. Both the German New Objectivist Max Beckmann and the Austrian Expressionist Oskar Kokoschka came to lecture and teach at the Museum School in the late 1940s,[47] and it was evident that Zerbe's students, in the spirit of rebellion, preferred the collection of the Germanic Museum to the older Boston school of Impressionism.[48]

What held Zerbe's broad curriculum together was an emphatic and often anecdotal adherence to the figurative. His attitude towards futuristic aestheticization, the Cubists, and the Fauves was ambivalent at best, and the action-driven, abstract Expressionists he all but reviled.[49] Instead, Zerbe sought to preserve a reflective, contemplative tenor, a subtle articulation of his "innermost emotions" to which he attributed an ultimately mystical disposition.[50] As a painter primarily of landscapes and still lifes in his early career, Zerbe conveyed a measured tranquility that was reminiscent of the "overcoming" of Expressionism in the works of Karl Hofer (1878-1955) and the *Neue Sachlichkeit*, rather than the undulating, anxiety-filled, and at times apocalyptic surroundings that dominated the Expressionist movement in the aftermath of World War I.[51]

A similar calmness and objective distance characterized Zerbe's allegorical paintings of the middle period. In *Melancholia* of 1944, Zerbe chose the triptych—a form valued by many German Expressionists, particularly Max Beckmann,[52] and then used by Aronson as well—to arrange seemingly unrelated figures and objects in a quiet and dreamlike scene of yearning, contemplation, and unassuming anticipation. Both figures and objects become symbols of displacement, of a broken order. They are banished to their own spaces in a flat, fragmented landscape, their faces turned away from each other, motionless; some, it seems, have turned to plaster, one is reminiscent of the classical

Socrates. A harlequin, like a modernist intruder, hides his face behind a mask, a motif Zerbe repeatedly explored later in his life.[53] Framed portraits, like painted mirror images, reflect truncated memories. A broken wheel, a clock missing numerals on its face, dripping candles, a trumpet resting on its mouth, a half eaten loaf of bread, a piece of dried fish, a blurred figure in a top hat, all evoke a sense of an unfinished past. The ancient medium—encaustic—finally frames the symbols to an absurd assemblage of time and contemporality.

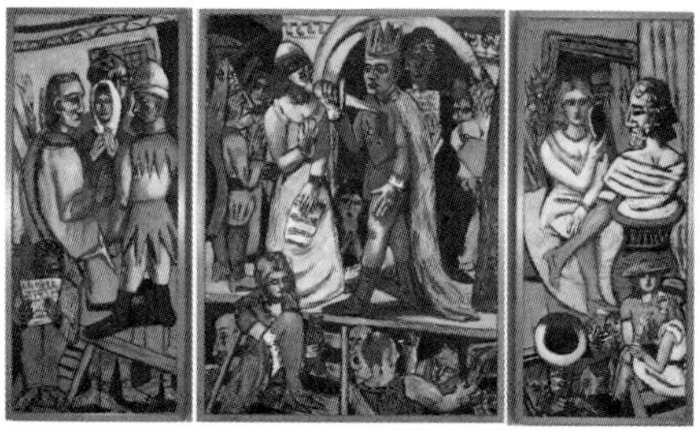

Figure 2

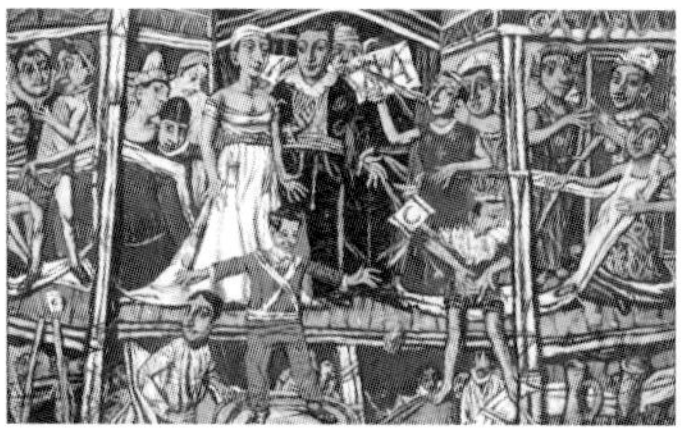

Figure 3

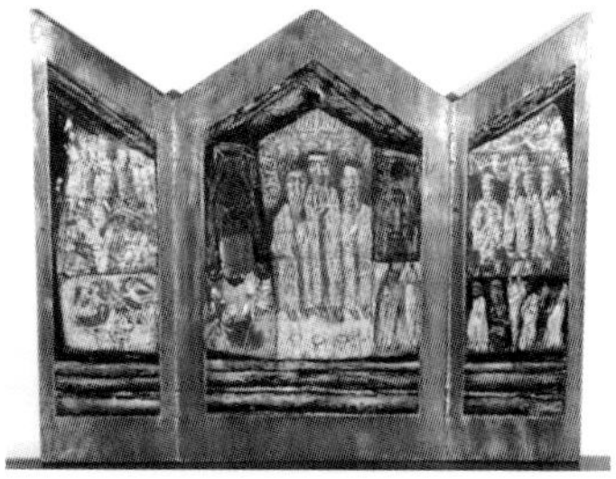

Figure 4

THE TRIPTYCH AS FORM

Zerbe's *Melancholia* most clearly invoked the symbolism in Beckmann's triptychs *Die Versuchung* (1936-7), *Blindman's Buff* (1945), and *Die Schauspieler* (1941-42; Fig. 2)[54] the latter presented in 1955 as a gift to the Busch-Reisinger Museum. *Die Schauspieler* also seems to have strongly inspired David Aronson's *Marriage at Cana* (1947-52; Fig. 3), which, though not a triptych itself, still follows Beckmann's compositional structure, dividing the scene into three panels as well as into an upper and a lower stage. Like Beckmann, Zerbe and Aronson use the triptych form to disperse narration and fracture centrality. Each panel contains a story of its own, yet is meaningless without the other two. A dialectical tension runs through the tripartite structure: The triptych implies discontinuities and contradictions, yet also a paradoxical unity.[55] It creates a simultaneity of narration rather than a linear development, and its parallel realities and scopic extension resemble the experience in a theater.[56] But the triptych also conveys a sacrality associated with the devotional role of the tripartite form in Western art and Christian theology. Beckmann deliberately applied these qualities to intensify the pathos of what he experienced as the *theatrum mundi*, the theater of the world. In their own ways, Zerbe and Aronson absorbed Beckmann's theatrical realism, Zerbe with introverted restraint, Aronson with a more satirical eye for human chaos. Emotional discord seems to reign in Aronson's *Marriage at Cana,* a work so important that it appeared in Ralph Pearson's volume *The Modern Renaissance in American Art* of 1954.[57] The canvas is populated with quizzical relatives, twisted spectators, chaffing servants, and wedding guests who have drifted off to forge their own relationships. Based on an episode in the life of the young Jesus (John 2:1-12), the painting has a religious subtext. But where the evangelist focuses on the miraculous transformation of water into wine and tells us little about the wedding itself, the artist revels in the ceremony and in the variety of human encounters. In accordance with the written source, the wonder goes unnoticed to the wedding company, and all that points to Jesus' "first sign" in public are the stone jars in the lower corner of the stage. It is the stage that defines the composition of the painting and lends structure to its chaotic forces. Bride and groom are positioned at the center of the stage, carefully choreographed and dignified like actors in a classical play. But the real actors have moved to the panels on the side, and the real source of their play is concentrated in the jester (who could also be the narrator or director) acting from the top of a table that emerges from the lower register. The painting, then, has two overlapping compositional centers, adding to the parallel narratives on stage a narrative *off* stage that travels towards an invisible audience. Even more than in Zerbe's work, Aronson's space has collapsed into a surface where all intimation of depth and perspectivity is compressed, if not reversed by size. The jester in the foreground seems farther away than the nuptial couple behind him. But unlike in the late mediaeval tradition where size often indicates importance and privilege, the protagonists in this painting are not clearly designated: They may be hiding behind shadows and doors.

Aronson experimented with the triptych form on other occasions, the most pronounced example being his *Triptych* of 1943 (Fig. 4) which, in fact, mirrors an open altar piece. But Aronson's technique of parallel narratives more often moves beyond the traditional tripartition into multiple images that appear in sharp, though frequently trespassed frames like on split-screen. We see this manifest already in the 1943 *Trinity* (Fig. 5), where frames are part of an hieratic pattern filled with grotesque human fragments; and we see a similar simultaneity in the Joseph paintings of 1954-55 (Fig. 6), *The Sacrifice of Isaac* (1957; Fig. 7), *Young Baal-Shem* (1959; Fig. 8), and even in the bronze relief *The Judges* of 1961 (Fig. 9). Each frame in these images opens another narrative, not an independent one but one that acts as a commentary, a series of footnotes, as they would appear on a rabbinic folio. The frame as a means of spatial constraint is consistently negated by its content, through penetrating limbs and objects. And time, the principle of all narration, thus conquers space or, as Beckmann put it in his *Three Letters,* "the palace of the gods."[58]

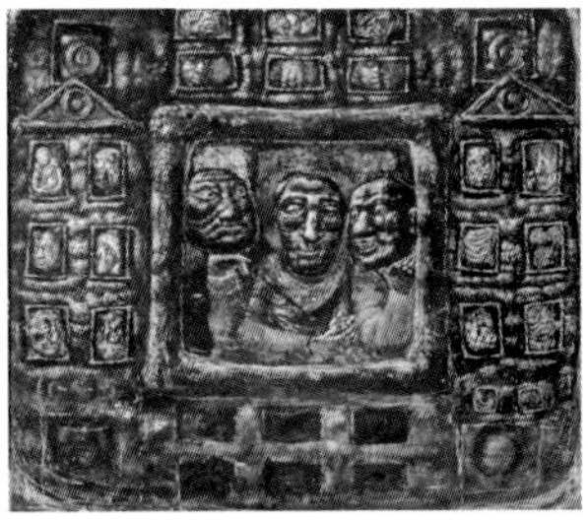

Figure 5

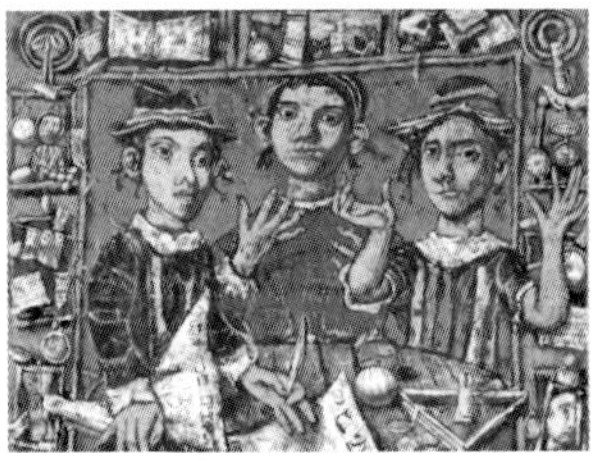

Figure 6

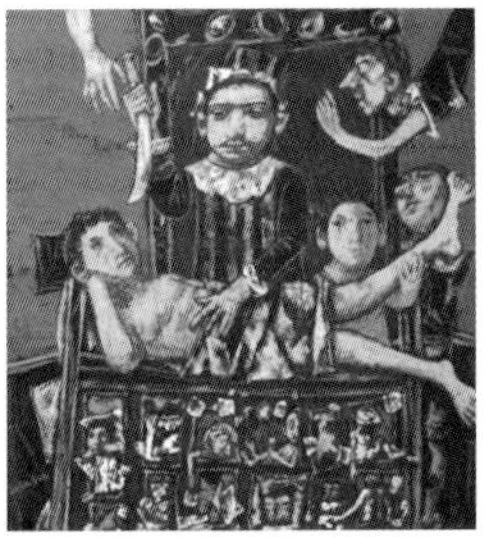

Figure 7

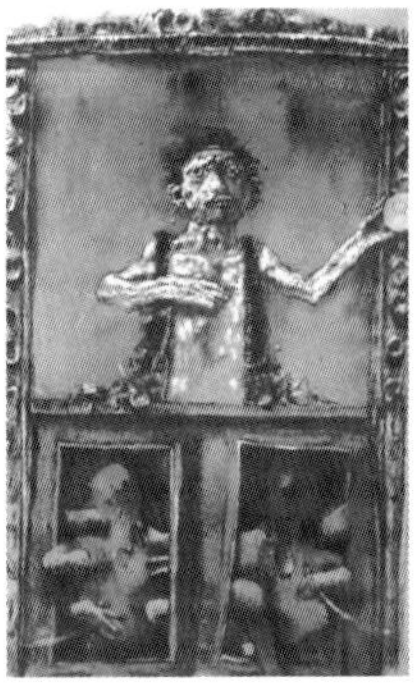

Figure 8

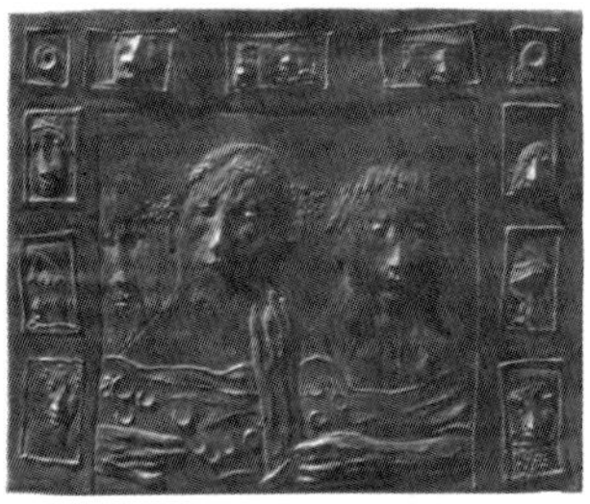

Figure 9

BOSTON EXPRESSIONISM

Beckmann's triptychs clearly exerted considerable influence on the young Aronson and his Boston contemporaries. No less obvious was Karl Zerbe's impact on his students. The rigorous training in technique, the objective-figural commitment, the conscious indebtedness to German and North European Expressionists were traits most of his pupils shared, among them Arthur Polonsky (b. 1925), Henry Schwartz (b. 1927), and of course David Aronson. It was this group that, along with Hyman Bloom, Mitchell Siporin (1910-1976), Jack Levine, and Zerbe himself formed the core of Boston Expressionism in the early 1950s. Three decades later, Robert Taylor, in the *Boston Globe,* referred to their work as "the first indigenous style to emerge here in this century."[59]

That such an "indigenous style" was born from the midst of a group of—for the most part—recent immigrants reflects a paradox not uncommon to the modern American experience. That a good portion of them were Jewish immigrants is a phenomenon that was no less unprecedented—one need only think of the "école juive" in the Montparnasse circle, or of the entire Russian Avantgarde—and is a subject that still remains to be addressed more fully in the scholarly literature.[60] The apparent "Jewishness" of early Boston Expressionism, however, rarely expressed itself in the subject matter of the art.[61] Rather, as was true for most Jewish families migrating from East to West, whether to prewar Vienna, Berlin, or to Boston, a phasing out of heritage or, at best, a rebellion against it, were common responses to the new environment and to the expectations of the "host-societies." Local artists of Jewish background, at this early stage of Expressionism in Boston, only seldom engaged with their religious and cultural heritage. Ideals of humanism and aesthetic universalism prevailed in their work instead. Like their modernist forbears, the Boston Expressionists felt connected by one global language of art, by a concept of humanity that transcended time and space, and by an intellectual rebelliousness that defeated the many parochialisms still found ingrained in American culture in the mid 20th century. Rebels against Boston's Puritan Brahmin culture by virtue of their backgrounds and cross cultural sensibilities, they constituted a regional avantgarde that nevertheless was part of international modernism. What Dorothy Miller wrote in 1946 about the artists she chose for the *Fourteen Americans* show at the New York Museum of Modern Art, which included Aronson, seemed particularly true of the Expressionist environment in Boston: "The mood is serious, even religious, but it has nothing to do with preaching. The idiom is American but there is no hint of regionalism or chauvinisitc tendency. On the contrary, there is a profound consciousness that the world of art is one world and that it contains the Orient no less than Europe and the Americas."[62] Only at a later stage in their careers do we encounter Bloom's rabbis, Levine's prophets, and Aronson's exploration of Biblical scenes and Jewish folklore, themes that we will discuss in a separate chapter.

The original core of Boston Expressionists was joined in subsequent years by Leonard Baskin (b. 1922), Alfred Duca (1920-1997), Sigmund Abeles (b. 1934), Jason Berger (b. 1924), Jack Kramer (1923-1984), Reed Kay (b. 1925), Conger Metcalf (1914-1998), Henry Schwartz and Joseph Ablow (b. 1928), artists who, among others, remained faithful to the figurative Expressionist orientation.[63] Only in the late 1960s did this orientation abate and was challenged by an era of gestural abstraction with roots in New York.[64] A new wave of Expressionism was seen in Boston at a time when Philip Guston (1913-1980) taught at Boston University, an appointment facilitated by David Aronson. Guston had himself lectured at the Museum School under Karl Zerbe. It was Aronson who, in 1955, fashioned the Division of Art at Boston University where he taught until his retirement in 1989. The Department of Painting at Boston University became one of the most important institutions for the development of figurative Expressionism. Not by accident did Aronson seek out former members of the Museum School for his faculty, including Arthur Polonsky, Reed Kay, Jack Kramer, John Wilson (b. 1922), Conger Metcalf, and Joseph Ablow.[65]

The legacy of Expressionism was aided by other institutions as well. At a time when Boston's museum culture was still indifferent, if not hostile, to the local avantgarde, Boston Expressionists found a refuge in private galleries, first in New York, then in their native city. The prestigious exhibition *Americans 1942* at the New York Museum of Modern Art, featuring eighteen artists from nine states, served as a catalyst for Hyman Bloom, Jack Levine, and Mitchell Siporin. In 1946, a very young David Aronson appeared in the sequel *Fourteen Americans.*[66] Bloom, Levine, Aronson, and Zerbe were already represented by New York galleries by the time the Boston art market developed, spearheaded by the Boris Mirski Gallery, originally a little frame shop on Charles Street that moved to the heart of Newbury Street in 1935.[67] Mirski, a well traveled immigrant from Vilna, established what Dorothy Abbott Thompson called the "nucleus of the modern art world of Boston."[68] He represented, among other artists, Karl Zerbe, Jack Levine, Arthur Polonsky, Barbara Swan (b. 1922), Leonard Baskin, and David Aronson, with whom he shared a lifelong friendship. The gallery closed its doors in 1974 upon Mirski's death. In 1953, one of Mirski's closest assistants, Hyman Swetzoff, opened his own gallery on Newbury Street, showing the work of Boston Expressionists, including Hyman Bloom and Lawrence Kupferman (1909-1982). Another gallery on Newbury Street opened in 1945, the Margaret Brown Gallery, which featured both contemporary New York and New England artists. Both the Swetzoff and the Brown galleries closed with the deaths of their owners in 1968 and and 1957, respectively. In the following decades, the Nielsen Gallery (opened in 1964), the Alpha Gallery (founded in 1967 by Alan Fink, a former assistant to Boris Mirski), and the Pucker/Safrai Gallery (opened in 1967) became new fixtures on Newbury Street. Along with other private galleries and with a small number of committed public institutions, in particular the Institute of Contemporary Art (formerly the Institute of Modern Art), the DeCordova Museum (opened to the public in 1950), and the Rose Art Museum at Brandeis University (founded in 1961), they have kept the heritage of Boston's own modernism alive.

In fact, the Institute of Modern Art brought to Boston its first showing of European Expressionists such as Kokoschka, Soutine, Amedeo Modigliani

(1884-1920), Rouault and Marc Chagall (1887-1985). During his tenure at Boston University, Aronson was able to bring Boston its first one-man exhibitions of some of the most important American (and some European) expressionists, whose work surely had an impact on Boston artists. Among them were the exhibitions of Jacques Lipchitz (1891-1973), Max Weber (1881-1961), Raphael Soyer (1899-1987), Germaine Richier (1902-1959), Rico Lebrun (1900-1964), Yasuo Kuniyoshi (1893-1953), Paul Burlin (1886-1969), and Philip Guston.

The trajectory from the beginnings of Boston Expressionism to its contemporary inheritors is neither linear nor uninterrupted. Its diverse sources, with a strong (though not limited to) European element at its center,[69] and its subsequent alliances with realism, Surrealism, and abstraction has rendered the Expressionist tradition in Boston heterogeneous and dynamic. Yet, as Nicholas Capasso summarized the movement between 1950 and 2000, "expressionism was the only truly coherent painting style in Boston, with an integrity based on shared intentionality, pedagogy, emulated masters, documented lines of generational influence, and institutional support systems within academia and museums."[70] David Aronson's vital connection with Expressionism in Boston is a necessary context for the interpretation of his work. The coherence of style that has been attributed to Boston Expressionism is nowhere as evident as in Aronson's consistent struggle with figure and feeling. ■

II YOUNG CHRIST

WE ARE LOOKING AT *YOUNG Christ* of 1945 (Fig. 10). The lonely and fragile figure of the young Jesus is placed in the center, his opaque, luminous skin quietly glowing against the warm, loamy colors of the background. A stark contrast sets face and hands against the dark hair and the dark garment hanging loosely from virtually non-existent shoulders. Out of this vacuous body grow hands that are uncertain of their place, brittle fingers engaged in a nervous, uneasy play, and an elongated, nearly one-dimensional neck, too weak to bear the accentuated plasticity of the head. This young man, it seems, is not here to stay. Rather, he seems to have floated to the center against his will, dangling, as it were, from what appear to be the charcoal traces of an eclipsed halo. There is no redemptive iconography, none of the monumental glory of a *Christos pantocrator*—the all-ruling Christ—whose image is familiar to the visitor of Byzantine churches. On the contrary, this young Christ has shrunk to a melancholy, introverted boy, whose lips seem too small to form words and whose big, dark eyes are directed away from us, away, in fact, from anything in the outside. Yet, he is not quite disconnected from the world: He hears. To say he listens would be saying too much. He hears with awkward, foreign ears, accentuated to the degree of caricature. He hears and seems exposed rather than immersed. The black traces now become sound strokes descending from above, visible only in the negation of light. But while all hearing occurs in the flow of time, sound upon sound, this hearing seems to be timeless, captured perhaps in the moment between sound and sound, or in anticipation of sound; or in a moment of fear of sound. It is like the frozen image of time itself, of the anti-image. Devoid of all traditional Christological language, the *Young Christ* is removed not only from the visual sacredness of iconic representation but also from the dimension of space altogether, of which he only occupies a mere tinge. Captured in a nervous tranquility, he appears to us as deeply and painfully human, yet also as too ethereal to be solely of this world.

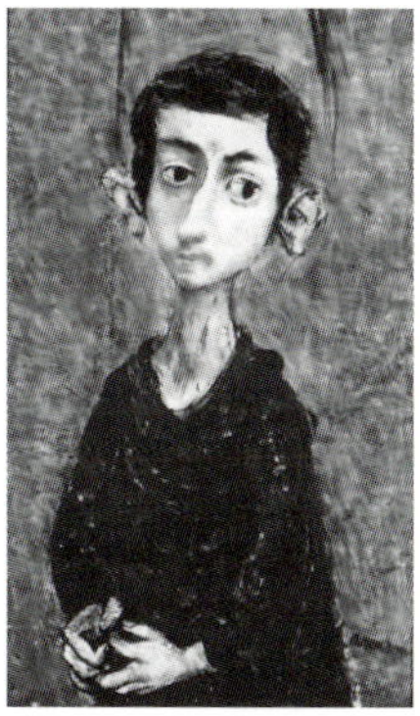

Figure 10

AN ANCIENT TECHNIQUE

For Aronson, *Young Christ* marked a distinct departure from his earlier work, both in technique and composition. "I found a very meaningful fusion of technique and message," he would later explain. "The luminous, waxy colors offered a deeply religious aspect to the proceedings, like a stained glass window in a church that thrusts you into a mood or state of mind."[1]

It was the ancient Greek technique of encaustic, literally, "burning in," that allowed the luminosity and translucidity of the painting. In its modern version, layers of raw pigments, hot wax, and resin are applied to the surface and, in the last stage, ignited with an electrical heat lamp.[2] The mixture can vary from thick, ropy impasto to a thin glaze of superimposed nuances. It hardens quickly but can be reheated and refashioned many times. Once dried, the colors are locked in a controlled coalescence, layer upon layer, creating a unique contrast of diaphanic volatility and earthly permanence. The result is a surface of strangely archaic quality. The painting seems endowed with an indefinite past; it no longer belongs to a particular moment in time, and we are startled by the precarious balance between the pastness of the medium and the presentness of the image. In this balance, the medium becomes a primary point of reference to what is perceived as old and new. Enshrined in sheer timelessness, the figurative image always appears a bit rebellious against its medium, as an anachronism that must define itself anew with each encounter by the viewer. Yet, what may be seen as a retro effect is not intended to be an effect at all. Despite its stark presence, the medium does not transcend its boundaries. Rather, it contains the image, in the dual sense of the word, not more, not less. The specific credibility of David Aronson's encaustics lies in their internal history, in the tempered engagement of two opposite directions in time, and it is this inner frame of reference that has kept his style largely independent of changing artistic movements and moods.

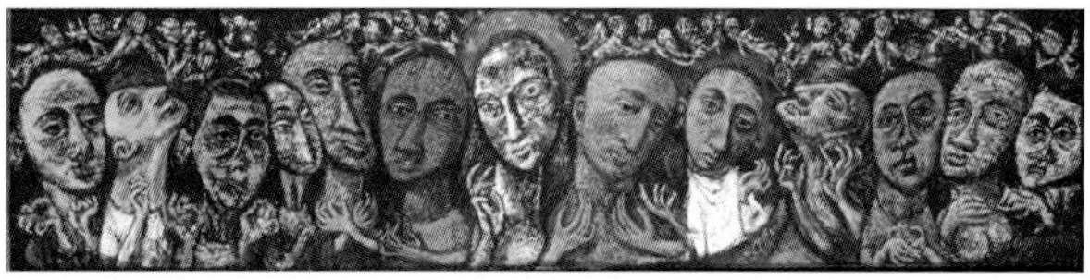

Figure 11

The technique of encaustic demands a high degree of skills and experience that is seldom seen in the history of modern art. Aronson acquired these skills early in his career, as a pupil of Karl Zerbe who himself was a master of the medium. Zerbe, however, abandoned the technique when it became clear that the fumes released during the heating process increasingly affected his health. For Aronson, who continually improved the process, encaustic remained a technique used alongside with oil, charcoal, and, in his later period, oil pastel and mixed media. The material quality of Aronson's paintings, therefore, varies with his deliberate choice of technique.

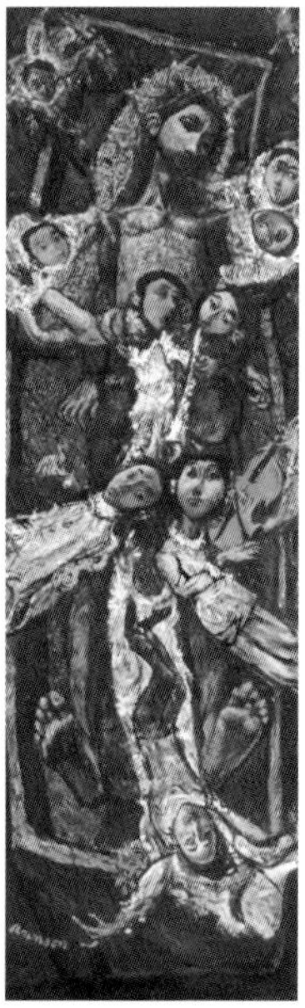

Figure 12

"CHRIST OR CARTOON"?

But it was not only the unusual technique that distinguished *Young Christ,* which was part of Aronson's first one-man show at the New York Niveau Gallery, in the eyes of the critics. *Newsweek Magazine* ran a full page review of the exhibit, referring to the work as "highly controversial religious pictures" and posing the rhetorical question "Christ or cartoon?"[3] Speaking of *The Last Supper* (1944; Fig. 11), which won both the first Judges' Prize and the first Popular Prize of the Boston Institute for Contemporary Art in 1944, Lawrence Dame of the Boston Herald sneered that "this oil is an abomination of cartoon portraiture" worthy to serve as "footboard for the devil's bed."[4] The painting was promptly purchased by the Art Institute of Chicago and, in 1946, included in Dorothy Miller's exhibition *Fourteen Americans* at the Museum of Modern Art in New York.[5]

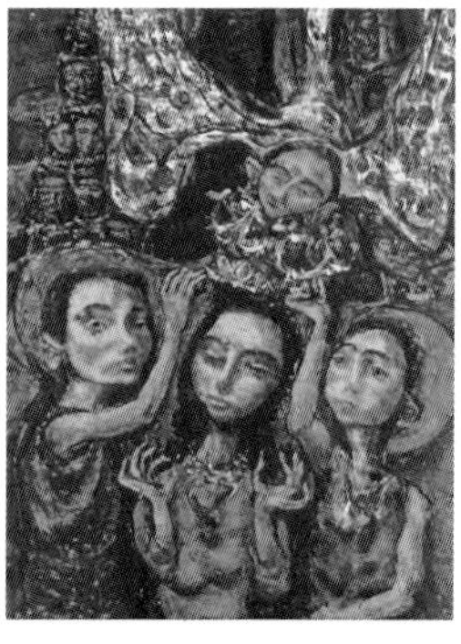

Figure 13

Aronson devoted about twelve years of his career to classical New Testament motifs. *Trinity* of 1943 (Fig. 5), *Resurrection* of 1945 (Fig. 12), *Coronation of the Virgin* of 1945 (Fig. 13), *Madonna and Child with Saints* of 1946 (Fig. 14), *Adoration of the Magi* of 1947 (Fig. 15), *Crucifixion* of 1946 (Fig. 16) are among the paintings that belong to this period. They mirror and reflect upon a visual canon that has become the foundation of Western art since the Middle Ages and the early Renaissance. Known to the visitor of all great museums, Christological symbolism is inextricably entwined in the history of art, as well as in the training of young artists around the world who continue to look to the old masters for insights into composition, style, and technique. Aronson, too, studied the old masters. In 1946 he was awarded a scholarship for European study and travel. In 1949 and 1951, he traveled through Europe and the Near East, seeking out the works of Leonardo (1452-1519), Raphael (1483-1520), El Greco (1541-1614) Caravaggio (1571-1610) and Rembrandt (1606-

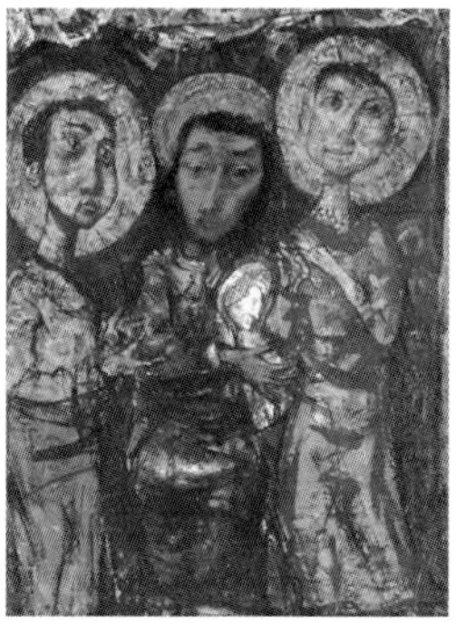

Figure 14

1669).[6] He writes fondly of the all too human elements in Paolo Veronese's (1528-1588) *Christ in the House of Simon* which resurge in his own version of the subject (1945-50; Fig. 17).[7] He admires Leonardo's *Adoration of the Magi,* 1481-82, for its stark monochromatic contrasts that later influenced his own charcoal sketches and pastels.[8] And he feels an overall affinity to the painting styles of the Renaissance tradition.[9] To this we could add the obvious allusions to Early Christian art, Byzantine mosaics, and to a long history of Greek and Russian Orthodox Iconism that is most evident in *Adoration of the Magi* (Fig. 15), but no less present in *Young Christ* (Fig. 10).

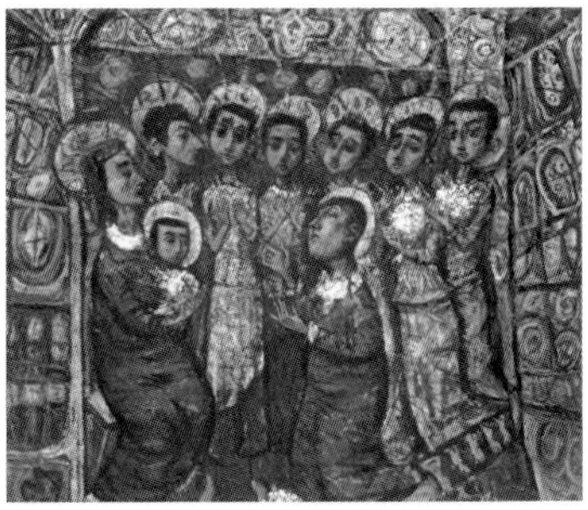

Figure 15

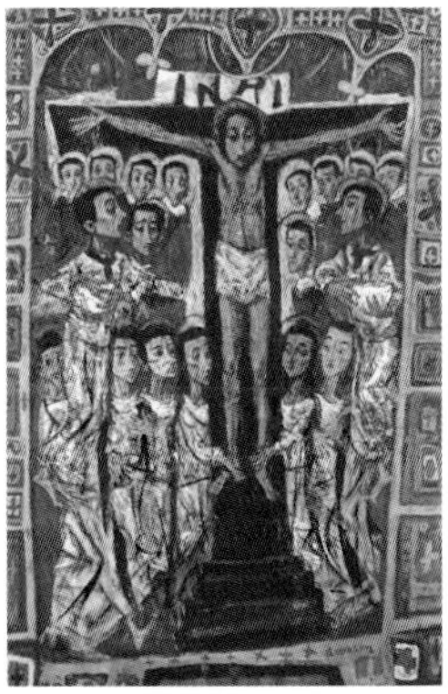

Figure 16

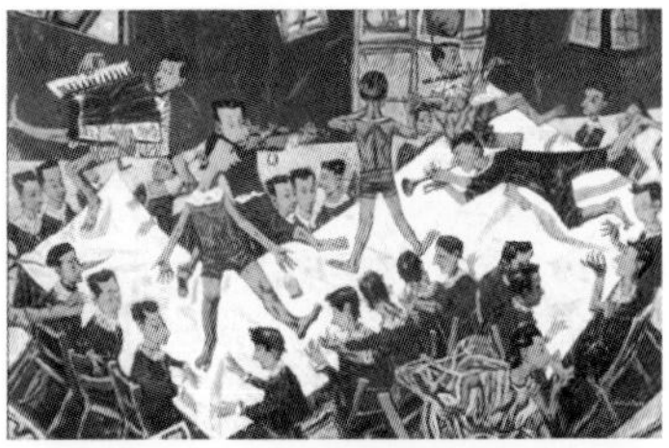

Figure 17

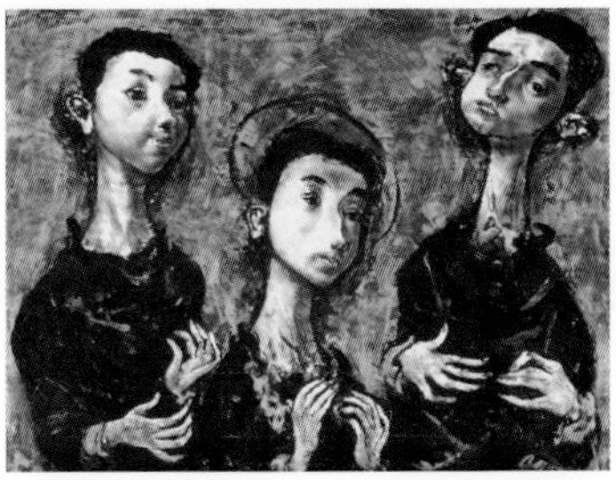

Figure 18

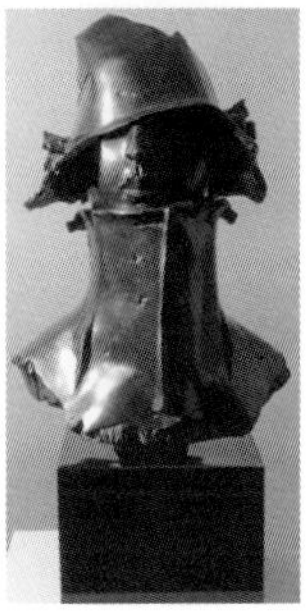

Figure 19

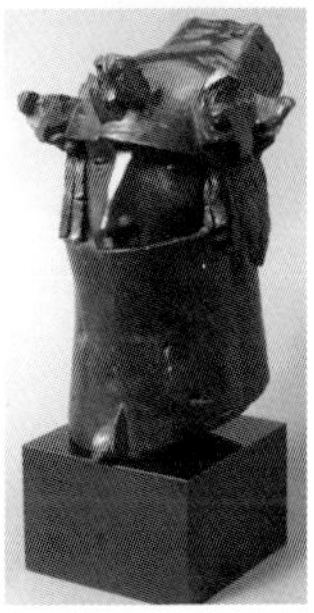

Figure 20

ICONIC ICONOCLASM

Once again, we are faced with a paradox. *Adoration of the Magi* immediately evokes a strong iconic presence. An assembly of halo bearing figures is framed by a richly textured ornamental border that culminates in an early design of the Christian cross. The weight of ornamentation contributes to a "hieratic distance and rigidity" often associated with early Christian art.[10] In a skillful setting of the scene, our eyes are led from the kneeling figure in front to the sitting Mary with child, to a standing and ultimately soaring group in the background. Step by step, then, the human body ascends from the ground into the air, anticipating the redemptive course of the protagonist. Yet, something also seems to fundamentally disturb the iconic harmony of the devotional scene. We begin to be vexed by the odd features of the figure kneeling in front, a foreshortened profile that seems utterly out of place in the tradition of devotional icons. We begin to feel moved by the innocent gesture of the infant Jesus clinging to his mother and casting a suspicious, fearful look to his visitor while a proud, confident Mary parries unsubmissively the acts of adoration. And the group of devout bystanders seems to disband into ever more uniconic individuals once we become acquainted with their faces. On a second tour with our eyes, the fixed forms of the icon dissolve quickly into a flux of undisguised humanness, into the same fragility that surrounds the *Young Christ.*

David Aronson's iconism is self-overcoming. The impressionistic ornamentation that envelops the *Magi* shrinks to a symbolic foil that is penetrated by the expressionistic realism of the figure. The halo becomes a mere trim of the face, just as the religious symbolism remains all but a context. In *Young Christ Disputing with the Doctors* (1945; Fig. 18), the halo is reduced to a dark rim surrounding the luminous features of Jesus and inverting the order of light that the religious icon with its often darkened faces establishes. The iconic representation of sacredness has moved from the interchangeable symbol, from the halo as visual topos to the irreducable human face; to the face that the 20th century philosopher Emmanuel Levinas regarded as "pure expression," as ultimate "nakedness" and "destitution," as a "pure vulnerability" which eludes our grasp and yet demands our response.[11] When Aronson begins to explore the subject of the warrior, as in his later sculptures (Figs. 19 and 20), the face hides its vulnerability behind impenetrable layers of armor.

But it is not only the face that conveys affection and expressivity. Like the earlier Expressionists, Oskar Kokoschka above all, Aronson pays much attention to the expressivity of the hands. In *Young Christ,* we have noted hands engaged in nervous play. In

Young Christ Disputing with the Doctors, these hands have opened into a pair of delicate corals that seem to shield the young Jesus' heart from the heat of the dispute. But the dispute itself carries on in a silent manner, without speech and retort; it has, in fact, been translated into a quiet language of gestures, a ballet of conversing hands. Likewise, in *Adoration of Magi,* words have become hands, and it is in the hands of the kneeling figure that the painting finds its compositional center. *The Last Supper* (Fig. 11), cause of much ire among conservative critics, as we have noted above, is a painting composed of almost nothing but faces and hands, the faces colorful and painfully individual, the hands like licking flames consuming them. In *Coronation of the Virgin* (Fig. 13), the hands seem to be the real receptacles of the crown; they are opened towards the above whereas the eyes of the Virgin are cast to the ground. And in *Young Christ with Phylacteries* (1945; Fig. 21), the hands become bearers of signs not normally seen on depictions of Jesus: A ring and the straps of the *tefillin shel yad,* the ritual box observant Jews mount on their arms during morning prayers. A second box, the *tefillin shel rosh,* which, like the first, contains Scriptural passages, appears firmly on the young Jesus' forehead. All that remains of iconic imagery has vanished behind a canopy-like drapery; the halo has become a woven ring that may not be a halo at all. What is sacred has now been encased in darkness. Image has become text. The icon has become the anti-icon.

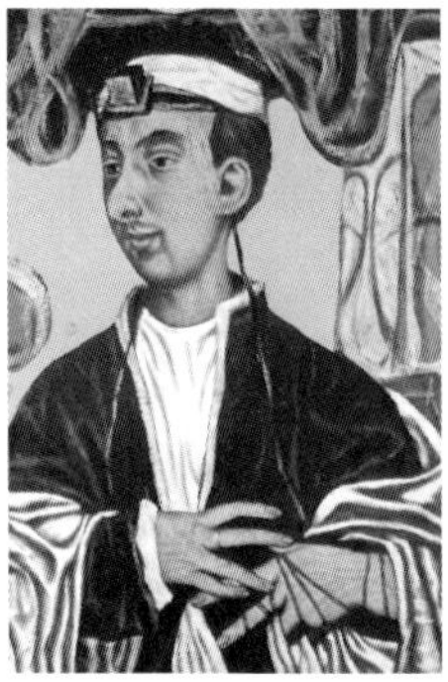

Figure 21

DISCONTINUOUS CONTINUITIES

With his emphasis on human physiognomy as an expression of individuality and physicality, Aronson transplants the Byzantine and mediaeval canon of the religious icon into the pictorial territory of the Renaissance and its late obsessions with the grotesque and the mannerisms of the human form. Earlier studies of this era have depicted the Renaissance artist as a self-declared inheritor of the classical ideal who asserted not only human creativity over canonical tradition but also himself as a creator of semi-divine nature. Ever since the studies of Jacob Burckhardt (1818-1897) and the writings of his disciple Friedrich Nietzsche (1844-1900), the Renaissance has served as the historical incubator of individuality, human ingenuity, moral liberation, and emancipation from religion.[12] In the Middle Ages, Burckhardt wrote, the human consciousness lay "dormant" beneath a veil of "faith, infantility, and delusion." But in Italy, he continues, this veil was lifted into the air: "Man becomes a cognitive *individual* and recognizes himself as such."[13] From the *uomo singolare* it was only a small step to the *uomo universale,* the universal genius, and to the artist who is no longer copying artisan—like the painter of icons—but capricious maker of art.[14] When the Italian painter and architect Giorgio Vasari (1511-1574) published his famous *Lives of the Great Painters, Sculptors, and Architects* in 1550, he celebrated this very individuality of the Renaissance artist, culminating in the work and person of Michelangelo (1475-1564), who also happened to be his life-long friend.[15] It was Vasari who first interpreted the art of the Renaissance as a revolt against the crude and infantile expressions of mediaeval artisanship, which, for him, was the result of the barbarian invasions in Italy and the rise of a new artless religion that had no sympathy for the creative pagan: Christianity. In the middle of the thirteenth century, however, a new generation of artists in Tuscany began to "abandon the old style, imitating the works of antiquity with all ardor and industry."[16] "The arts," Vasari continues, "were freed from that rust of old age which still clung to them."[17] The faces became human, the eyes sensual, the manner harmonious and passionate. And with Giotto (1266-1337), the "monstrosity of those Byzantine painters" was finally "done away with."[18]

Vasari's assessment of the Italian Renaissance as an emancipation from, and radical break with, the mediaeval regression into formalism defined the historical and art historical thinking of many centuries.[19] A substantial revision of this interpretation occurred only at the beginning of the 20th century, chiefly as the result of a scholarly problematization of the term "Renaissance," a new interest in "primitive art" and mysticism, and the rise of a nationalism, particularly in Germany, which helped generate a new, if also often misguided, appreciation for the Middle Ages and the Gothic.[20] Unlike in Vasari's perception of the Renaissance, contemporary scholarship has come to see a continuity rather than a rupture between the Middle Ages and the early age of modernity. While the Renaissance architect could study the ancient ruins of Rome and recreate the splendor of antiquity, the painter had no immediate access to the ideal archetypes of art and was left with nothing but the "crude style" of his Byzantine predecessors.[21] It is no surprise, then, that we find the early masters of the Renaissance training their hands at the very icons of the despised "dark age" that they sought to overcome.[22]

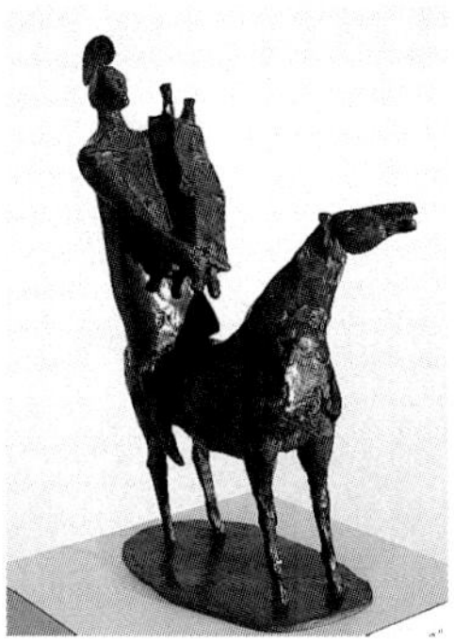

Figure 22

A similar line of continuities—rather than ruptures—defines David Aronson's work. Like the analytic scholar, he identifies patterns of continuity between the Byzantine icon and the Renaissance portrait, infusing one with the other. Like the early Expressionists, he absorbs moments of authentic feeling and existential reality from the seeming clumsiness and imperfection of "art before art." What must have appeared as an embarrassment to the refined artist of the Renaissance becomes a source of true expression for Aronson. A mediaevalizing modern, he infuses movement with rigidity, the quotidian with the mystical, depth with ornament.

A mediaeval exteriority also surrounds much of Aronson's sculptural work: Cumbersome coats and funny-shaped hats and the armor of knights interact with baroquish contortions, classical contraposts, and even—as in the *Rider with Torah* (1976-78; Fig. 22)—with the intriguing simplicity of ancient Phoenician statuettes. "Although cast in mediaeval garb and aglow with the epicurean colors of Rembrandt, the art of David Aronson merely stages modern problems in ancient dress," wrote *Time Magazine* in 1963.[23] A century earlier, however, Charles Baudelaire made a similar observation about modern artists seeking to "distil the eternal from the transitory". "Casting an eye over our exhibitions of modern pictures," he writes, "we are struck by a general tendency among artists to dress all their subjects in garments of the past."[24] The outward persistence of the past, then, seizes the transient, fugitive nature of modernity.

What renders Aronson's continuities so—for lack of a better word—discontinuous is that they are unexpected. They are different from epigonous mannerisms and different from the post-modern affection for the historical quote. The Renaissance as a rebellious continuity against its will has become a conscious struggle with continuity itself in symbol and form. As in *Young Christ*, Aronson's art stands at an ever new crossroad between time and form. His images are like open windows to different eras: diachronic commentaries. They are timekeepers, and yet themselves chronoclastic. Unobtrusively, the history of art passes through them not as a succession of static epochs but as a continuum of emotions.

ART AND RELIGION

Mediaeval art, almost by definition, was religious. Religion was the overall fabric that created the Renaissance, albeit in a sensual, worldly fashion.[25] Should David Aronson's art be called religious as well? And what is the religious significance of *Young Christ*, *Trinity*, or *The Last Supper?*

Newsweek Magazine stamped the 22 year young painter of Christological scenes a "New Testament Teacher."[26] Beginning in the 1950s, Aronson returned to what is commonly known as the Old Testament, or the Hebrew Bible. He "returned" to it, he said, because it was in the spirit and tradition of the Hebrew Bible that he was reared in his youth. "My father was a rabbi," he writes in his now often quoted lecture of 1967, "and I was destined to be the same [...]."[27] Yet, he became a painter of young Christs and resurrections instead. "I was attracted to the mystical and physical splendor of Catholic ritual and pomp with its processionals and pageantry, magnificent ceremonial objects, pontifical miters, ecclesiastical vestments and precious embroideries," he reminisces in the same lecture, continuing that "all the while my preoccupation with New Testament texts was neither devotional nor anecdotal."[28]

One can well imagine the stupor that grasped both the Jewish and the Christian audiences when the son of an observant Jew from Lithuania began his career as a painter with a series of daring depictions of New Testament characters. Inevitably, the fictional Asher Lev, the "notorious and legendary Lev of the *Brooklyn Crucifixion*" in Chaim Potok's novel of the same name comes to mind. Both the fictional Lev and the real Aronson not only become artists against the will of their fathers, but also penetrate the ultimate forbidden sanctuary of a rival religion. "[I]n choosing this subject," Aronson spoke about his New Testament paintings in 1967, "I, as a painter with an intense Jewish background, was doing something daring and dangerous, which had a great appeal to a young artist, full of enthusiasm and with new worlds to conquer. [...W]hat better way to punish my father for the years of restrictions?"[29]

To be sure, the young Aronson was hardly the first artist of Jewish background to conquer this foreign territory. Marc Chagall's famous crucifixions in response to the Holocaust, and his church windows of the 1960s and 1970s are well known examples of "Jewish art" intersecting with Christianity, both in form and function.[30] Jewish artists of the modern period routinely employed Christian motives. The early paintings of Moritz Daniel Oppenheim (1800-1882),[31] the controversial *12 Year Old Jesus in the Temple* (1878) by Max Liebermann (1847-1933),[32] Maurycy Gottlieb's (1856-1879) scenes from the life of Christ,[33] Moses Jacob Ezekiel's (1844-1917) *Christ in the Tomb* for the Chapel of Notre Dame (1890),[34] are only a few of many such instances, indicating that the link between a Jewish artist and "Jewish art" is not a necessary one.

But Aronson's concern with religion does not grow from a tradition of academic and historical painting, nor does it leave the same Jewish imprint on all religious symbolism that we consistently encounter in Chagall.[35] Rather, for Aronson, the concern with religion is a concern with "truth," with religion as such, and art becomes a medium to separate truth from duplicity. His statement for the 1946 *Fourteen Americans* reflects this concern: "Religion and art are two ways of seeking ultimate truth. Religion has affinity for a great cross-section of humanity. Art is sympathetic to fewer numbers. A sincere art comes to judgment in unequivocal face value, endowed with effective power to stir a quest for the true. How fitting, therefore, to give expression through the medium of art, for freedom from imposed thinking in religion. Once freedom is attained, we would say, religion gives peace of mind without premeditated dogma."[36]

At their core, Aronson maintains, religion and art are pursuits of the same quest for truth. But religions have relinquished their core. And for the young Aronson, art becomes a way to free oneself from the tutelage of religion. But what might easily be seen as a rebellion against dogma and a thrust towards the secular is—quite to the contrary—an attempt at a humanistic resacralization of art. Where the initial teachings "have often been twisted, like the faces in some of my pictures," art steps in to expose, through "the gentle and the grotesque," the double nature of word and text. It clears away the layers of contorted commentary; it is a form of critique.

Written in the spirit of enlightenment, optimism and certain "pantheistic tendencies,"[37] David Aronson's statement of 1946 was a response, perhaps, to a war whose human and religious dimensions had not yet been fully grasped by the world. A humanist by conviction, Aronson used his artist's statement not to speak about his art and not to speak about himself, but to speak about the universality of human truth. "There is a man," he concludes, "who, above all, preaches tolerance and understanding to himself. He is a religious man."[38] ■

III YOUNG BAAL-SHEM

A *YOUNG BAAL-SHEM* (1964; FIG. 23) stands before us, his right hand pointing to his heart, an amulet in his left. He emerges, like a puppeteer, from a stage within the frame, the grass and thicket of his mysterious whereabouts still clinging to his coat. His hair unkempt, his chest bare, an earring dangling from his ear, he anticipates a movement of counter-culture still four hundred years away. And this is what a Baal-Shem does: He heals with miraculous hands, he invokes the secret names, he plays the numbers of the Hebrew *Alef-bet,* he inscribes amulets for all occasions, he summons spirits and exorcizes others, he cures madness and brings rain and may charge a small fee for all that. His wondrous deeds are recorded in the two insets below, but the testimonies are as blurry as the miracles. The Hebrew letter *Yod* looms on the circular amulet. It is the first letter of the Divine name, its numeric equals ten, the number of spheres, or *Sefirot,* which, for the mystic, connect the worldly world with the Divine. The young Baal-Shem clasps the amulet with his left hand, but it also eludes him, drifting off the framed stage and becoming a fixture in the frame itself. With its thinly penciled outline, the letter *Yod* all but floats above the charcoal landscape of the painting. And yet, it is in this letter, in the verism of script, that the image also becomes a reality of its own reference: In writing, image and object are the same.

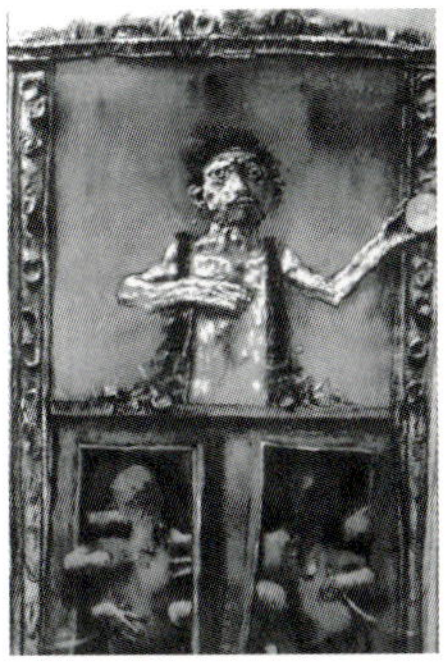

Figure 23

MAGIC JUDAISM

David Aronson has left the rich images of the New and "Old" Testaments to explore folk traditions. "In my search for a more speculative approach to Scripture," he writes, "I considered the place of the Talmud with its parochial definitions, rigid disputations and rational systems."[1] But the Talmud, a compilation of rabbinic rulings and counter rulings over the course of almost five centuries, did not yield enough material to be visualized. Instead, Aronson turned to the history of Jewish heterodoxies. In Jewish folklore and in the intricate architecture of Jewish mysticism, or Cabbala, he found an inexhaustible well of untainted, all too human beliefs, hopes and fears: "This numerological jugglery along with the writing of amulets, trust in the efficacy of charms, conjuration of devils, frenzied rituals, and sublime levitations provoked dazzling images and provided a wealth of visual material for my work."[2]

Between 1958 and 1960, Aronson devotes much attention to the subject of Jewish magic and superstition. He is interested in the magician, the conjurer, the bearer of amulets, the Cabbalist and the Hasid. His scenes revolve around exorcism, consultations from the Dybbuk, the cleaving migrant soul that possesses its victims, and the creation of Golems, shapeless heaps of clay brought to life through the power of divine names. Subject of countless folk fantasies, these areas of Judaism have typically been shunned by the inheritors of the rational rabbis who once helped father the Jewish Enlightenment *(Haskalah).* In their demand for a purified, rational, and outwardly presentable form of Judaism, the Jewish enlighteners, from the 18th century onward, preferred to distance themselves from what they regarded as an embarrassing legacy of Cabbalistic teachings and their popular renderings: "Bone-dry ideas were plucked apart, pretentiously presented as novel discoveries and decked out in the motley tatters of fantasy," wrote Abraham Geiger (1810-1871), one of the spiritual ancestors of modern day reform Judaism, of the writings that came to be known as the Zohar.[3] The Zohar, an esoteric commentary on the Hebrew Bible laced with prophetic insights, whose author most likely was the 13th century mystic Moses de Leon, advanced to an almost canonical book for a Jewish movement that arose in mid 18th century Eastern Europe: Hasidism. With its firm roots in Cabbalistic messianism, oral legends, folk customs, and wonder-working leadership, Hasidism gripped much of the Jewish population in Galicia, Volhynia, and the Ukraine. From there, it quickly spread north, toward Lithuania, until, in the 1770s, a bitter strife broke out between the "mystical" Hasidim and their "rational" opponents (Mitnagdim), headed by the Gaon of Vilna (1720-1797), in whose name the Hasidic "sects" were repeatedly excommunicated. But while Lithuania became the stronghold of anti-Hasidism, the teachings of the Hasidic masters continued to shape Polish Jewry before, in 1939, the shadow of a violent end fell upon it.

In *Young Baal-Shem,* Aronson created a memorial for a world irrevocably lost. A Baal-Shem (literally, master of the Name) is a Hasidic teacher. Generations of Hasidic teachers, however, identified themselves with one particular Baal-Shem—the Baal Shem Tov, or Master of the Good Name (1698-1760). Born under miraculous circumstances and learned in the teachings of the practical and theoretical Cabbala, the Baal Shem Tov is said to have exorcised demons, brought rain, and magically lit a tree with his bare hands, and even to have communicated with the prophet Elijah in his dreams.[4] His legendary, though humble, life turned the Baal Shem Tov into a model for all subsequent leaders of Hasidism, his humility, however, soon to be replaced by wealthy dynasties.

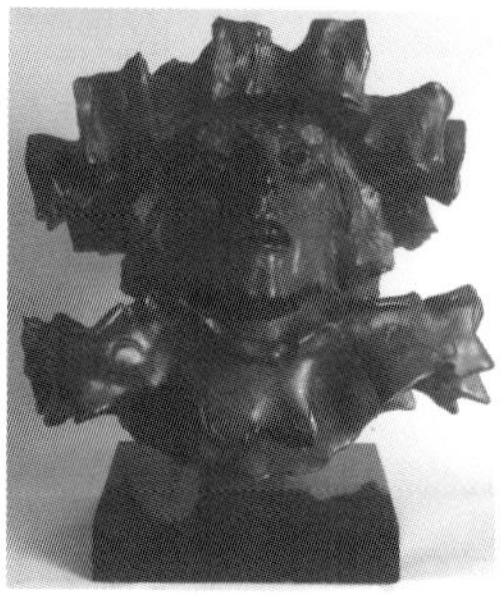

Figure 24

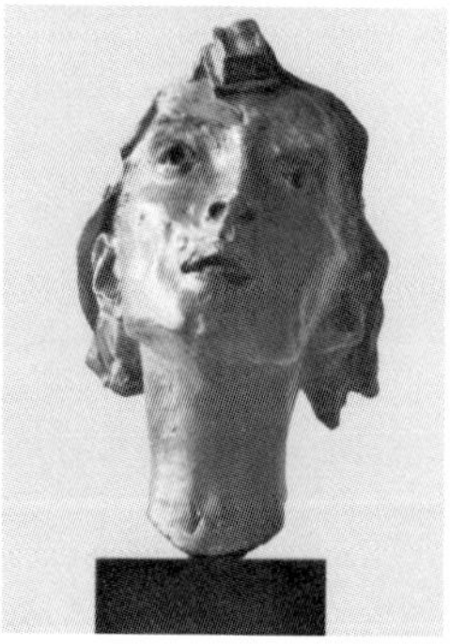

Figure 25

THE BAAL SHEM AS REBEL

The Jewish thinker Martin Buber (1878-1965), who can be credited with bringing the literature of Hasidism—if also in his own "re-narration"—to wider audiences around the world, rightly mentioned the Baal Shem Tov in one breath with the philosopher Baruch Spinoza (1632-1677) and the infamous messianic pretender Sabbatai Zvi (1626-1676).[5] Both Spinoza and Sabbatai Zvi were radicals in opposite ways, and both emerge in David Aronson's sculptural work (*Spinoza* [1965-69; Fig. 24], *False Messiah* [1964-68; Fig. 25]). They challenged tradition authorities and the authority of tradition, Spinoza through the self-empowered intellect, Sabbatai Zvi by empowering himself. Spinoza was excommunicated for his teachings by the Jewish council of Amsterdam in 1656;[6] Sabbatai Zvi was declared messiah in 1666 and commanded a large following among Jews throughout Europe and Asia Minor. Some remained faithful to him even after he embraced Islam to retire gracefully at the mercy of the Sultan.[7]

For Buber, the Baal Shem Tov was neither a messianic pretender (though parallels undoubtedly exist), nor a philosopher. Rather, he saw the Baal Shem Tov as a corrective rebel to the "late-exilic catastrophe of Judaism" that Spinoza and Sabbatai Zvi had triggered: A rebel against reason and a rebel against human haughtiness—but a rebel all the same.[8] Indeed, the Baal Shem stands out as a religious innovator. Hasidism not only undermined the traditional study of Talmud but also reformed the aesthetics of prayer and dramatically subverted the social fabric of Polish Jewry. At its origins, Hasidism blossomed as a religion of the people, just as the Baal Shem was born in a home of utter poverty without access to the established forms of society. "He lived in a small village and made his living by keeping a tavern [...]," the legend has it. "His brother-in-law, Rabbi Gershon of Kuty, thought him to be an ignorant and boorish person [...]."[9]

It is this anti-establishment youth whom we meet in Aronson's *Young Baal-Shem.* As in *Young Christ* (Fig.

10), weakness and fragility seem to threaten his physical existence. He appears to be connected to nature more than to society, just as the young Baal Shem Tov used to seclude himself in a mountain crevice beyond the river. The sacralization of nature and, indeed, of all profane becomes one of the major tenets of Hasidism. And yet, the *Young Baal Shem* is no Spinoza. He reaches out, reaches beyond nature, to the divine Name. Creation is still a mystery. "Genuine religious movements," wrote Martin Buber of Hasidism, "do not want to offer man the solution of the world mystery, but to equip him to live from the strength of the mystery."[10]

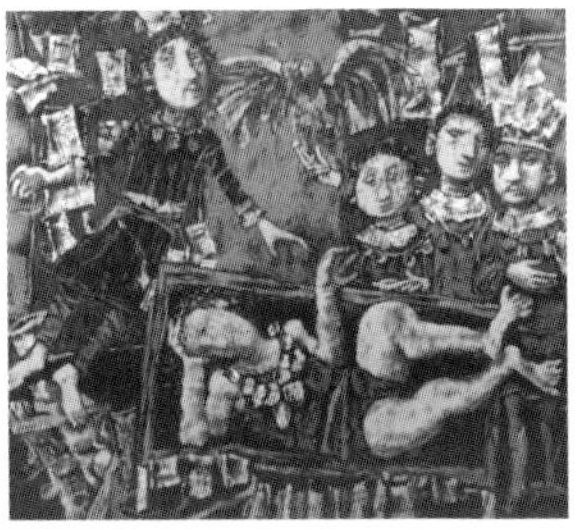

Figure 26

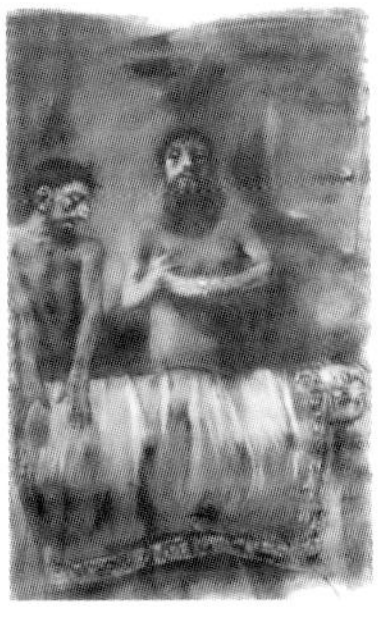

Figure 27

But there are also forbidden mysteries. The Talmud prohibits by punishment of death all magic that produces a visible effect or a visual illusion through the "performance of an act."[11] The shapelessness that reigns in the lower register of the drawing, however, invokes the mystery of the shapeless Golem who is brought to life by the secret formula once used in the creation of Adam from the earth. In *The Golem* of 1958 (Fig. 26), David Aronson already addressed the magic story of making a homunculus. "While the apprentices, properly adorned with amulets and charms, chant magical incantations, the sorcerer, in a state of ecstatic levitation, hovers over the figure of the emerging *golem*," he later wrote about this painting.[12] In *Rabbi Judah Loew* (1959; Fig. 27), Aronson returns to the topic from the eyes of the maker, Rabbi Yehuda Loew ben Bezalel of Prague. The colorful gaiety of the 1958 Golem encaustic has made room for a more somber mood in the charcoal *Rabbi Judah Loew*. And while the Golem of 1958 reclines uncovered on his bed, the Golem of 1959 resembles a corpse taking shape underneath an embroidered sheet that seems to oscillate in front of our eyes. Life and death are intertwined in the Golem legend: Only one letter—the letter *Aleph*—separates truth *(emet)* from death *(met)*; and when the insolent rabbi erases the letter from the forehead of his Golem, a mass of shapeless clay buries him underneath.

The Baal Shem now begins to strike us as dubious. On the one hand, he reflects a form of Judaism that proved inspirational to David Aronson: "Piety became joyous, ritual became spiritualistic instead of formalistic."[13] On the other hand, he yearns for the ultimate boundary of Jewish mysticism, for the role of the Creator. It is this very tension that accompanies the parable of hubris in Rabbi Yehuda Loew, whose father's name, not by accident, was Bezalel—the name of the first "Jewish artist" in the book of Exodus. Bezalel is "singled out" by God to create the Tabernacle (Ex. 35:30). Rabbi Yehuda Loew singles himself out to create, through the secrets of Cabbala, a Golem. And here, Jewish folk spirituality seems strangely fused with the spirit of the Renaissance. The Baal Shem, patriarch of Jewish pietism, appears as a rebellious creator, as a religious heretic—that is a chooser of his own beliefs—and, finally, as an independent individual outside the convention of community. The mystic turns into an artist.

THE ARTIST

It would be all too simple to establish biographical parallels between the artist David Aronson and his penchant for rebellious characters. To be sure, Aronson speaks of his own "perhaps immature but necessary rebellion against an authoritarian, orthodox environment chafed by its claims of exclusive salvation."[14] His New Testament scenes and the exploration of motifs from the fringes of Judaism certainly seem to testify to such rebelliousness. In traditional Jewish orthodoxy, where the biblical commandment against "graven images" (Ex. 20:4) still retains significance, being an artist alone can be a rebellious gesture.

Yet, Aronson's rebels are not quite so rebellious. They are self-conscious, thrown into rebellion, contemplating rather than acting. They are gentle revolutionaries, radicals in the clouds, or "anti-heroic heroes," as one critic poignantly remarked.[15]

Thrown into rebellion may be an apt metaphor for David Aronson himself. Born in 1923 in the Lithuanian village Shilova, Aronson immigrated to the United States in 1929, together with his mother and four siblings. Sponsored by relatives in Boston, his father, a Rabbi, had already arrived in 1924 to establish himself as a local *Mashgiach* (inspector of Jewish ritual slaughter and dietary laws) under the supervision of Rabbi Joseph Soloveitchik. Like most Jewish immigrants from Eastern Europe, the family kept a strictly observant household, spoke Yiddish, and subscribed to the *Jewish Daily Forward,* while following the course of American politics with great interest. The Aronsons lived in a tenement house in Dorchester, Massachusetts, and the sons and daughters attended a traditional Hebrew school in addition to the Boston public schools. From his young age on, Aronson was accustomed to the daily routine of laying *Tefillin* during morning prayers and to all aspects of observant Jewish life. At the time of his Bar Mitzvah, however, he began to question the value of "formal ritual." "I experienced enormous conflict, and what was to be the beginning of a significant rebellion," Aronson remembers in an interview for the magazine *Moment* in 1978.[16] For his Bar Mitzvah, he reluctantly read a passage from the Torah, as is the custom. But a celebration never took place.

We encounter this questioning, inner conflict, and imminent rebellion in *The Confirmation*, 1999 (not reproduced in this volume), where the Bar Mitzvah boy has isolated himself from the celebration that marks his transition into adulthood, the balloons and Hebrew letters dangling like a wreath of weights around his head, his prayer shawl slipping off his shoulders, held in place by passionless arms. "His moment of confirmation is transformed into a moment of doubt," writes Judith Bookbinder about the boy in the painting.[17] It was at this time of doubt (1936) that Aronson began to take art lessons with the artist and teacher Harold Rotenberg, his first mentor, at the Hecht House, a community center located in Mattapan, then one of the Jewish neighborhoods in the Boston area. Despite his conflicted relationship with tradition, he attended, like all his siblings, the Hebrew Teacher's College in Roxbury; but unlike his siblings, he dropped out after two years (1938-39). "I did a tremendous amount of drawing in the margins of my textbooks," he remembers of his time there. Encouraged by his teacher and later Dean of the Hebrew Teacher's College, Dr. Eisig Silberschlag (who was a poet himself)[18], he left high school early three times a week to continue his lessons in art classes for gifted students offered at the Boston Museum of Fine Arts. In 1941, he began his professional art training under Karl Zerbe at the Boston Museum School.

The world of traditional Jewish learning was now no longer his world. Aronson left the home of his parents and, inevitably, a distance grew between them. "My interest in making images—a violation of the second commandment—provoked a lack of understanding if not downright antagonism among those with whom I lived," he recalls in the interview for *Moment*. "The very notion of images, to a strictly Orthodox family, was threatening, to say the least."[19]

ART AND JUDAISM

The "threatening notion" of images in Judaism deserves to be qualified. For already in biblical times, the fundamental prohibition against "graven images" was an ambiguous law at best. The Cherubim, winged creatures sitting on top of the Ark of the Covenant (Ex. 25:10), with human faces (as many as four each, according to the prophet Ezekiel [Ez. 1:5; 10:1]), the twelve oxen bearing the weight of the Brazen Sea in the Salomonic Temple (1 Kg. 7), and the striking figural decorations of post-biblical synagogues defy the abhorrence against the "likeness" of anything above and below (Ex. 20:4). At the same time, severe measures are taken to punish the fashioning and worship of a golden calf (Ex. 32-33), and it is understood that the decline of the northern kingdom of ancient Israel has its roots in the reversion to idolatrous practices. Idolatry becomes perhaps the primal concern of the Mosaic legislation. Purviewing the canon of Jewish law, the mediaeval Jewish philosopher Moses Maimonides (1135-1204) wrote that "it is the object and centre of the whole Law to abolish idolatry and utterly uproot it."[20] Since in biblical and rabbinic times idolatry was primarily associated with seeing, all visual aspects of life were regarded as potentially dangerous: "Only over what a person's eye sees, does the evil impulse bear sway," the Sages stated in the Talmud.[21]

The primacy of hearing in Judaism over seeing in Greek culture is a common notion that informed many thinkers in the modern period. Ever since the German idealist philosopher Hegel (1770-1831), the freedom of seeing and the bondage of hearing served as distinguishing marks between West and East. Matthew Arnold, in his famous essay "Hebraism and Hellenism" of 1868, did much to ingrain this notion in the English speaking world when he wrote: "The uppermost idea with Hellenism is to see things as they really are; the uppermost idea with Hebraism is conduct and obedience."[22] Still in 1902, Martin Buber did not hesitate to speak of the "ancient Jew" as a "person-of-the-ears (Ohrenmensch) rather than person-of-the-eyes (Augenmensch),"[23] which was promptly echoed by the Prague philosopher Hans Kohn in 1924: "[The Jew] hears more than he sees."[24] For some, the virtual absence of the visual in Judaism quickly became proof for the unenlightened character of an entire people.[25] But others, like the neo-Kantian Jewish thinker Hermann Cohen (1842-1918), used the absence of Jewish art to reaffirm the spiritual and rational purity of prophetic Judaism: "[...] prophetic monotheism is necessarily opposed to, necessarily contradicts art."[26] In contrast to polytheism and pantheism, Cohen concludes, the Jewish form of expression is auditive and most manifest in poetry. "The plastic arts and painting were kept at a safe distance from the pure worship of God."[27] Traditional Judaism, for much of its history, tried to maintain this distance.

Much less concerned with the "pure worship of God," the Zionist movement of the fin-de-siècle and its accompanying forms of Jewish cultural revival became perhaps the single most driving force behind the rehabilitation of the visual in Judaism. Having established that the "ancient Jew" had a "degenerate sense of space" which led to his "utilitarianism" and "intellectualism," the early Martin Buber welcomes the "creative spirit of Hasidism": "Hasidism is the birth of a new form of Judaism. The human body becomes a devotion of the world, beauty a ray of God, seeing a unity with God."[28] This quiet, mystical, and yet so worldly spirit of Hasidism, Buber contends, still glows in the creativity of Jewish artists today. "Our tribe, which has for so long produced scholars who hated life, began to create artists."[29]

It was primarily the cultural Zionist movement and its rootedness in European modernism that gave birth to the idea of the "Jewish artist" as a producer of "Jewish art."[30] With "Jewish art" at its disposal, Zionism aimed at returning pride and culture to a downtrodden people whose creativity, as the cultural Zionists argued, had been stifled by life in exile. But it was in the creation of "culture" that the secular and Orthodox camps of Judaism also clashed most. For "culture" associated itself with national, tribal authenticity, with "Hebraism" rather than Judaism. "To be the last Jews or the first Hebrews," was Micha Berdichevski's (1865-1921), famous question.[31] For him, the survival of the people was contingent upon the liberation of the individual. And who else could embody individuality more than the independent artist? "Our people," Berdichevski concluded, "can continue to exist only if there will be created among us a spiritual atmosphere and material possibilities for artists and builders."[32] The artist as quintessential individual and breaker with tradition soon advanced to the urban hero of cultural Zionism, and represented the "Jew of the future." And in the struggle for a culture more vital than the "semi-life" of Exile, art became the preferred medium of self-expression and self-knowledge. "We will look at it," wrote Buber in 1901, "and recognize ourselves."[33]

The transition from the "pure worship" of hearing to the culture of seeing was nothing short of a revolution. Judaism, as we have indicated above, was never fully hostile to the visual. Depending on whether the image was two- or three-dimensional, intaglio or relief, on the floor or on walls, to be used in mundane or in sacred contexts, the rabbis showed a surprising degree of flexibility.[34] Nor were Jews banned from the artistic professions, though, for centuries, they were barred from Christian artisan guilds. On the contrary, artisans of all trades were respected members of the traditional Jewish community. But artists in a modern sense were not. They were not for the same reasons the *apikores*—the freethinker—was not. For it was the modern artist, as Zionism well recognized, who was most suited to become an individual and to subvert the beliefs and practices of the group. In Judaism, the artist turned revolutionary not so much on account of his work than on account of his style of life. A participant in all walks of urban culture, living at the pulse of all transvaluation of values, and exposed to the many venues of assimilation, the modern Jewish artist was destined to be a rebel long before his rebellion.

RECONCILIATION AND RESISTANCE

The nature of David Aronson's conflict now appears more clearly. Being an artist not only challenged the aniconic tendency of traditional Judaism but also undermined the expected curriculum of Jewish learning and, indeed, the entire socio-cultural fabric of the community. Finally, and no less significant for a generation of immigrants, the choice of an artistic profession threatened the prospect of a secure livelihood.

Aronson's early success, however, made it possible for him to pursue and indeed live the life of an artist. And even though the alienation from his family was real, he never denied a Jewish undercurrent in his work. "[T]hese are Jewish paintings," he says of his New Testament motifs. "My own religious background was deeply woven into the fabric of the work."[35] His turning point towards Jewish subject matter, however, came from a source associated with secular culture. It was Aronson's wife, Georgianna Nyman, a serious painter in her own right with an acute artistic sensibility who gave him Thomas Mann's (1875-1955) *Josephslegend*, which he read in 1954. This served as the catalyst that turned him back to his early roots. That same year, he began a series of paintings devoted to the life of the biblical Joseph, taking liberties he had not taken before: "I could allow my imagination to roam freely through time and to shuffle like the mediaeval metaphysical conjurers," he writes.[36] The turn to Jewish folklore marked a final step towards reconciliation with what the young Aronson remembered as an anti-figurative religion. He was able to reconcile himself with Judaism because the Judaism he uncovered was not the religion of reason and spiritual purity the German *Maskilim* (enlighteners) and Lithuanian *Mitnagdim* (opponents to Hasidism) had fabricated, but a religion of material creativity and sensual imagination.

Just as Aronson found a way to reconcile himself with his heritage, his father found an explanation for the aberrant son. Aronson likes sharing an anecdote that took place on the Jewish Day of Atonement: "One Yom Kippur, I looked for my father in the synagogue, just to see how he was doing with the fast. I spied him looking up and smiling. I don't think I had ever seen him smile before. I asked him if he was feeling okay. He turned to me and said: 'It all came from your mother's side of the family.'"[37] And indeed, Aronson's maternal grandfather was known to have carved tombstones and played the fiddle.

But the inner reconciliation in the Aronson family had only little effect on the outward resistance in conservative Jewish and Christian circles. The harsh criticism Aronson's New Testament themes had earned in the 1940s was still present more than thirty years later when the Jewish Museum in New York arranged a retrospective show of his work in June 1979.[38] The Jewish Museum, which emerged during the first decade of the 20th century from a side room at the library of the Jewish Theological Seminary before it moved to its present quarters at the Warburg House on Fifth Avenue in 1947, already had an impressive, though not always untroubled history of exhibiting Jewish (and non-Jewish) modern artists.[39] Marc Chagall, Jacques Lipchitz, and Max Weber were among the featured artists at the opening exhibit of May 1947; Robert Rauschenberg (b. 1925) and Jasper Johns (b. 1930) were among those shaking the conservative foundations in the 1960s. But when David Aronson's work was prepared to be shown, the chancellor of the Jewish Theological Seminary, Gershon Cohen, decided shortly before the opening to remove 19 of Aronson's early paintings because of their "Christian symbolism." "A display of Christological paintings at the Jewish Museum," Cohen's statement read, "would be offensive to the Jewish community and would show both lack of respect for and lack of sensitivity to the perspective of our Christian friends."[40] Worried to offend Christians and Jews alike, a perhaps not entirely unfounded concern at the time, the conservative—not Orthodox—Jewish Seminary, with which the Jewish Museum has been affiliated from its beginnings, permitted to show only the "Jewish" Aronson, while the "Christian" Aronson was moved one block further to the National Academy of Design, whose director was "pleased to cooperate with a neighboring museum and to assist Mr. Aronson."[41] Once again, Aronson felt "a Jew among Christians and a Christian among Jews,"[42] while the *New York Times* noted bitingly that "the Jewish Museum should recognize that art, like freedom, is indivisible."[43] ■

IV THE DOOR

JOSEPH ABLOW CALLED *THE Door* (1963-69; Fig. 28) the "fullest statement of his [David Aronson's] aesthetic and allegorical concerns."[1] *The Door* is a monumental relief measuring eight feet by four feet and cast in solid bronze. Inspired by the Renaissance perfection of cast doors—such as the famous doors of the Florentine Baptistry—it has the plasticity of a sculpture and the composition of a painting. It is a door, as well as the image of a door. Divided into seven panels, *The Door* echoes and most fully realizes Aronson's multi-paneled paintings. Seven figural groups move in and out of their frames with great ease and elasticity, some soaring, some falling, as if the panels were revolving doors within the image of the door. We can recognize individual, recurring themes: The moonworshipers in the top register, a choir of angels in the left panel below, the levitation of a Golem next to it, the exorcism of a Dybbuk in the center, apprentices belonging to the Golem legend in the lower left panel, two musicians in the lower right panel, and, finally, a group of musicians absorbed by the power of music in the bottom register. The figures occupy varying spaces: Some are blended into the surface, appearing in the faintest relief, others pertly stick out their limbs, still others are fully sculptured. In *The Door,* the painterly and the sculptured are not only juxtaposed to evoke a rhythmic score that is harmonious as much as counterpoint; in *The Door,* the painterly is also *transformed* into the sculptured, and what we see is the frozen image of this metamorphosis, a metamorphosis from door to "door," from object to subject, from painting to sculpture. And just as the door comes to life as an image of itself, the figures seem to slyly step outside their painted existence into a corporeal chaos, like a horde of little golems escaping the drawing board of their master. For it is the independence of the figures that lends a quasi accidental composition to the door. The paradox of a sculptured surface that *The Door* puts before us, is resolved by the playful obstinacy of the figures who all but ignore the panels and frames to which they belong. In the crowded top panel, moonworshipers gaze into the skies above them, in the panels below an angel choir seems to return from a heavenly excursion, while the Golem next door, artfully mirroring the movement of the angels, is about to be lifted beyond the rim of his panel. In the center, exorcisers exorcise a Dybbuk who floats away to the left while the exorcee gains support on the shoulders of the musician in the lower panel. A tired observer reaches down to pull the nose of an apprentice whose leg dangles into the bottom panel where the musicians are sitting precariously along the edge, ready to slip out of their panel and, if nothing holds them back, fall off the door altogether.

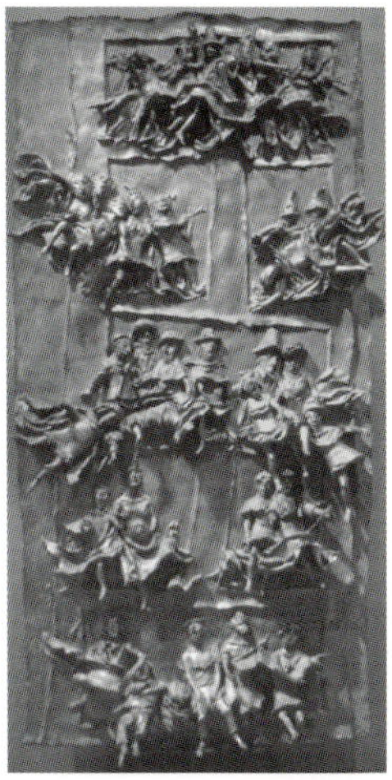

Figure 28

What all these figures have in common is their uncertain balance. They seem to be captured in a moment between falling and leaping, giddy with vertigo, intoxicated by a staggering carelessness. "*The Door* offers an unexpected view of those who dare to leap," writes Ablow in his now classic commentary on the work. It reveals, he continues, "the absurdity of man's aspiration to divinity."[2] The population of *The Door* is enveloped in ecstasy, leaping beyond the boundaries of the door as much as beyond themselves, and leaping towards a distant divine, charmed and conjured through magic and music. But despite all music and magic, despite all leaping and falling, and despite all denial of their own limits and boundaries, the figures remain figures on a door they cannot penetrate, on a door that remains closed to them, even if it turns in its real hinges. Unwittingly, the figures on *The Door* become guardians of a mystery they thought to have unlocked.

INTO THE THIRD DIMENSION

For David Aronson, sculpture emerged almost naturally from his painting: "I approached sculpture much as I did drawing and painting," he writes, "and the transition was natural and developmental."[3] We can best see a process of "sculpturization" in Aronson's charcoal and pencil drawings of the early 1960s. *Moonworshipers* of 1959-60 (Fig. 29) illustrates this transition most starkly. Against the dim walls of a room whose open window reveals the full moon in the back, two figures float up and down as if the room were filled with a viscous liquid. A third person, only partially visible, slowly descends from a nebulous ceiling and remains suspended in the air. Soaring figures, to be sure, have long been a stylistic topos in Aronson's work. They stand on their toes and hover weightlessly above ground. But unlike in his earlier paintings, the moonworshipers remove themselves not only from the ground beneath and above but from the very surface through which they enter an illusive space. The figures become sculptures to our eyes, and we cannot but observe utter astonishment in their faces as they suddenly fall into the third dimension.

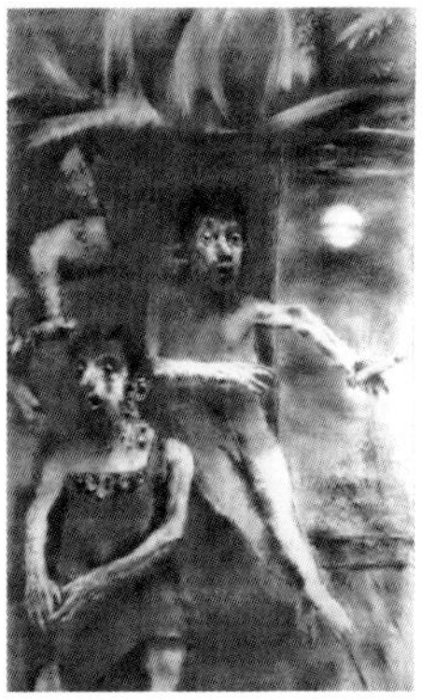

Figure 29

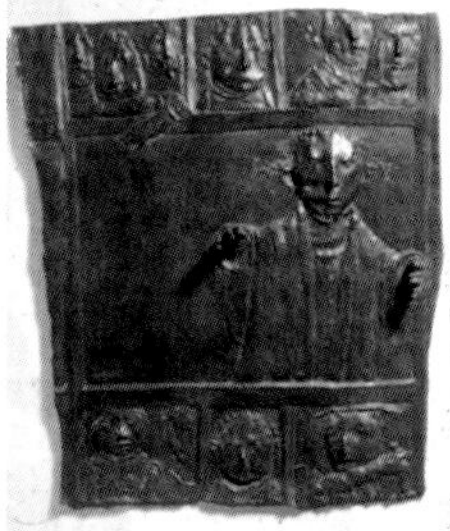

Figure 30

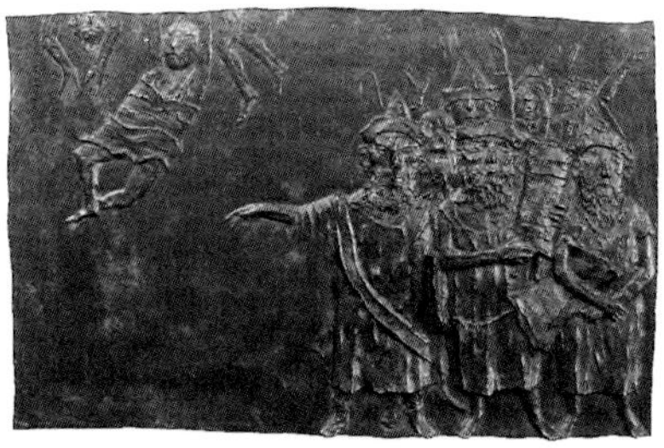

Figure 31

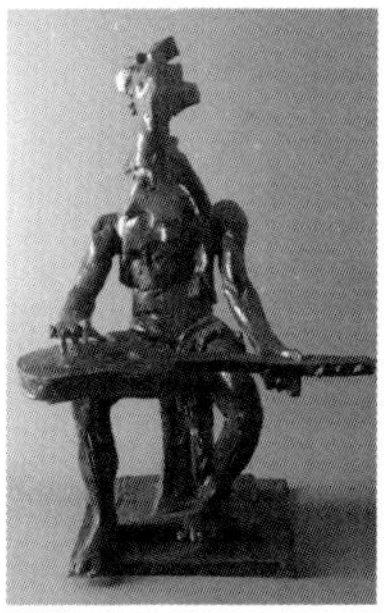

Figure 32

What remains skillful illusion in Aronson's paintings—beginning with *The Paradox* (Fig. 1)—is transformed into tangible space in his sculptures. His reliefs, in particular *The Judges* of 1961 (Fig. 9), *Edmund Burke* of 1963 (Fig. 30), and another version of the *Moonworshipers* (1963; Fig. 30), still echo the illusionism of his charcoal works, in fact, reverse it into an illusionism of two-dimensionality: The reliefs fool us into reading them as paintings. But in *The Door*, the illusionism has mastered itself. The figures have extended their limbs into the all-encompassing air that is between them and us, leaving behind the illusion of the door and the ground to which they are affixed.

SCULPTURE AND IDOLATRY

The Door opened the way to the free-standing sculptured image. From the 1960s on, painting and sculpture began to exist independently—as well as simultaneously—in Aronson's work.

But the transition to sculpture revealed yet another conflict to the artist: "As I produced reliefs and pieces in the round of moonworshipers, troubadours, scribes and Biblical figures," Aronson writes, "I was well aware that it was primarily against such images, the three-dimensional ones, that the popular interpretation of the Biblical prohibition was directed."[4] With the Golden Calf as the archetype of forbidden sculpture, the three-dimensional image has yet to be rehabilitated in the history of Judaism. Idols, in the Biblical experience, were sculptured images, and idolatry was primarily—though by no means exclusively—associated with their worship.[5] The Talmud knows an abundance of laws regarding *avodah zarah*, literally "foreign worship," many of them specifically concerned with the ubiquitous presence of statues in Greco-Roman culture. As in most examples of idolatry, it is not the object itself that warrants a prohibition but the possibility of its being worshiped. From the youthful patriarch Abraham smashing the clay idols in his father's workshop to the destruction of Baal temples upon the conquest of Canaan, Jewish iconoclasm has served as a powerful fence around what the Torah laboriously established as the irrefrangible oneness of God. Where idols could not be smashed the Sages developed a complex corpus of guidelines for how to live with them. "If a splinter has gone into his [foot] while in front of an idol," the Talmud (*Avodah Zarah* 12a) suggests in a well known passage, "he should not bend down to get it out, because he may appear as bowing to the idol." The *Shulkhan Arukh* (167:9) adds to this that if, however, a splinter must be removed at once, it should be done sitting down with one's back turned towards the image. The image itself, most sources agree, remains forbidden, even if its purpose is not designated to worship. But here, too, the prohibition is not absolute. A three-dimensional image whose realistic features have somehow vanished or been removed becomes, under certain circumstances, permissible. Fragments of an image, even if it was known to be an idol, are permitted as well, with the exception of an intact foot or a hand (cf. *Avodah Zarah* 41b). And, finally, idols annulled by the idolater are seen fit to decorate the Jewish home. "How does he annul it?" the Mishnah (*Avodah Zarah* 53a) asks. "If he cut off the tip of its ear, the tip of its nose or the tip of its finger; or if he defaced it." To the rabbis, imperfection was the most potent antidote to idolatry.

FRAGMENTS RESTORED

Imperfection, of course, is not the attribute to describe Aronson's sculptures. On the contrary, his sculptured work deliberately invokes the Renaissance mastery of draftsmanship, material, and patina. He fully identifies with the universal artist whose sculptures are logical extensions of his paintings. As in his encaustics, Aronson recovers an ancient technique, *cire perdu* (literally, lost wax) to cast objects of great detail and texture. An affinity exists, as Ablow pointed out, to the late Gothic of Tilman Riemenschneider (1460-1531) and to the eclectic Baroque of Gianlorenzo Bernini (1598-1680).[6] Aronson admires the spatial contours and the richness of patina in the sculptures of Auguste Rodin (1840-1917) and in the 16th century West African Benin bronzes.[7] Yet, he also favors the fragment which, too, evolves from his paintings where figure and form seem to continuously renew themselves in a shattered cosmos. Aronson's sculptures are fragments restored to space; their compactness is torn apart and recomposed in a fragile balance of broken pieces. This technique of restored fragmentation is especially evident in the *Seated Angel With Guitar* (1977-78; Fig. 32) whose upper body and oddly elongated neck appear to be composed of stacked scraps of sculpture, a crude reconstruction, it seems, of a battered, fractioned, tormented torso. We see this again in the *Fallen Angel* of 1987 (Fig. 33) where blocks of body are fused into an almost cubist figure at once monolithic and fragile, pinned to the ground by its own weight and unable to raise its clumsy, dislocated arms to the skies from where it came. The same sense of dislocation is apparent in the *Violinist II* (1987; Fig. 34) whose fractured arms seem to rest freely against the rounded torso, disconnected and yet strong enough to clasp the instrument. The chest itself is split open while deep clefts invade the sides of the neck. A pattern of clefts, cracks, and craters covers the *Warrior* heads (1989-95, Figs. 19 and 20) and, indeed, most of Aronson's sculptures, disrupting all smooth patina and violating the

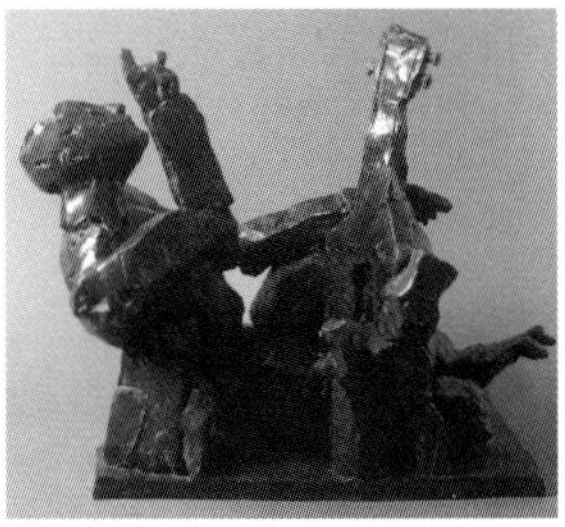
Figure 33

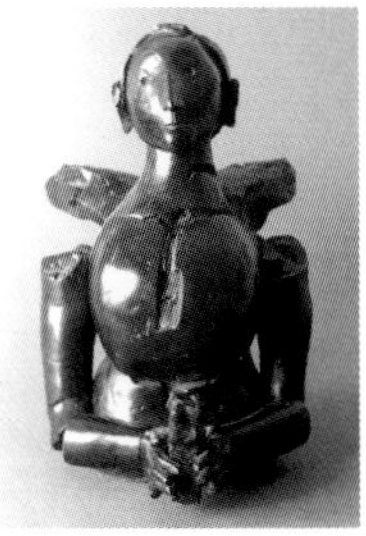
Figure 34

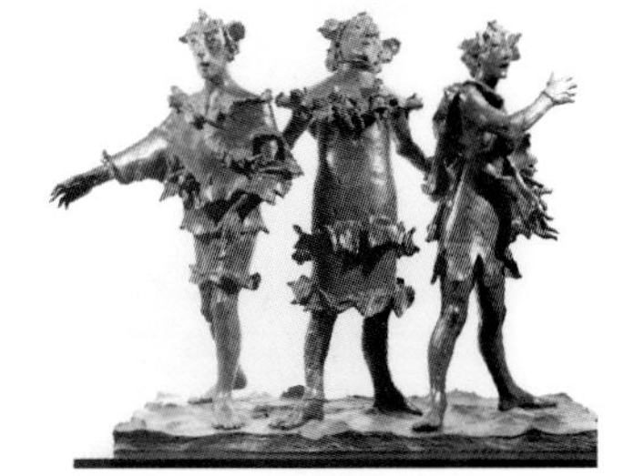
Figure 35

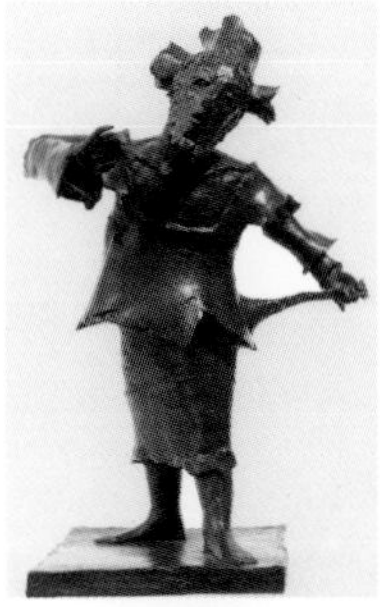
Figure 36

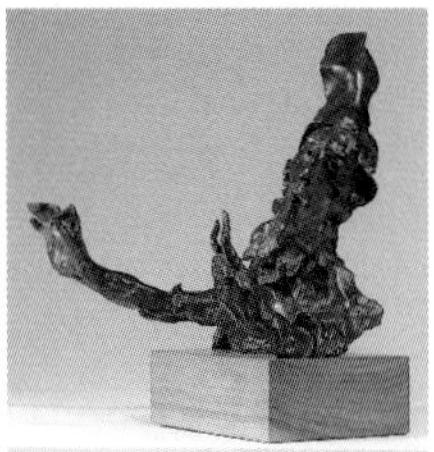
Figure 37

common perception of the perfect. These cracks and nicks cut into the beauty of the torso. They are wounds from the outside, traces of exteriority inflicted by an invisible space surrounding the sculpture. They remind us, then, that the space the sculpture occupies and fills is not a space of its own, but a space borrowed from a world that encompasses us all. Rather than being set apart, the sculpture becomes exposed, weathered by reality. No armor can shield the sculpture inside. The battered warriors hide their faces, but they cannot hide their humanity.

Why, then, was imperfection an antidote to idolatry? Because idolatry presupposes the power of the idol. "They bow down before empty emptiness and pray to a god who cannot save," the prophet Isaiah says of the idolaters.[8] But a shattered idol is no longer an idol of power. It is, in fact, more powerless than no idol at all. Hence, the power of iconoclasm does not lie in the mere removal of the object but in the shattering itself; in the visible act of disenchantment. The fracture negates idolatry. In this sense, David Aronson's sculptures can be seen as annulled idols, fallen idols whose illusory power has vanished just as, in his paintings, the icon has transcended itself to become the anti-icon.

HEARING IMAGES

And what is the anti-icon? "The prophets," writes the philosopher Hermann Cohen, "would not have been able to carry on the fight against art in the images of God if they themselves had not been able to lead it as artists."[9] But the prophets were not artists in a visual sense. To Cohen, they were "poet-thinkers," artists with a powerful "poetic imagination," masters of the spoken word. Their medium was speech, the sound of spokenness that continues to penetrate the poetic tradition of Psalms and hymns. The hearing idolater, Cohen continues, becomes "ashamed" of his images. But even more, the images become ashamed of themselves, as in Isaiah (44:9): "That they may be ashamed." Because they defy all visible form, poetry and music, for Cohen, became the most powerful instruments of iconoclasm. Expanding upon the thoughts of his teacher, the Jewish thinker Franz Rosenzweig (1886-1929) writes a few years later that "among the arts it is music that is coordinate with revelation. For in revelation the ray of time bursts through the aperture of the moment into the broad basin of created space, and music is that art which spins a time period out of the moment."[10] "Melodies," Rosenzweig concludes, "preserve words."[11]

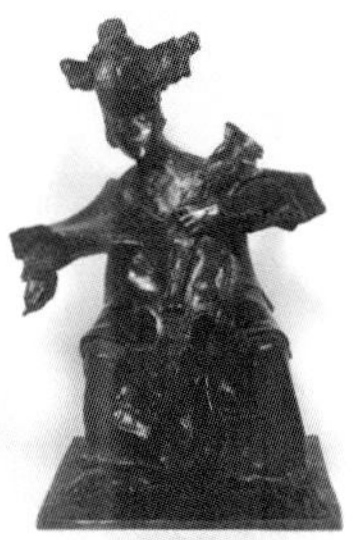

Figure 38

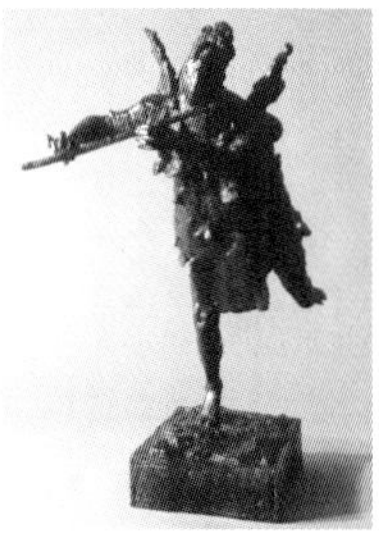

Figure 39

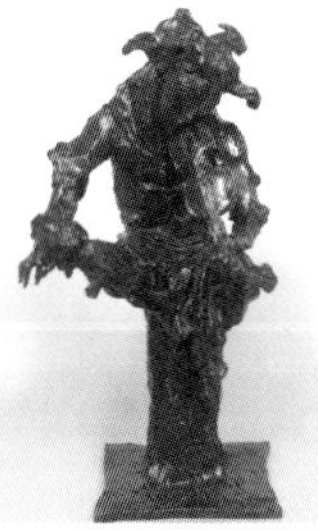

Figure 40

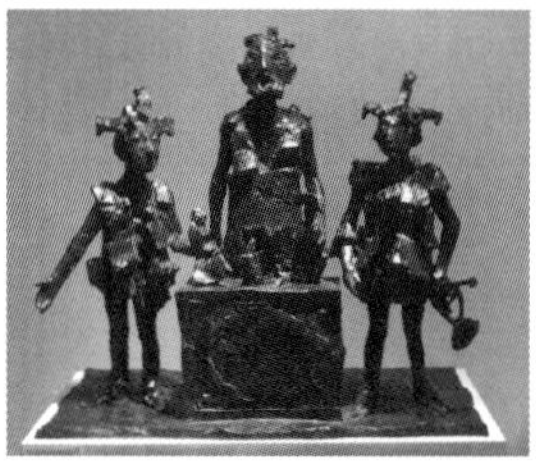

Figure 41

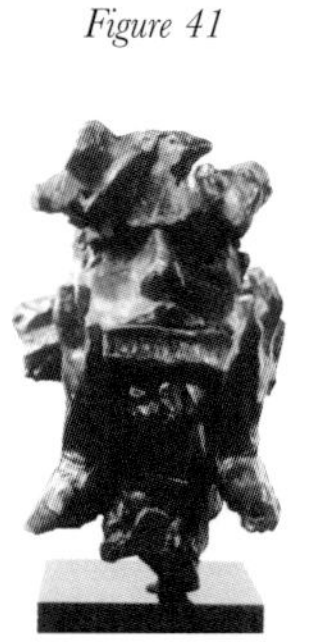

Figure 42

A peculiar affinity exists between image and music in Aronson's sculptures. Already *The Door* is populated with musicians and singing angels. In one of his most accomplished works, *Three Singers* (1963-69; Fig. 35) are seen performing, each one with asserted independence, claiming individual spaces for their movements and sounds. We can see the group as much as we can "hear" it. Indeed, a silent sound rolls from their postures and gestures, and it spills beyond the spatial boundaries of their sculptured likeness. We see similar images evoking sound in *Troubadour* of 1964 (Fig. 36), in *Virtuoso* of 1969 (Fig. 37) and in *Cellist* of 1974-76 (Fig. 38), who is generating music as much as being absorbed in it. In *Angel with Flute* (1971; Fig. 39), sound and movement and are fused together in a body of sheer weightlessness: The angel seems to travel with the fleeting lightness of his music. In *Fiddler* (1974; Fig. 40), whose pose almost invokes the classical Spinario (Thornpuller), music flows through the physical relationship between the fiddle and its player. In the *Violinist II* of 1987 (Fig. 34) we encounter the same physical closeness between player and instrument. *The Entertainers* (1976-78; Fig. 41) have lowered their instruments to engage with the audience, but we can still catch faint echoes of their play. A *Harmonica Player* (1987; Fig. 42) forces air through his harmonica. The rugged sound of his instrument repeats itself in the rugged landscape of his hands and hair.

One is tempted to conclude that David Aronson's sculptures play music to annul their last traces of idolness; that music, or the mere presence of a musical instrument, disperses the solidity of the figure; that sound is yet another leap toward fragmentation. It is his play that throws the otherwise robust *Kneeling Rider with Violin* (1977-78; Fig. 43) off balance, and it is, perhaps, the rhythm of the same play that also keeps him *in* balance. To the viewer, the absurd juxtaposition of a violinist and a horse, as also in *Rider with Violin* (1976-78; Fig. 44), is reason enough for a spell of queasiness. In *Rider with Torah* of the same period (1976-78; Fig. 45), the act of balance becomes even more acrobatic while the object—the Torah—becomes more displaced in the absurd synthesis of sacred and profane. A Torah must not fall, but the rider, we fear, cannot possibly remain kneeling on the back of his horse. His balance is all but a paradox.

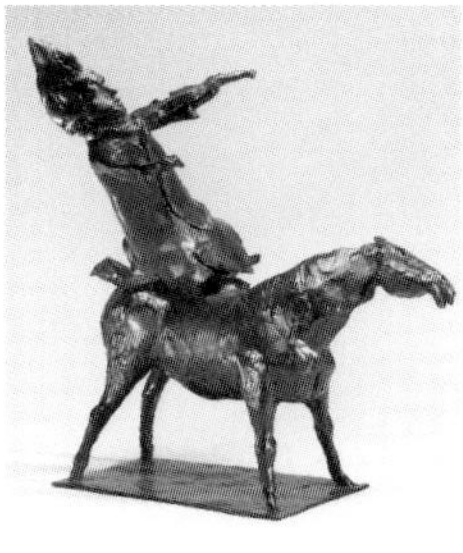

Figure 43

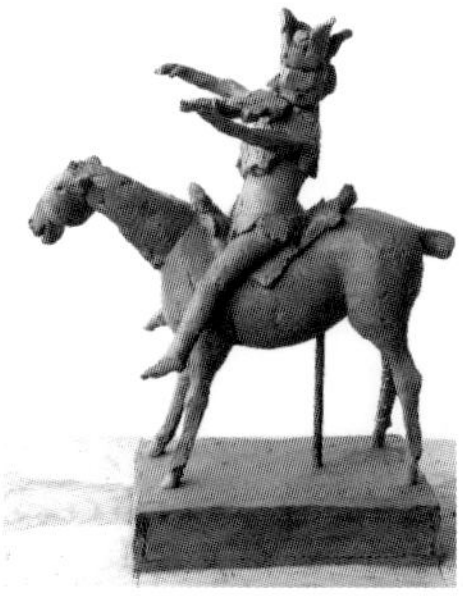

Figure 44

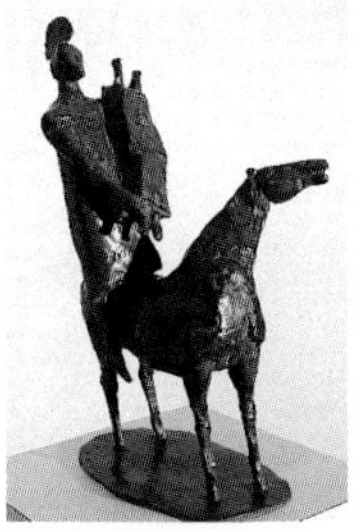

Figure 45

THE HUMANIST PARADOX

The Paradox (Fig. 1) opened our reflections. A paradox, we saw then, encompasses an experience both beyond reason and beyond delusion. A paradox reveals and conceals. It creates realities and shatters them. It points beyond and misleads. It enables to see, and obscures. To the Surrealists, the paradox represented an existential credo. For Aronson—despite his sympathies for Surrealism—it is no more than a reality. He remains a realist; not a realist of realism, but a realist in the mystical, transcendental, paradoxical sense that we have encountered above all in the Expressionism of Beckmann and his Boston inheritors. The reality of his realism is magical, capricious, unpredictable. But it is also fragile, fleeting, and ambiguous. Again and again Aronson returns to the theme of the entertainer, the harlequin, the charlatan and magician; in short: to the artist who creates illusions, but whose illusions are as real as reality. We look at *Entertainer* of 1998 (Fig. 46) and see a musician captured in the moment between her music and her private life, clutching a violin in one hand, feeling the surface of a table with the other. She is torn, it seems. But if she is torn, then she is also at peace with her tornness, immersed in an eternal moment of introversion. The entertainer turns inward, and we turn with her.

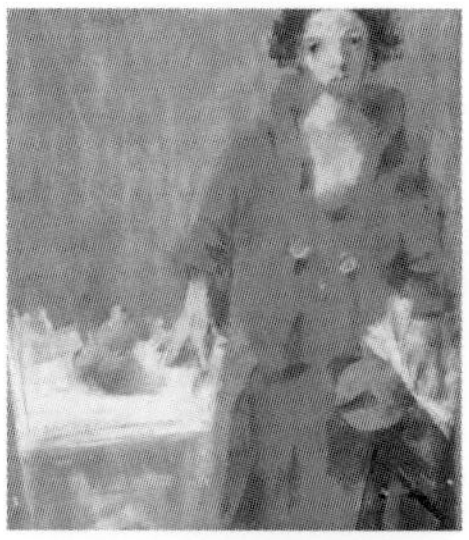

Figure 46

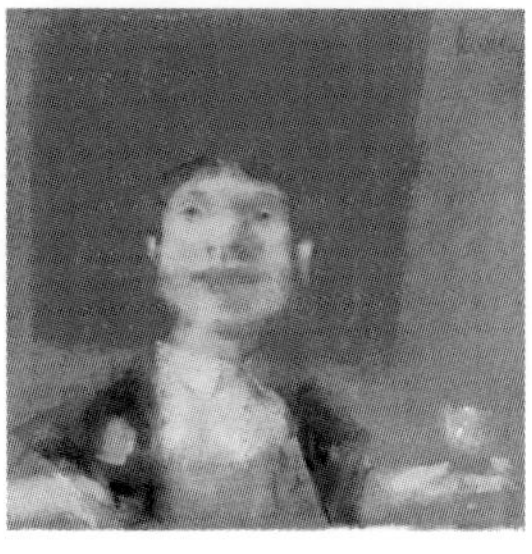

Figure 47

There is a persistent duality in Aronson's figures, an ambiguity between active and passive life, between expression and contemplation. His figures appear in a constant in-between, in an endless state of turning. They are not settled, not at home in the exterior world. Falling and leaping, they are caught in mid-air, as it were, hurled into the depths of their thoughts. The moment of their depiction, the *kairos* in Aronson's art, is a moment where the inner and outer worlds face each other with great astonishment, even alienation, knowing that they can never be reconciled.

It is here, in this moment of free-fall contemplation, that David Aronson finds what art and religion seek with equal but often misguided ardor: Humanity. Humanity as a delicate, ephemeral balance between a chaos of things and a confusion of feelings. His realism is a gentle unmasking of this humanity, so gentle that it must hide what it unmasks. And so his characters, whether from the midst or from the fringes of society, must hide as well. It is as if they were ashamed of themselves, ashamed to be. And if they are not ashamed, like *The Hedonist* (1999; Fig. 47), they frighten us as tragic fools. ■

NOTES TO CHAPTER I (pages 3-12)

[1] On the Boston Museum of Fine Arts see Roberta A. Sheehan, "The Boston Museum School: A Centennial History." Diss., Boston College, 1983.

[2] David Aronson, "Real and Unreal: The Double Nature of Art," p. 144— in this volume.

[3] Ibid., p. 144.

[4] Ibid., p. 144.

[5] Ibid., p. 144. No less apparent is the influence of Rembrandt and Chaim Soutine in Aronson's work. "There are also two truly important heroes of mine—Rembrandt and Soutine whose ghosts always hover as I work." (David Aronson, Letter to author, Dec. 2, 2003). "[M]y greatest inspiration came, and still comes, from Rembrandt. I find the most profound characterizations and the greatest humanity in a Rembrandt head. And what he did with light and dark affected me deeply, even more than Caravaggio, the master of chiaroscuro who influenced Rembrandt." (Interview, quoted in Gail D'Angelo, "An Ancestral Aesthetic. The Fine Art of David Aronson," *Bostonia,* Spring 1992, p. 47).

[6] Cf. Stephen Robert Frankel (ed.), *Jack Levine,* New York: Rizzoli 1989, p. 29f.

[7] "Without being too dogmatic, one may still distinguish the divergence of tendencies in the history of art and recognize that Aronson must clearly be an expressionist by virtue of both his artistic and actual heritage." Paul T. Nagano, "The Expressionism of David Aronson." in *Aronson* (Exhibition catalogue), Boston: Pucker/Safrai Gallery, 1976, p. 6.

[8] On the origins of the term Expressionism see Victor H. Miesel, "The Term Expressionism in the Visual Arts," in *Uses of History: Essays in Intellectual and Social History, presented to William J. Bossenbrook,* ed. by Hayden V. White, Detroit: Wayne State University Press, 1968; and Marit Werenskiold, *The Concept of Expressionism. Origin and Metamorphoses,* Oslo et al: Universitetsforlaget, 1984, p. 5-34. It seems that the art dealer Paul Cassirer coined the term (cf. ibid., p.6).

[9] *Katalog der XXII. Ausstellung der Berliner Sezession,* Berlin, 1911, p. 11: ". . .Werke jüngerer französischer Maler, der Expressionisten. . ."

[10] Reprinted in Thomas Anz/Michael Stark (eds), *Expressionismus (Manifeste und Dokumente zur Deutschen Literatur 1910-1920),* Stuttgart: J.B. Metzler, 1982, p.18. For the relation between Expressionism and the German cultural pessimism that emerged around World War I and permeated the Weimar Republic see Bernd Hüppauf (ed.), *Expressionismus und Kulturkrise,* Heidelberg: Carl Winter, 1983; Peter Gay, *Weimar Culture: The Outsider as Insider,* New York and Evanston: Harper & Row, 1968, pp. 102-118; Walter Laqueur, *Weimar: A Cultural History,* New York: G. P. Putnam, 1974, pp. 162-182. On the connection between Expressionism and German nationalism see George L. Mosse, *The Crisis of German Ideology: Intellectual Origins of the Third Reich,* New York: Schocken, 1981, esp. pp. 186f. For an account of German cultural pessimism see Fritz Stern, *The Politics of Cultural Dispair: A Study in the Rise of the Germanic Ideology,* Berkeley and Los Angeles: University of California Press, 1961.

[11] Franz Marc, "Die 'Wilden' Deutschlands," in *Der Blaue Reiter,* ed. by Franz Marc and Wassily Kandinsky, Munich, 1912, p. 4. Reprinted in Anz/Stark, *Expressionismus,* p. 27f. Similarly, Max Beckmann stated in 1914: "My program is short, for I do not have one. The most I can say is that I detest all theory and all principles of painting." ("Vielleicht doch ein Programm." Faltblatt zur Ausstellung im Kunstverein Hamburg, 1914, reprinted in *Die Realität der Träume in den Bildern. Schriften und Gespräche 1911 bis 1950,* ed. by Rudolf Pillep, Munich: Piper 1990, p.16.). The group *Der Blaue Reiter* (The Blue Rider), named after a painting by Wassily Kandinsky (1866-1944), emerged in December 1911 as a breakaway from the *Neue Künstler-Vereinigung München e.V.,* originally founded in 1909 by Kandinsky, Alexej Jawlensky (1864-1941), Alexander Kanoldt (1881-1939), Alfred Kubin (1877-1951), and others. The first exhibition of the group included works by Kandinsky, Franz Marc (1860-1916), Kubin, and Gabriele Münter (1877-1962). The almanac was intended to provide a forum for the theoretical foundations of the movement. However, only one volume of the almanac appeared, with a second in preparation, before the oncoming war destroyed all further efforts. Kandinsky returned to Russia whereas Franz Marc died at the Western front in 1916.

[12] Cf. Rudolf Blümner, "Expressionismus und Impressionismus," in *Der Geist des Kubismus und die Künste,* Berlin, 1921, pp. 65-7.

[13] Paul Fechter, *Der Expressionismus,* Munich: Piper & Co, 1914, p. 21f.

[14] Ibid., p.22.

[15] Ibid., p.23.

[16] Wassily Kandinsky, *Concerning the Spiritual in Art and Painting in Particular* (1912), trans. by Michael Sadleir et al, New York: Wittenborn & Schultz, 1947, p. 23f. On this subject see also David Pan, *Primitive Renaissance: Rethinking German Expressionism,* Lincoln and London: University of Nebraska Press, 2001, esp. pp. 98-120.

[17] Kandinsky, *Concerning the Spiritual in Art,* p. 24.

[18] Fechter attributed "intensive" Expressionism as "expression of its own" to Kandinsky: "What he wants to give us is his human existence of feeling *(Gefühlsexistenz),* isolated from all environment, removed from all relation to nature and form." (Fechter, *Der Expressionismus,* p. 24f.). The "extensive" variant he associated with Max Pechstein: "He experiences himself not in isolation, not in contemplation of his own profundity, but in the submission to the experience of the world around him. As a man of this-worldliness, he takes in the environment and creates a new life for it from his own emotions [...]. He expresses his life in the felt existence of things, expressing in this way their essence." (Ibid., p. 26).

[19] Hermann Bahr, *Expressionismus,* Munich: Delphin, 1916, p. 123. *Der Mensch schreit* (Man Screams) was also the title of a collection of poems by the expressionist writer Albert Ehrenstein, published in 1916 (Leipzig).

[20] Max Beckmann, *Bekenntnis* (1918), reprinted and ed. by Hans Voss, Berlin: Friedenauer Presse, 1966, p.4.

[21] Kurt Hiller, "Vom Aktivismus," in *Die weißen Blätter* 4 (April-June 1917), p. 88. Reprinted in Anz/Stark: *Expressionismus,* p. 284.

[22] Cf. "Rat geistiger Arbeiter," in *Die Weltbühne* 14, No. 47 (November 21, 1918), p. 473-478. Reprinted in Anz/Stark: *Expressionismus,* p. 288-291.

[23] Ernst Bloch, *Der Geist der Utopie,* Munich: Drucken & Humboldt, 1918 (reprint Frankfurt/M.: Suhrkamp, 1971), p. 9. On the utopian, messianic ideals of the inter-War period see also Paul Mendes-Flohr, "'The Stronger and the Better Jews': Jewish Theological Responses to Political Messianism in the Weimar Republic," in Jonathan Frankel (ed.), *Jews and Messianism* in the *Modern Era: Metaphor and Meaning* (Studies in Contemporary Jewry VII [1991]), pp. 159-185.

[24] Kasimir Edschmid, "Bilanz," in *Die doppelköpfige Nymphe. Aufsätze*

über die Literatur und die Gegenwart, Berlin: Paul Cassirer, 1920, p. 209.

[25] Cf. Iwan Goll, "Der Expressionismus stirbt," in *Zenit* 1, No. 8 (Oktober 1921), pp. 8-9. Reprinted in Anz/Stark, *Expressionismus,* pp. 108-109.

[26] Franz Roh, *Nach-Expressionismus. Magischer Realismus (Probleme der neuesten europäischen Malerei),* Leipzig: Klinkhardt & Biermann, 1925, p.24.

[27] Ibid., p.36.

[28] Beckmann, *Bekenntnis,* p.3.

[29] Ibid., p.5.

[30] Roh, *Nach-Expressionismus,* Preface n.p.

[31] Emil Utitz, *Die Überwindung des Expressionismus. Charakterologische Studien zur Kultur der Gegenwart,* Stuttgart: Ferdinand Enke, 1927, p. 39.

[32] The term *Neue Sachlichkeit* was most likely coined by the art historian Gustav Hartlaub in a letter to Max Beckmann of May 1923. Cf. Dennis Crockett, *German Post-Expressionism: The Art of the Great Disorder 1918-1924,* University Park, PA: Pennsylvania State University Press, 1994, p. 155.

[33] Paul Westheim, "Beckmann: Der wahre Expressionismus," in *Für und Wider,* Potsdam, 1923, p.104f. Westheim, however, did not consider Beckmann a true member of *Neue Sachlichkeit.*

[34] Cf. Gustav F. Hartlaub, "Zur Einführung in die Neue Sachlichkeit: Ausschnitt aus der deutschen Malerei seit dem Expressionismus" (exhibition catalogue), Dresden, 1925.

[35] Roh, *Nach-Expressionismus,* p.35.

[36] Cf. Beckmann, "Der Künstler im Staat," in *Die Realität der Träume,* p. 39: "It is essential that also the workers appear in a dress coat."

[37] Emil Utitz noted that the new aesthetic and moral worldview of post-Expressionism would culminate in the "German man." *(Die Überwindung des Expressionismus,* p. 100). On the latter interpretation see, for instance, Waldemar George, "Frankreich und die Neue Sachlichkeit," in *Das Kunstblatt 11* (November 1927), p. 395: "The *Neue Sachlichkeit* is Americanism, the cult of the objective, the hard fact, the predilection for functional work, professional consciousness, usefulness." A similar contradiction surrounded the initial reception of Expressionism. In the infamous *Protest of German Artists* of 1911, the painter Carl Vinnen and 118 signatories denounced the influence of French "Expressionist" art as a "große Gefahr für unser Volkstum" (a great danger for our national culture) (Cf. Carl Vinnen, *Ein Protest deutscher Künstler,* Jena: Diederichs, 1911, p. 8). In response, a group of artists (including the director of the Berlin Secession, Max Liebermann, Karl Hofer, Beckmann, Pechstein, Kandinsky, and others), art historians (including Wilhelm Worringer), and art dealers (including Paul Cassirer) published a volume of statements (*Im Kampf um die Kunst. Die Antwort auf den Protest deutscher Künstler, Munich:* Piper, 1911) defending the internationality of art. Ironically, as we have seen in Fechter's *Expressionismus* of 1914, Expressionism soon advanced to a "national art" in Germany, if only temporarily. On the Vinnen incident and the German resistance to French modernism see also Peter Lasko, *The Modernist Roots of Expressionism,* Manchester and New York: Manchester University Press, 2003, p. 9.

[38] Among the many examples, one could name Otto Dix' *An die Schönheit* of 1922 and Georges Grosz' *Vor Sonnenaufgang* of 1922, or *The Café* of 1925, the latter at the Busch-Reisinger Museum.

[39] On the history of the Debschitz Schule see Dagmar Rinker, *Die Lehr- und Versuchs-Ateliers für Angewandte und Freie Kunst (Debschitz Schule): München 1902-1914.* Munich: Tuduv, 1993. Helga Schmoll gen. Eisenwerth, "Die Münchner Debschitzschule," in Hans M. Wingler (ed.), *Kunstschulreform 1900-1933: Bauhaus Weimar, Dessau, Berlin, Kunstschule Debschitz, München, Frankfurter Kunstschule, Akad. Breslau, Reimann-Schule Berlin.* Berlin: Mann, 1977, pp. 68-92. For a biography of Karl Zerbe and further references to his work see Judith A. Bookbinder, "Figurative Expressionism in Boston and Its Germanic Cultural Affinities: An Alternative Modernist Discourse on Art and Identity." Ph.D. Diss., Boston University, 1998, pp. 31-50; idem, "Boston Modern: Figurative Expressionism in the 1940s," in *The Visionary Decade: New Voices in Art in 1940s Boston,* ed. by Sinclair Hitchings and Stephanie Mayer, Boston University Art Gallery, 2002, pp. 30-34.

[40] At the time of Zerbe's student years, Debschitz and Obrist were no longer involved in the school, which, after 1920, was called "Münchner Lehrwerkstätte" and had lost much of its original momentum. (Cf. Helga Schmoll gen. Eisenwerth, "Die Münchner Debschitzscule," p. 79). On the work of Eberz see Leopold Zahn, *Josef Eberz.* Leipzig: Klinkhardt & Biermann, 1920. For Karl Casper see Peter-Klaus Schuster (ed.), *"München leuchtete": Karl Caspar und die Erneuerung christlicher Kunst in München um 1900,* Munich: Prestel, 1984.

[41] Cf. Sheehan, "The Boston Museum School," p. 130f. Zerbe, in fact, looked with certain delight at his students smashing the plaster casts in an iconoclast orgy. Cf. Bookbinder, "Boston Modern," p.31. On the didactic reforms introduced by Iacovleff see Bookbinder, "Figurative Expressionism in Boston," p. 273f.

[42] Jason Berger, interview with Dorothy Thompson, February 28, 1986. Quoted in Dorothy Abbott Thompson, *Origins of Boston Expressionism: The Artist's Perspective,* Lincoln, MA: DeCordova and Dana Museum, 1986, p. 19. Cf. also Bookbinder, "Boston Modern," p. 30.

[43] "Boston art was parochial and conservative and removed from what was happening in the rest of the world." (Dorothy Thompson, "The Spirits of Hyman Bloom: The Sources of His Imagery," in: Dorothy Abbott Thompson, *Hyman Bloom,* New York: Chameleon Books, 1996, p. 12). The "academic impressionism" of turn of the century painters like Edmund Tarbell (1862-1938), Frank Benson (1862-1951), William Paxton (1869-1941), or John Singer Sargent (1856-1925) still dominated the Boston scene in the 1920s and 1930s. (See Patricia Jobe Pierce, *The Ten: Frank W. Benson, Joseph R. DeCamp, Thomas W. Dewing, Childe Hassam, Willard L. Metcalf, Robert Reid, Edward Simmons, Edmund C. Tarbell, John H. Twachtman, J. Alden Weir and William Merritt Chase (who replaced Twachtman, 1902);* Concord, N.H.: Rumford Press, and North Abington, MA: Pierce Galleries, 1976. Idem, *Edmund C. Tarbell and the Boston School of Painting 1889-1980;* Hingham, MA: Pierce Galleries, 1980. Susan Strickler (ed.), *Impressionism Transformed: The Paintings of Edmund C. Tarbell;* N.H.: Currier Gallery of Art, and Hanover, N.H.: University Press of New England, 2001. Ellen Wardwell Lee (ed.), *William McGregor Paxton, 1869-1941 (Member of the National Academy);* Indianapolis: Indianapolis Museum of Art, 1979). When the historic Armory Exhibition of 1913, which included works by Henri Matisse, Georges Braque, Marcel Duchamp (1887-1968), and many others of the European avant-garde, traveled from New York City—where it had been a great, if also controversial success—to Boston, it hardly received attention. (Cf. Thompson, *Hyman Bloom,* p.12). This, however, needs to be qualified. As J. M. Mancini has recently indicated, the Armory show did have a significant influence on young artists and intellectuals not only in New York but also in Chicago and Boston. On this point and a reevaluation of the reception of the show see idem, "'One Term is as Fatuous as Another': Responses to the Armory Show Reconsidered," *American Quarterly* 51.4 (1999), pp. 833-870; on the Armory Show see Milton Brown, *The Story of the Armory Show,* Greenwich, CT, 1963.

[44] See Bookbinder, "Figurative Expressionism in Boston," pp. 12-29 and p. 82f.

[45] Cf. Bookbinder, "Boston Modern," p. 28 and "Figurative Expressionism in Boston," pp. 25-29. On the history of the Busch-

Reisinger Museum see Peter Nisbet and Emilie Norris, *The Busch-Reisinger Museum: History and Holdings*, Cambridge: Harvard University Museums, 1991. Also: Charles Kuhn, *German Expressionism and Abstract Art: The Harvard Collections,* Cambridge: Harvard University Press, 1957 (supplement, 1967).

[46] Frankel, *Jack Levine*, p. 13. Levine called himself "one of the first native Brechtians in America" (ibid., p. 20).

[47] Beckmann visited Boston from March 10 to 17, 1948, Kokoschka in the fall of that year and again during the summer session at the Berkshire Museum in Pittsfield, Massachusetts, in 1949 (cf. Capasso, "Expressionism," p.149). In his diary (March 9, 1948), Beckmann noted that he did "not expect much from Boston" (cf. *Die Realität der Träume in den Bildern. Aufsätze und Vorträge aus Tagebüchern, Briefen, Gesprächen, 1903-1950,* Leipzig: Reclam jun., 1984, p. 309). Beckmann's work, however, had already been presented at the Germanic Museum in November 1940 (cf. Bookbinder, "Figurative Expressionism in Boston," p. 282, n.39). In 1946, Karl Zerbe initiated an exhibition of Beckmann's drawings and paintings for the Museum School, a project that David Aronson helped assemble (cf. Bookbinder, "Boston Modern," p. 32). Two major exhibitions at the Germanic Museum in 1935 and 1941 were devoted to George Grosz (1893-1959). By the 1950s, the Germanic Museum had acquired a substantial collection of European Expressionists including works by Ernst Barlach (1870-1938), Otto Dix (1891-1969), Erich Heckel (1883-1970), Ernst Ludwig Kirchner (1880-1938), Emil Nolde (1867-1956), and Wassily Kandinsky (1866-1944) (cf. Capasso, "Expressionism," p. 150; and Charles L. Kuhn, *German Expressionism and Abstract Art. The Harvard Collection*).

[48] "We often went to the Germanic Museum and the Fogg. We had no interest in the Boston School of Impressionism (with the exception of [John Singer] Sargent who was a great painter)." (David Aronson, interview quoted in Bookbinder, "Figurative Expressionism in Boston," p. 274). This view was corroborated by Hyman Bloom and Jack Levine (cf. ibid., p. 65f.).

[49] On Zerbe mocking the action painter Jackson Pollock (1912-1956) see Capasso, "Expressionism," p. 149, and Nancy Stapen, "Showcasing the Artist Who Recast Hub Scene," *The Boston Globe* (Feb. 9, 1995), p. 66.

[50] Cf. Karl Zerbe, "Expressionism and Symbolism," *Art Panorama* (Jan./Feb. 1945), p. 11.

[51] On Karl Hofer's impact on Zerbe see Gillian Levine, Stephen Prokopoff, Elisabeth Sussman, *Boston Expressionism: Hyman Bloom, Jack Levine, Karl Zerbe,* Boston: Institute of Contemporary Art, 1979, p.7, and Bookbinder, "Figurative Expressionism," p. 46f. Hofer was portrayed as a conservative who rejected the "ecstasies of Expressionism" and described himself as a "romantic in search of the classic." (Cf. Laqueur, *Weimar*, pp. 167f.).

[52] On the use of the triptych in Beckmann see Peter J. Gärtner: *Der Traum von der Imagination des Raumes: Zu den Raumvorstellungen auf einigen ausgewählten Triptychen Max Beckmanns,* Weimar 1996; and Reinhard Spieler, *Max Beckmann. Bildweld und Weltbild in den Triptychen,* Köln: Dumont, 1998.

[53] *Harlequin* (1944) and *Hooded Figure* (1952) are striking examples of Zerbe's interest in this motif.

[54] See Heinz Jatho, *Max Beckmann: Schauspieler-Triptychon. Eine Kunst-Monographie,* Frankfurt: Insel Verlag, 1989.

[55] On the dialectics of the triptych form see Spieler, *Max Beckmann*, p. 49f.

[56] On the theatrical quality of Beckmann's triptychs see Claude Gandelmann, "Max Beckmann und die Simultanbühne der 20er Jahre," in *Max Beckmann. Die Triptychen im Städel* (exhibition catalogue), Frankfurt/M., 1981, pp. 102-113.

[57] Ralph M. Pearson, *The Modern Renaissance in American Art. Presenting the Work and Philosophies of 54 distinguished American Artists,* New York: Harper and Brothers, 1954, pp. 133-134.

[58] Beckmann, "Drei Briefe an eine Malerin," in *Die Realität der Träume* (1984), p. 182.

[59] Robert Taylor, "Boston Expressionists," *Boston Globe* (January 14, 1979), p. B-1. Cf. Thompson, *Origins of Boston Expressionism*, p.3.

[60] Citing Max Weber, Bloom, and Levine, Pamela Edwards Allera asserts a link between figurative Expressionism and the Jewish response to World War II and Nazism (cf. Idem, "The Humanist Vision: Expressionist Art in Boston, 1945-1985," in *Expressionism in Boston: 1945-1985,* Lincoln, MA: DeCordova Museum, 1986, p.12). It is interesting to note that Joseph Paul Hodin described "Jewish art" as "entirely the product of painters who have not only Jewish origin, but also a Slavonic background." (Joseph Paul Hodin, "The Problem of Jewish Art in its Contemporary Aspect," in J. P. Hodin, *Modern Art and the Modern Mind,* Cleveland: Case Western Reserve University, 1972, p. 149).

[61] To refer to the first phase of Boston Expressionism as "on the whole, a Jewish phenomenon," as Robert Taylor does, therefore, needs to be qualified (cf. Robert Taylor, "The Humanist Tradition in Boston," in *Humanism in New England Art,* Lincoln, MA: DeCordova Museum, 1970, n.p.).

[62] Dorothy C. Miller (ed.), *Fourteen Americans,* New York: The Museum of Modern Art, 1946, p. 8.

[63] With the exception of Joseph Ablow, who later turned to "other aesthetic concerns." Joseph Ablow, Letter to author, June 20, 2004.

[64] Hence, Pamela Edwards Allera distinguishes three periods of Boston Expressionism: The figurative phase (1940-55), the phase of gestural abstraction (1968-1975), and a third phase of neo-Expressionist figuration (1975-1985) (cf. Pamela Edwards Allera, "The Humanist Vision", pp. 10-49). Nicholas Capasso sees a "second wave of expressionist painting" following the decline of neo-Expressionism and extending from the mid 1980s to the twenty-first century (cf. Capasso, "Expressionism," p. 169f.).

[65] On David Aronson and the School for the Arts at Boston University see Judith Bookbinder, "Figurative Expressionism in Boston," pp. 367-388.

[66] Cf. Dorothy Miller, *Americans 1942-1963: Six Group Exhibitions,* New York: The Museum of Modern Art (Reprint). 1972.

[67] On the Boris Mirski Gallery see Dorothy Abbott Thompson, *Origins of Boston Expressionism,* pp.22-24. And Rachel Rosenfield Lafo, "The Boston Art Scene: A Community and its Institutions," in Lafo/Capasso/Uhrhane (eds.), *Painting in Boston: 1950-2000,* pp. 24-26.

[68] Dorothy Abbott Thompson, *Origins of Boston Expressionism,* p. 23.

[69] David Aronson points out the influence of the Mexican painters and muralists José Clemente Orozco (1883-1949) and David Alfaro Siqueiros (1896-1974) as well (cf. Aronson, "Real and Unreal," p. 144 in this volume).

[70] Capasso, "Expressionism," p. 170.

NOTES TO CHAPTER II (pages 13-18)

[1] Quoted in Carol Kur, "David Aronson's Art," in *Moment*, Vol. 4, No. 1 (November 1978), p. 28.

[2] On the technique of encaustic see Frances Pratt and Becca Fizel, *Encaustic: Materials and Methods*, New York: Lear, 1949; Gail Stavitsky, *Waxing Poetic: Encaustic Art in America*, Montclair, NJ: Montclair Art Museum, 1999. See also David Aronson, "Encaustic," in *The Artist*, Vol. 64, No. 4, Iss. 382 (December 1962), pp. 78-79.

[3] *Newsweek*, Vol. XXVI, No. 22 (November 26, 1945), p. 114.

[4] Cf. ibid., p. 114; see also Aronson, "Real and Unreal," p. 147 in this volume.

[5] Cf. Chapter I, n62. At 22, Aronson was the youngest artist to participate in the show. His work, however, was among the most controversial. A response to his *Coronation of the Virgin* (1945; Fig. 13) published in *Newsweek* read: "[...] the people in Aronson's 'Coronation of the Virgin' seem to be ill, both mentally and physically. The picture presents an aroma of decay, the degeneration of faith. It should not, I believe, be labeled 'Art' but, rather, 'exhibit A' in a psychologist's casebook." (*Newsweek*, Sept. 30, 1946, p.7).

[6] Cf. Aronson, "Real and Unreal," p. 150 in this volume.

[7] Cf. Ibid., p.144.

[8] Cf. Ibid., p. 150.

[9] Cf. Ibid., p. 150.

[10] Cf. Hans Belting, *Likeness and Presence: A History of the Image before the Era of Art*, Chicago: University of Chicago Press, 1994, p. 23. On the history of Early Christian Art see David and Tamara Talbot Rice, *Icons and their History*, Woodstock, N.Y.: Overlook Press, 1974; Kurt Weitzmann, *The Icon: Holy Images – Sixth to Fourteenth Century*, New York: George Braziller 1978; Kurt Weitzmann, Gaiané Alibegasvili, et al., *The Icon*, New York: Knopf, 1982; John Lowden, *Early Christian and Byzantine Art*, London: Phaidon, 1997.

[11] On Emmanuel Levinas' ethics of the Face see Emmanuel Levinas, *Totality and Infinity: An Essay on Exteriority*, Pittsburgh, PA: Duquesne University Press, 2001, Section III, pp. 187-219; and idem, *Entre Nous. On Thinking-of-the-Other*, New York: Columbia University Press, 1998, p. 167.

[12] On the reception of the Italian Renaissance see Wallace K. Ferguson, *The Renaissance in Historical Thought. Five Centuries of Interpretation*, Cambridge, MA: Houghton Mifflin, 1948.

[13] Jacob Burckhardt, *Die Kultur der Renaissance in Italien. Ein Versuch (Gesammelte Werke III)*, Basel and Stuttgart: Schwabe & Co 1970, p. 88.

[14] Though, as Leonard Barkan has recently shown, imitation of the ancients, the "creation of an official replica," was of crucial significance for the making of Renaissance culture. Leonard Barkan, *Unearthing the Past: Archeology and Aesthetics in the Making of Renaissance Culture*, New Haven and London: Yale University Press, 1999, p. 277.

[15] An abridged version appeared as Giorgio Vasari, *Lives of the Artists: Biographies of the Most Eminent Architects, Painters, and Sculptors of Italy*, New York: Simon and Schuster, 1946. A more complete version of the introduction is printed in Giorgio Vasari, *Lives of the Artists.* A Selection, transl. George Bull, New York: Penguin Classics, 1977

[16] Vasari, *Lives of the Artists* (1977), p. 45.

[17] Vasari, *Lives of the Artists* (1946), p. 42.

[18] Ibid., p. 42.

[19] Cf. Ferguson, *The Renaissance in Historical Thought*, p. 66f.

[20] Note in particular the works of the art historian August Schmarsow, *Kompositionsgesetze in der Kunst des Mittelalters* (Leipzig 1915-22) and *Die Gotik in der Renaissance: Eine Kunsthistorische Studie* (Stuttgart, 1921). See also Ferguson, *The Renaissance in Historical Thought*, pp. 329-385.

[21] Cf. Vasari, *Lives of the Artists* (1977), p. 45: "During the time we are discussing good paintings and sculptures remained buried under the ruins of Italy, unknown to the men of that time who were engrossed in contemporary rubbish."

[22] Cf. Belting, *Likeness and Presence*, p. 23f. The same observation was already made by Vasari: "Thus, the Italians learned how to copy their clumsy, awkward style and for a certain time continued to employ it. . ." (Vasari, *Lives of the Artists* [1977], p. 45). Yet, what may appear as evidence of continuity to us, to Vasari, represented the last obstacle before the Renaissance could begin.

[23] *Time Magazine*, Vol. 82, No. 21 (November 22, 1963), p. 72.

[24] Charles Baudelaire, "The Painter of Modern Life" (1863), idem, *The Painter of Modern Life and Other Essays*, trans. and ed. by Jonathan Mayne, London: Phaidon Press, 1994, p. 12.

[25] On the worldliness of religion see Burckhardt, *Kultur der Renaissance*, p. 339.

[26] *Newsweek*, Vol. XXVI, No. 22 (November 26, 1945), p. 114.

[27] Aronson, "Real and Unreal", p. 144 in this volume.

[28] Ibid., p. 147 in this volume.

[29] Quoted in Emery Grossman, *Art and Tradition*, p. 23.

[30] On the figure of Christ in Chagall's paintings see Benjamin Harshav, "The Role of Language in Modern Art: On Texts and Subtexts in Chagall's Paintings," in *Modernism & Modernity*, Vol. 1, No. 2 (April 1994), esp. pp. 66-71. It should be noted that Chagall rejected the attribute "Jewish art" for his work. (Cf. Chagall, "On Jewish Art—Leaves from my Notebook [1922]," in Benjamin Harshav (ed.), *Marc Chagall on Art and Culture*, Stanford, CA: Stanford University Press, 2003, pp. 38-40.

[31] See Georg Heuberger and Anton Merk (eds.), *Moritz Daniel Oppenheim. Die Entdeckung des jüdischen Selbstbewußtseins in der Kunst*, Frankfurt, 1999.

[32] See Karl Scheffler, *Max Liebermann*, Munich: Piper & Co., 1922. On the reception of Liebermann's *Jesus in the Temple* see Irit Rogoff, "Max Liebermann and the Painting of the Public Sphere," in Ezra Mendelssohn and Richard I. Cohen (eds.), *Art and its Uses: The Visual Image in Modern Jewish Society* (Studies in Contemporary Jewry VI, New York and Oxford: Oxford University Press, 1990, esp. p. 103f.

[33] See Hyman Lewbin, *Rebirth of Jewish Art: The Unfolding of Jewish Art in the Nineteenth Century*, New York: Shengold 1974, esp. pp. 76-89; Larry Silver, "Jewish Identity in Art and History: Maurycy Gottlieb as Early Jewish Artist," in Catherine M. Soussloff (ed.): *Jewish Identity in Modern Art History*, Berkeley, Los Angeles, London: University of California Press, 1999, pp. 87-113.

[34] See Joseph Gutmann and S. F. Chyet, *Moses Jacob Ezekiel: Memoirs from the Baths of Diocletian*, Detroit, 1975; A. Greenwald (ed), *Moses Jacob Ezekiel and the Classical Tradition*, Philadelphia, 1985; Zvi Amishai-Meisels, "The Jewish Jesus," in *Journal of Jewish Art 9* (1982), pp. 81-104; Alice M. Greenwald (ed.), *Ezekiel's Vision: Moses Jacob Ezekiel and the Classical Tradition* (catalogue), Philadelphia: National Museum of American Jewish History, 1985.

[35] Aronson, however, maintains that even his New Testament paintings were "Jewish paintings. My own religious background was deeply woven into the fabric of the work." Interview, quoted in Carol Kur, "David Aronson's Art," *Moment* Vol. 4, No. 1 (November 1978), p. 26. Cf. Chapter III, note 34 of this essay.

[36] Dorothy Miller, *Fourteen Americans* (1946), p. 11.

[37] Cf. Aronson, "Real and Unreal", p. 150 in this volume: "...the pantheistic tendencies of religion with which I wished my work to identify."

[38] Dorothy Miller, *Fourteen Americans* (1946), p. 11.

NOTES TO CHAPTER III (pages 19-23)

[1] Aronson, "Real and Unreal", p. 150 in this volume.

[2] Ibid., p. 151 in this volume.

[3] Abraham Geiger, "Judaism and Its History" (1865), reprinted in *Abraham Geiger and Liberal Judaism: The Challenge of the Nineteenth Century,* Philadelphia: Jewish Publication Society, 1962, p. 213.

[4] For an account of the Baal Shem Tov's wonder works see *In Praise of the Baal Shem Tov (Shivhei ha-Besht),* transl. and ed. by Dan Ben-Amos and Jerome R. Mintz, Bloomington: Indiana University Press, 1970.

[5] Martin Buber, "Spinoza, Shabbatai Zvi, and the Baal Shem," in Martin Buber, *The Origin and Meaning of Hasidism,* New York: Horizon Press 1960, pp. 89-112.

[6] On Spinoza's excommunication and the reception of his thought see Yirmiyahu Yovel, *Spinoza and Other Heretics* (Vols. I & II), Princeton: Princeton University Press, 1989. Note that Spinoza was a common source of influence for many young Jewish artists. Hyman Bloom, for instance, remembers reading Spinoza in his youth: "His definition of God was the first that made sense to me." (quoted in Frederick Wight, *Hyman Bloom,* Boston: Institute of Contemporary Art, 1954, p. 8. Cf. Bookbinder, "Boston Modern," pp. 29f.).

[7] On the life of Sabbatai Zvi see Gershom Scholem, *Sabbatai Zvi: The Mystical Messiah 1626-1676,* Princeton: Princeton University Press (Bollingen Series XCIII), 1973.

[8] Cf. Buber, "Spinoza, Shabbatai Zvi, and the Baal Shem," p. 90.

[9] *In Praise of the Baal Shem Tov,* p. 34.

[10] Martin Buber, "Spirit and Body of the Hasidic Movement," in Asher D. Biemann (ed.), *The Martin Buber Reader: Essential Writings,* New York: Palgrave, 2002, p. 64.

[11] *Talmud Bavli,* San. 67b. Cf. Joshua Trachtenberg, *Jewish Magic and Superstition: A Study in Folk Religion,* New York: Ateneum, 1977, p. 19.

[12] David Aronson, "Real and Unreal", p. 151 in this volume.

[13] Ibid., p. 151.

[14] Ibid., p. 145.

[15] Alfred Werner, "Perception of the Beautiful," in *David Aronson: Sculpture* (exhibition catalogue), New York: Bernard Dannenberg Galleries, 1969.

[16] Quoted in Carol Kur, "David Aronson's Art," *Moment* Vol. 4, No. 1 (Novemer 1978), p. 26.

[17] Judith Bookbinder, "david aronson: the artist as warrior," in *David Aronson: The Artist as Warrior* (exhibition catalogue), Boston: Pucker Gallery, 1999.

[18] Silberschlag was also a well respected historian of modern Hebrew literature and an expert on the radically secular, "paganizing" poetry of Saul Tschernichovski (1875-1943). His books include *Saul Tschernichovsky: Poet of Revolt.* Ithaca, NY: Cornell University Press, 1968; and *From Renaissance to Renaissance: Hebrew Literature from 1492-1970* (2 vols.), New York: KTAV Publishing, 1973.

[19] Carol Kur, "David Aronson's Art," p. 26.

[20] Moses Maimonides, *The Guide for the Perplexed,* Book III, ch. 37, transl. M. Friedlaender, New York: Dover, 1956, p. 333.

[21] *Talmud Bavli,* Sotah 8a.

[22] Matthew Arnold, "Hebraism and Hellenism," in *Selections from the Prose Writings of Matthew Arnold,* New York: Henry Holt, 1898, p. 183.

[23] Martin Buber, "Kunst und Judentum," in Martin Buber, *Die jüdische Bewegung. Gesammelte Aufsätze und Ansprachen (Erste Folge 1900-1914),* Berlin: Jüdischer Verlag, 1920, p. 245.

[24] Hans Kohn, *Die Politische Idee des Judentums,* München: Meyer & Jessen, 1924, p. 12.

[25] For a recent treatment of this theme see Kalman P. Bland, *The Artless Jew: Mediaeval and Modern Affirmations and Denials of the Visual,* Princeton and Oxford: Princeton University Press, 2000, pp. 13-36.

[26] Hermann Cohen, *Religion of Reason out of the Sources of Judaism,* Atlanta: Scholars Press, 1995, p. 53. Cohen, like most defenders of rational Judaism, regarded monotheism as the only perfectly rational religious position. We see this opinion already in the Jewish historian Heinrich Graetz (1817-1891): "In the strictest sense, absolute monotheism, as Judaism has revealed it, is rationalism; it is the negation of all absurdities by which the religious views and cults of the ancient nations were dominated." Idolatry, Graetz continues, must be "absurd and abominable to the present generation because Jewish rationalism has for centuries arrayed itself against it." (Heinrich Graetz, *The Structure of Jewish History and Other Essays,* ed. by Ismar Schorsch, New York: Jewish Theological Seminary, 1975, p. 284f.). Graetz's famous dictum "Paganism sees its god, Judaism hears Him" (cf. Ibid., p.68) reflects the rationalism typical of 19th century German Jewry and its aim at reinforcing an iconoclast "protestant" Judaism. "At the moment of its entrance into history," Graetz writes, "Judaism appears as a negative force. It negates paganism. It rises in protest." (Ibid., p. 66). To Graetz and Cohen, then, the notion of "visual" Judaism was an offense against reason. For a brief study on Hermann Cohen's aesthetics see Gerd Wolandt, "Hermann Cohens Verhältnis zur Kunst," Ekkehardd Mai, Stephan Waetzold, Gerd Wolandt (eds.), *Ideengeschichte und Kunstwissenschaft. Philosophie und Kunstgeschichte im Kaiserreich,* Berlin: Gebr. Mann, 1983, pp. 145-152.

[27] Cohen, *Religion of Reason,* p. 368.

[28] Buber, "Kunst und Judentum," p. 250f. For a recent assessment of Buber's aesthetic theory see Margaret Olin, *The Nation Without Art: Examining Modern Discourses on Jewish Art,* Lincoln and London: University of Nebraska Press, 2001, Chapter Four ("Martin Buber. Jewish Art as Visual Redemption"), pp. 99-126.

[29] Martin Buber, "Address on Jewish Art," in Gilya G. Schmidt (ed.), *The First Buber. Youthful Zionist Writings of Martin Buber,* Syracuse, NY: Syracuse University Press, 1999, p. 55.

[30] See Gavriel D. Rosenfeld, "Defining 'Jewish Art' in Ost und West, 1901-1908. A Study in the Nationalisation of Jewish Culture," *Leo Baeck Institute Year Book 39* (1994), pp. 83-110; Michael Berkowitz, *Zionist Culture and West European Jewry before the First World War,* Chapel Hill and London: University of North Carolina Press, 1996, Chapter 5 ("Art and Zionist Popular Culture"), pp. 119-143; Gilya Gerda Schmidt (ed.), *The Art and Artists of the Fifth Zionist Congress, 1901: Heralds of a New Age,* Syracuse, NY: Syracuse University Press, 2003. The debate on "Jewish Art," however, its essence and its existence, is ongoing and has been revived in the recent two decades. For one of the more instructive essays on this subject see Joseph Gutmann, "Is There a Jewish Art?" in Clare Moore (ed.), *The Visual Dimension. Aspects of Jewish Art,* Boulder, San Francisco, Oxford: Westview Press, 1993, pp. 1-23.

[31] Micha Berdichevski, "Wrecking and Building," in Arthur Hertzberg (ed.), *The Zionist Idea: A Historical Analysis and Reader,* New York: Atheneum, 1982, p. 293.

[32] Ibid., p. 299.

[33] Martin Buber, "Von jüdischer Kunst," in Martin Buber, *Die jüdische Bewegung,* p. 66.

[34] On a recent collection of rabbinic sources regarding art and Judaism see Vivian B. Mann, *Jewish Texts on the Visual Arts,* New York, 1999.

[35] Quoted in Carol Kur, "David Aronson's Art," *Moment* Vol. 4, No. 1 (November 1978), p. 26. Cf. Chapter II, n. 33.

[36] David Aronson, "Real and Unreal," p. 150 in this volume.

[37] Quoted in Bookbinder, "Figurative Expressionism in Boston," p. 385.

[38] The same retrospective, including more than a hundred works of painting and sculpture, had already been shown at the Rose Art Museum in Waltham, MA during the months of February and March.

[39] See Julie Miller and Richard I. Cohen, "A Collision of Cultures: The Jewish Museum and the Jewish Theological Seminary, 1904-1971," in Jack Wertheimer (ed.), *Tradition Renewed: A History of the Jewish Theological Seminary,* Vol. II (Beyond the Academy), New York: Jewish Theological Seminary, 1997, pp. 311-361.

40 Quoted in Grace Glueck, "Museum Drops 19 Aronson Paintings From Show Over Christian Themes," in *The New York Times,* May 25, 1979, p. C 7.

[41] Ibid., p. C 7.

[42] Cf. Aronson, "Real and Unreal", p. 147 in this volume.

[43] Culture Gaps, *The New York Times,* June 1, 1979.

NOTES TO CHAPTER IV (pages 25-29)

[1] Joseph Ablow, "The Art of David Aronson," in *David Aronson: A Retrospective* (exhibition catalogue), Boston and New York: Rose Art Museum and The Jewish Museum 1979, p. 6. See also idem, "David Aronson: Sculpture" (exhibition catalogue), New York and Boston: Lee Nordness Galleries and Boris Mirski Gallery, 1969, p. 4.

[2] Ibid., p. 5.

[3] Aronson, "Real and Unreal", p. 153 in this volume.

[4] Ibid., p. 153 in this volume.

[5] Among recent works on this subject are Moshe Halbertal and Avishai Margalit, *Idolatry,* transl. by Naomi Goldblum, Cambridge, MA, and London: Harvard University Press, 1992; and Lionel Kochan, *Beyond the Graven Image: A Jewish View,* New York: New York University Press, 1997; Anthony Julius, *Idolizing Pictures: Idolatry, Iconoclasm and Jewish Art,* New York: Thames & Hudson, 2001. For a comparative approach see Roger Burggraeve et al. (eds.), *Desirable God? Our Fascination with Images, Idols and New Deities,* Leuven and Dudley, MA: Peeters, 2003.

[6] Cf. "David Aronson: Sculpture," p. 4

[7] Cf. Aronson, "Real and Unreal", p. 153 in this volume.

[8] As it appears in the traditional Hebrew prayerbook. In Isaiah (45:20) the line reads: "They have no knowledge who carry about their wooden idols, and keep on praying to a god who cannot save." Found offensive by many Jews in the modern period, the line was removed from most Reform and Conservative prayerbooks.

[9] Hermann Cohen, *Religion of Reason,* p. 55.

[10] Franz Rosenzweig, *The Star of Redemption,* trans. William Hallo, New York et al.: Holt, Rinehart and Winston, 1971, p. 360. Rosenzweig stands here in a clearly neo-romantic tradition drawing from Arthur Schopenhauer and Friedrich Nietzsche. On the role of music in Schopenhauer and Nietzsche see, for example, Andrew Bowie, *Aesthetics and Subjectivity from Kant to Nietzsche,* Manchester and New York: Manchester University Press, 1990, esp. Chapter 8 ("Nietzsche: The Divorce of Art and Reason"), pp. 206-252. For a recent study on Rosenzweig's aesthetics see Leora Batnitzky, *Idolatry and Representation: The Philosophy of Franz Rosenzweig Reconsidered,* Princeton, N.J.: Princeton University Press, 2000.

[11] Franz Rosenzweig, *The Star of Redemption,* p. 362.

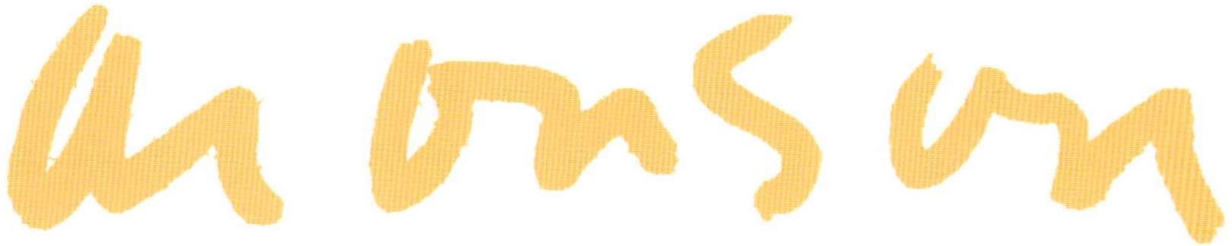

PAINTINGS, DRAWINGS, SCULPTURE

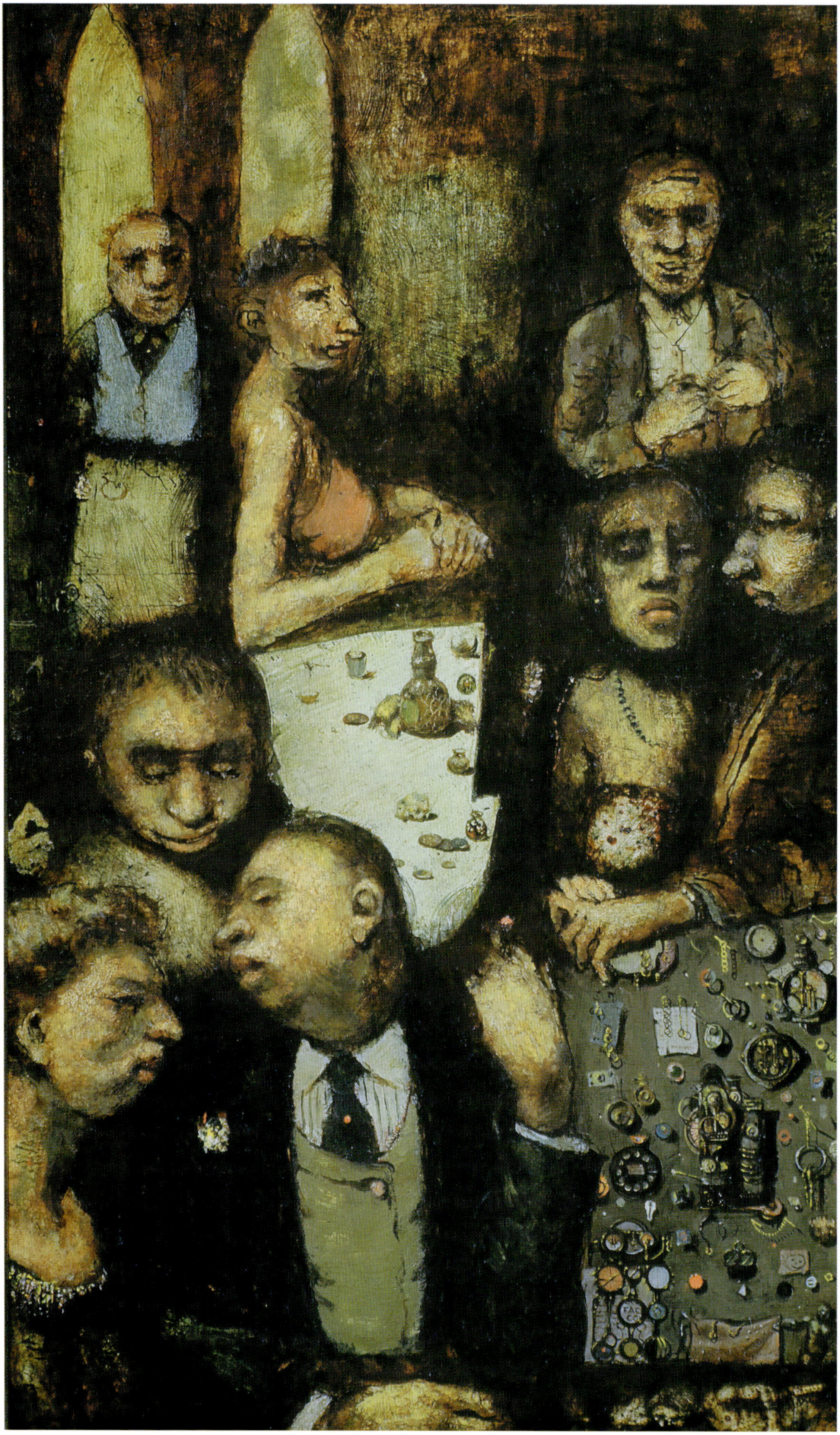

The Paradox, 1942
oil on panel
15 1/8 x 9 1/8"
Private Collection

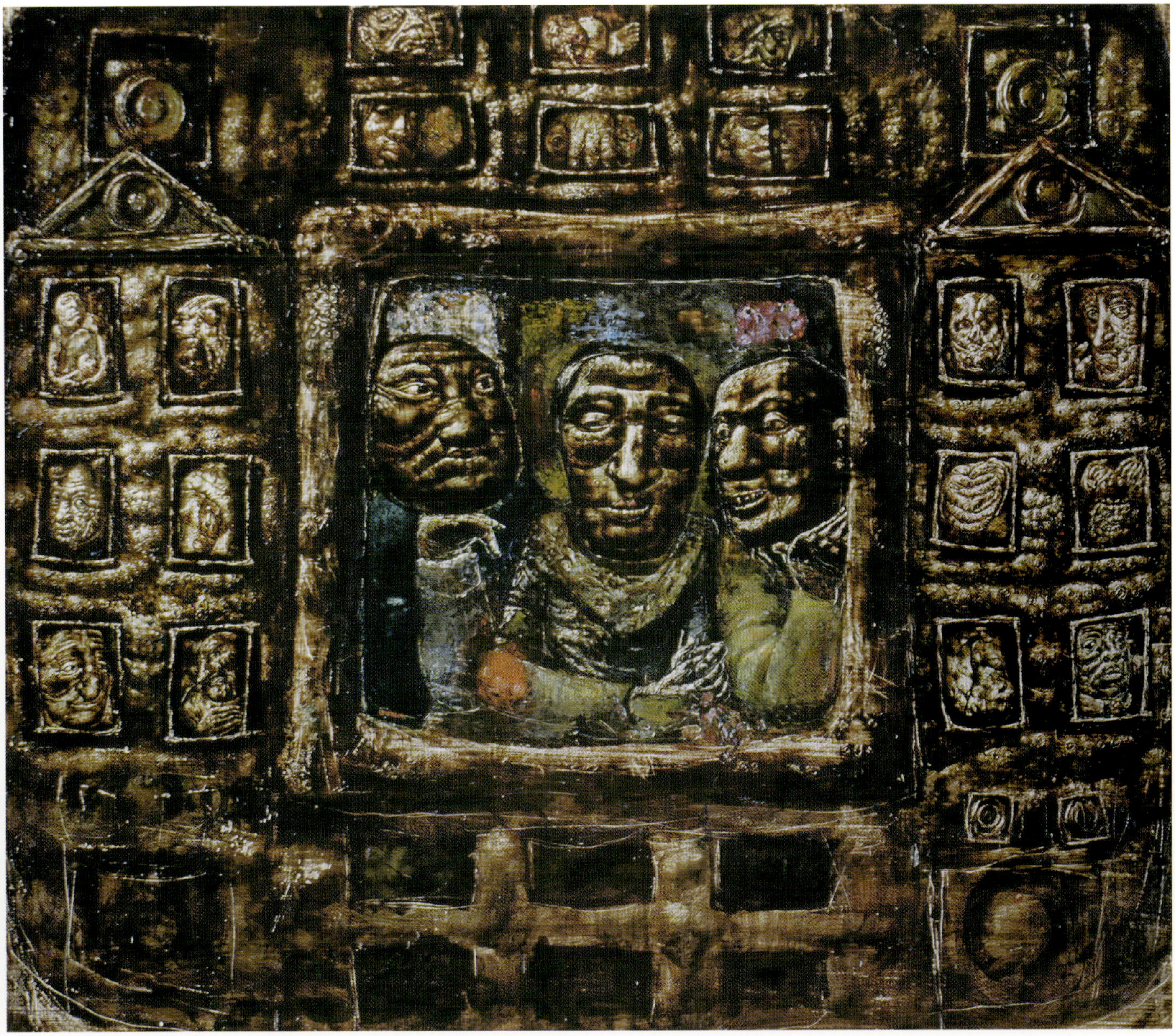

Trinity, 1943
oil on panel
23 1/4 x 26 1/2"
Private Collection

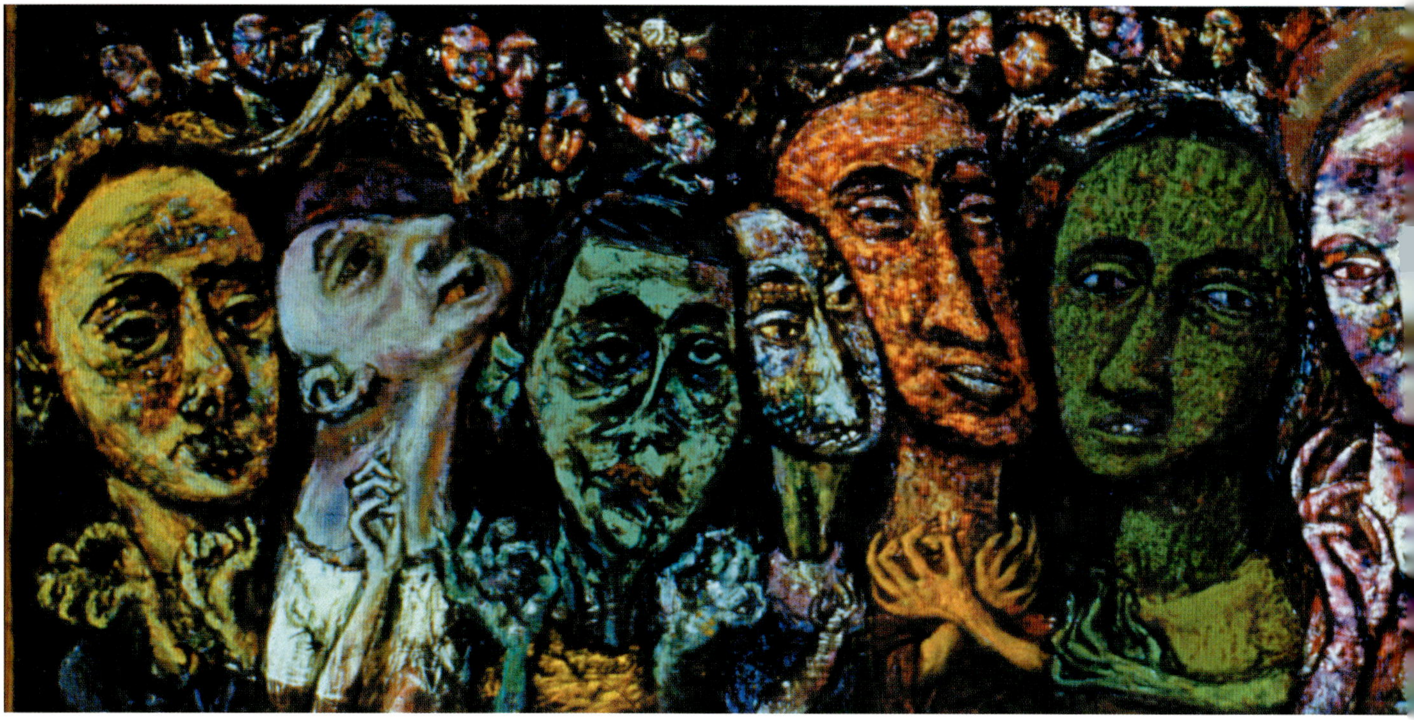

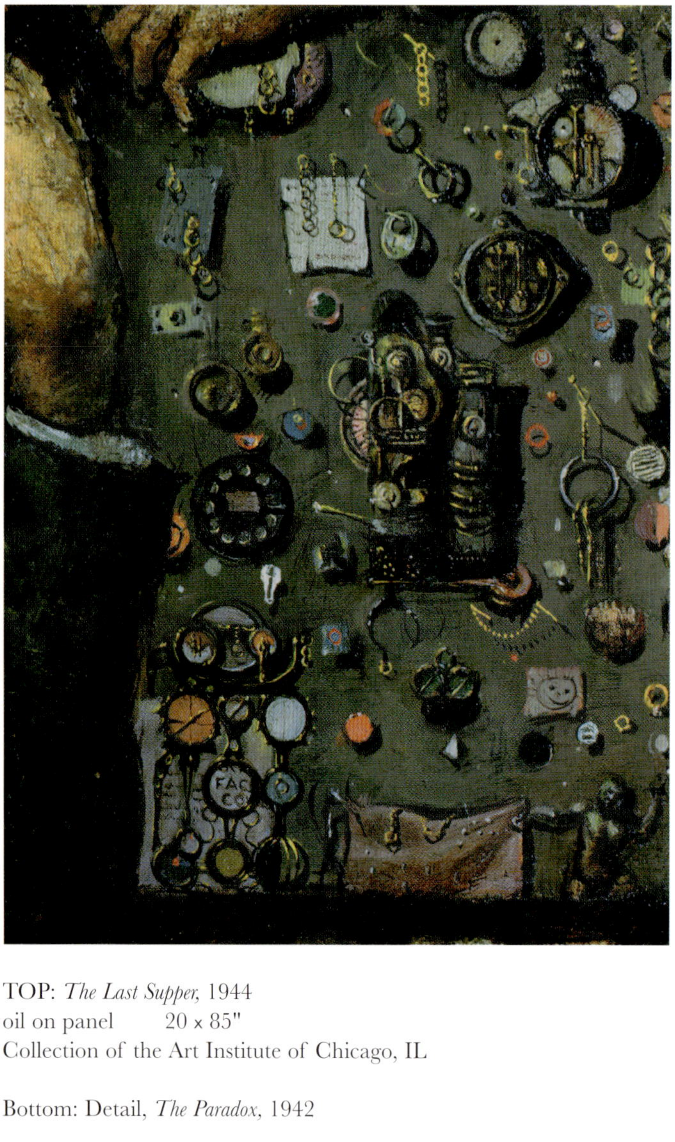

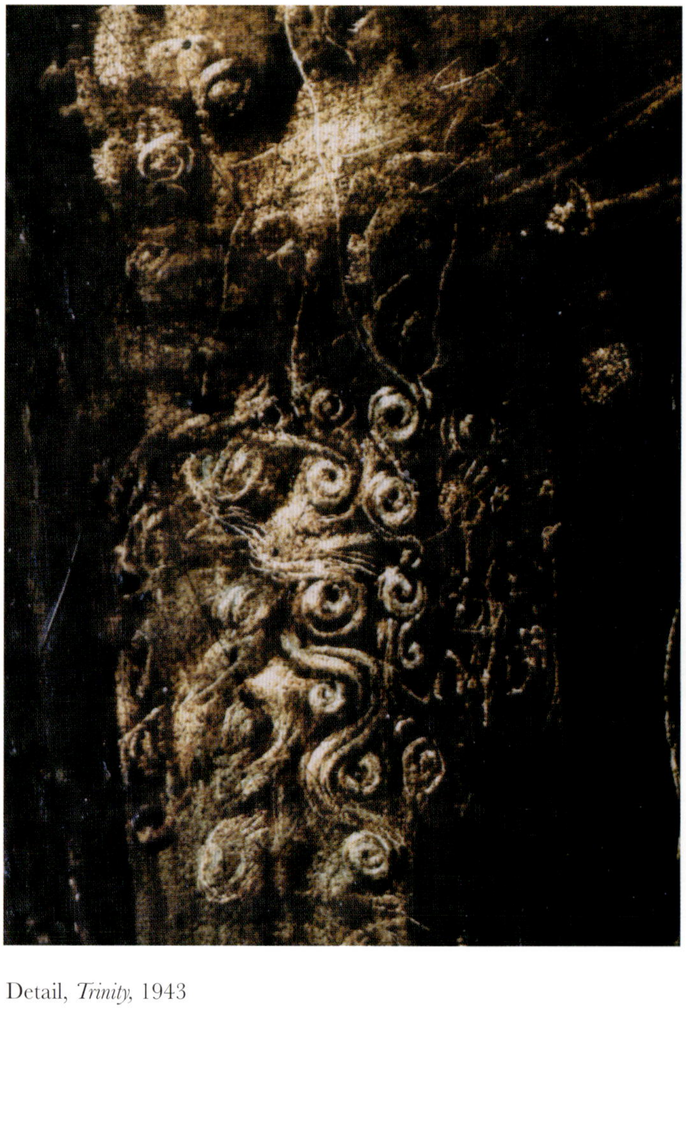

TOP: *The Last Supper,* 1944
oil on panel 20 x 85"
Collection of the Art Institute of Chicago, IL

Bottom: Detail, *The Paradox*, 1942

Detail, *Trinity,* 1943

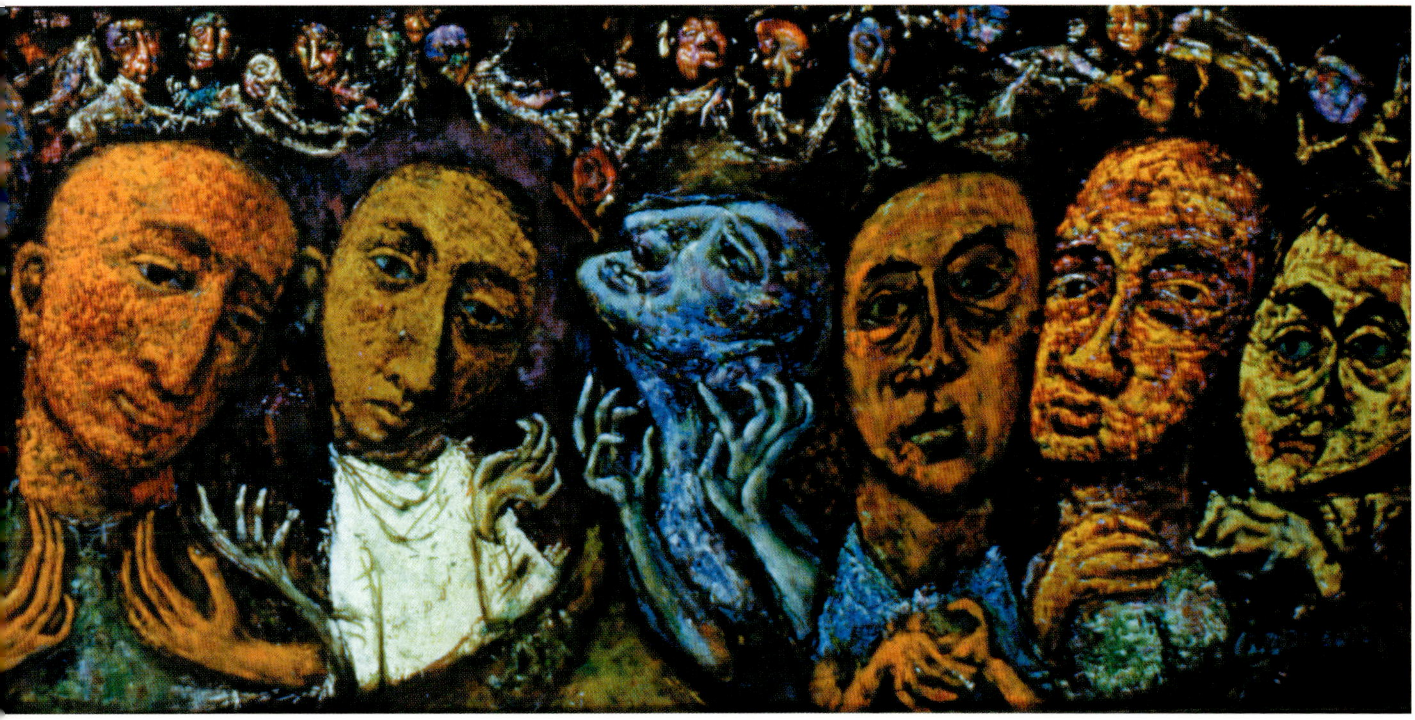

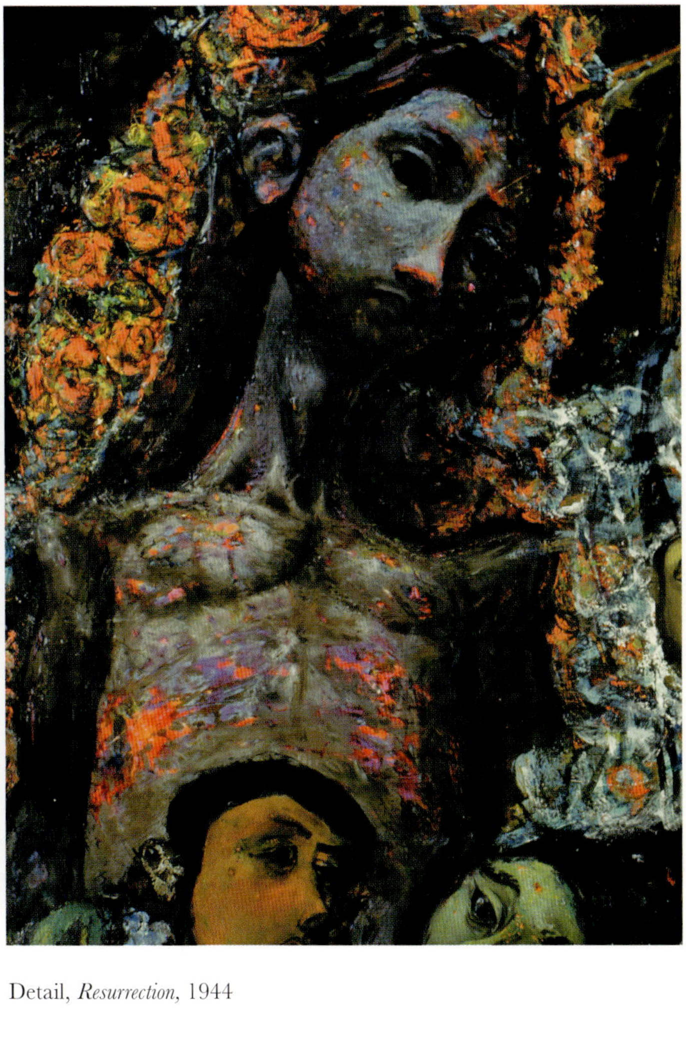

Detail, *Resurrection*, 1944

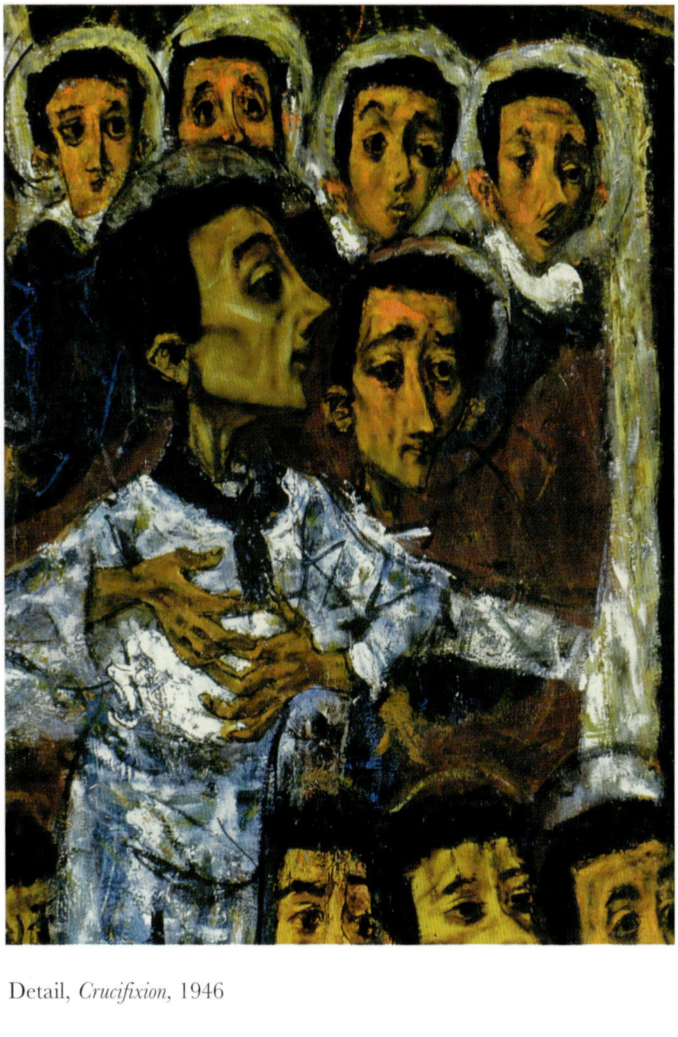

Detail, *Crucifixion*, 1946

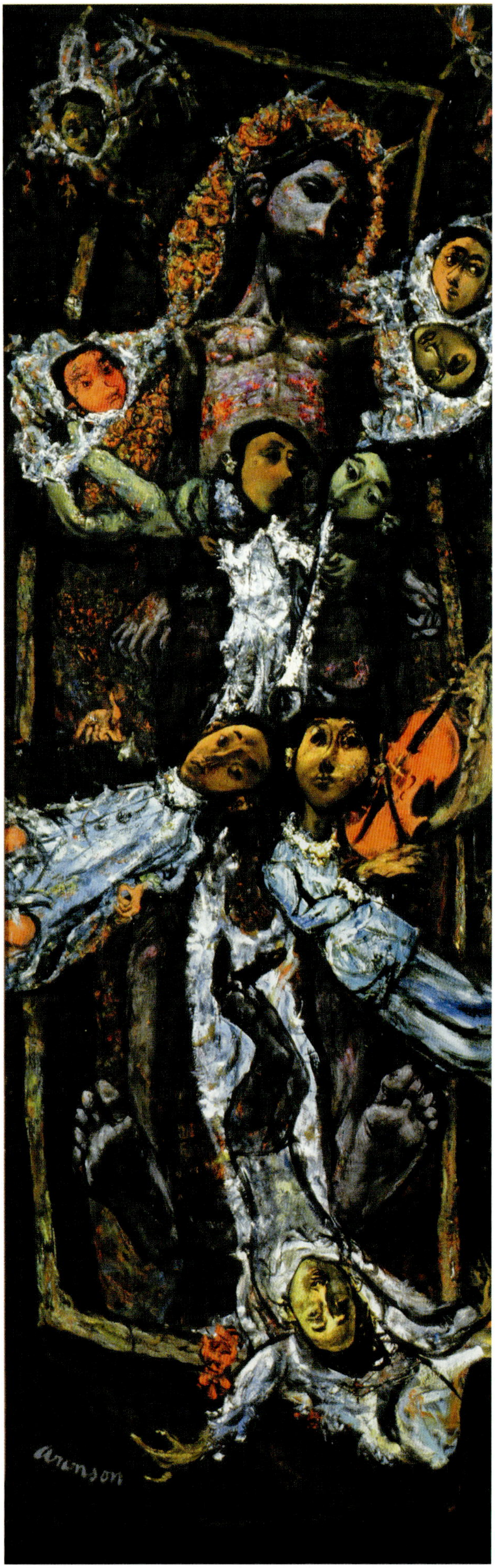

Resurrection, 1944
oil on panel 87 x 34"
Collection of the David and Alfred Smart Museum, Chicago, IL

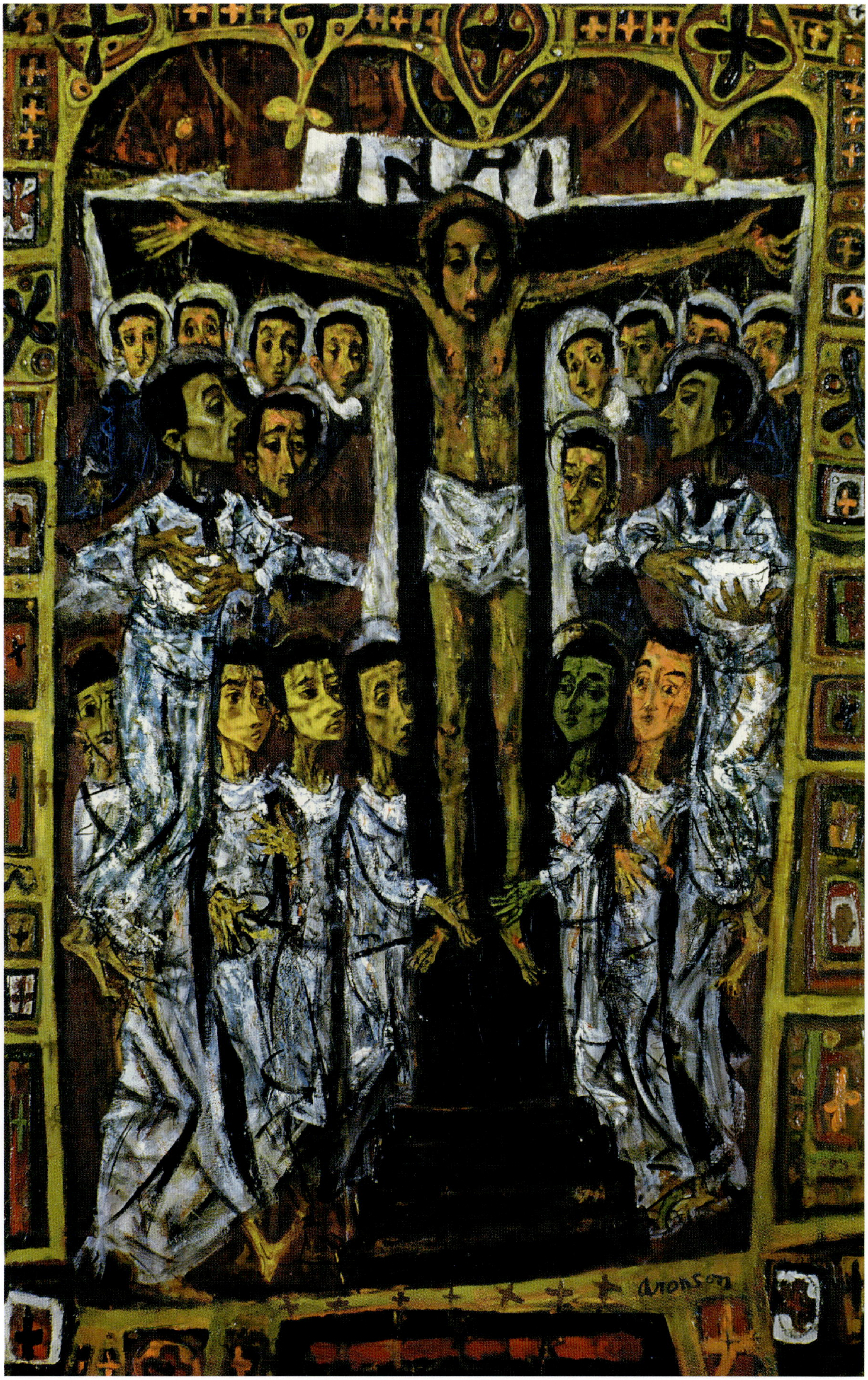

Crucifixion, 1946
oil on panel
72 x 48"
Collection of the
Corcoran Gallery of
Art, Washington, DC

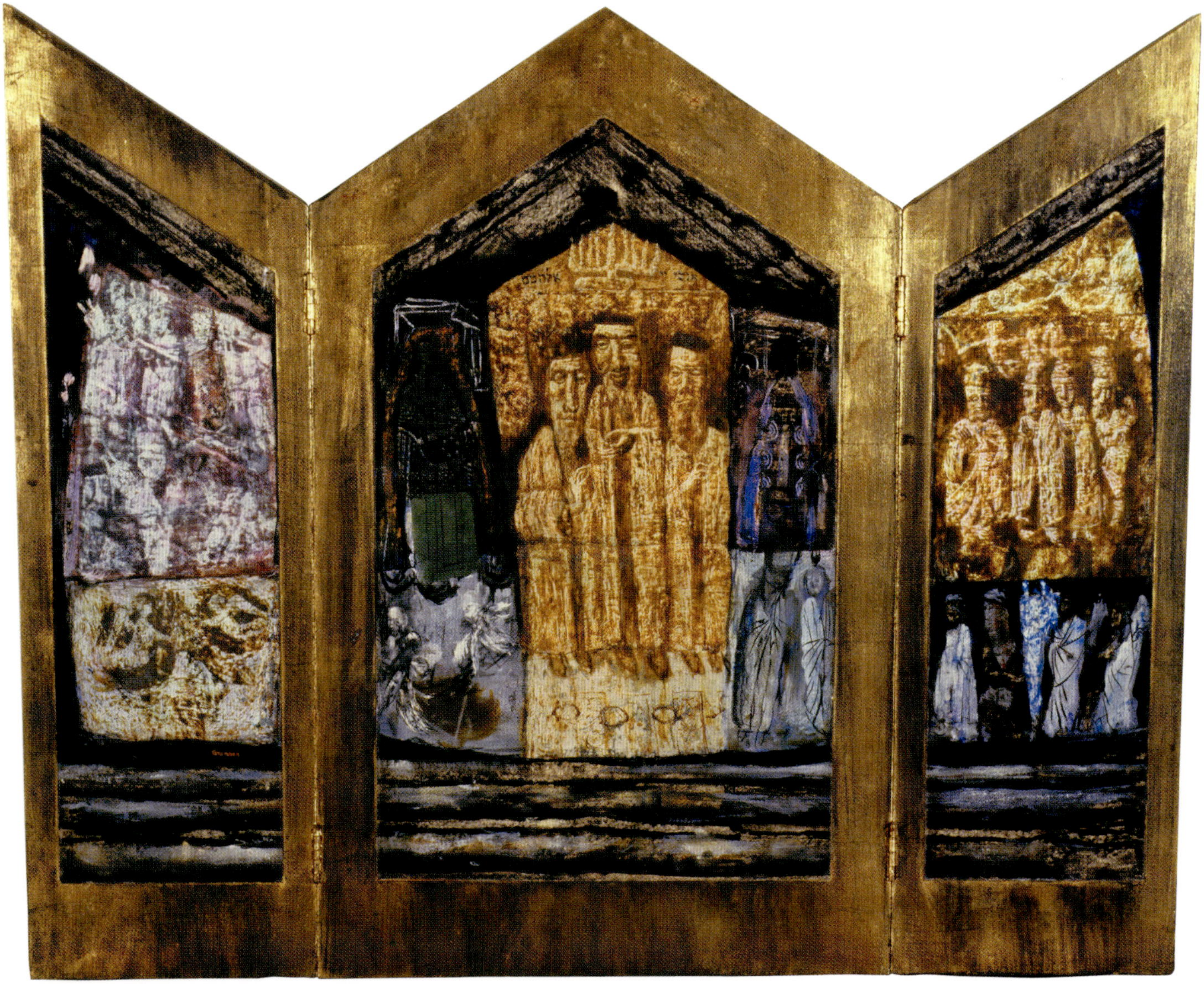

Triptych, 1944
tempera 24 1/2 x 30"
Collection of the DeCordova Museum, Lincoln, MA

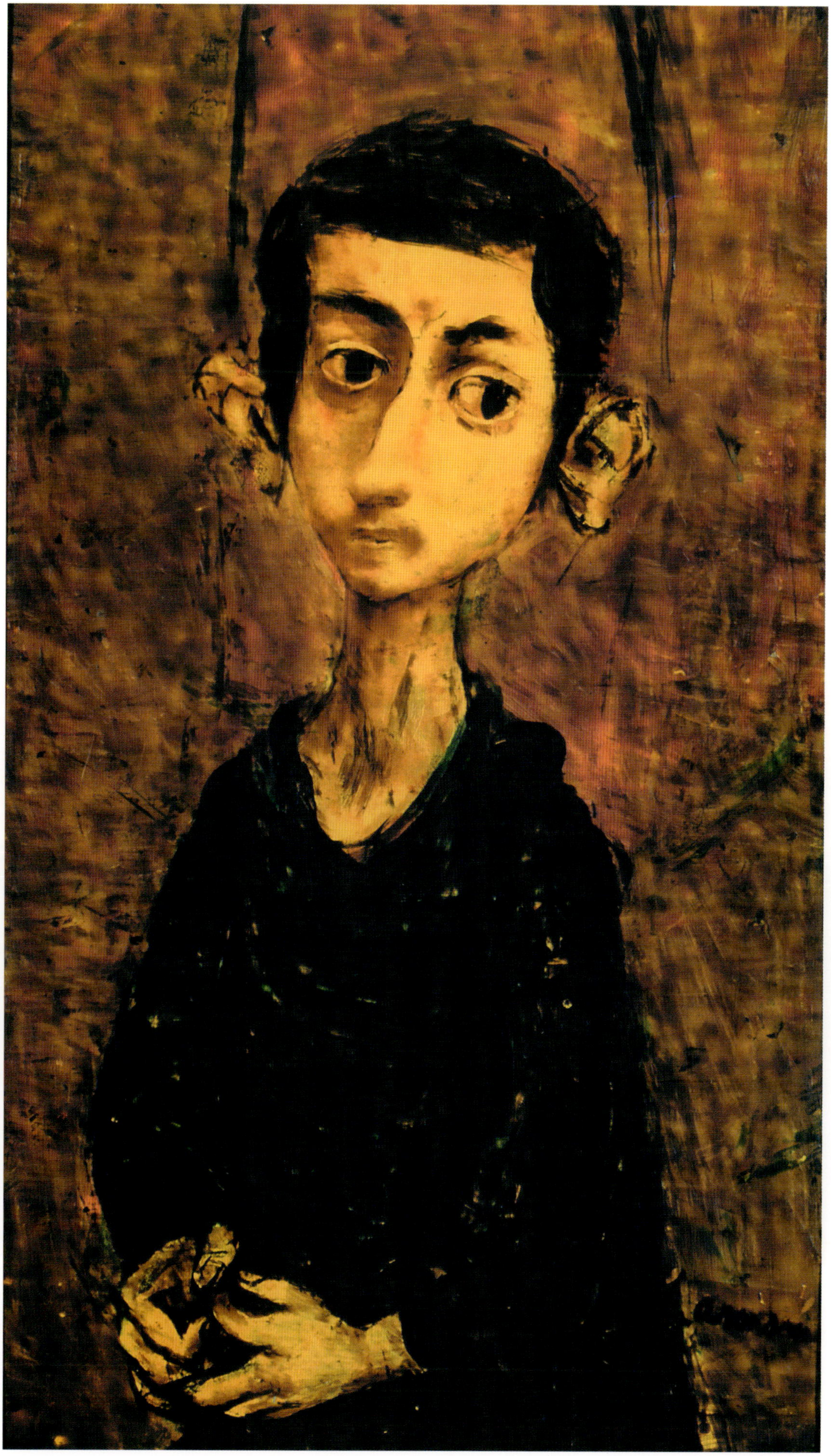

Young Christ, 1945
encaustic on panel
$25\frac{7}{8} \times 14\frac{5}{8}$"
Private Collection

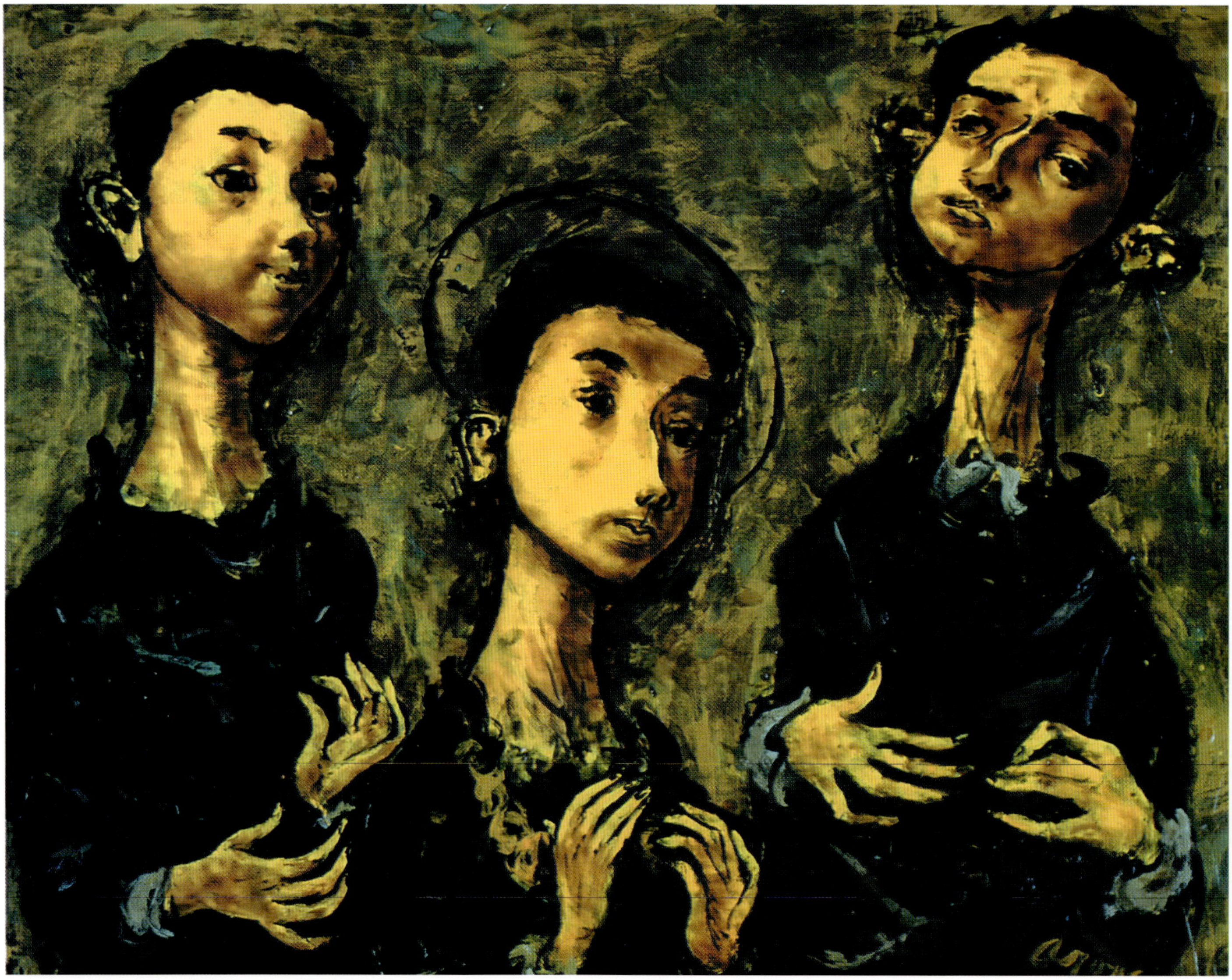

Young Christ Disputing with the Doctors, 1945
encaustic on panel 25½ x 32½"
Collection of Bryn Mawr College, Bryn Mawr, PA

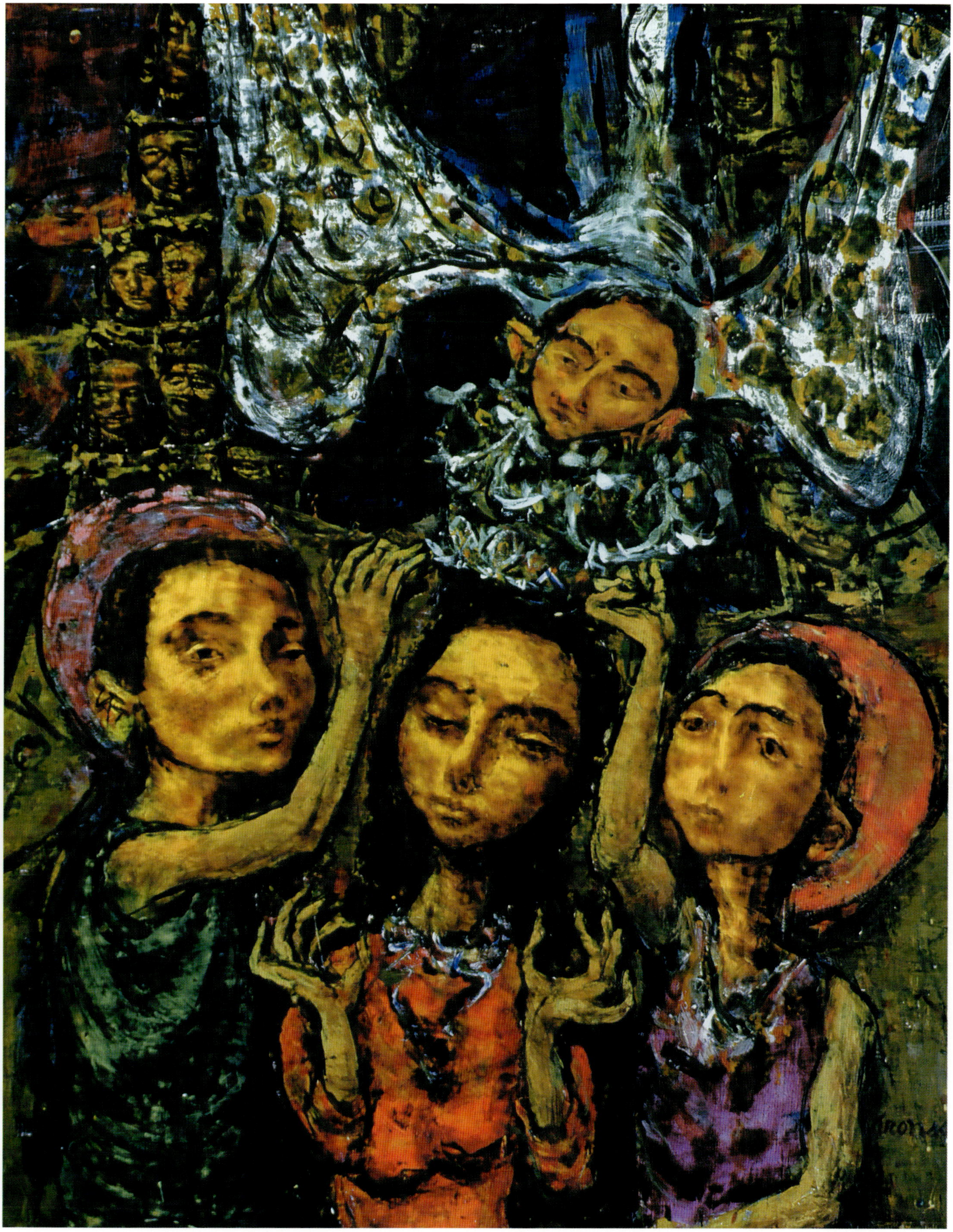

Coronation of the Virgin, 1945
encaustic on panel 38½ x 31⅝"
Collection of the Virginia Museum of Fine Arts, Richmond, VA

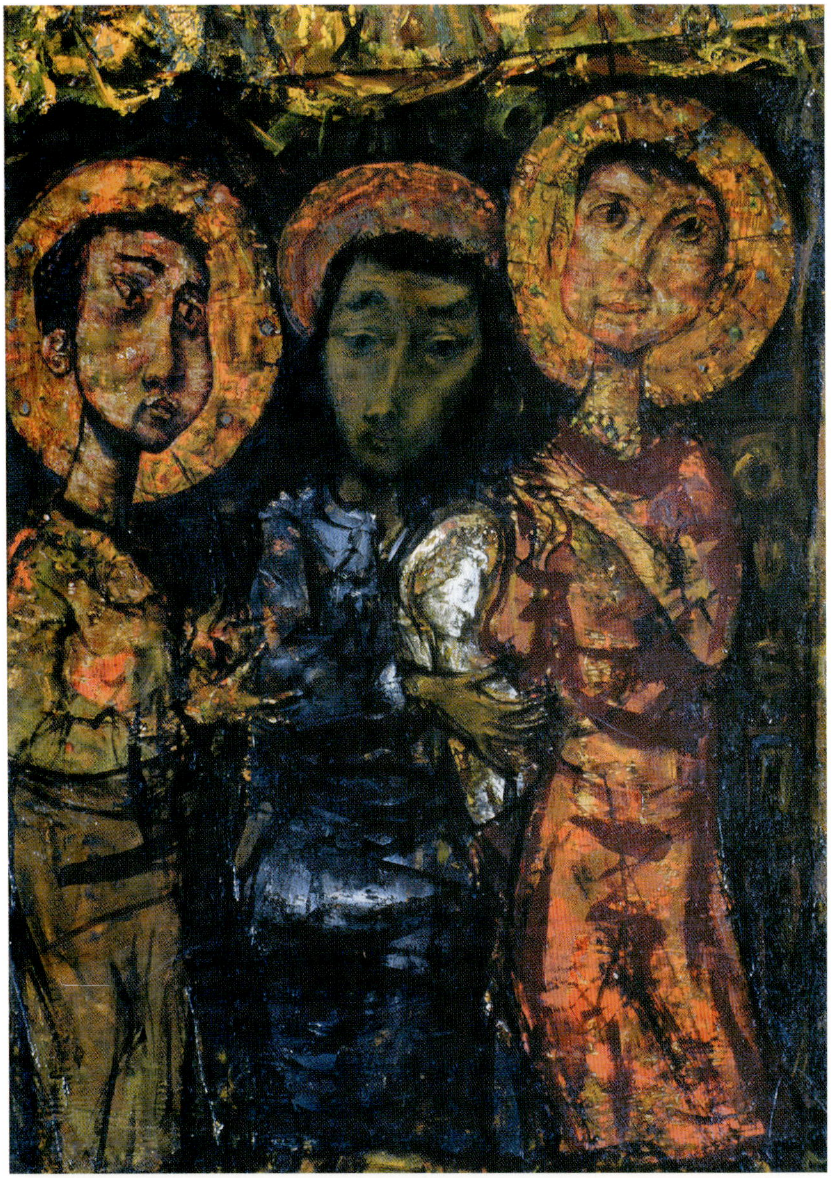

Madonna and Child with Saints, 1946
oil on panel 12 x 9"
Private Collection

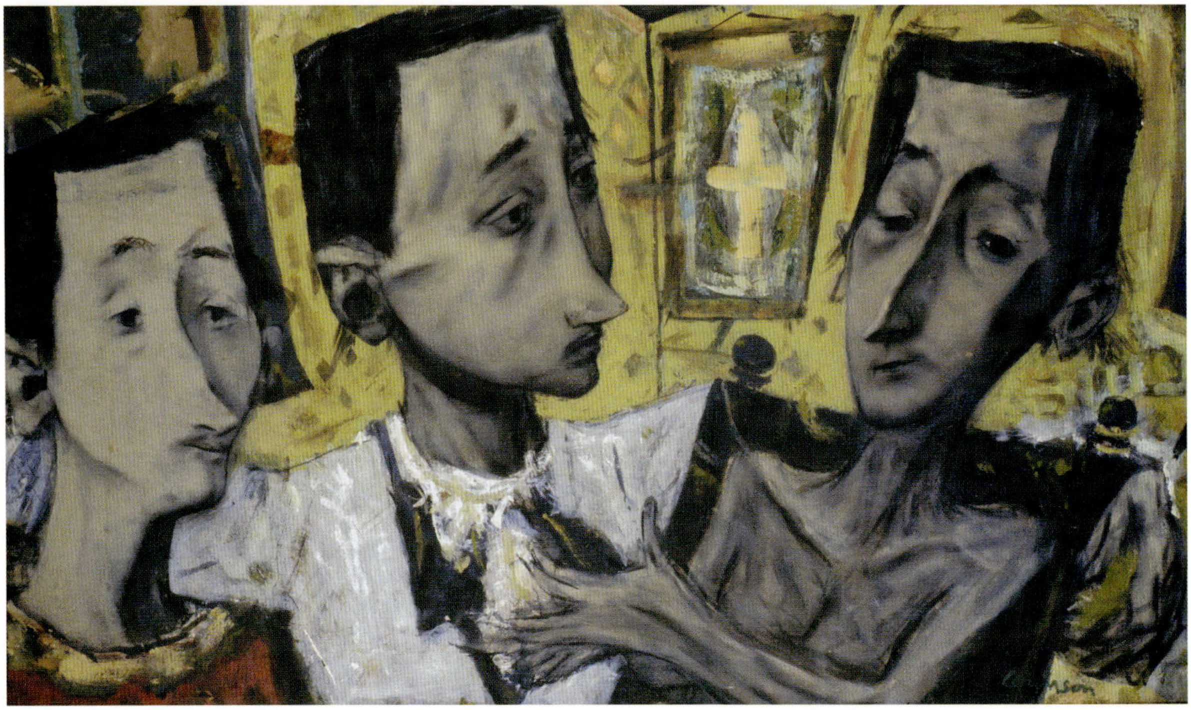

Christ Healing the Sick, 1947
tempera & oil on panel
8 5/8 x 15 1/8"
Private Collection

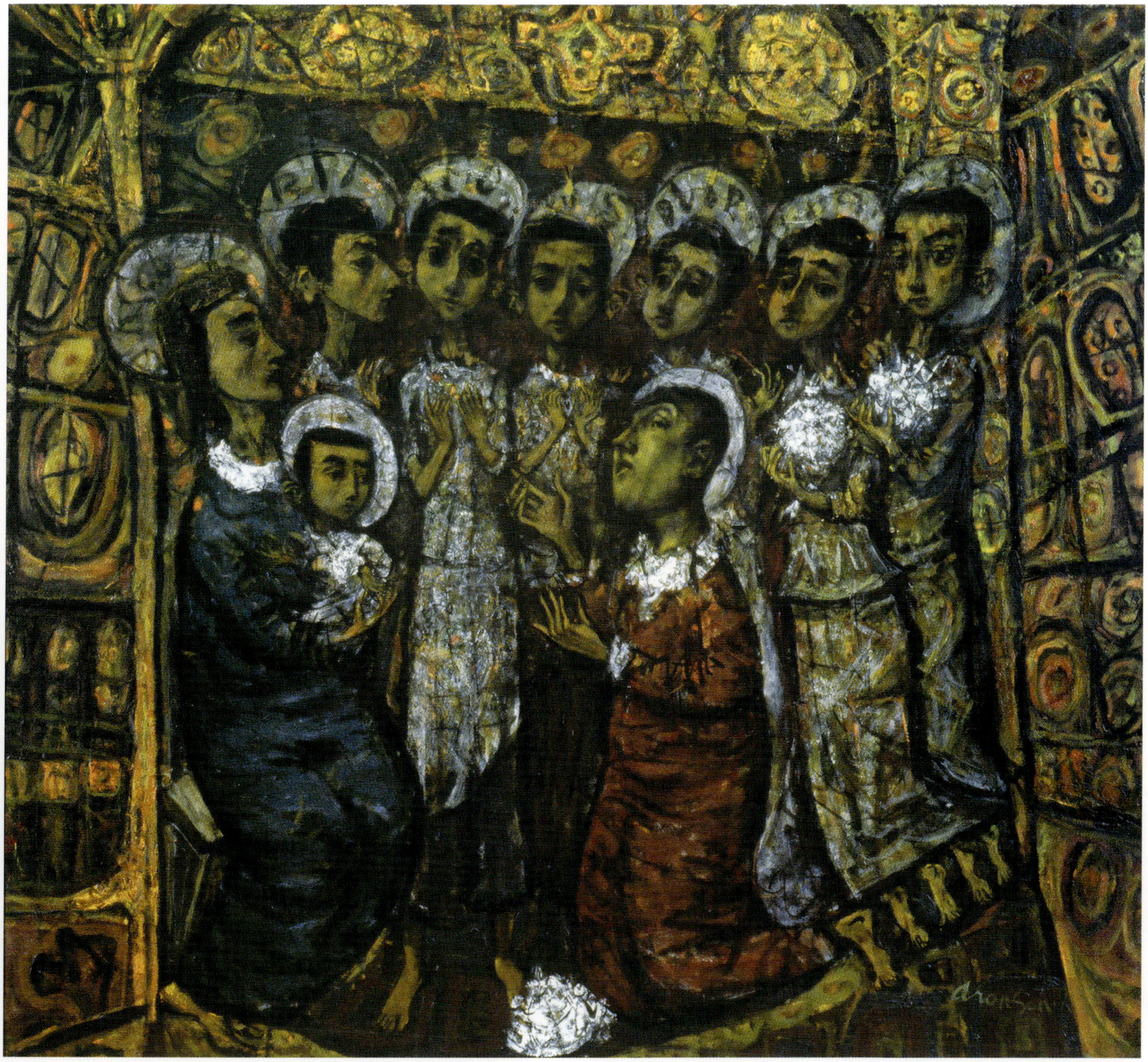

Adoration of the Magi, 1947
oil on panel 43 x 48"
Private Collection

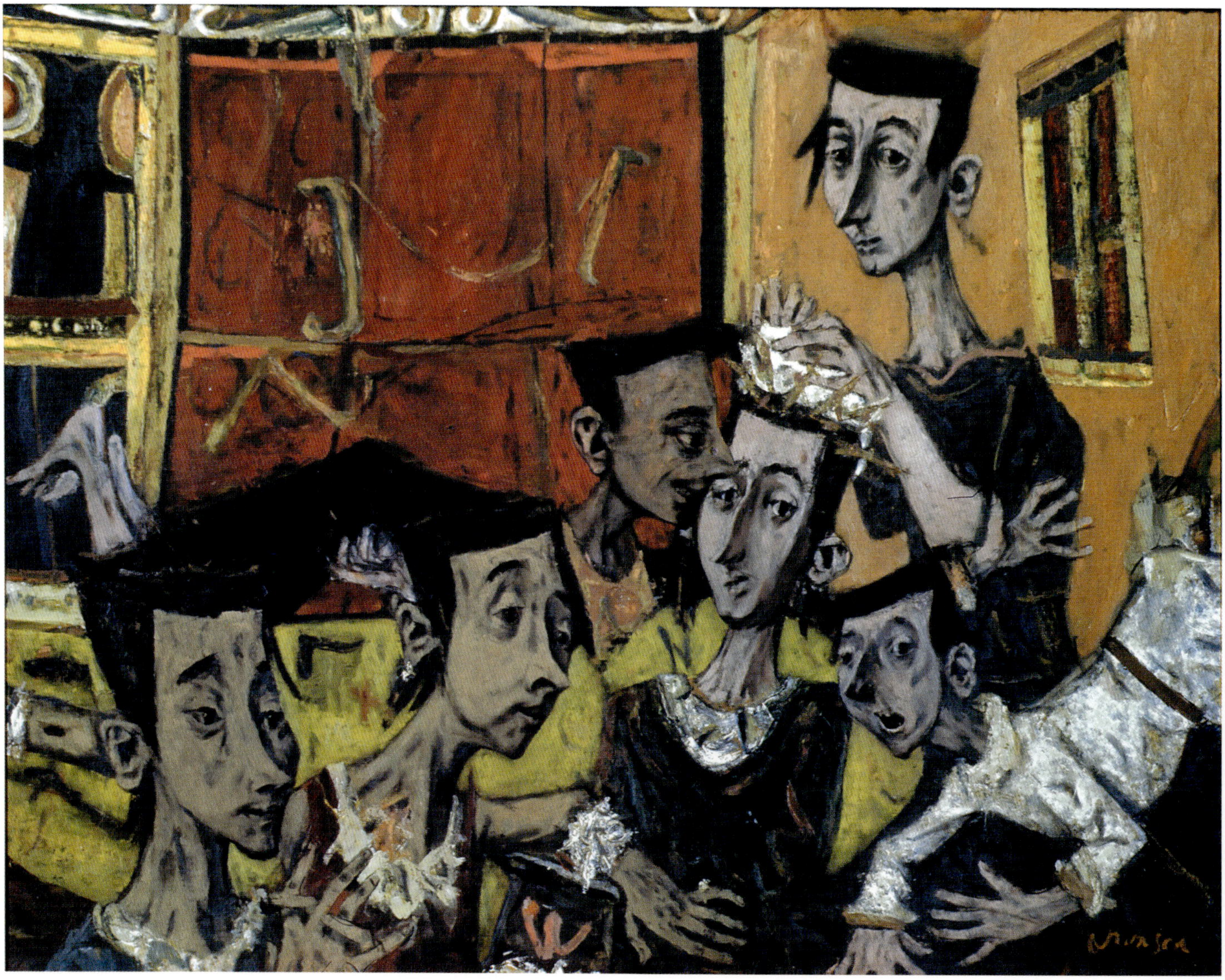

Crowning with Thorns, 1947
tempera & oil on panel
37 x 47"
Collection of the DeCordova Museum, Lincoln, MA

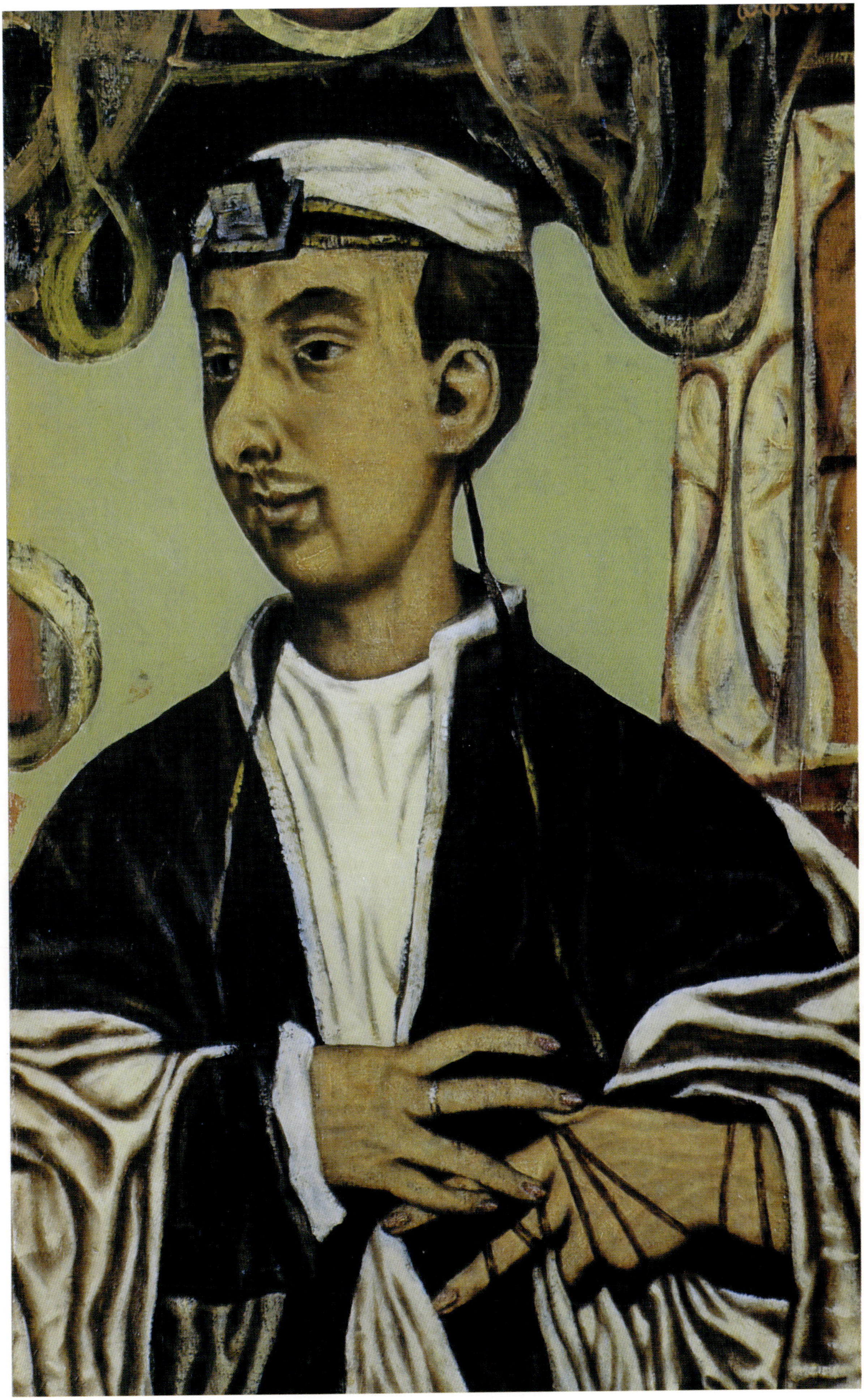

Young Christ with Phylacteries, 1949
oil on canvas
27 x 17"
Private Collection

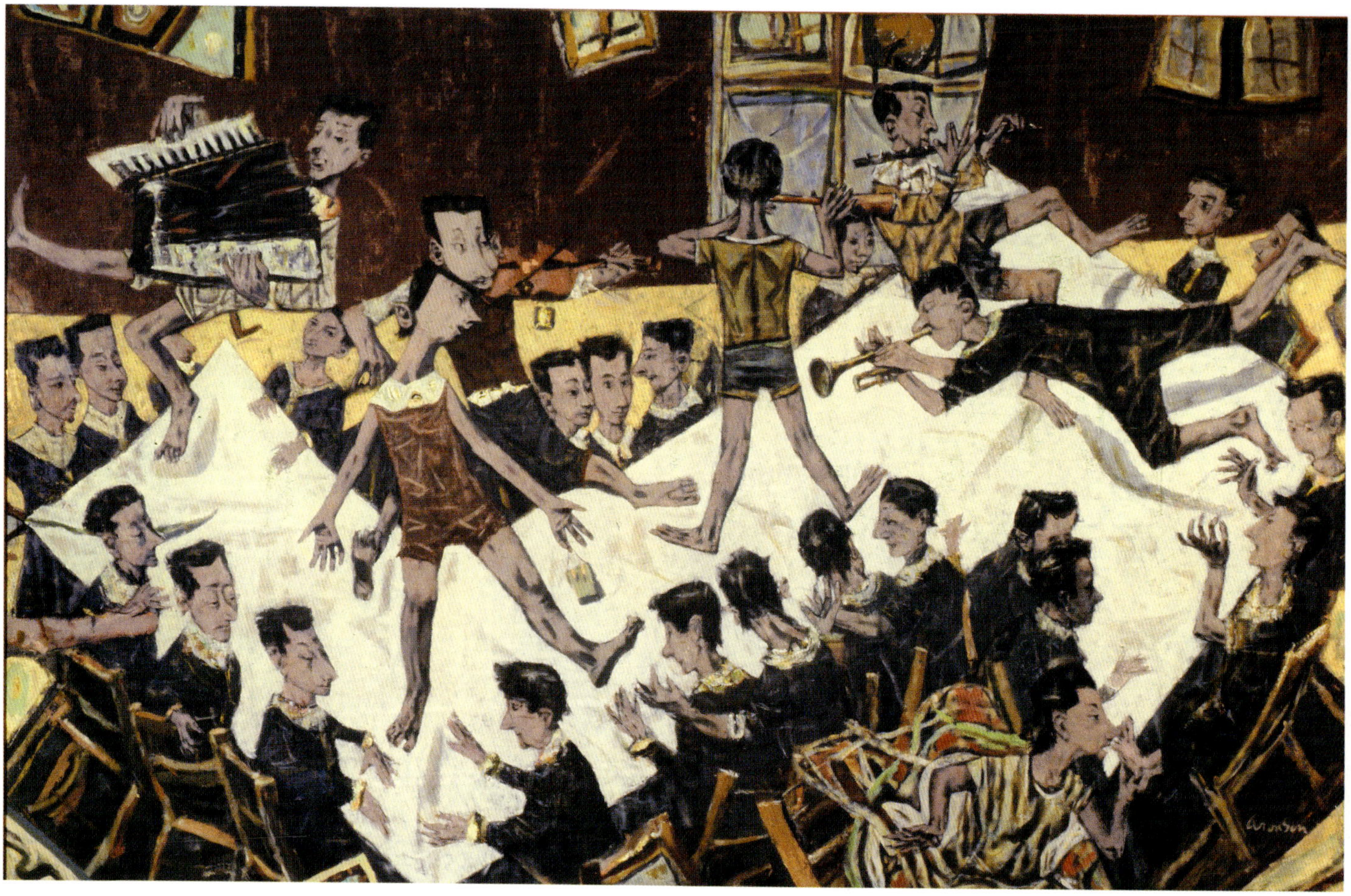

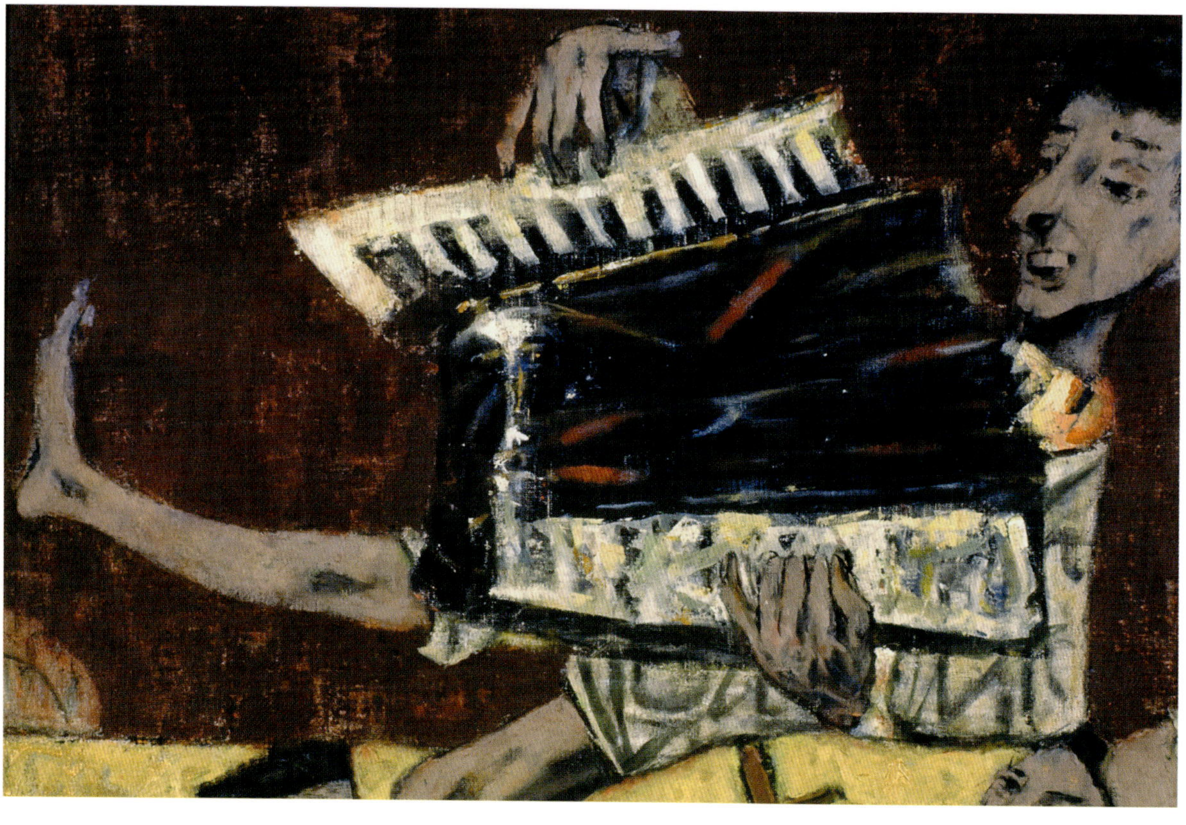

TOP: *Christ in the House of Simon,* 1947-1950
tempera & oil on canvas 60 x 96"
Collection of the DeCordova Museum, Lincoln, MA

BOTTOM:
Detail, *Christ in the House of Simon,* 1947-1950

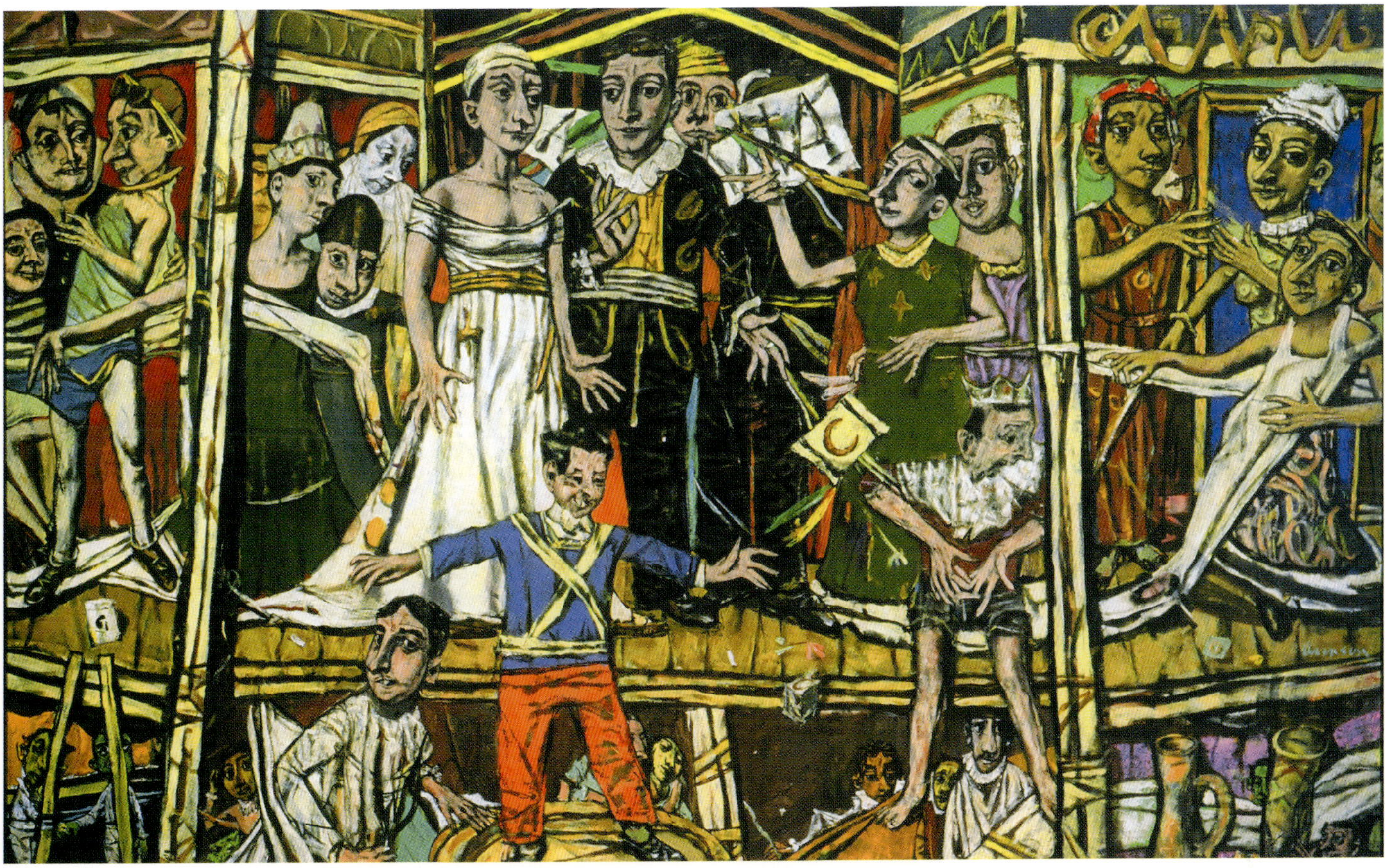

Marriage at Cana
1947-1952
oil on canvas
$60\frac{1}{8} \times 96\frac{1}{8}$"
Collection of the
University of New
Hampshire, Durham

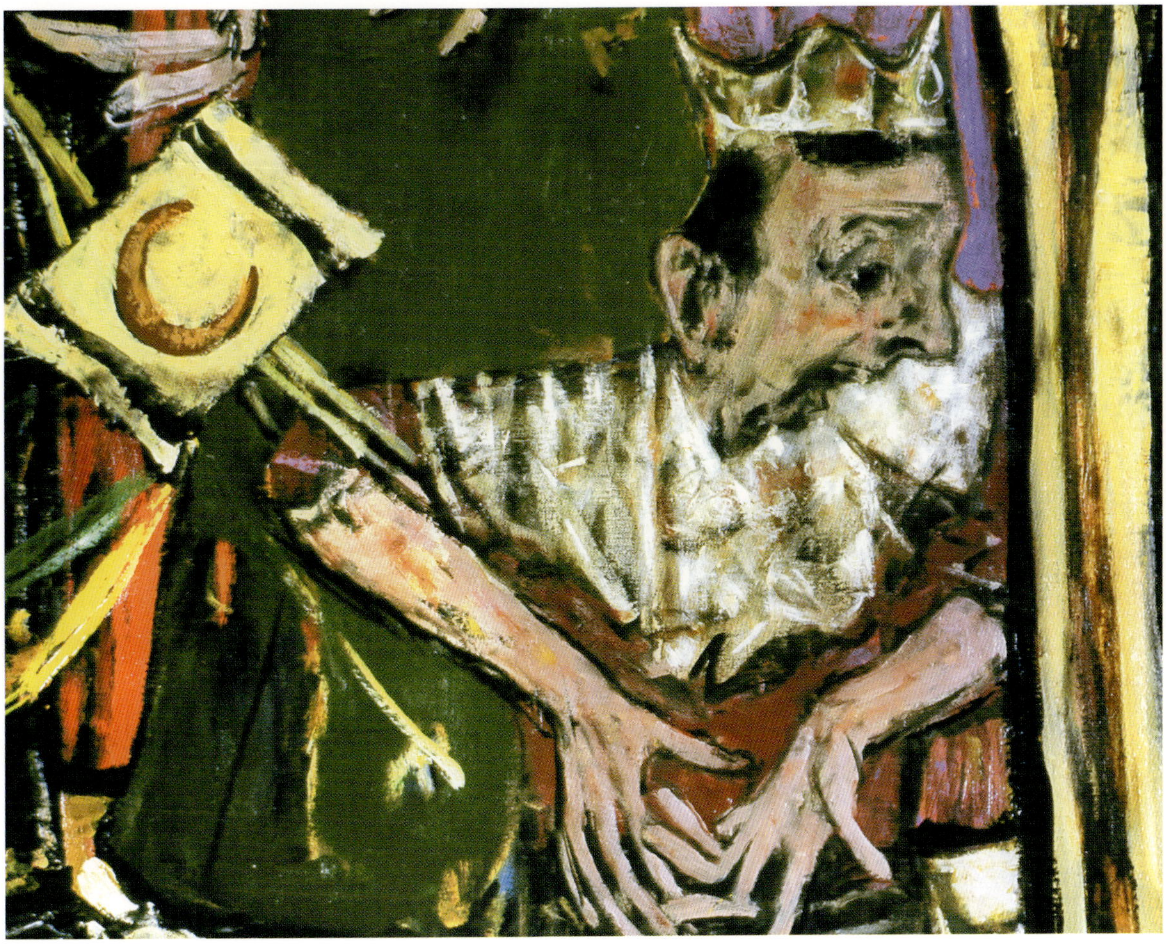

Detail
Marriage at Cana
1947-1952

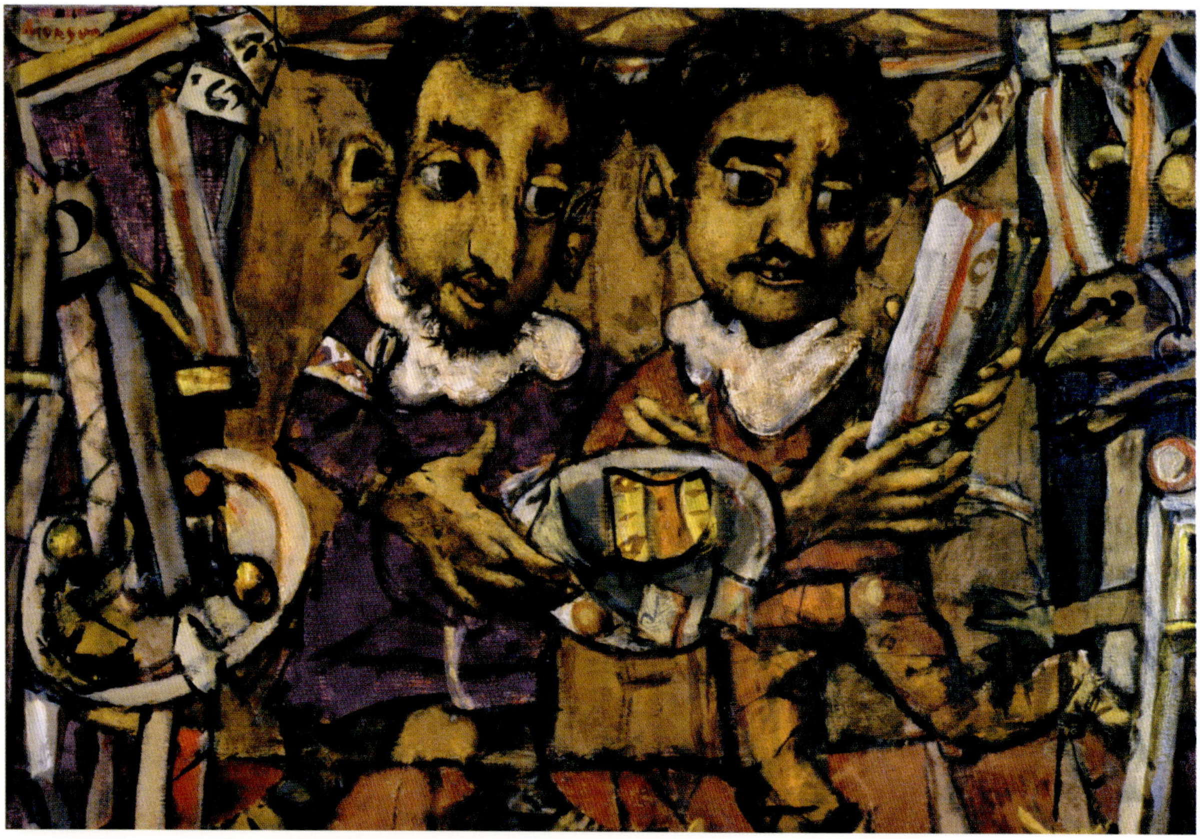

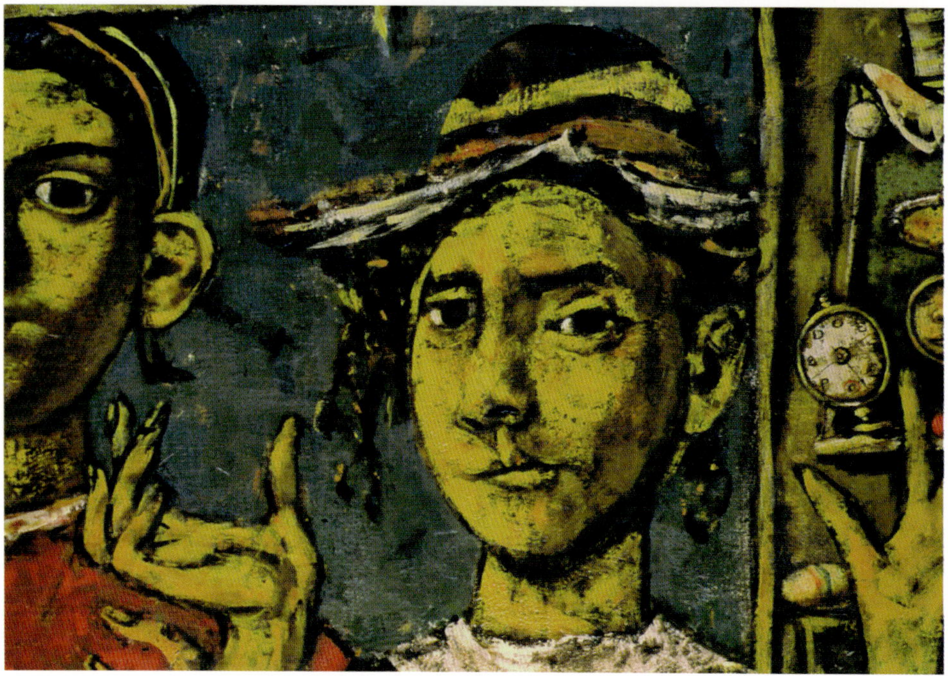

Dancing Ishmaelites
1955
tempera
12 x 17 1/2"
Private Collection

Detail 1
Joseph and the Ishmaelites, 1954

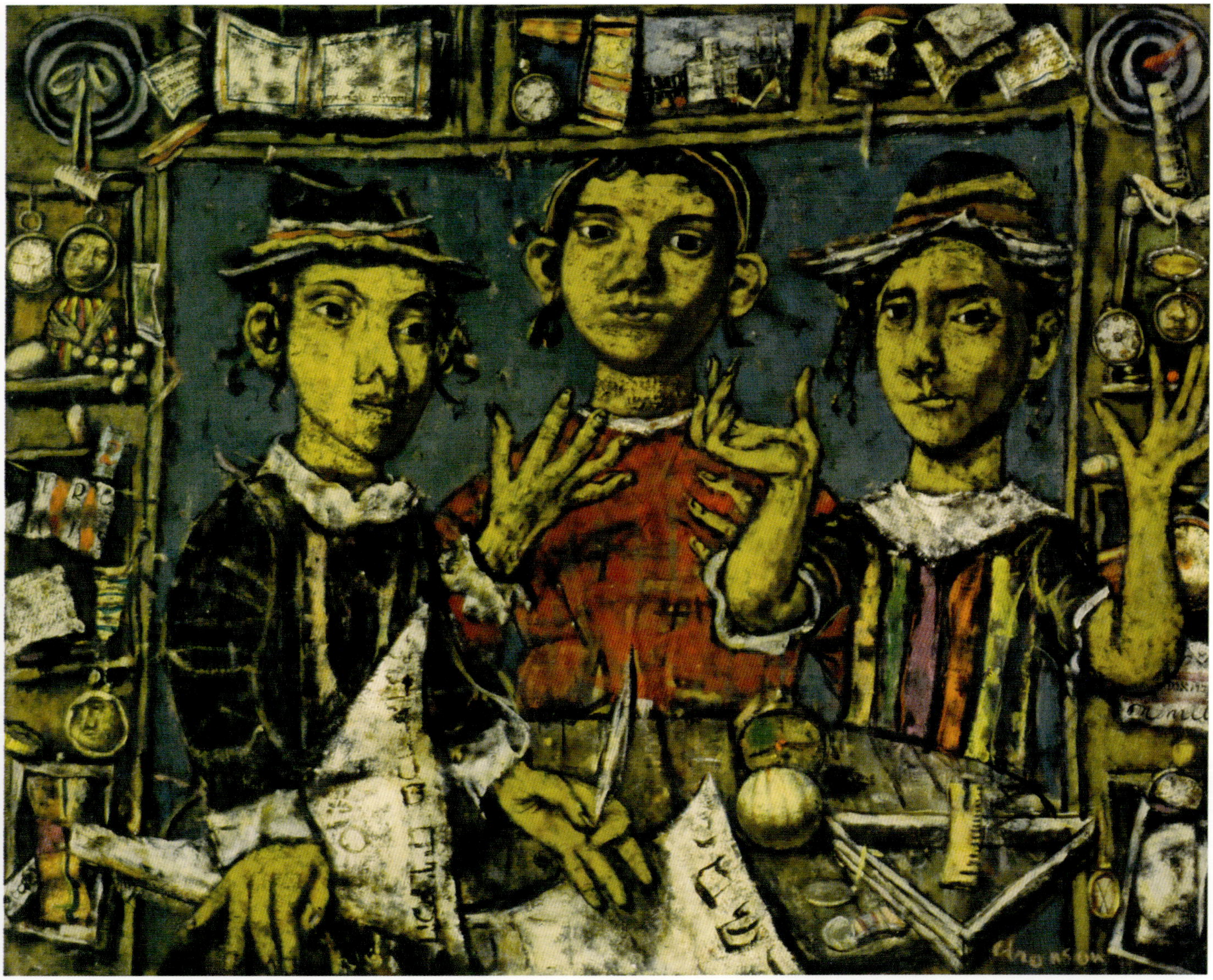

Joseph and the Ishmaelites, 1954
encaustic on panel   38 x 48"
Collection of the Krannert Art Museum, University of Illinois, Champaign, IL

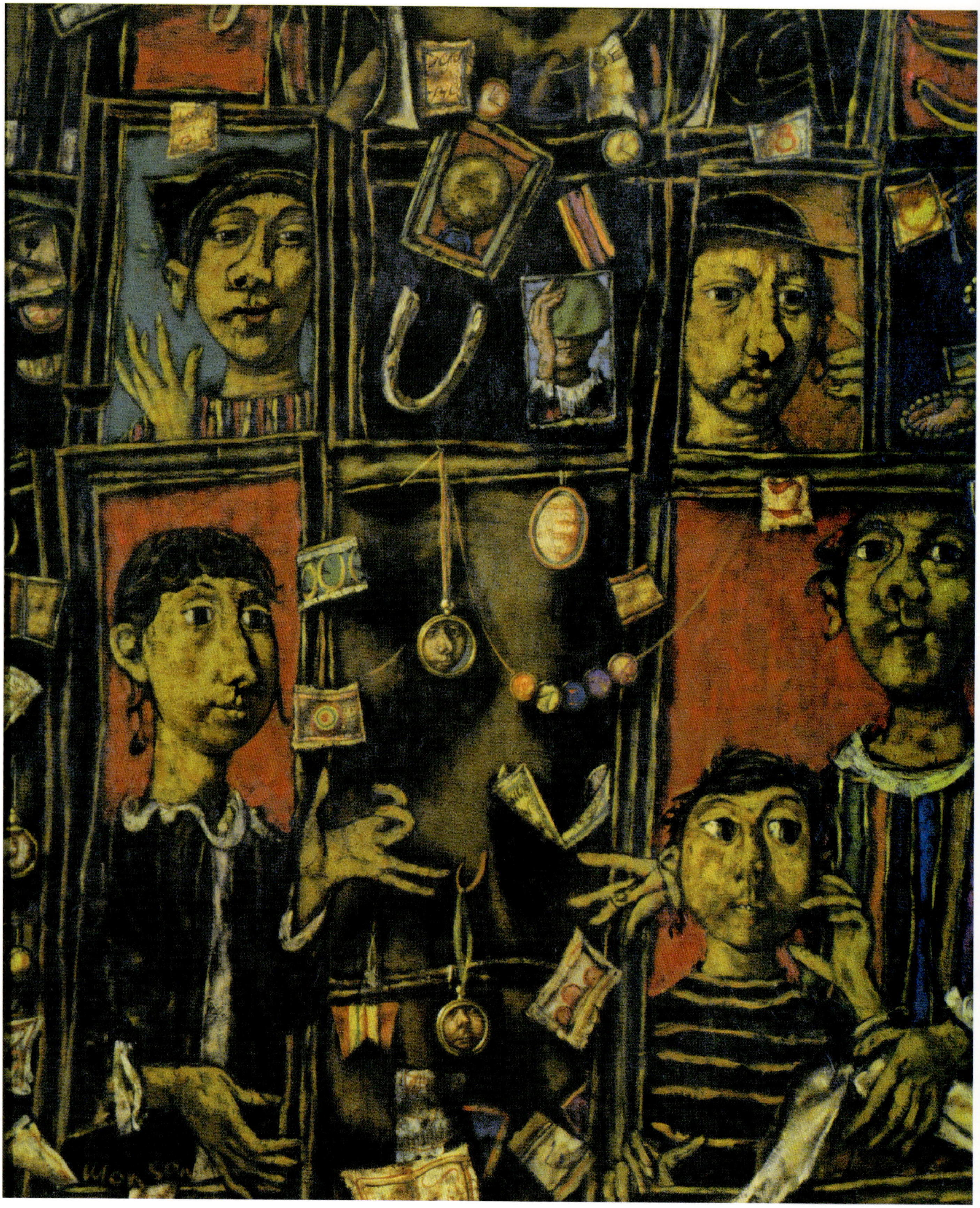

Joseph and the Ishmaelites II, 1955
encaustic on panel
52 x 48"
Collection of Temple Israel, Brookline, MA

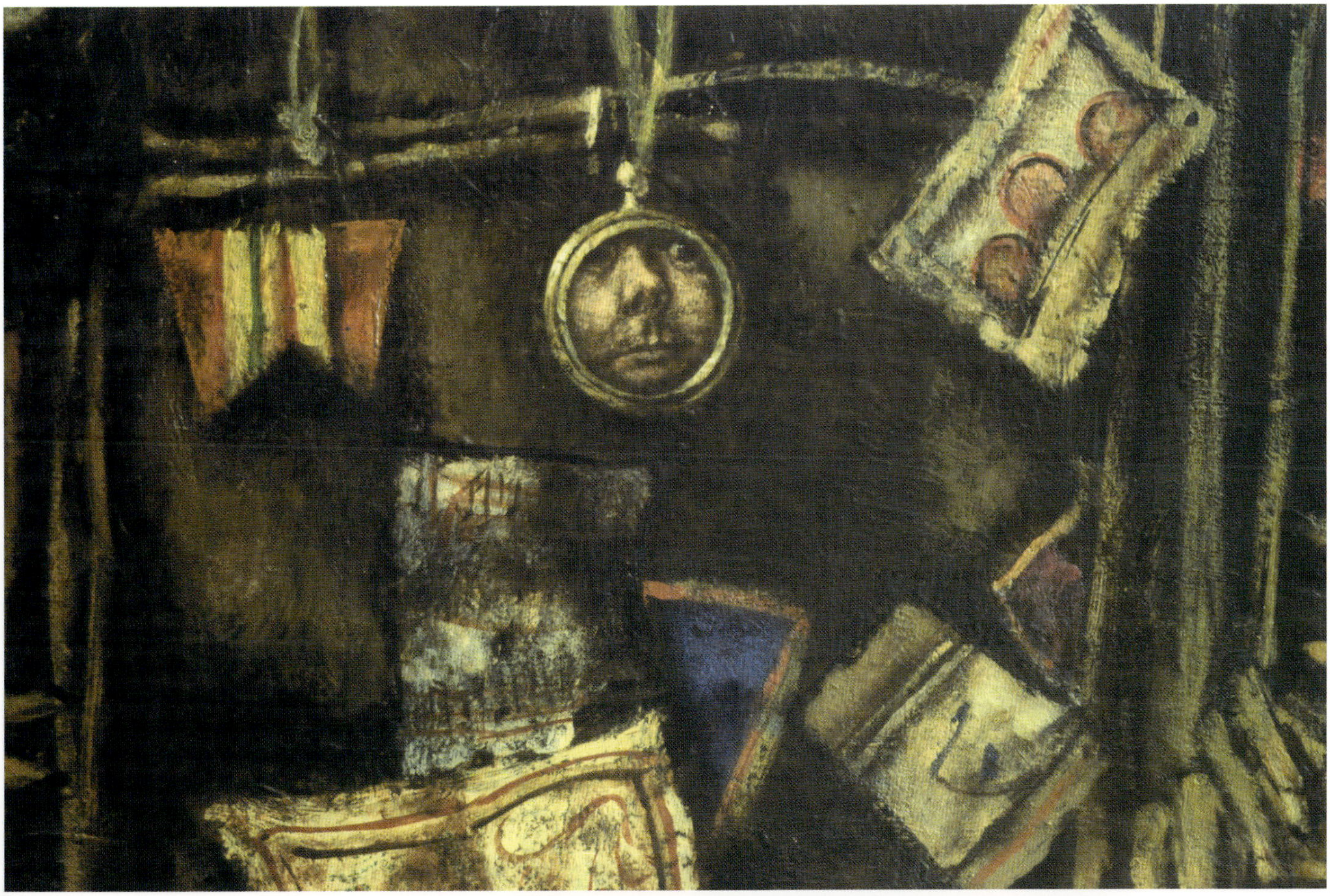

Detail
Joseph and the Ishmaelites II, 1955

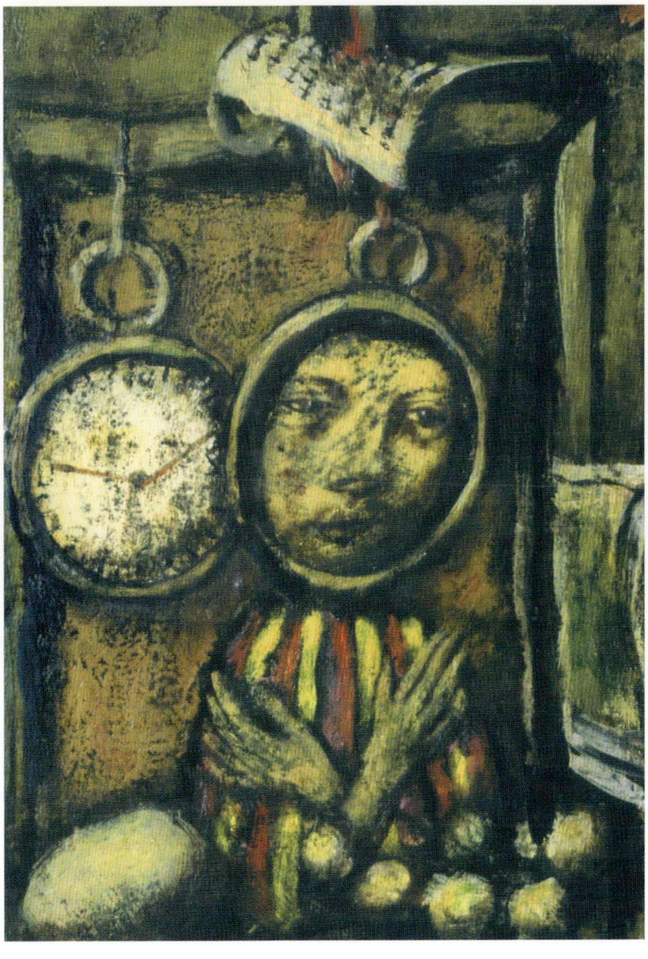

Detail 2
Joseph and the Ishmaelites, 1954

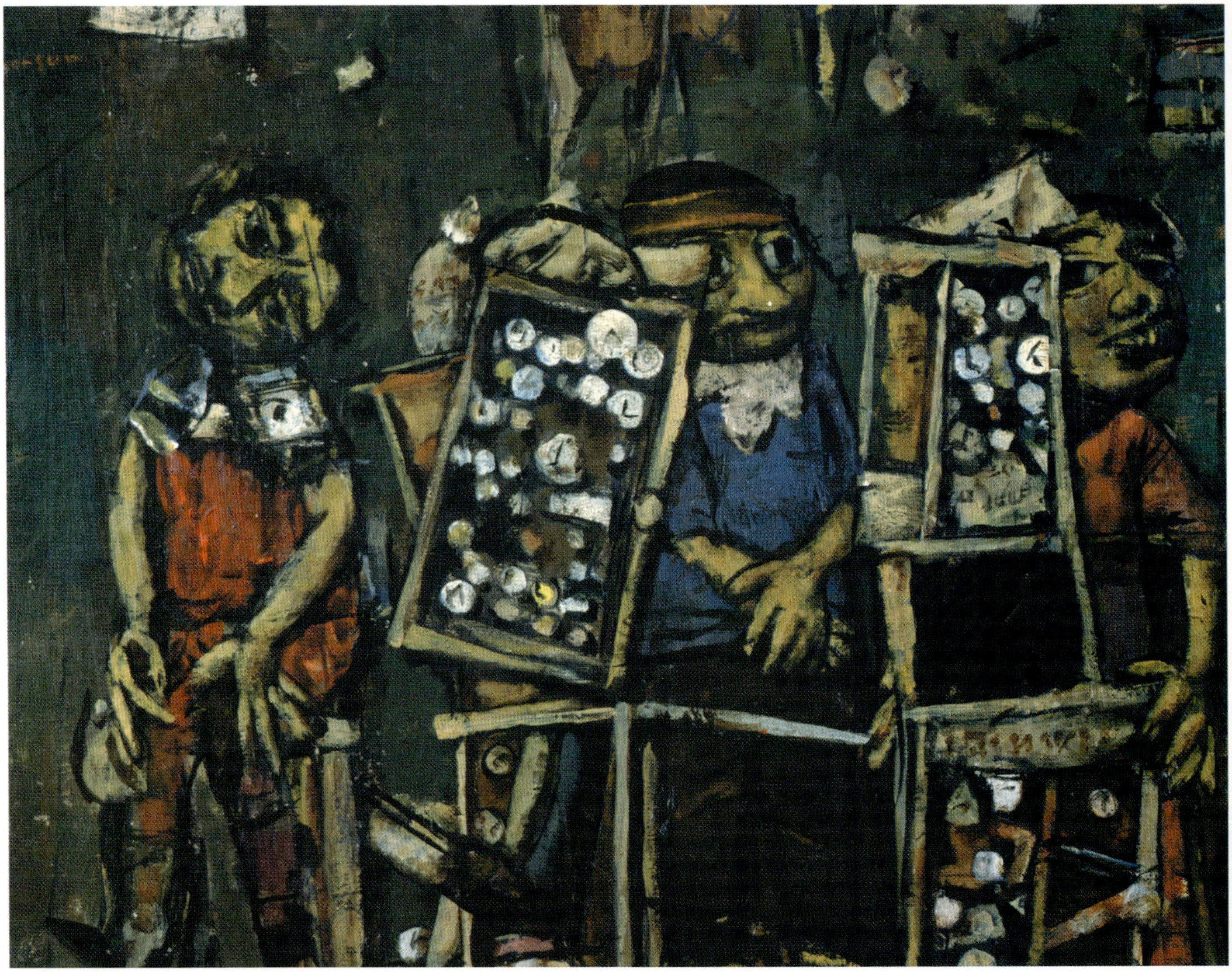

The Merchants, 1955
tempera
$10\frac{1}{8}$ x 13"
Private Collection

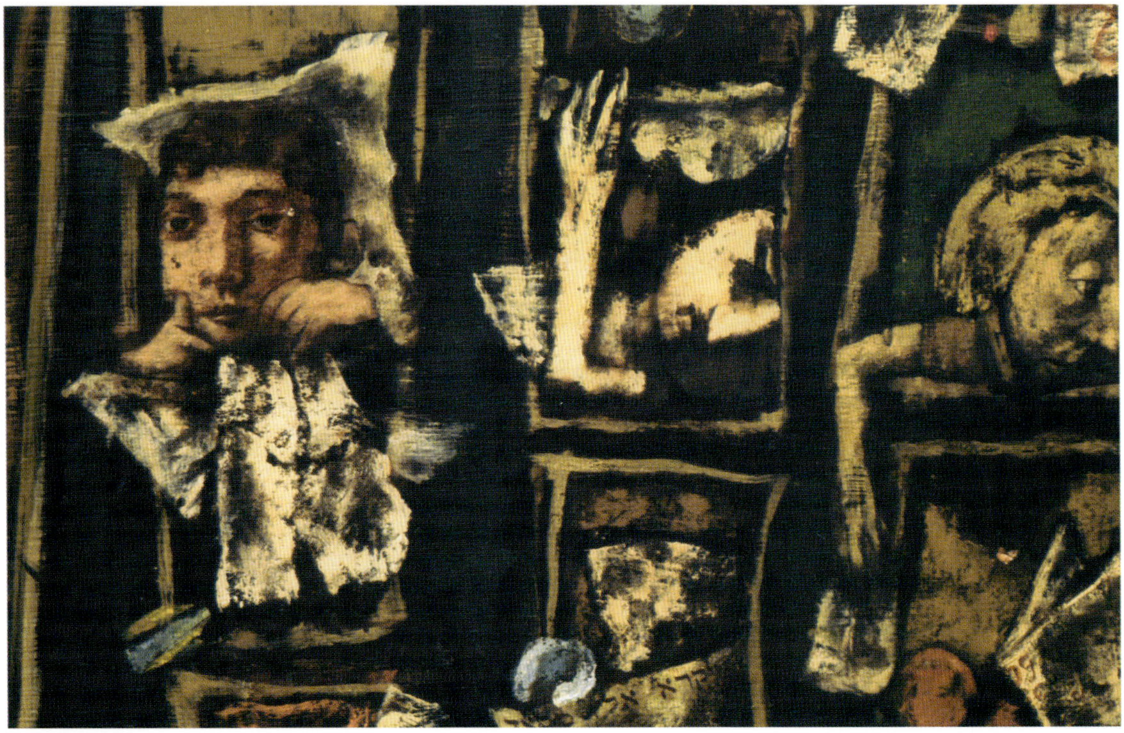

Detail
Sacrifice of Isaac, 1957

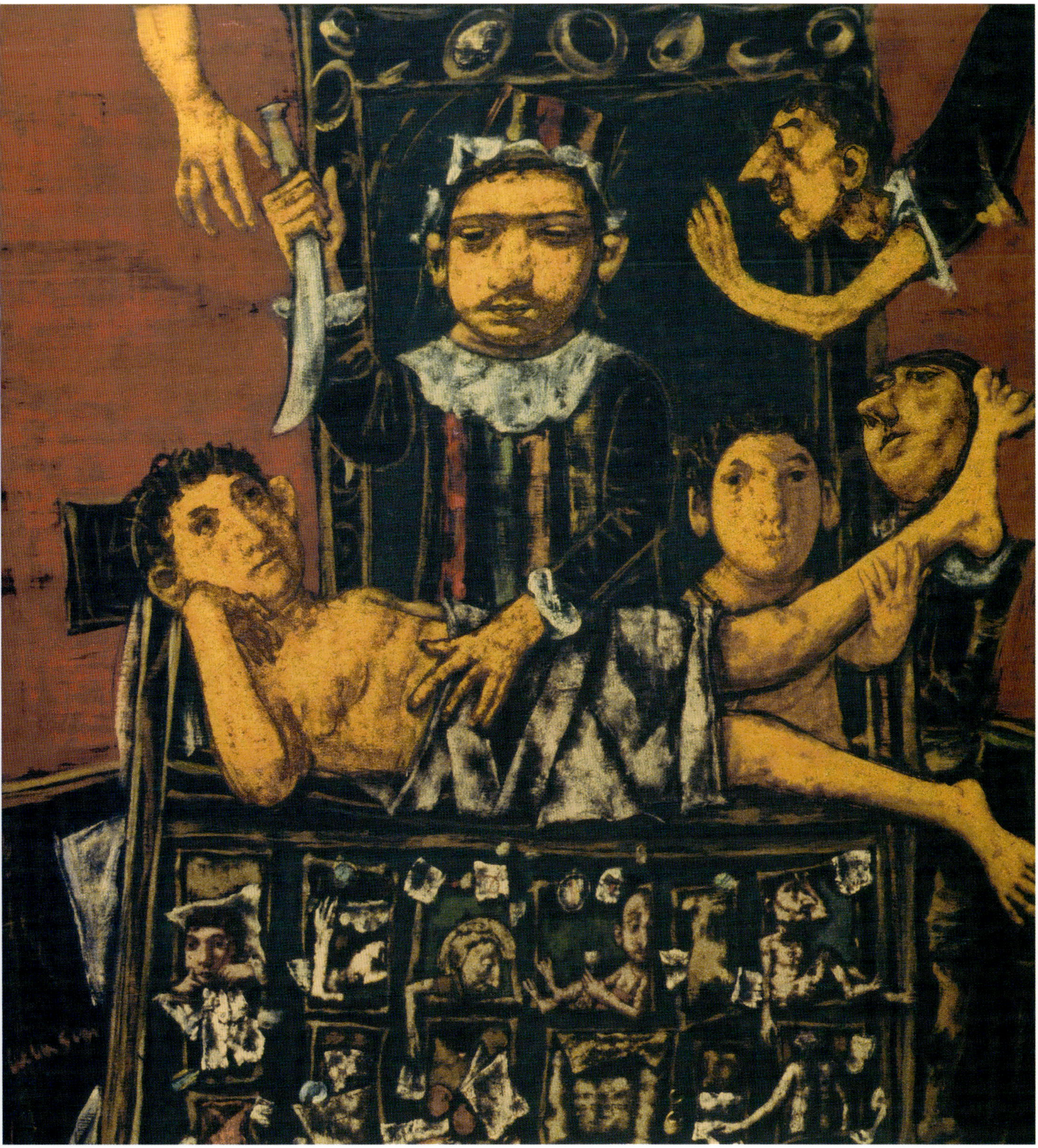

Sacrifice of Isaac, 1957
encaustic on panel 54 x 48"
Private Collection

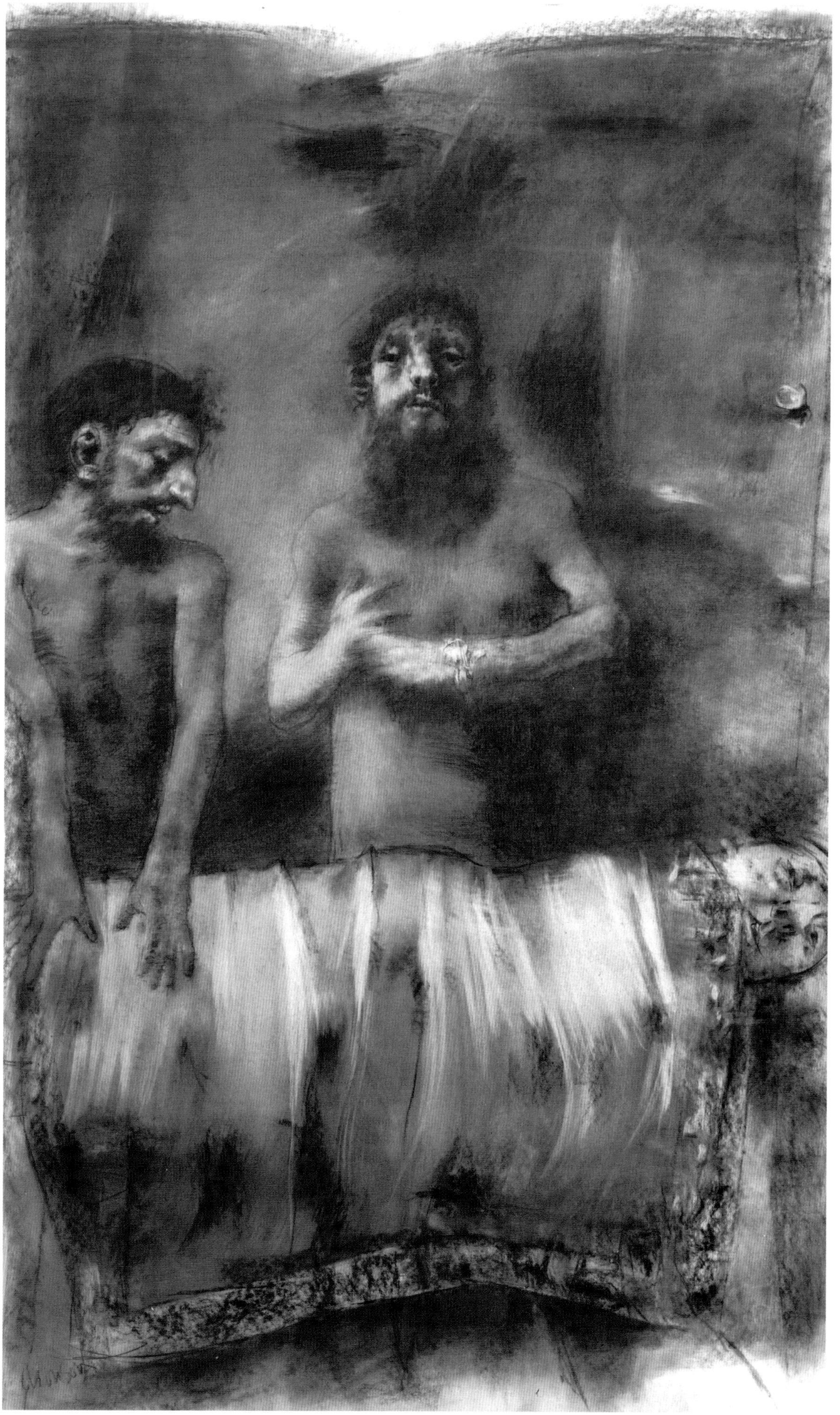

Rabbi Judah Loew, 1959
charcoal
78 x 48"
Collection of the American Friends of the Israel Museum, New York, NY

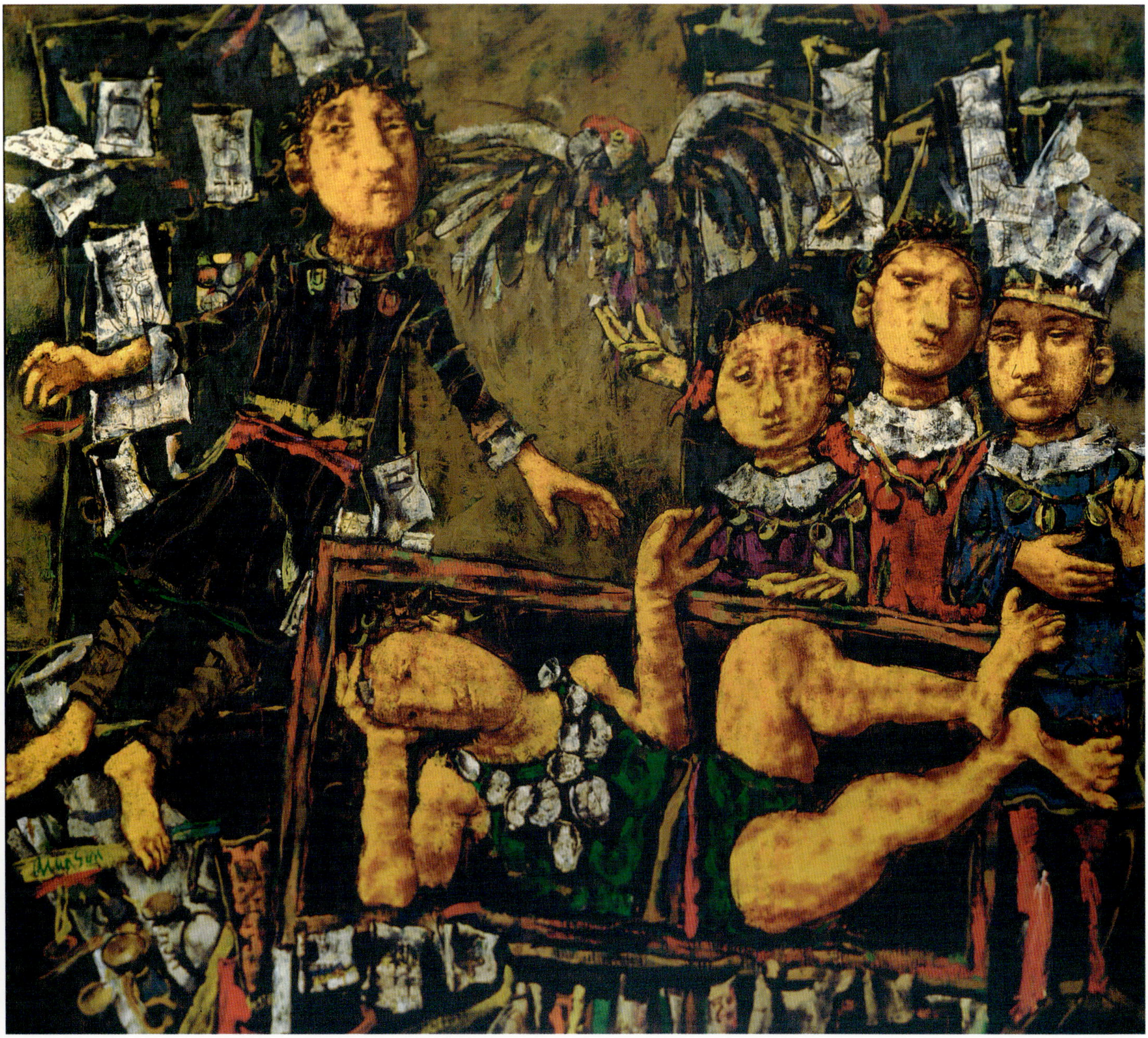

The Golem, 1958
encaustic on panel 57 x 64"

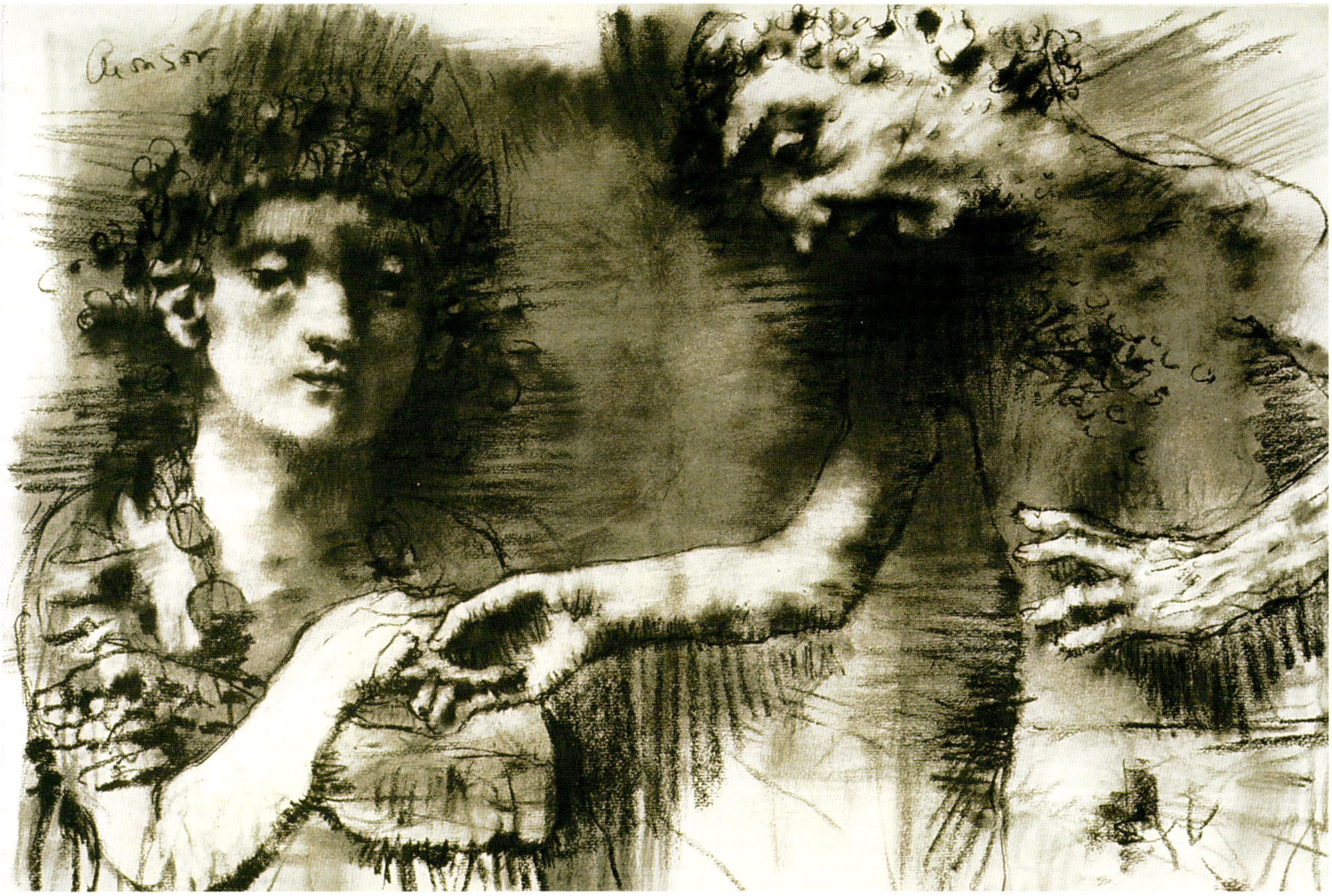

Consultation II (From the Dybbuk), 1959
pastel
26 x 40"
Private Collection

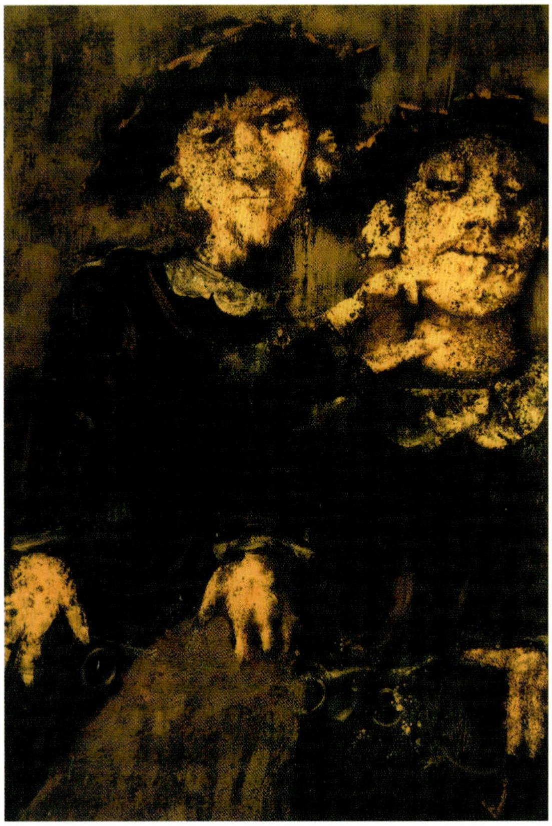

Levitation I, 1959
encaustic on panel 18 x 12"
Private Collection

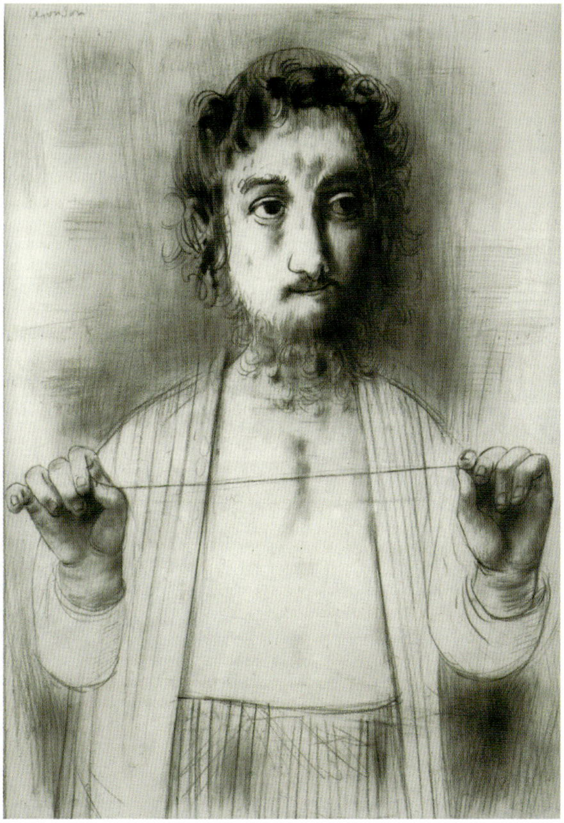

Ishmaelite, 1955
pencil 17 1/4 x 11 3/4"
Private Collection

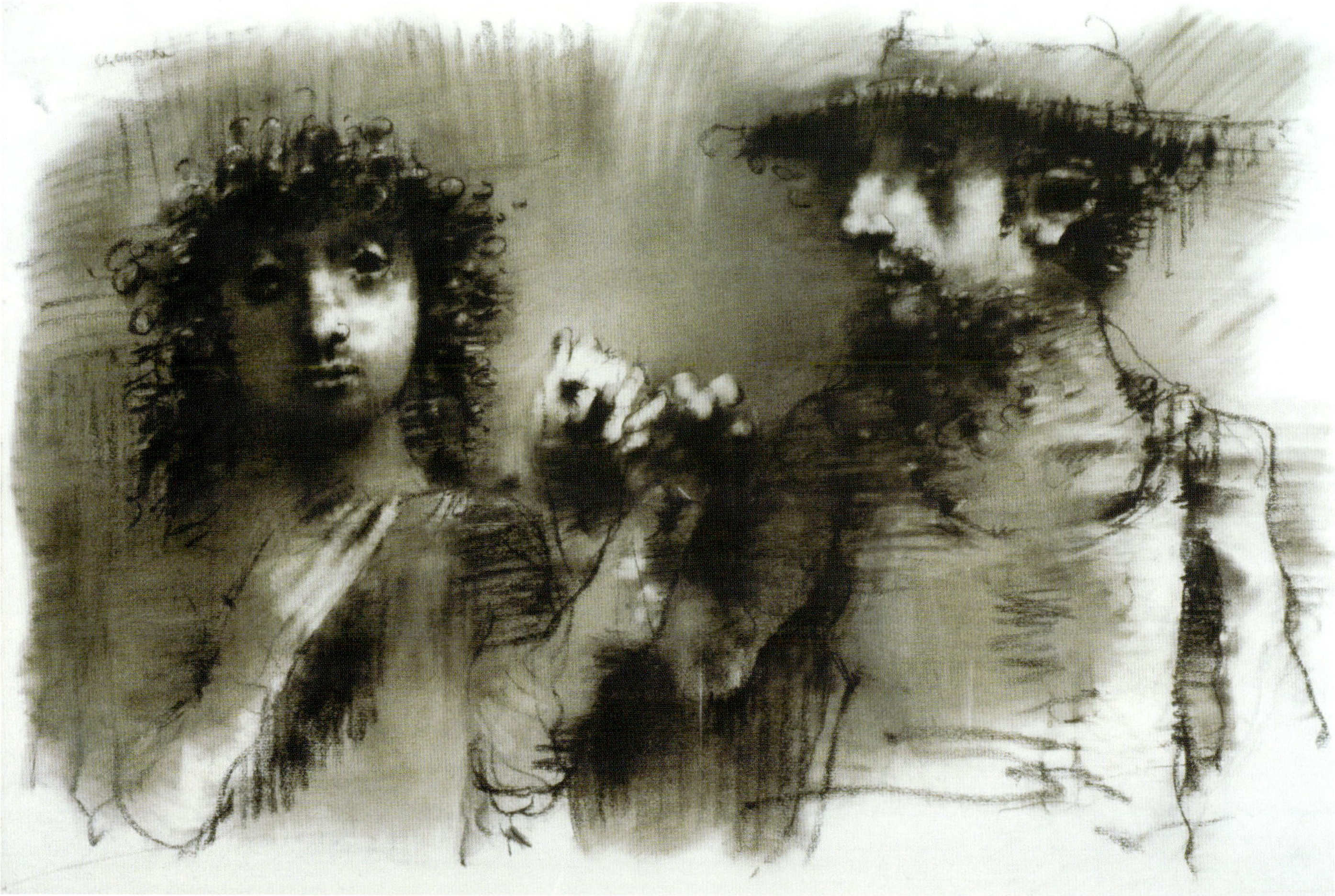

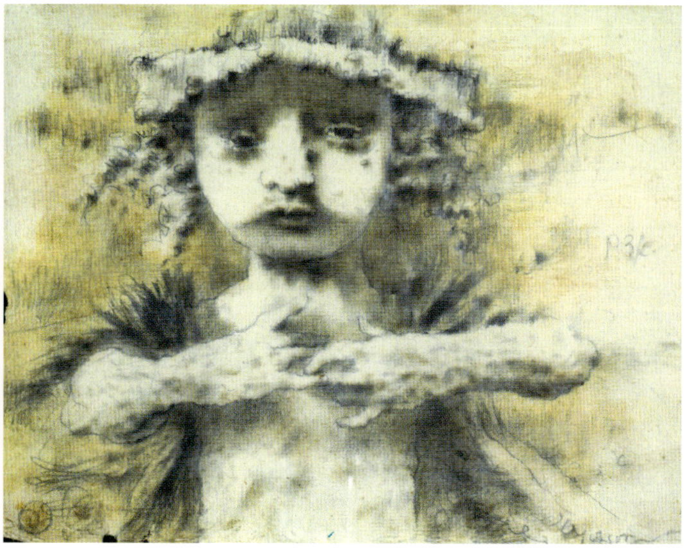

Adam, 1960
pencil & wash   8 3/8 x 10 3/4"
Private Collection

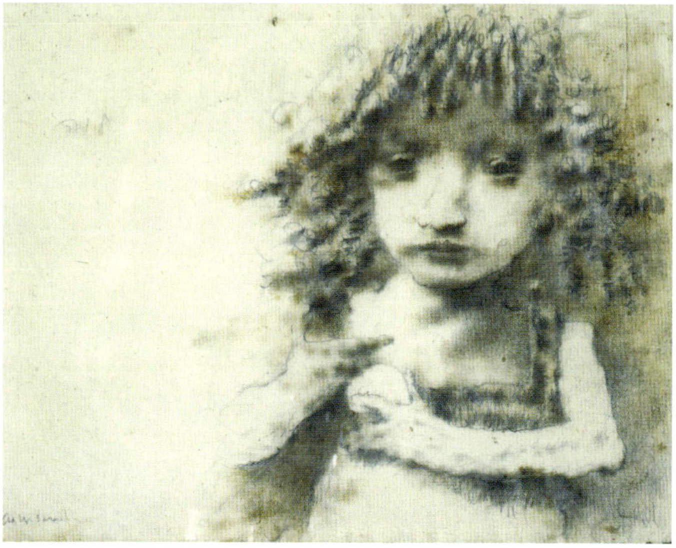

Eve, 1960
pencil & wash   8 3/8 x 10 3/4"
Private Collection

TOP: *Itinerant II,* 1960
pastel   26 x 40"
Collection of the Estate of Jerome Robbins, New York, NY

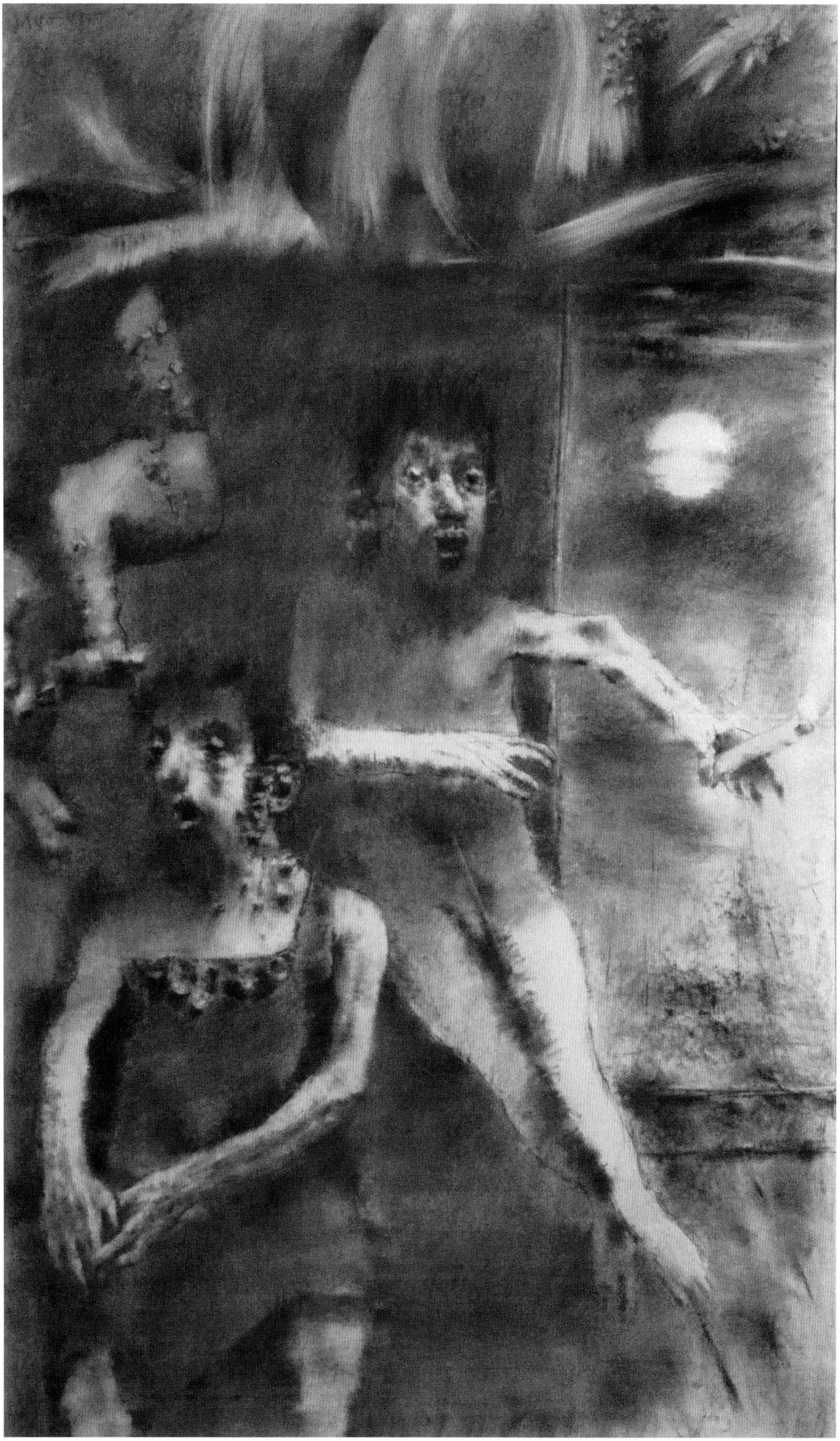

Moonworshipers, 1960
charcoal
80 x 48"
Private Collection

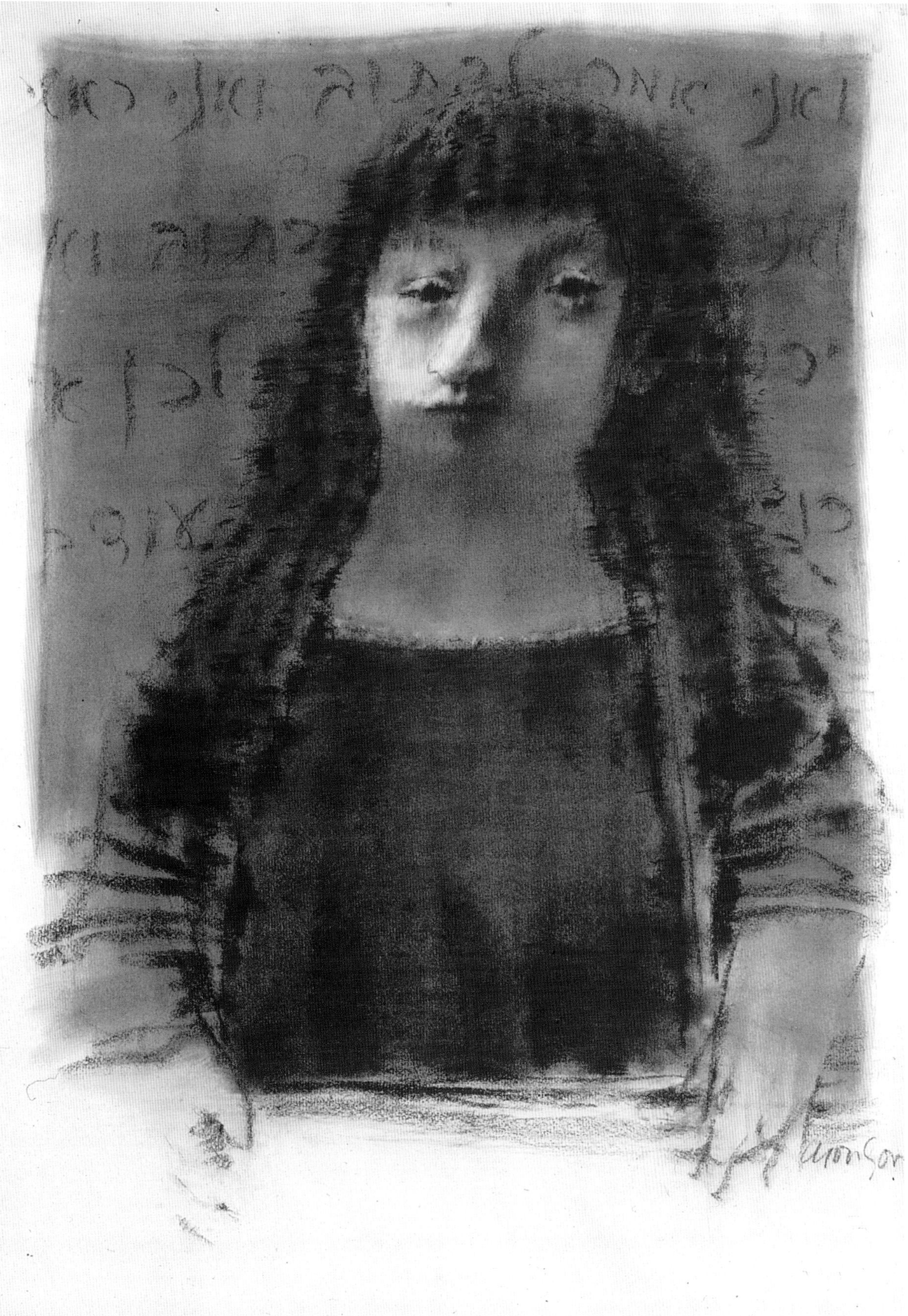

Scribe II, 1963
pastel
40 x 26"
Private Collection

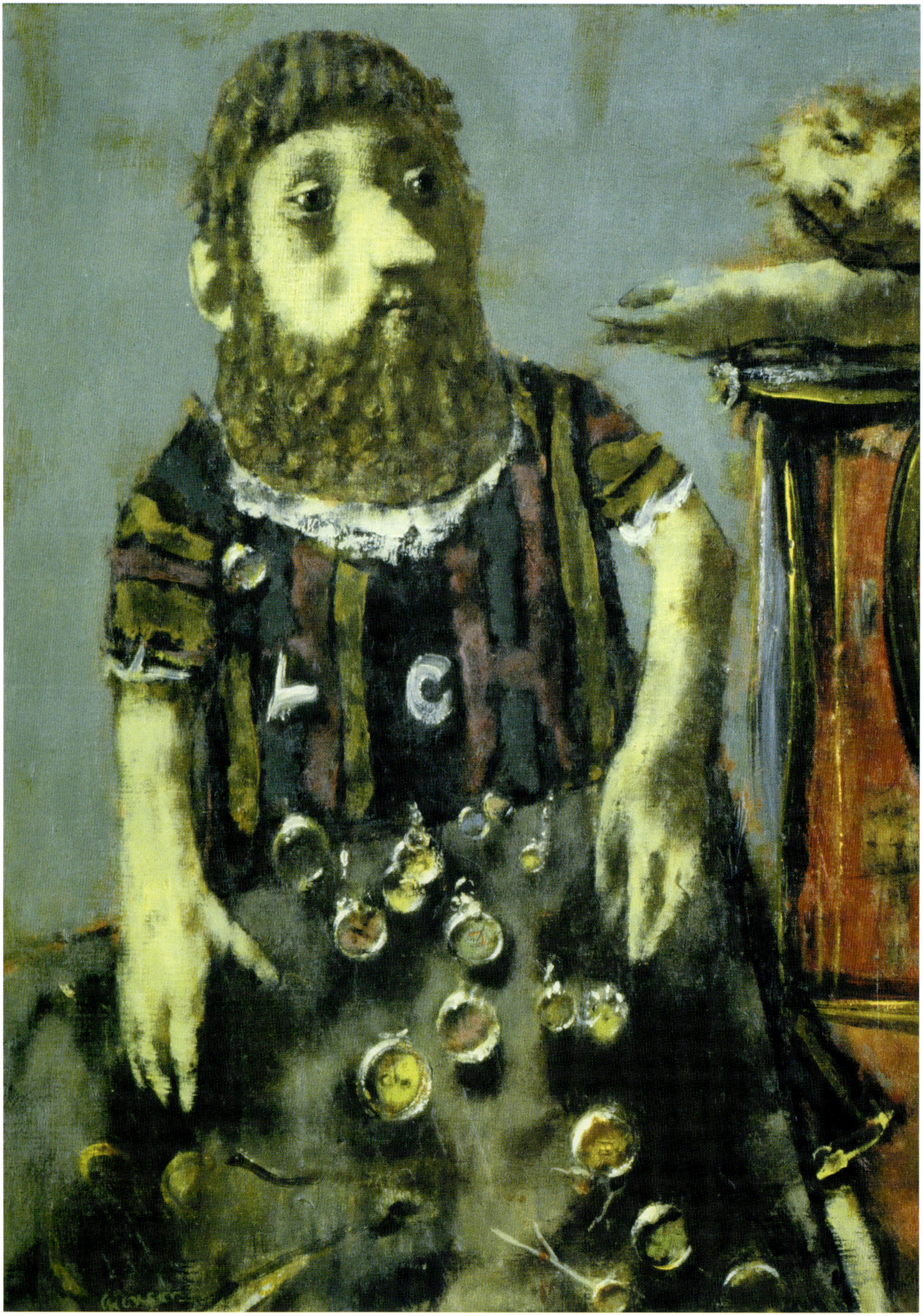

Conjurer, 1960
acrylic on panel 16 x 12"
Private Collection

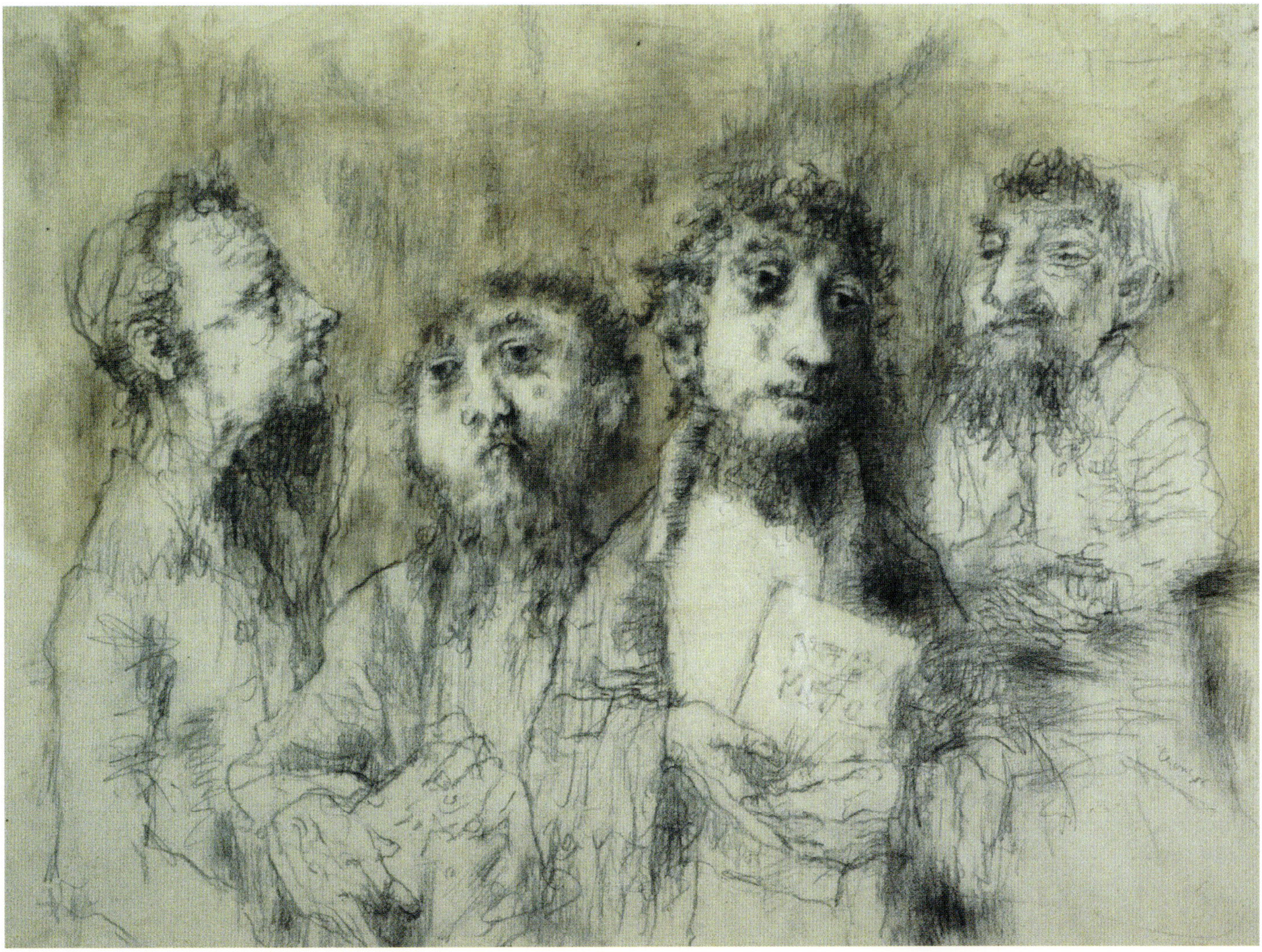

The Judges, 1959
pencil & wash
$22 \times 30\frac{3}{4}$"
Collection of the
Whitney Museum
of American Art,
New York, NY

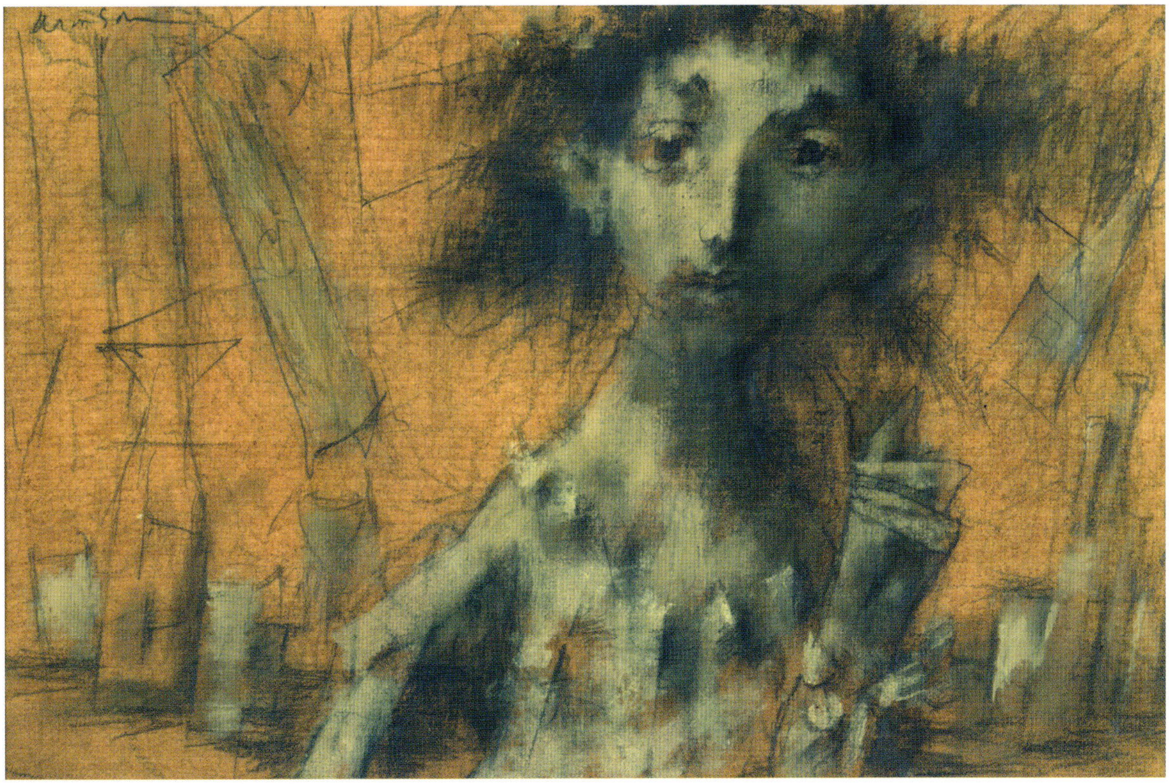

Alchemist, 1976
acrylic & pencil
$7\frac{1}{2} \times 11\frac{1}{2}$"
Private Collection

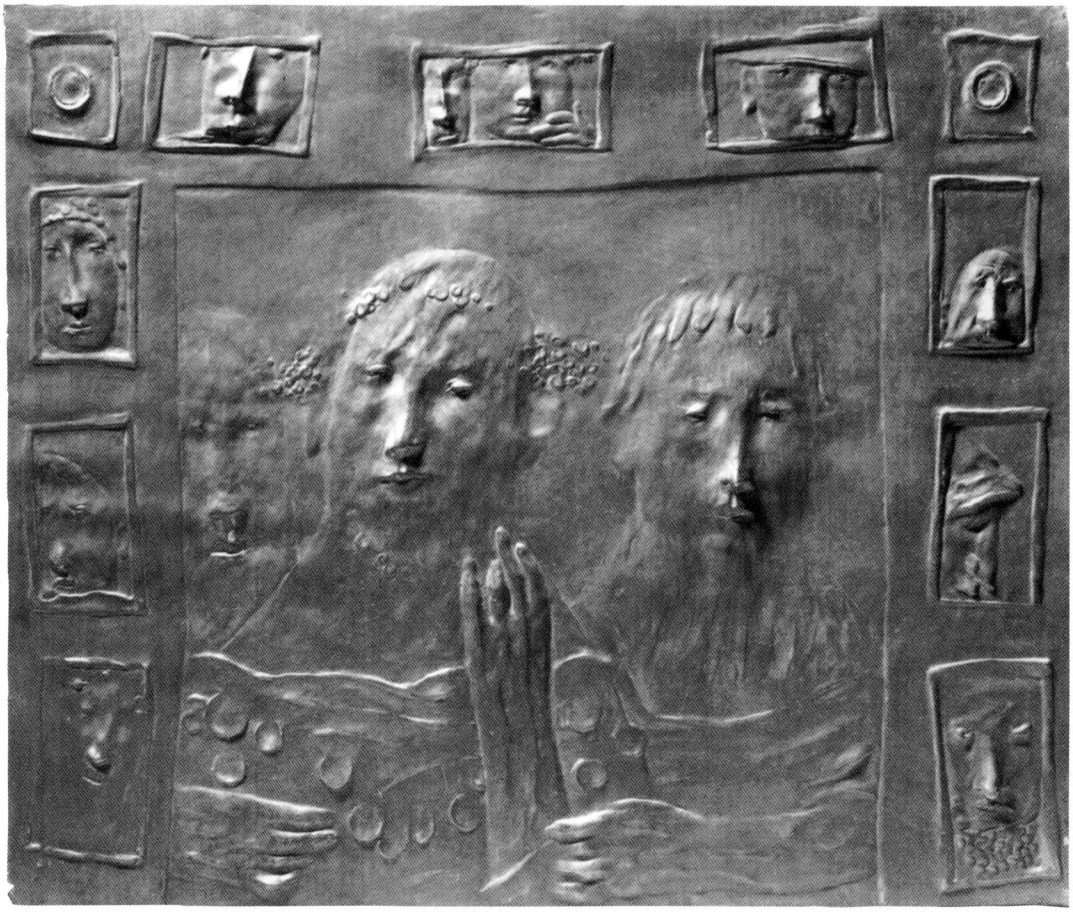

The Judges, 1961
bronze (relief)
$19\frac{1}{2} \times 23\frac{3}{4} \times \frac{3}{4}$"

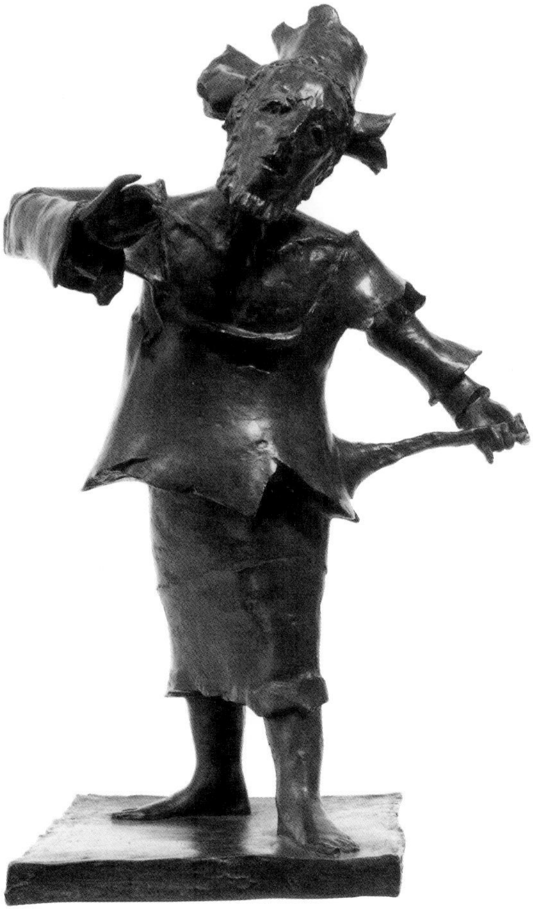

Troubadour, 1964
bronze $21\frac{1}{2} \times 13 \times 11$"

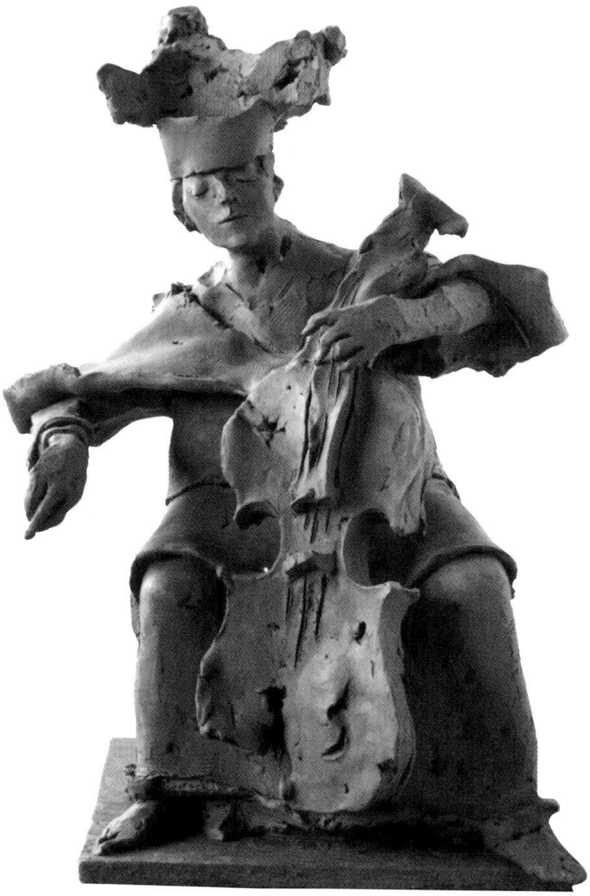

Cellist, 1974-1976 (photographed in clay)
bronze $20 \times 14 \times 11$"

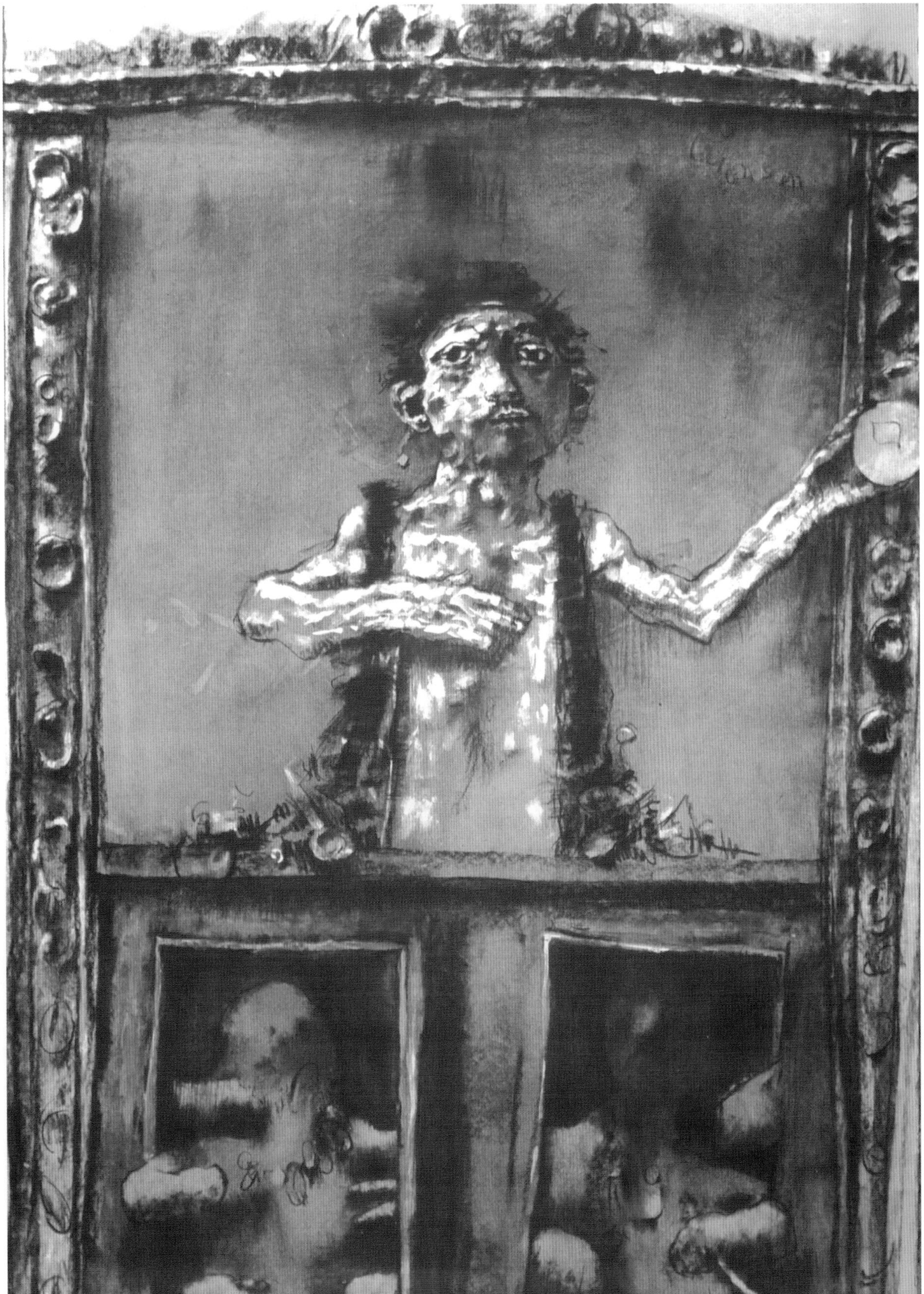

Young Baal Shem
1964
charcoal
60 x 48"

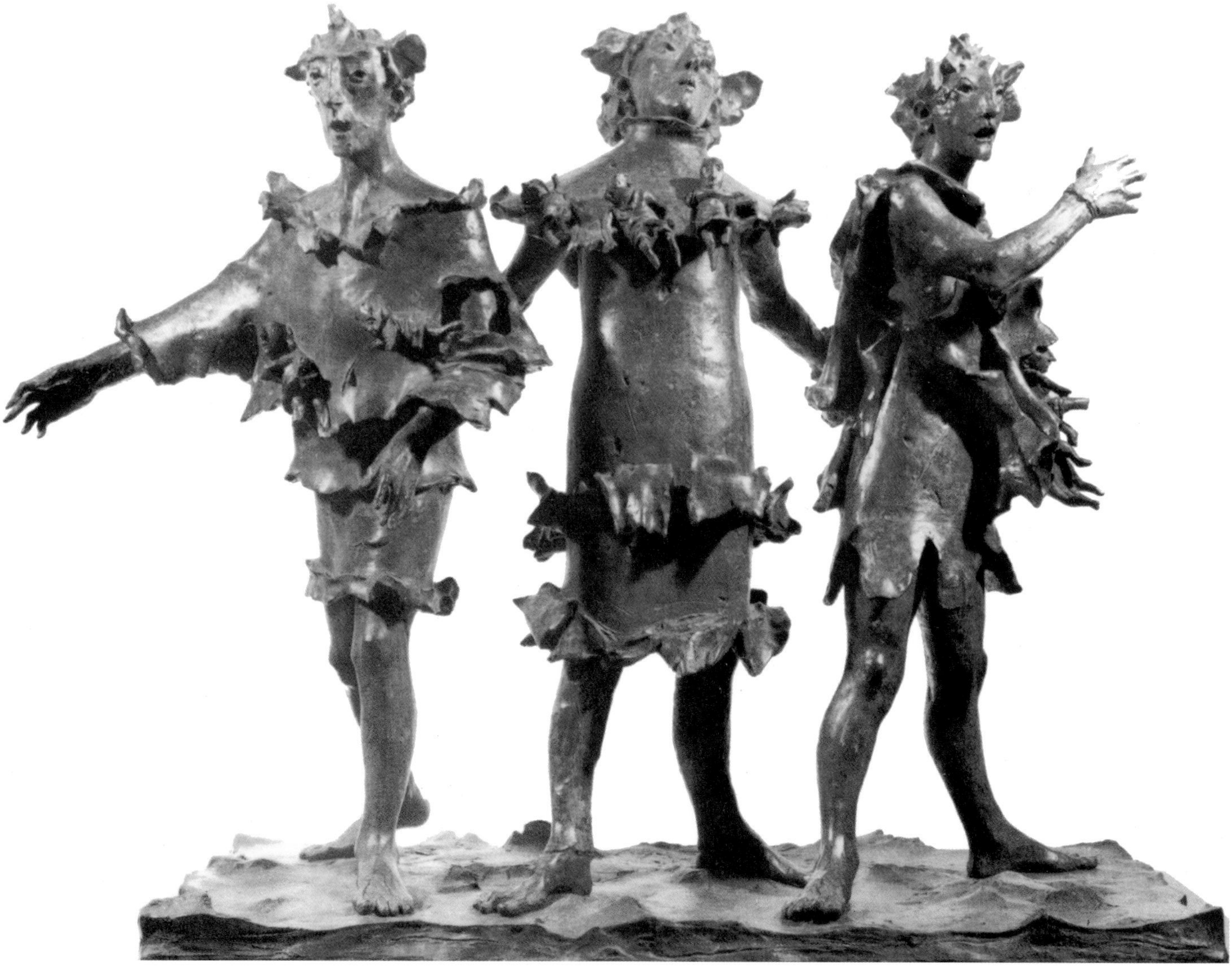

Three Singers, 1963-1969
bronze 58 x 68 x 30"

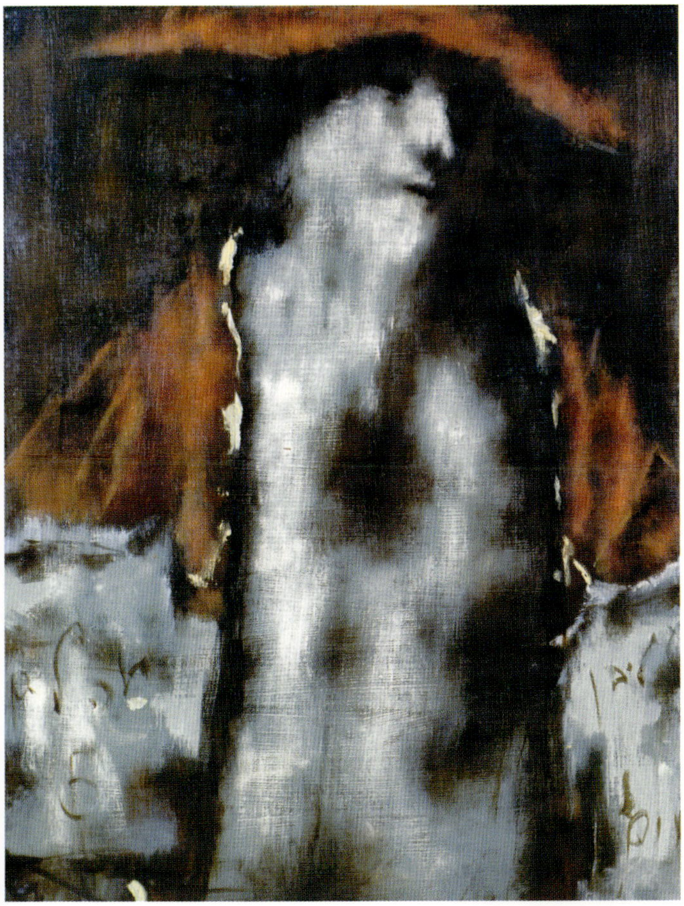

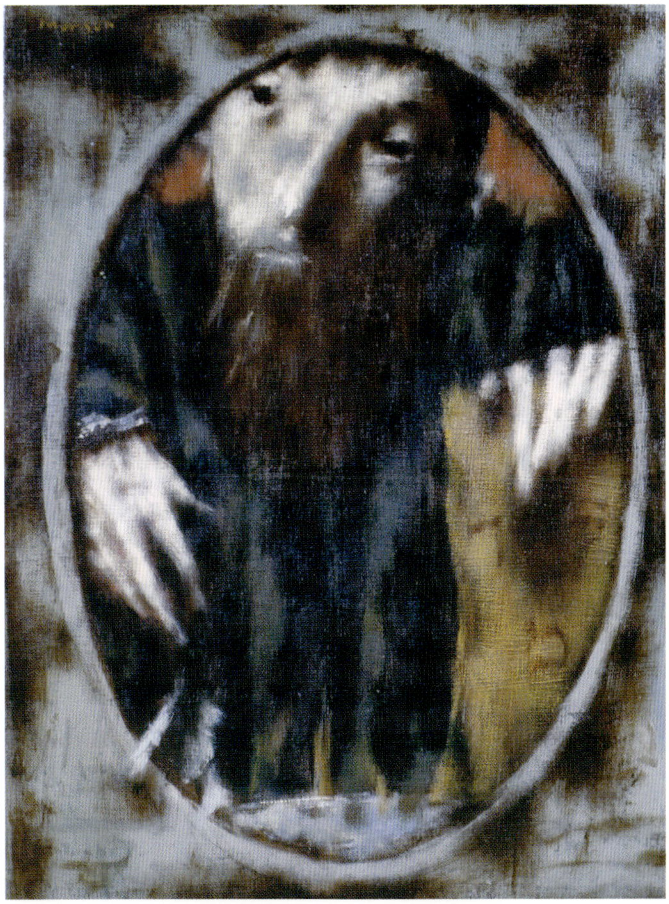

Man in Red, 1962
acrylic on panel 16 x 12"
Private Collection

Man in Oval Frame, 1962
acrylic on panel
16 x 12"
Private Collection

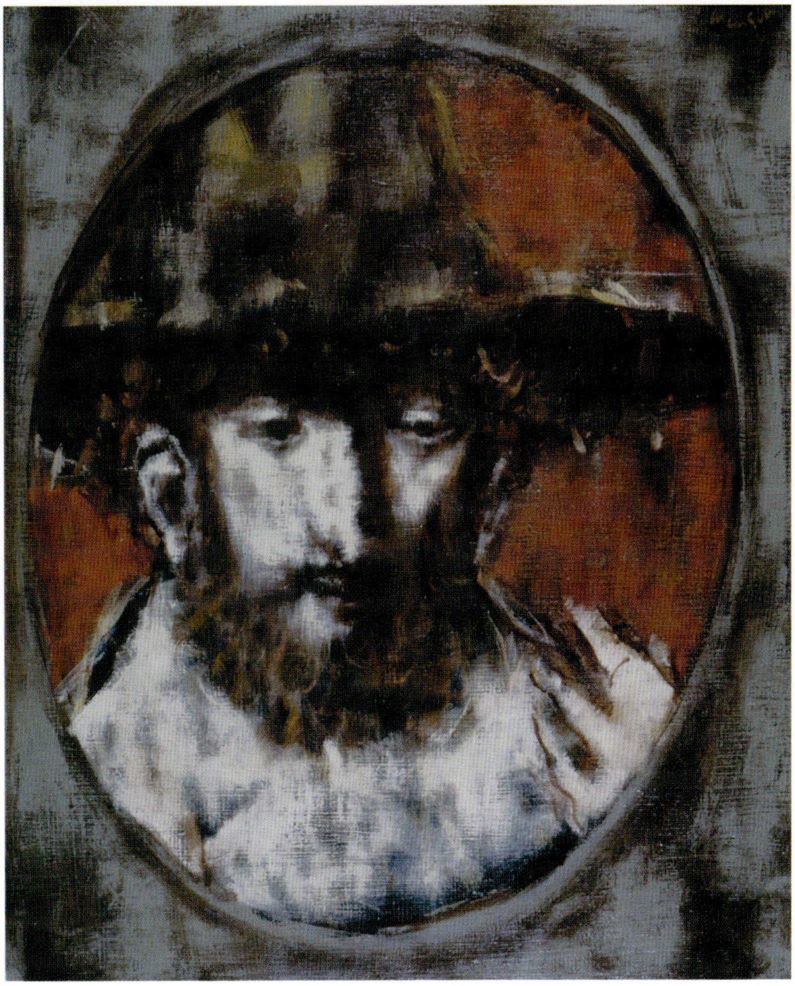

Moonworshiper, 1962
acrylic on panel
16 x 12"
Private Collection

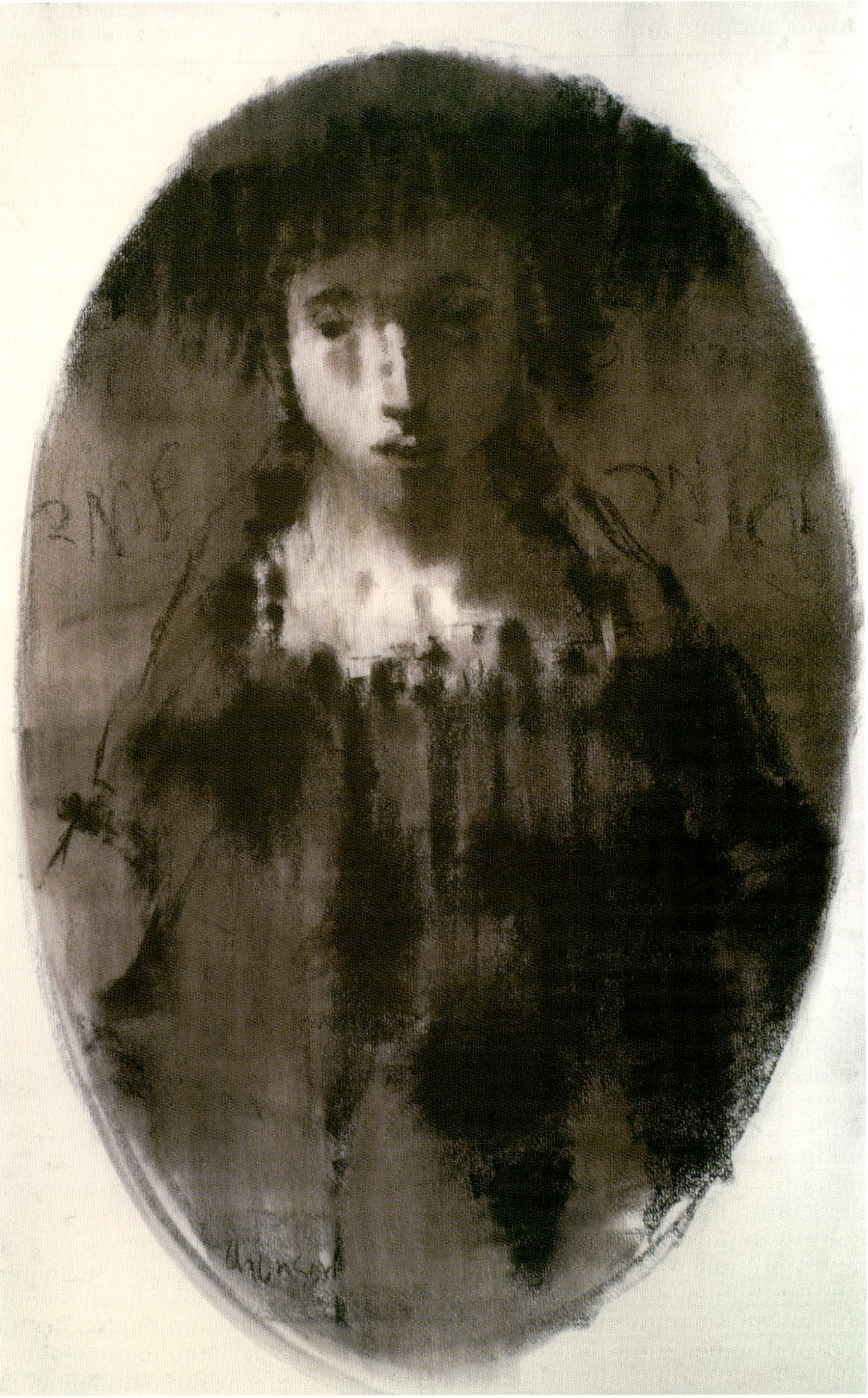

Rabbinical Student
1964
pastel
40 x 26"
Collection of the DeCordova Museum, Lincoln, MA

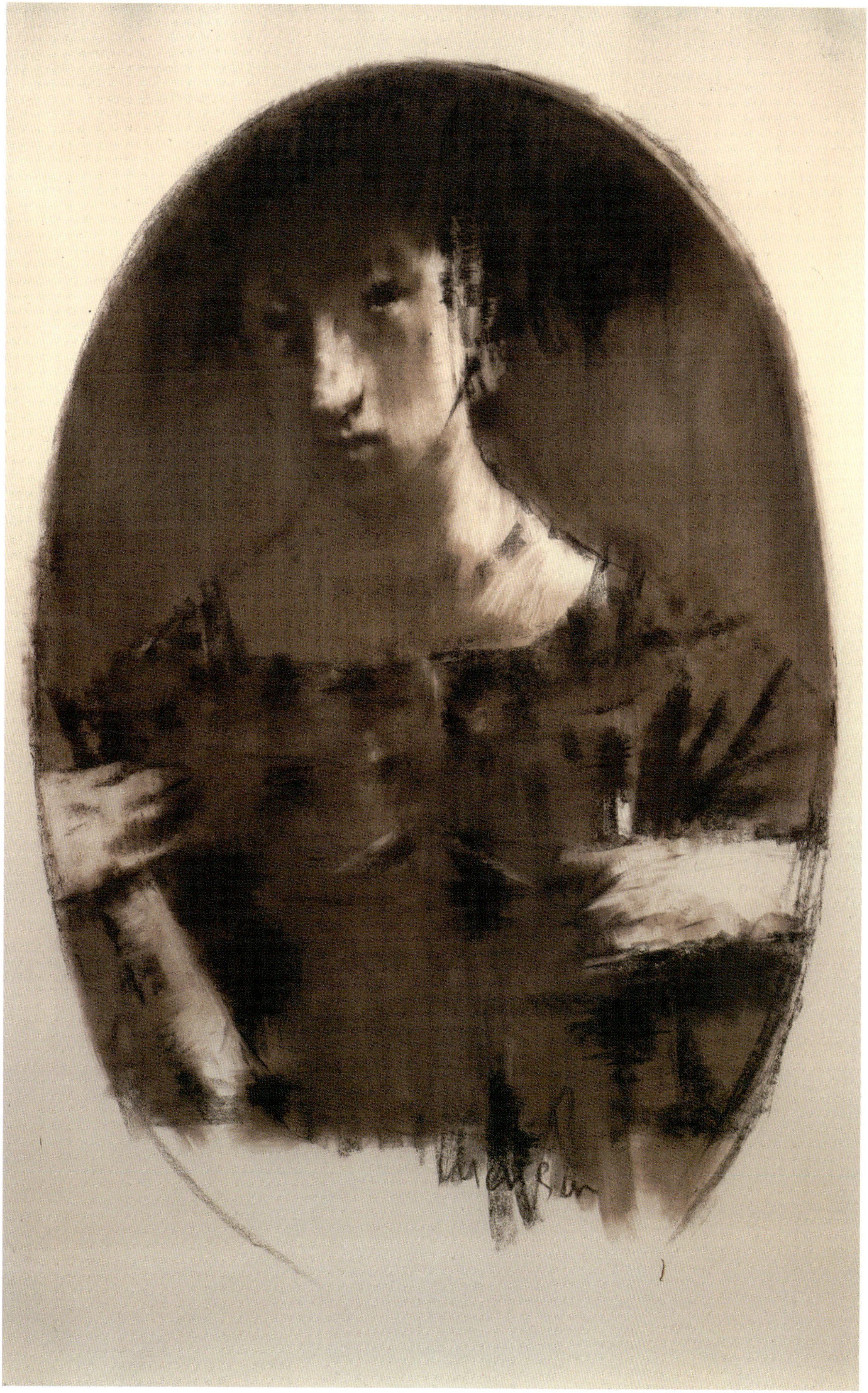

Young Magistrate
1964
pastel
40 x 26"
Private Collection

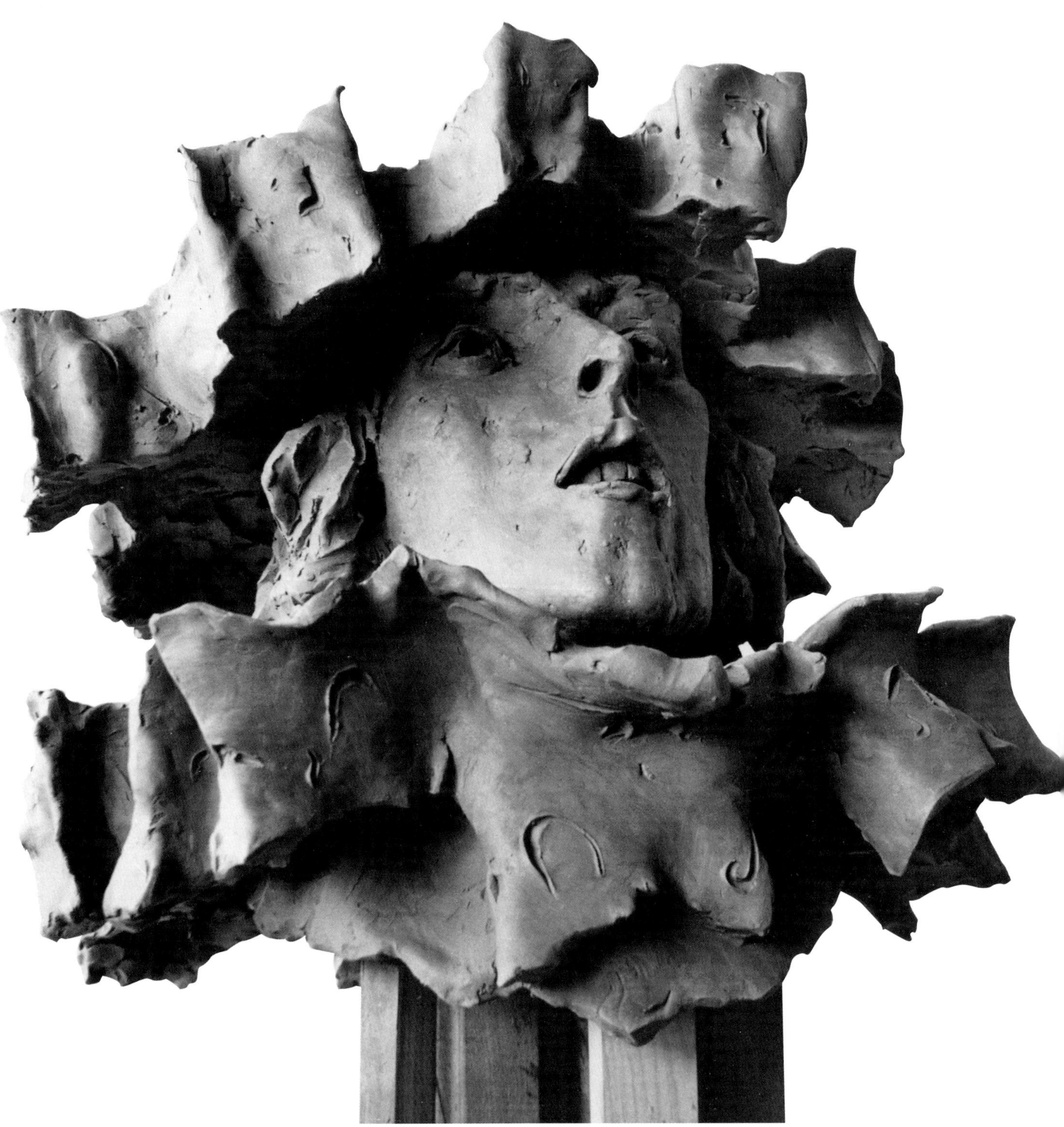

Spinoza, 1965-1969 (photographed in clay)
bronze 19 x 18½ x 19"

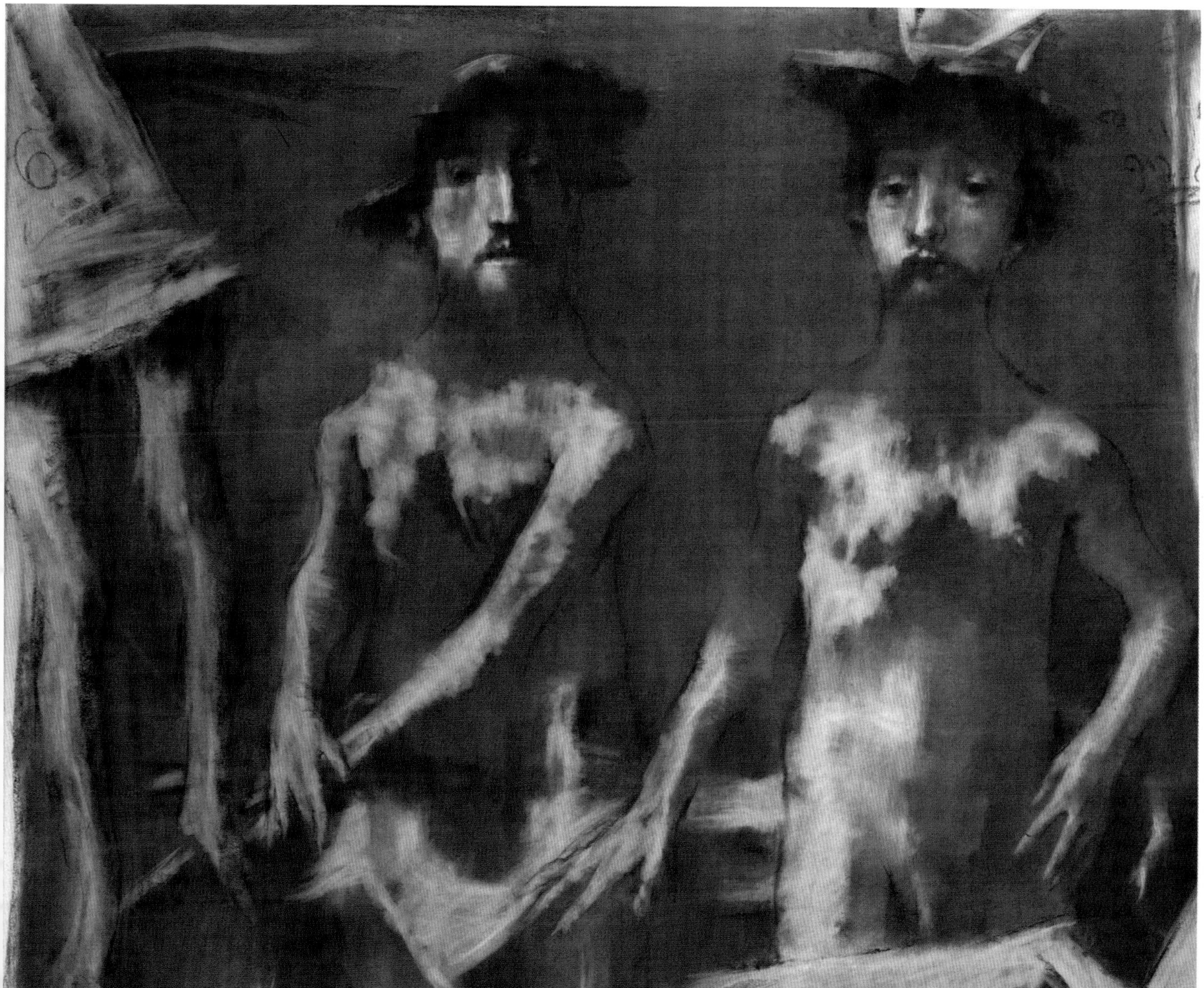

Rabbis with Birds, 1969
charcoal 51 x 44"
Collection of the Jewish Museum, New York, NY

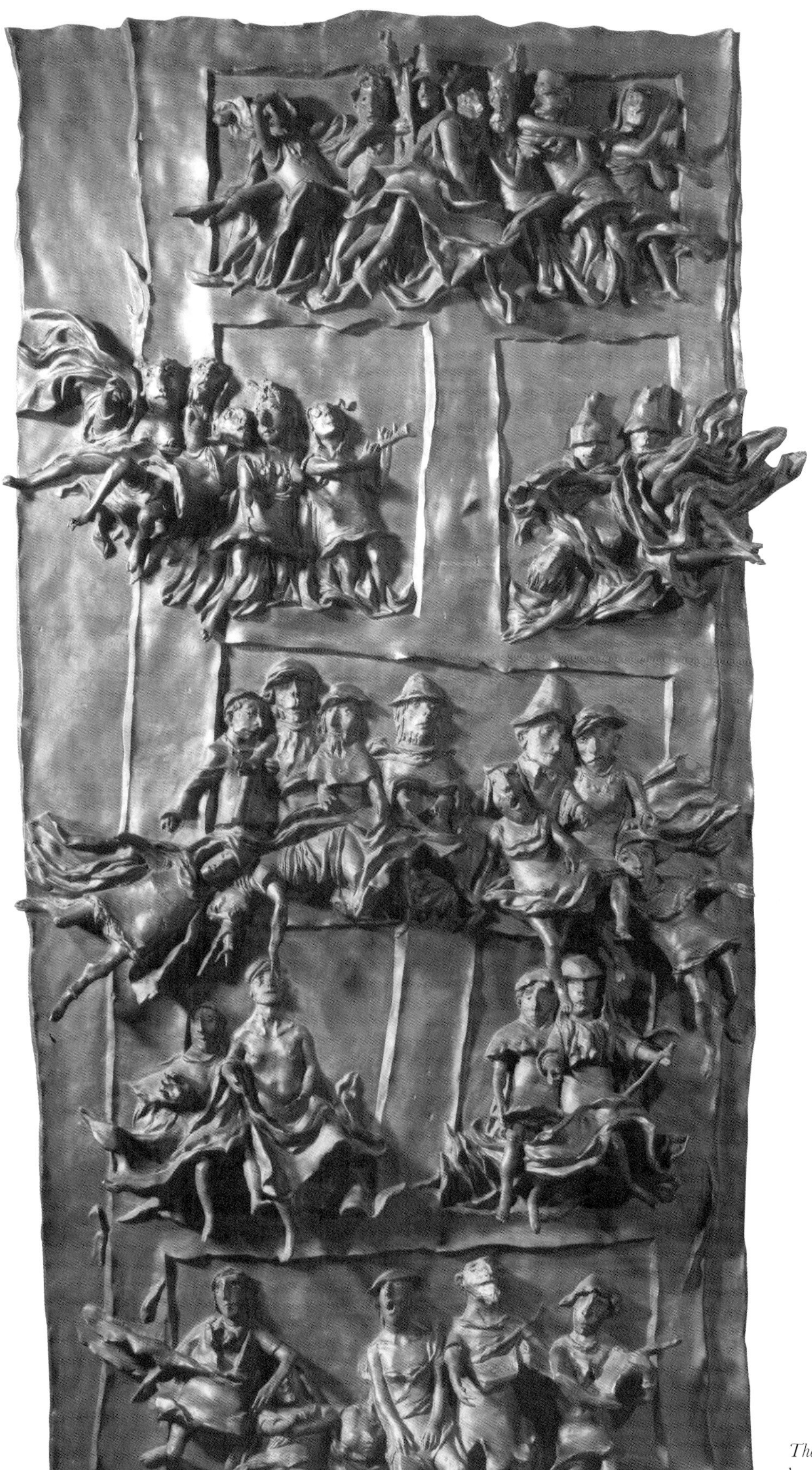

The Door, 1963-1969
bronze
94 x 50½ x 12¼"

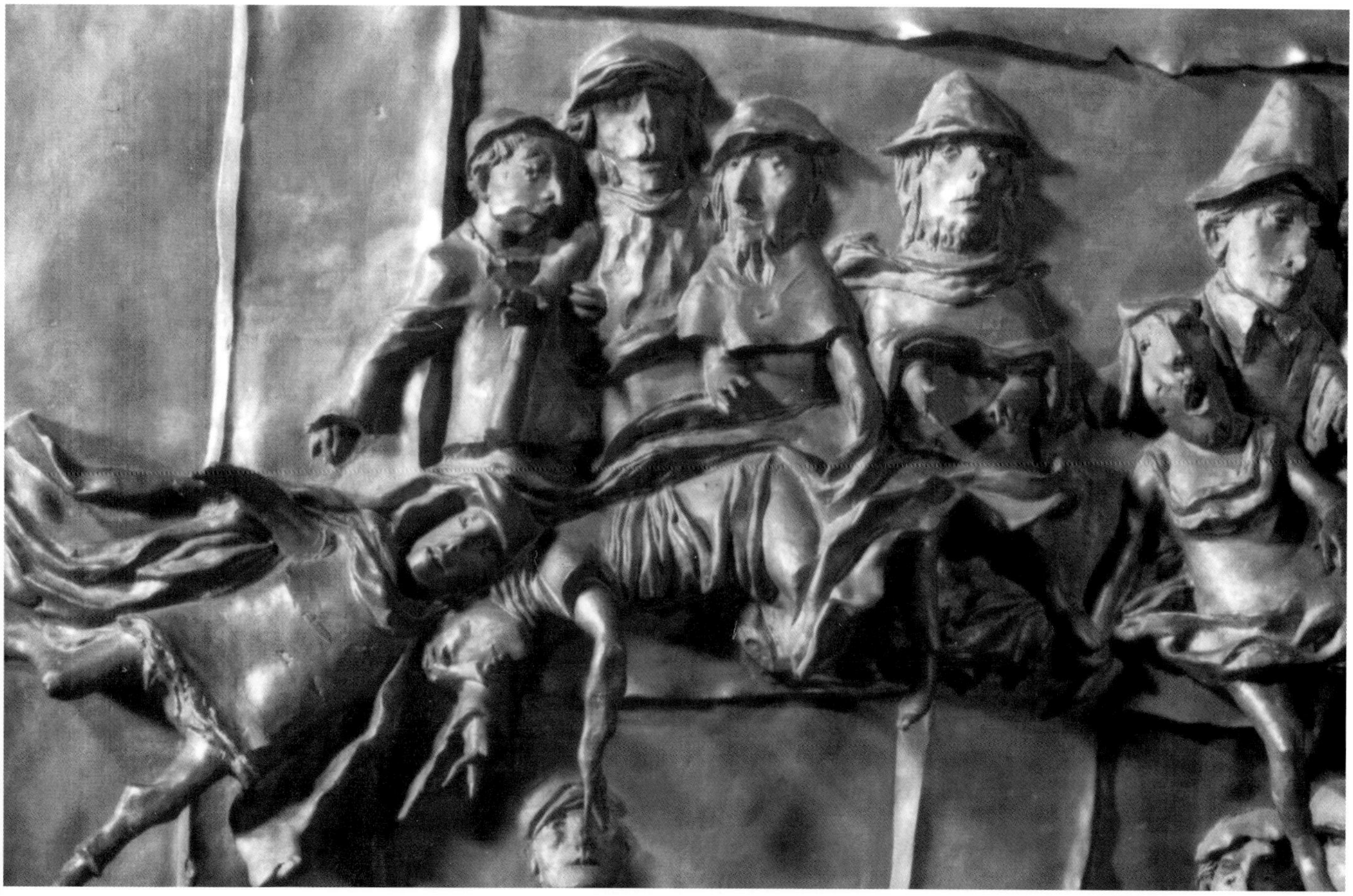

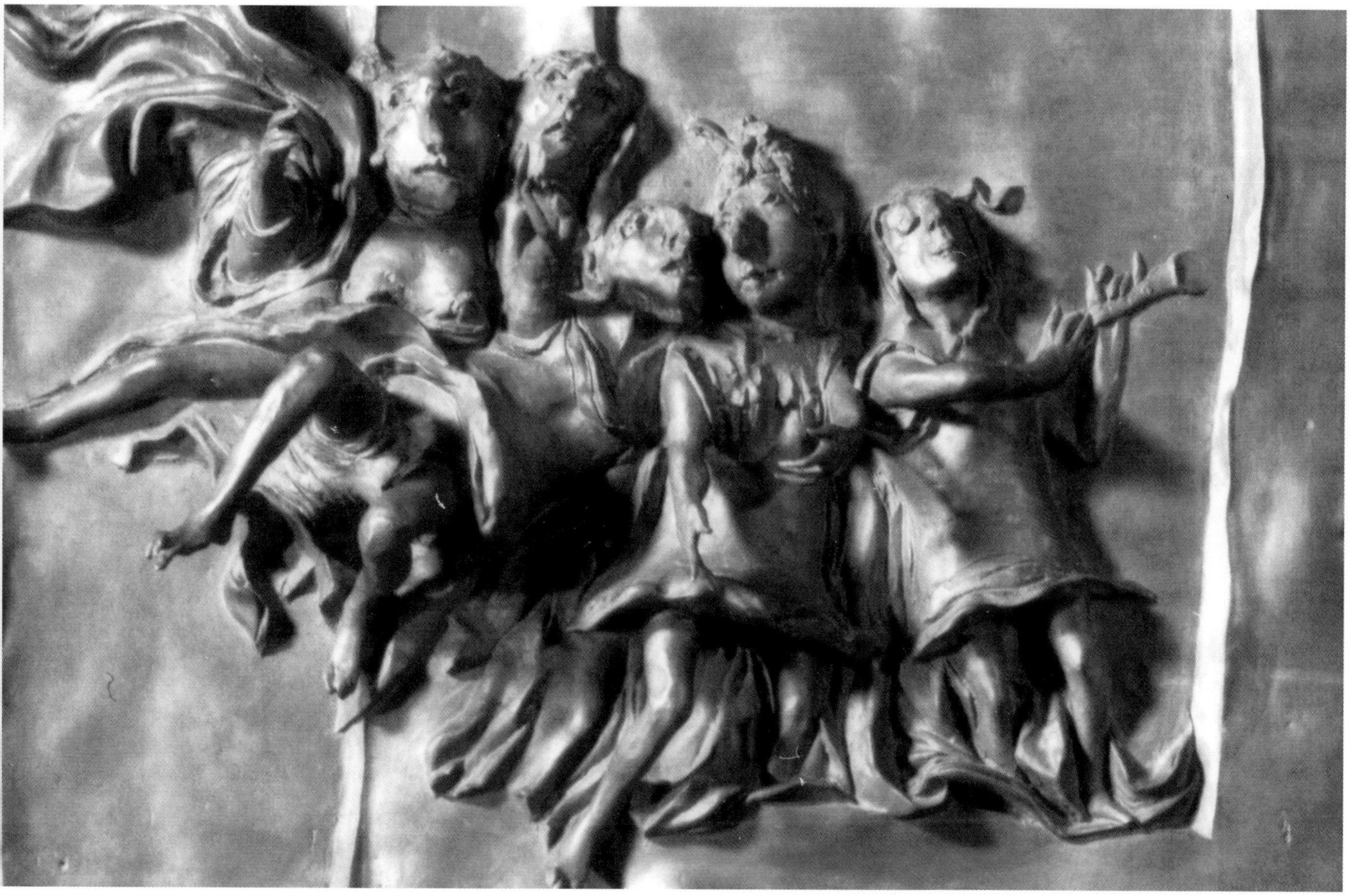

TOP: Detail 1, *The Door, (The Doctors)* 1963-1969

Detail 2, *The Door, (Angel Choir)* 1963-1969

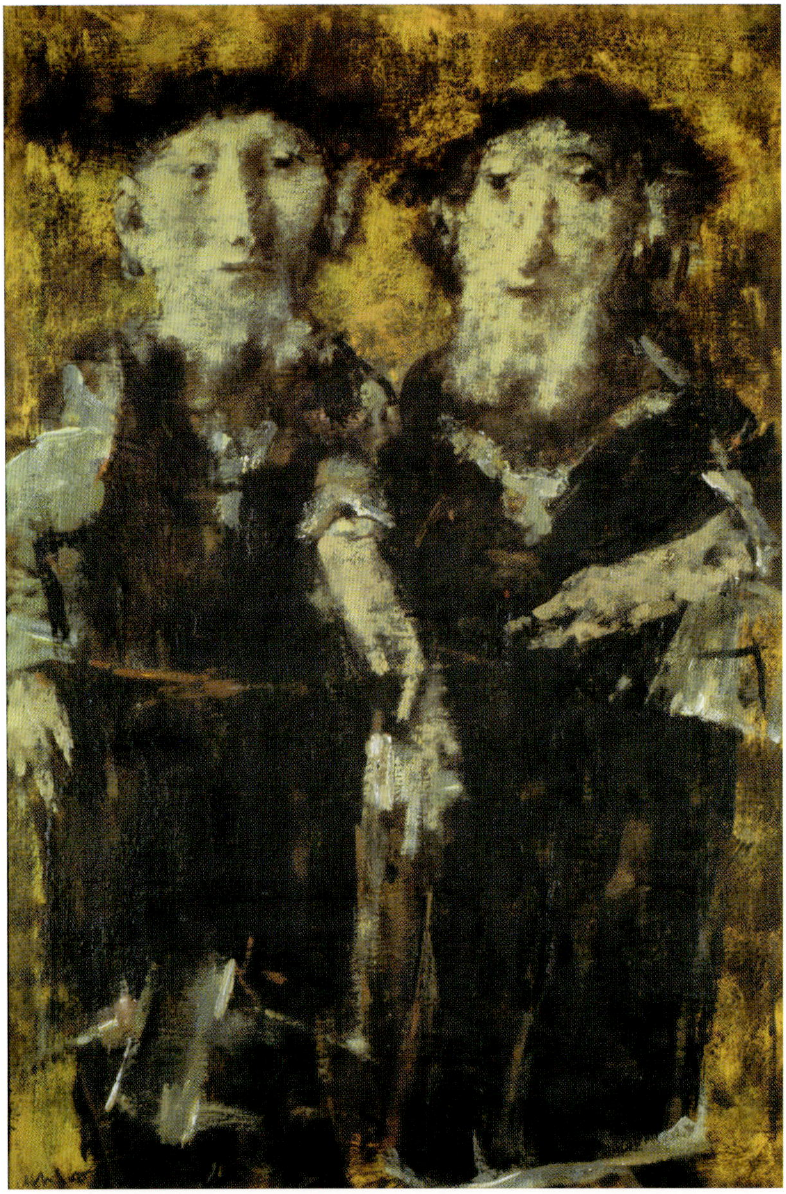

Dispute I, 1971
encaustic on panel 28 1/8 x 19"
Private Collection

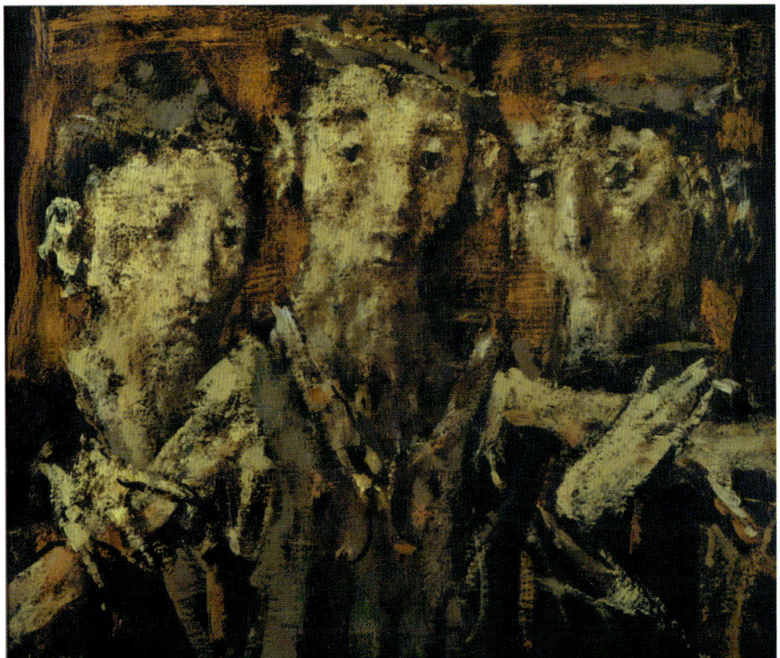

Dispute II, 1972
encaustic on panel 18 x 21"

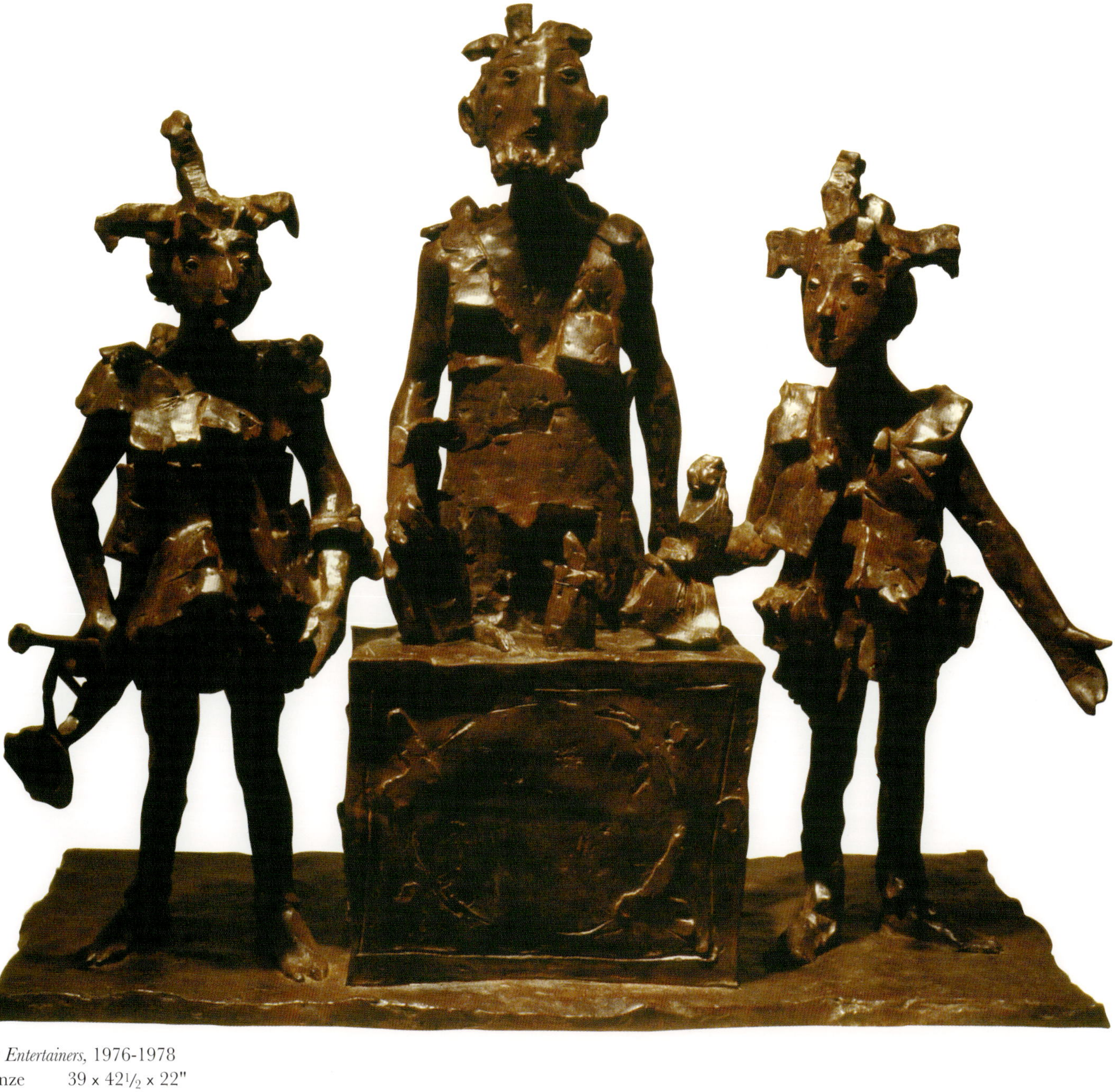

The Entertainers, 1976-1978
bronze 39 x 42½ x 22"
Collection of Syracuse University, Syracuse, NY

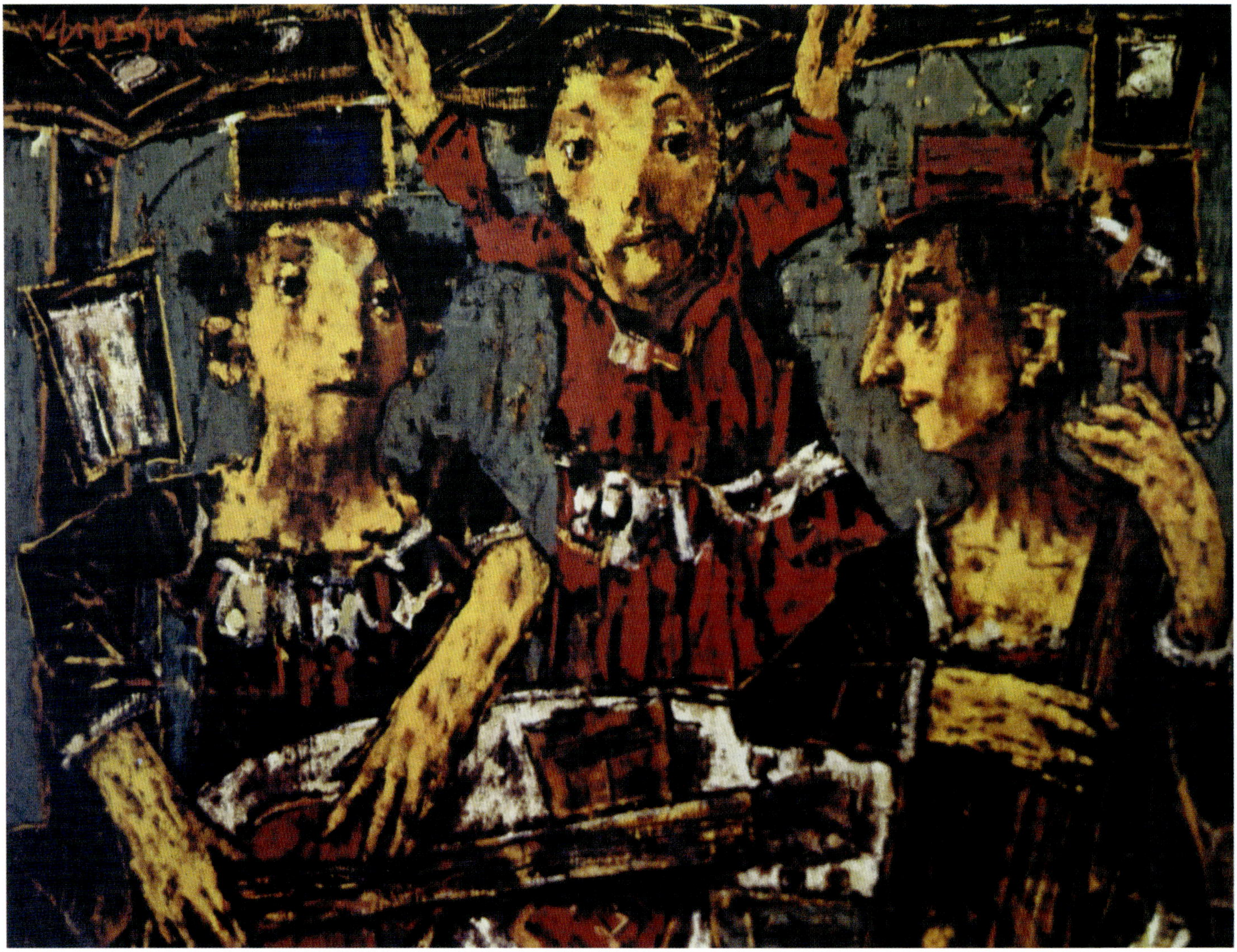

Three Musicians IV, 1972
encaustic on panel
43 x 52"
Private Collection

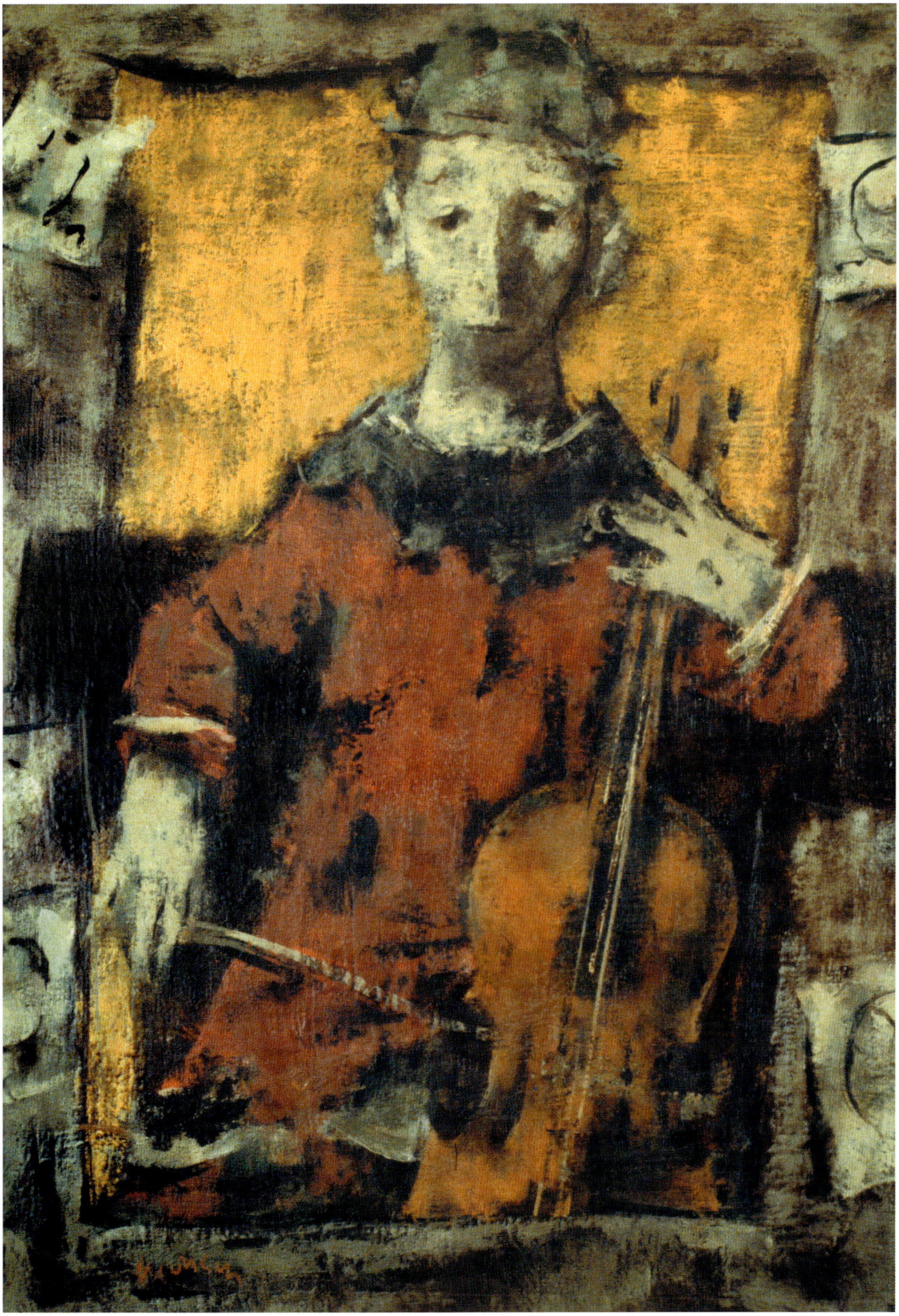

Cellist, 1971
encaustic on panel 30$\frac{3}{8}$ x 21$\frac{3}{4}$"
Private Collection

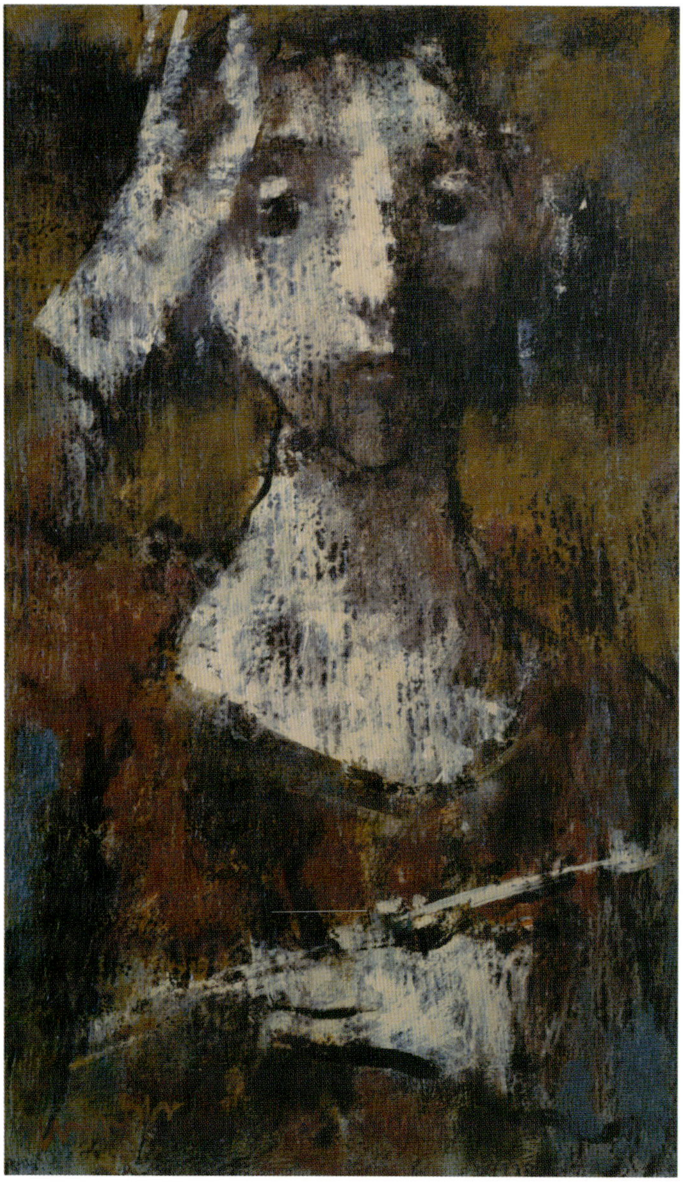

Young Flutist, 1972
encaustic on panel 15¾ x 9¾"
Private Collection

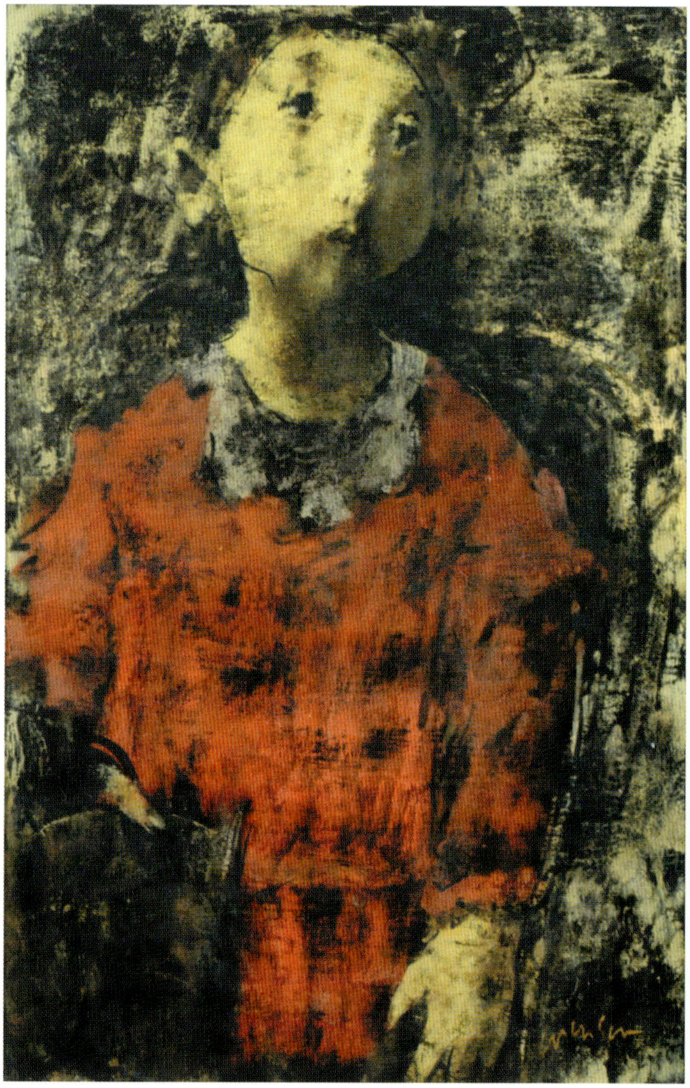

Young Man in Red Coat, 1972
encaustic on panel 24 x 16"
Private Collection

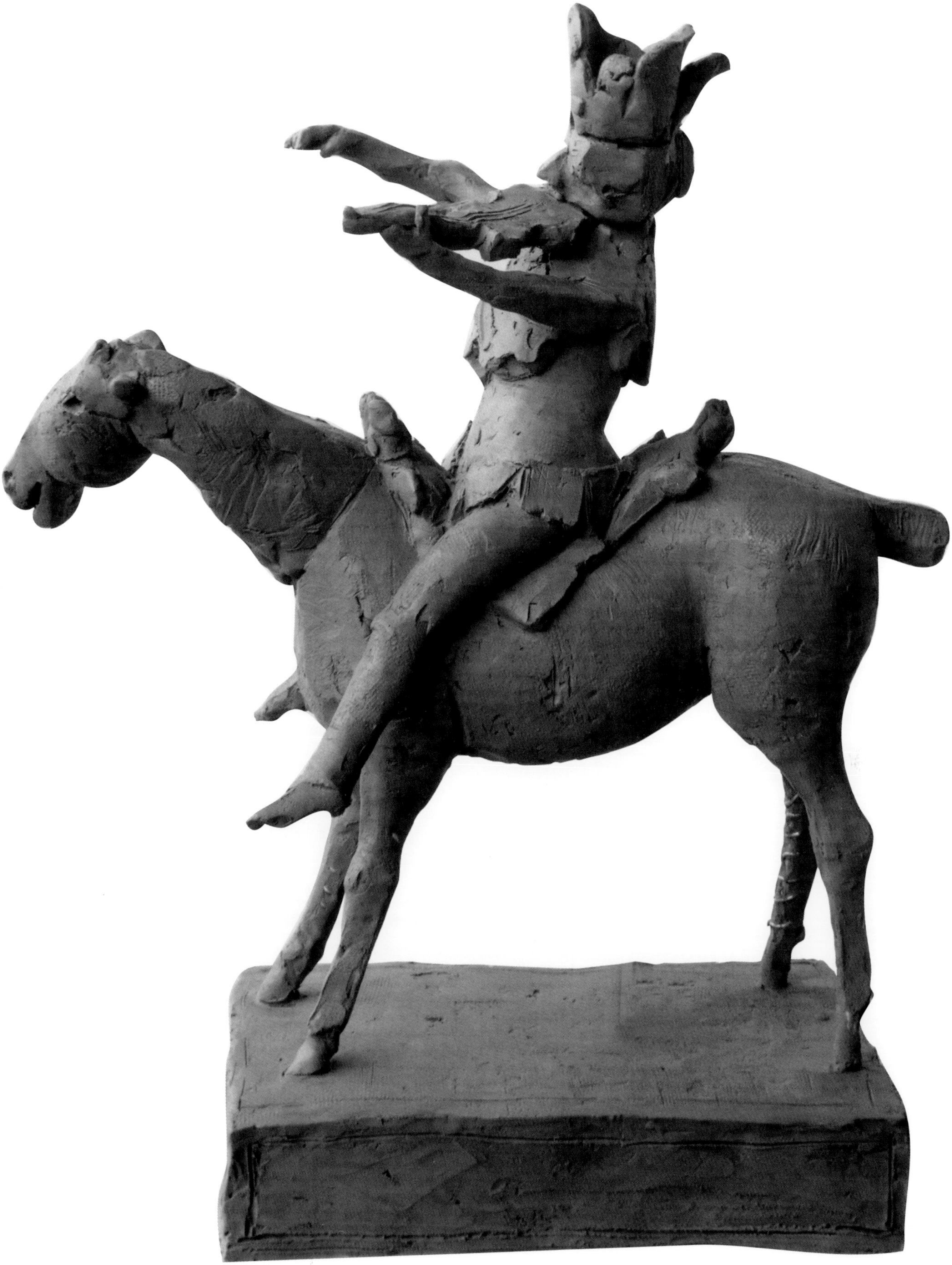

Rider with Violin, 1976-1978 (photographed in clay)
bronze 15½ x 9 x 8¼"

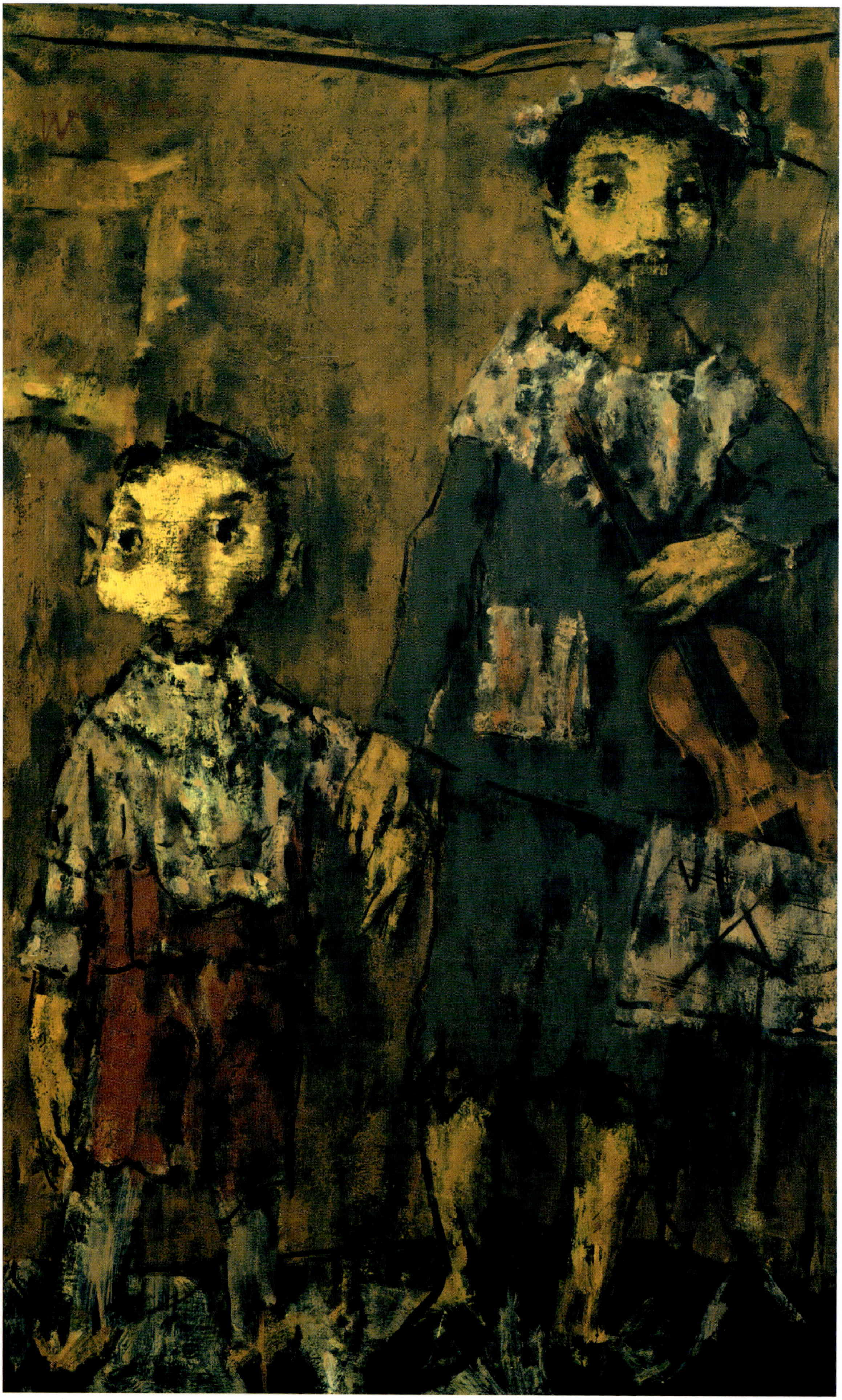

Teacher and Student I
1971
encaustic on panel
48 x 30"
Private Collection

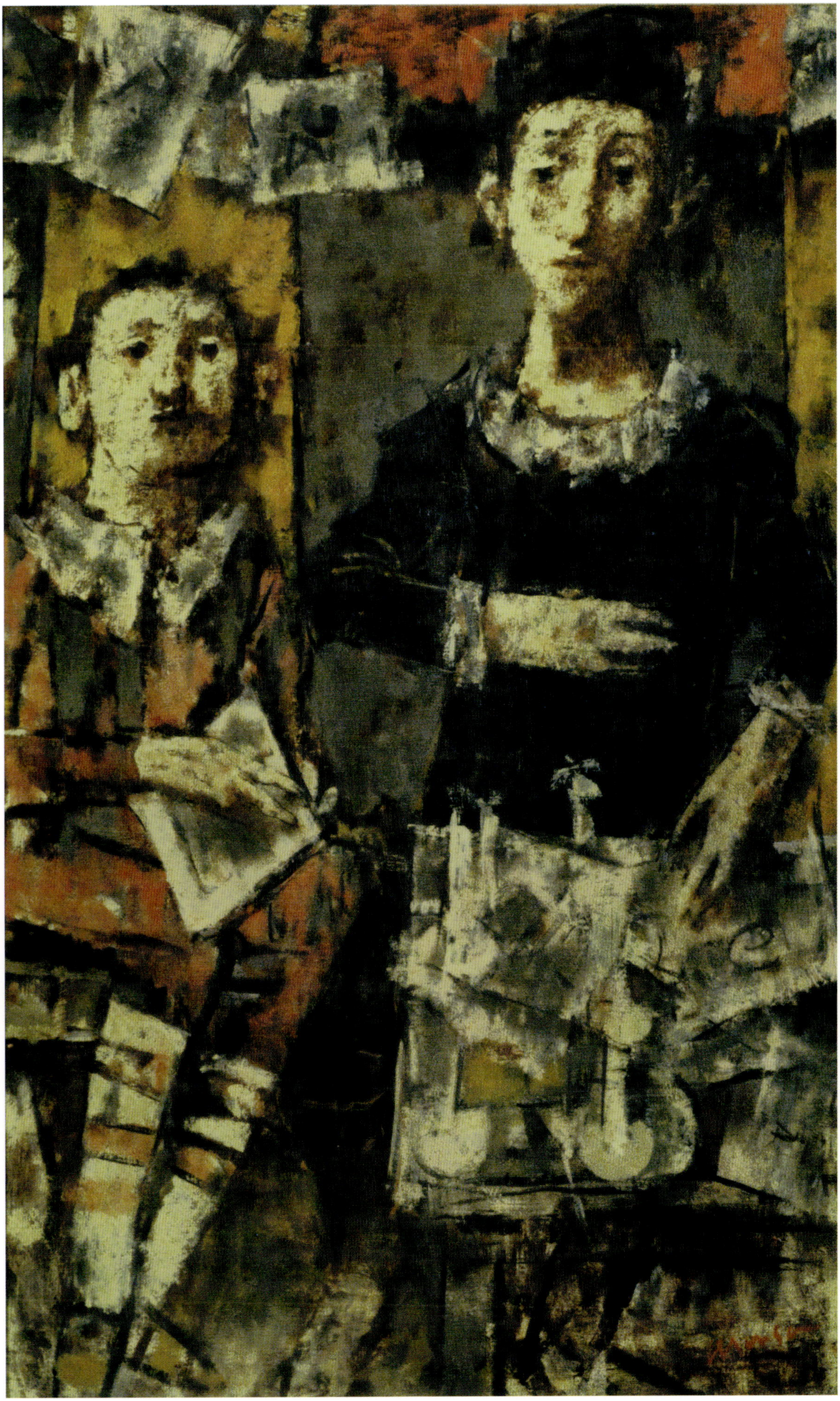

Teacher and Student II
1972
encaustic on panel
48 x 30"
Private Collection

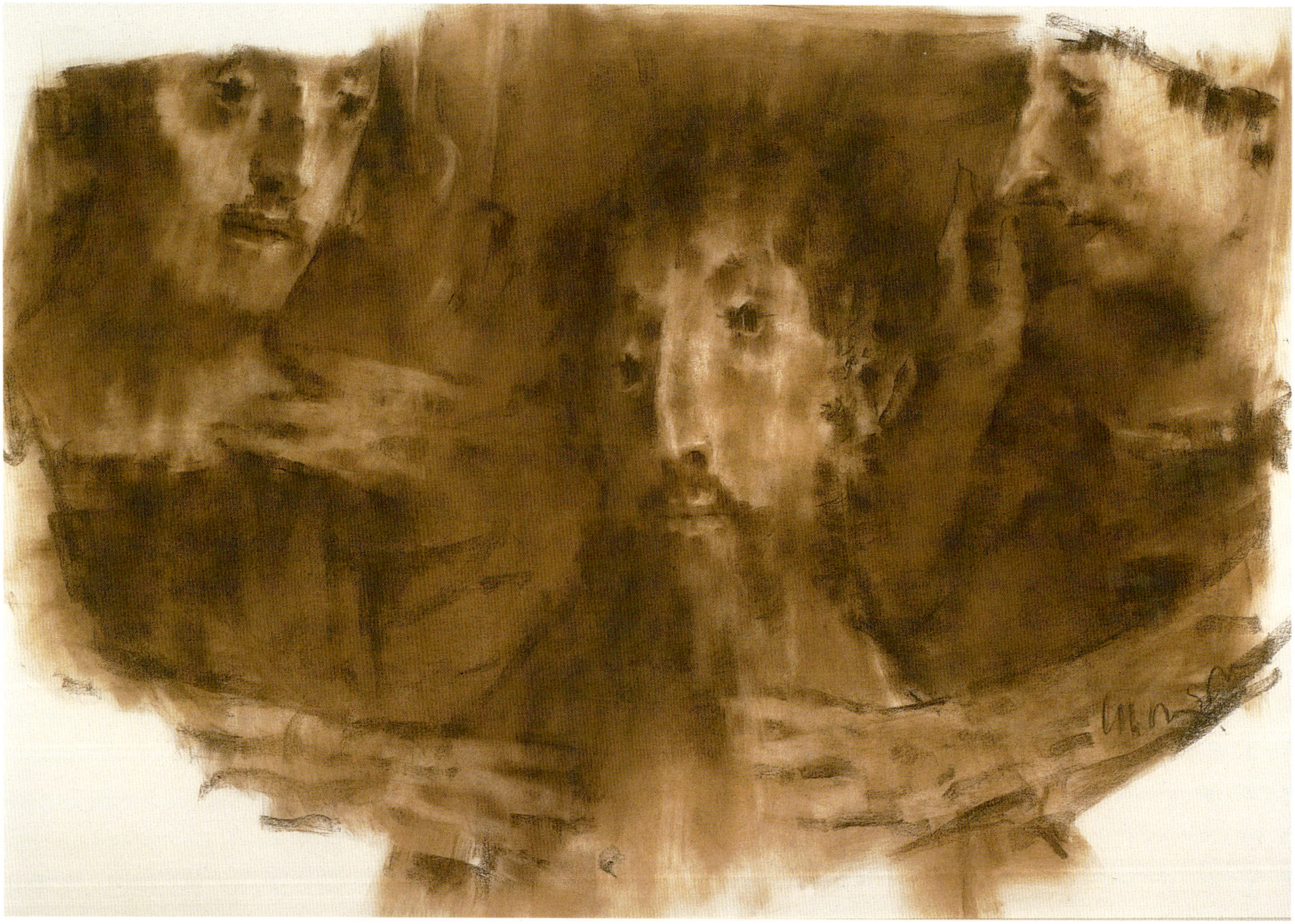

Conversation, 1969
pastel
26 x 40"
Private Collection

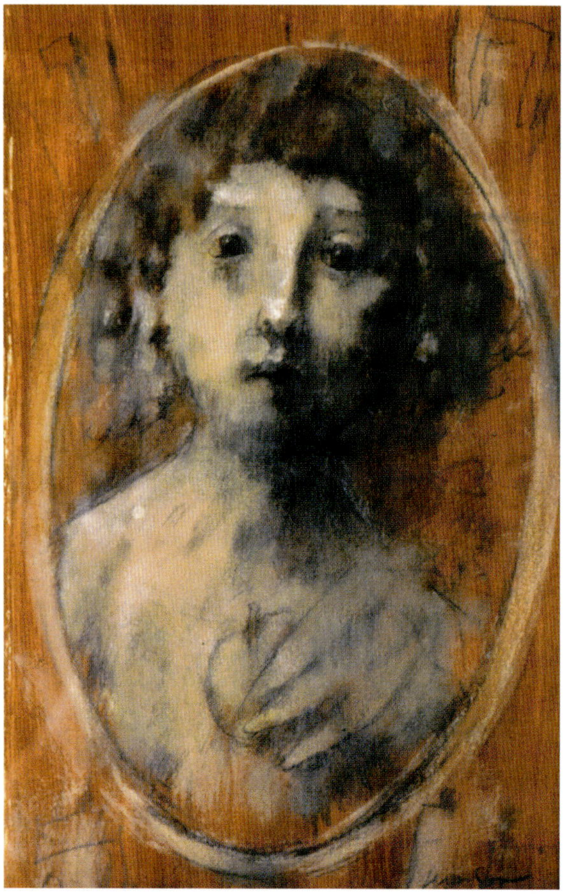

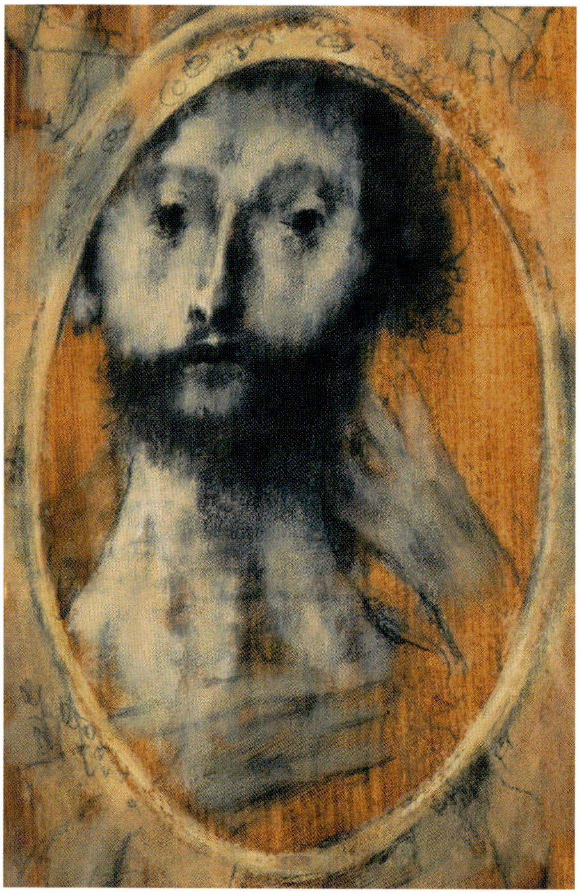

Eve, 1972
acrylic & pencil
11⅞ x 7⅝"
Private Collection

Adam, 1972
acrylic & pencil
11⅞ x 7⅝"
Private Collection

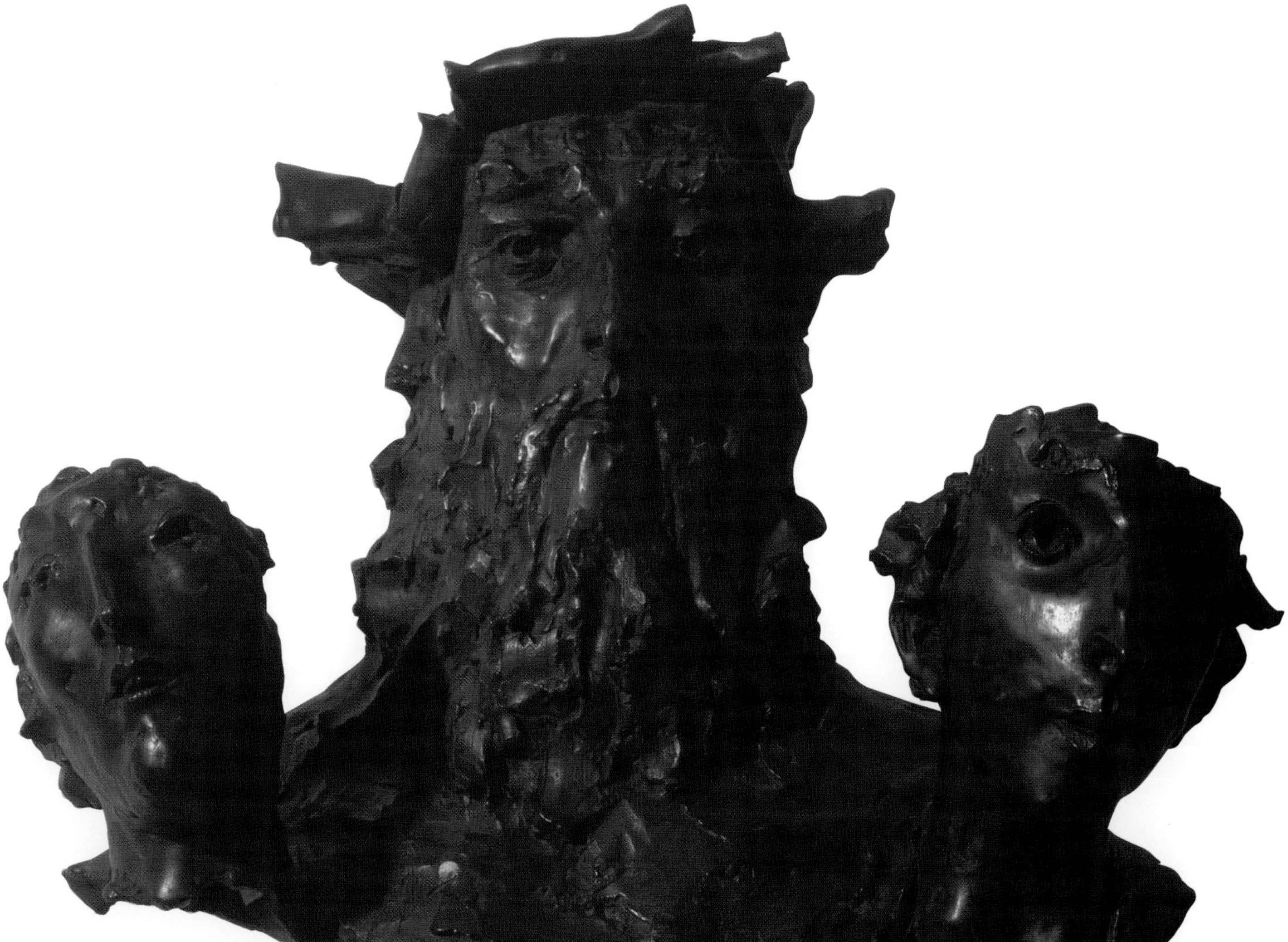

Teacher and Students, 1965-1969
bronze 26½ x 25½ x 20½"

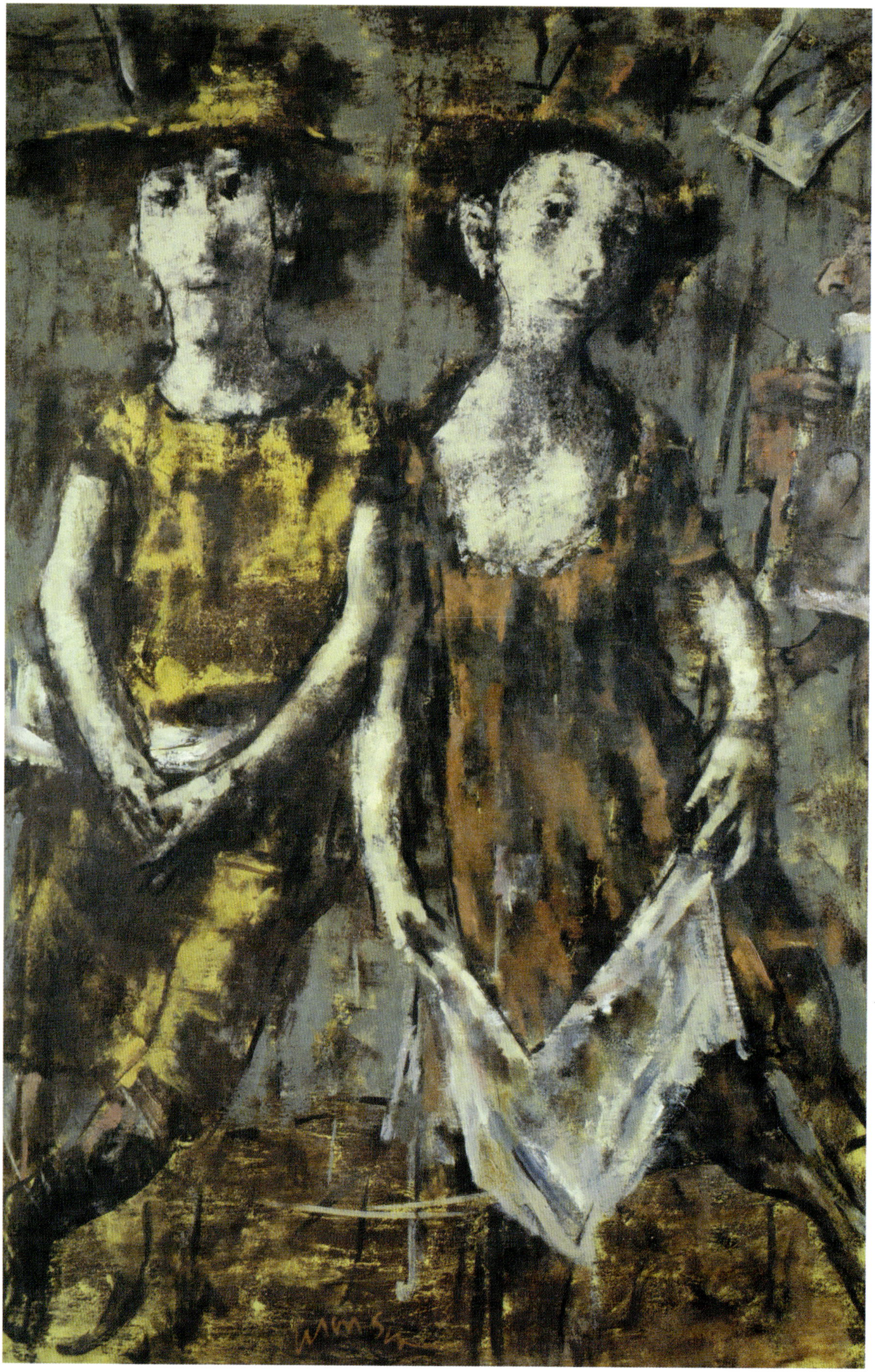

Levitation II, 1972
encaustic on panel
48 x 33"
Private Collection

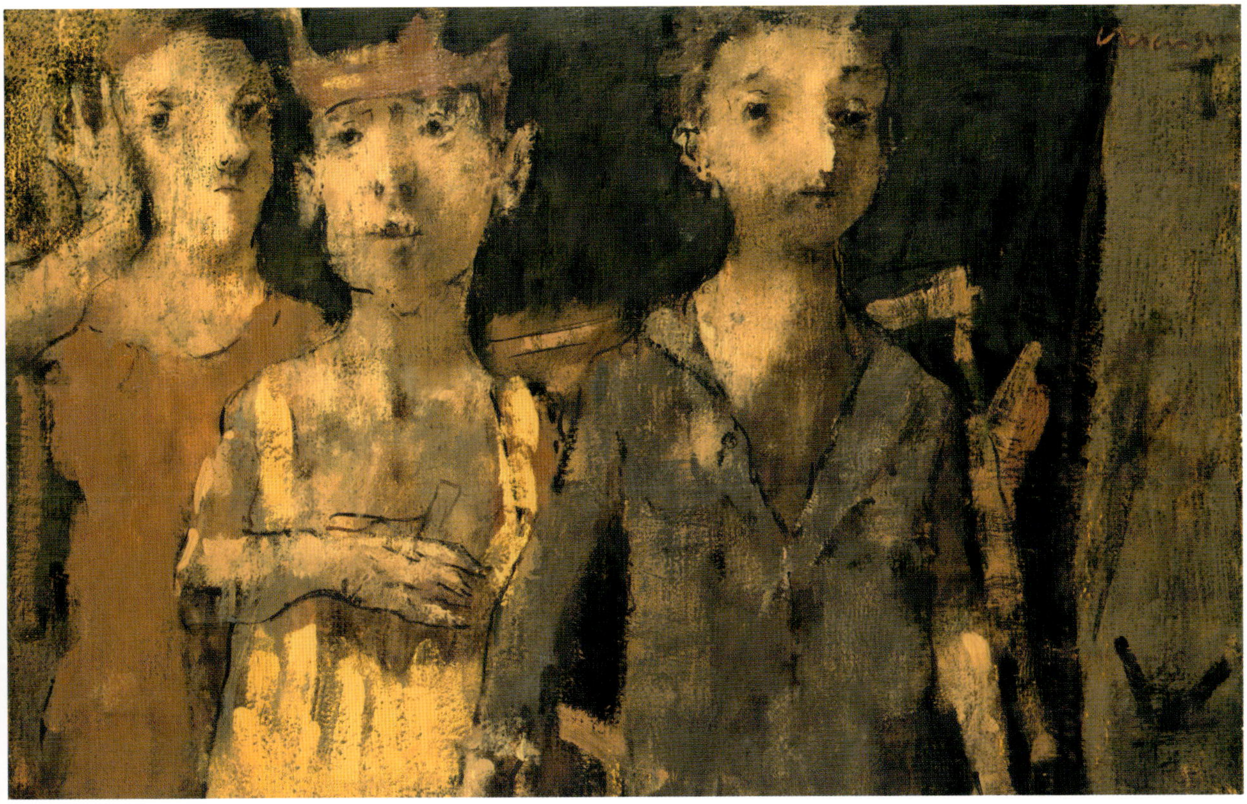

The Succession, 1975
encaustic on panel 19 x 29"
Private Collection

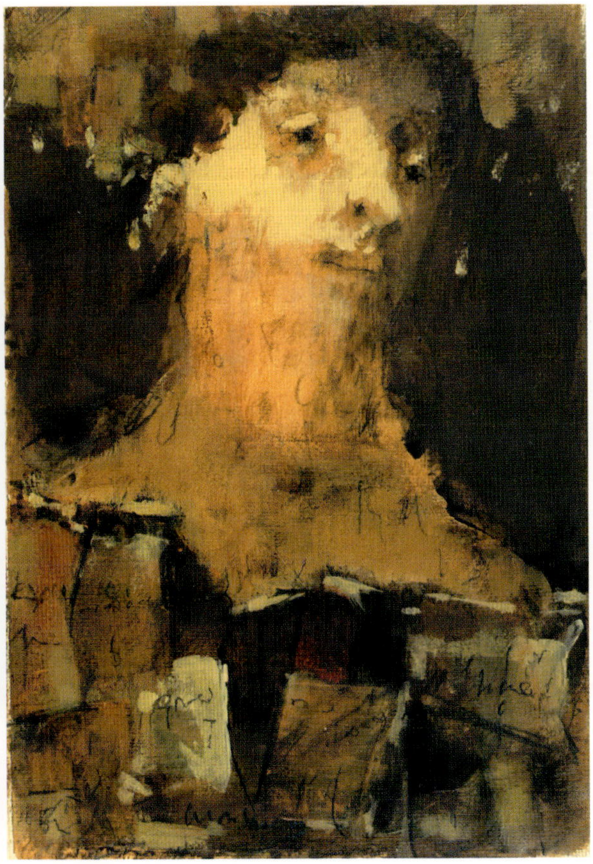

Man with Amulets, 1971
acrylic & pencil $11^1/_2$ x 8"
Private Collection

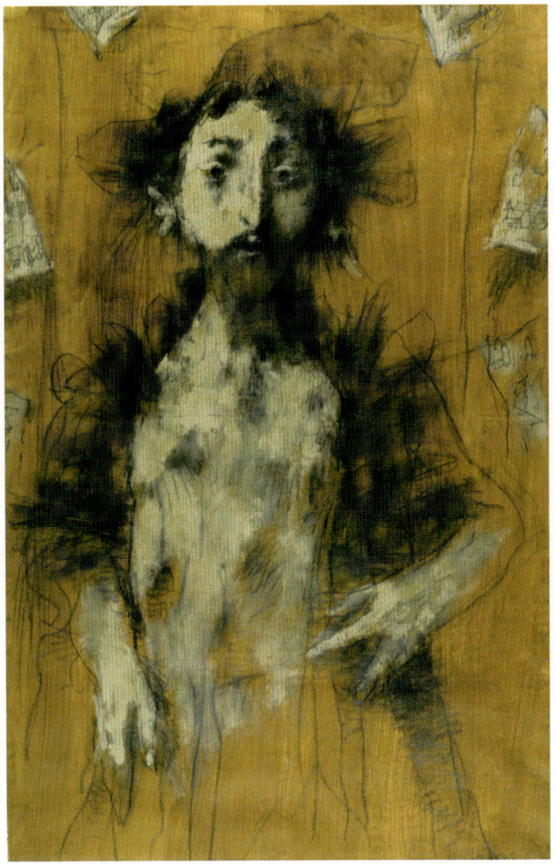

Conjurer, 1976
acrylic & pencil $11^1/_2$ x 8"
Private Collection

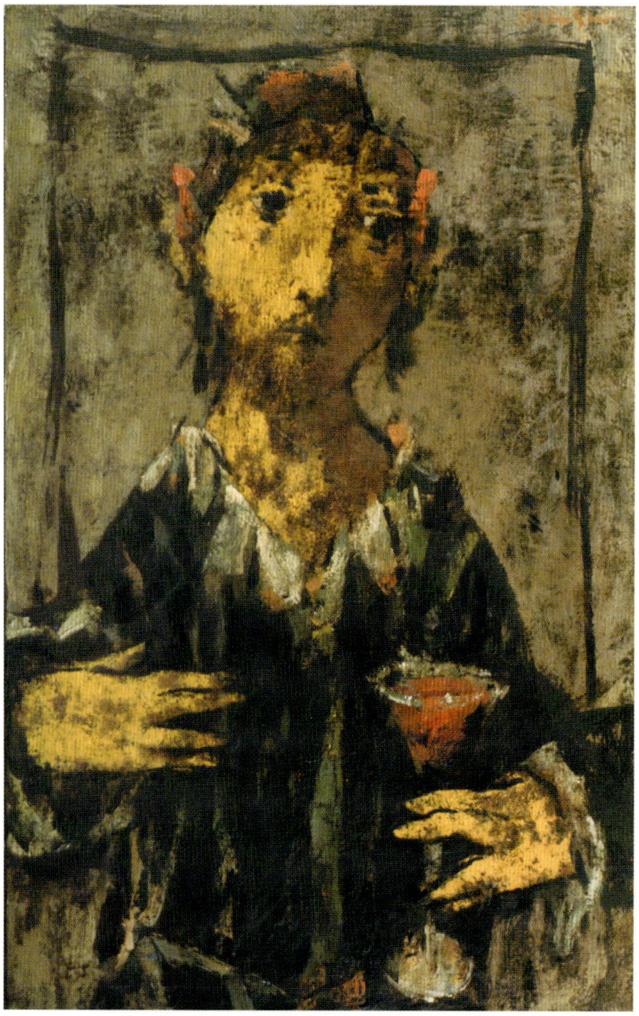

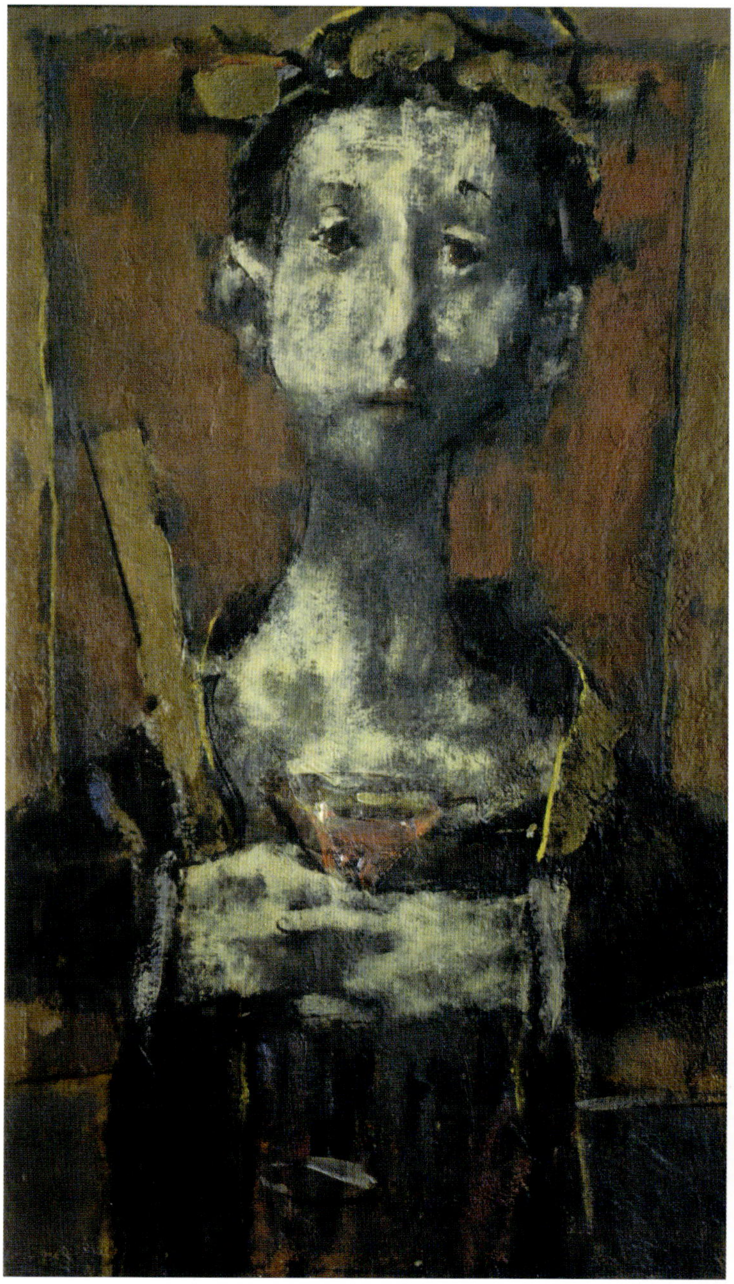

Boy with Glass of Wine II, 1975
encaustic on panel 26 x 18"
Private Collection

Boy with Glass of Wine, 1972
encaustic on panel 27 x 16"
Private Collection

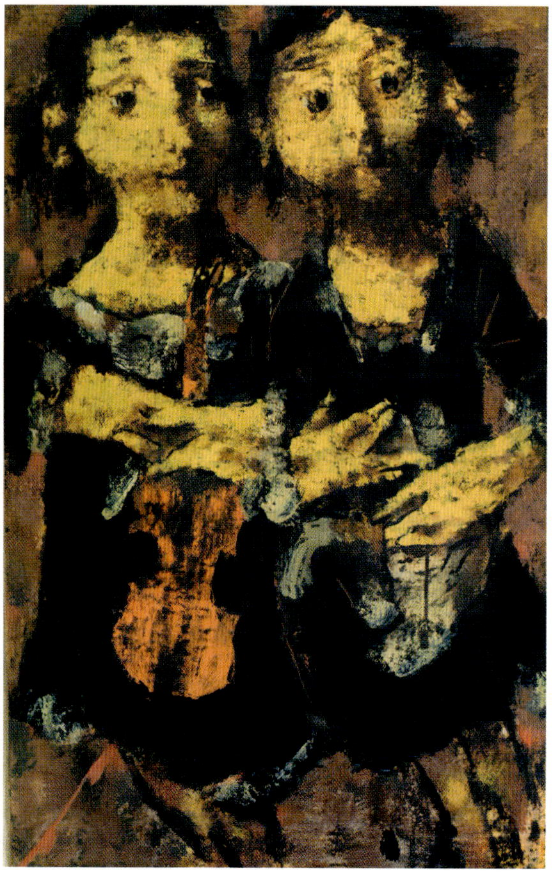

Wedding Couple, 1976
encaustic on panel 19 x 12"
Private Collection

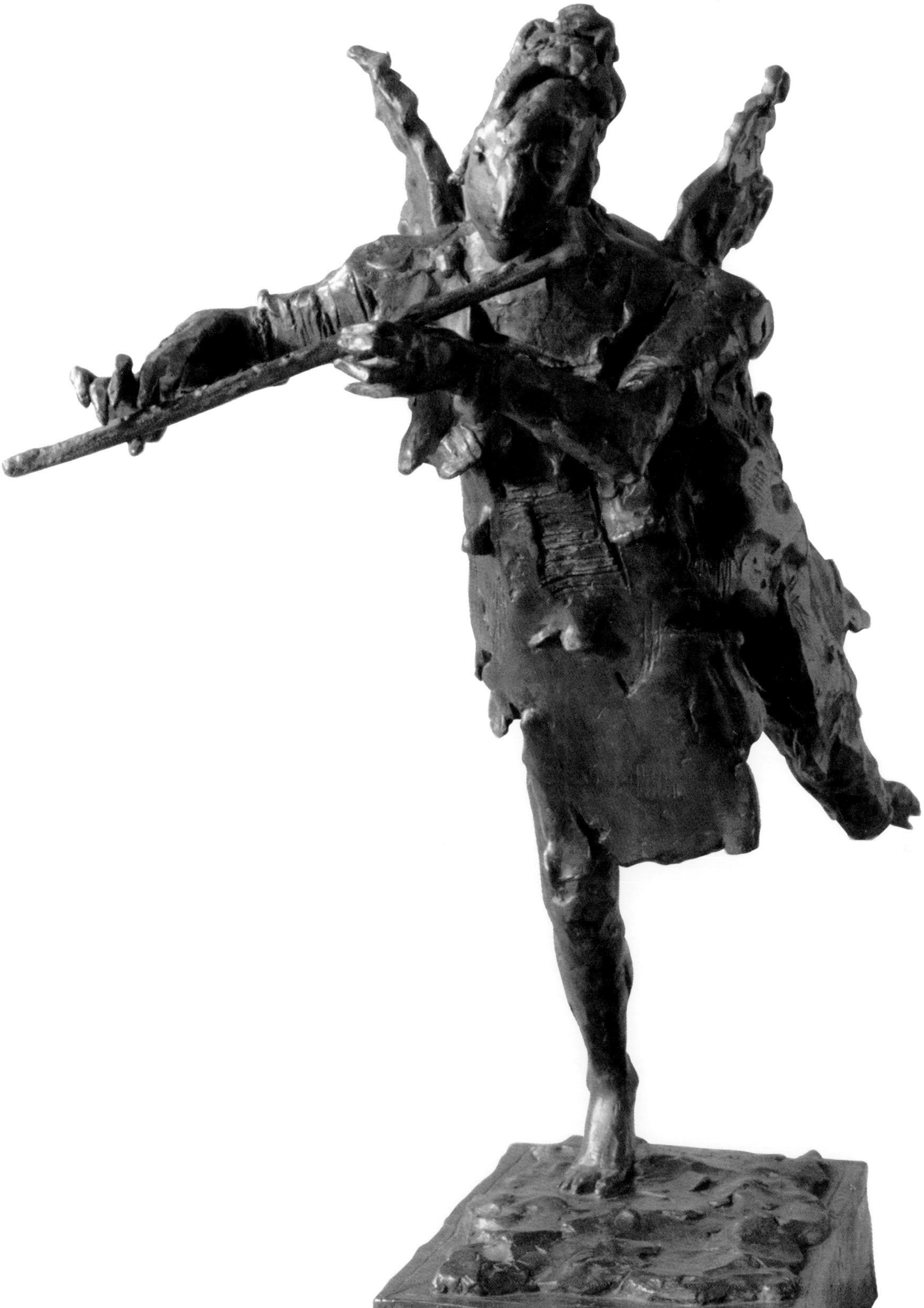

Angel with Flute, 1978
bronze 24 1/8 x 8 x 20"

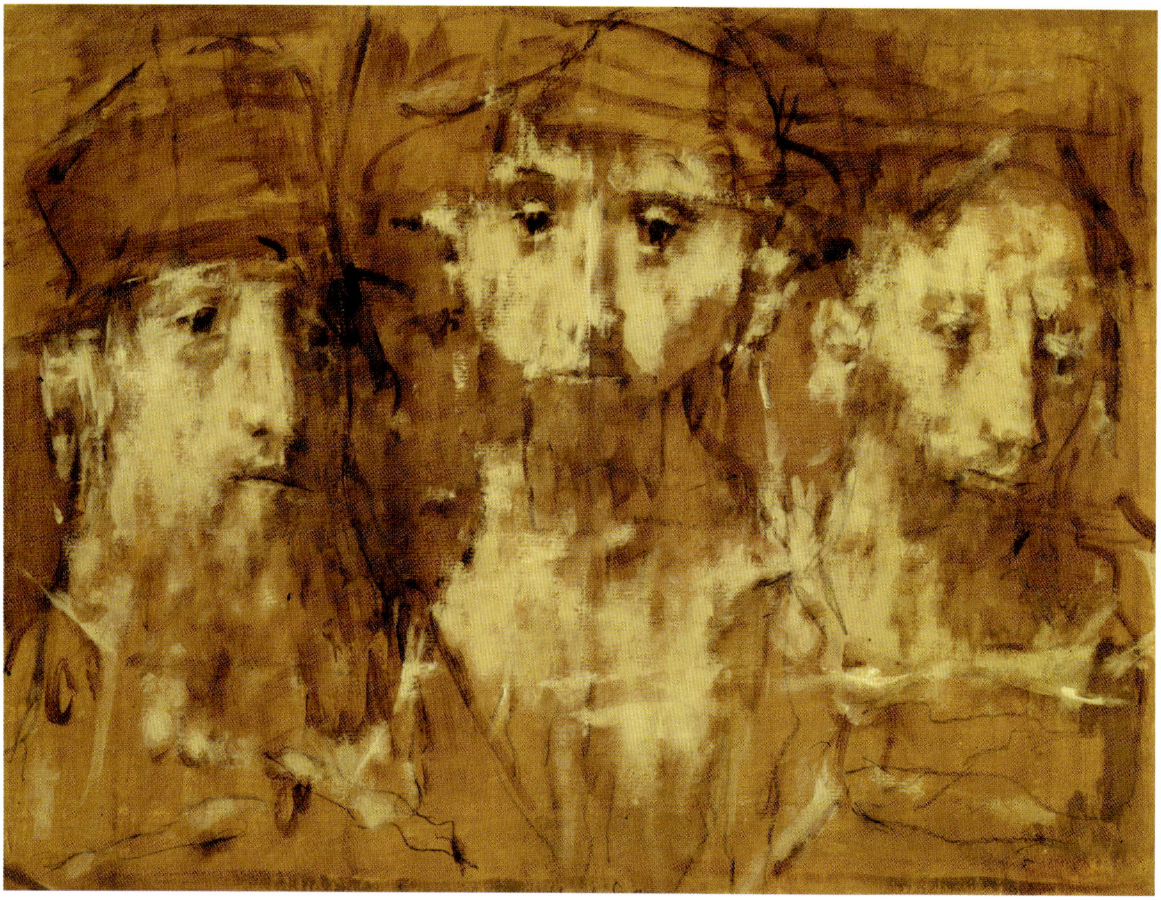

Three Judges, 1976
acrylic & pencil
17 1/4 x 22"
Private Collection

Man with Amulets
1976
acrylic & pencil
11 1/2 x 8"
Private Collection

Young Man with Newspaper, 1972
acrylic & pencil
11 7/8 x 7 5/8"
Private Collection

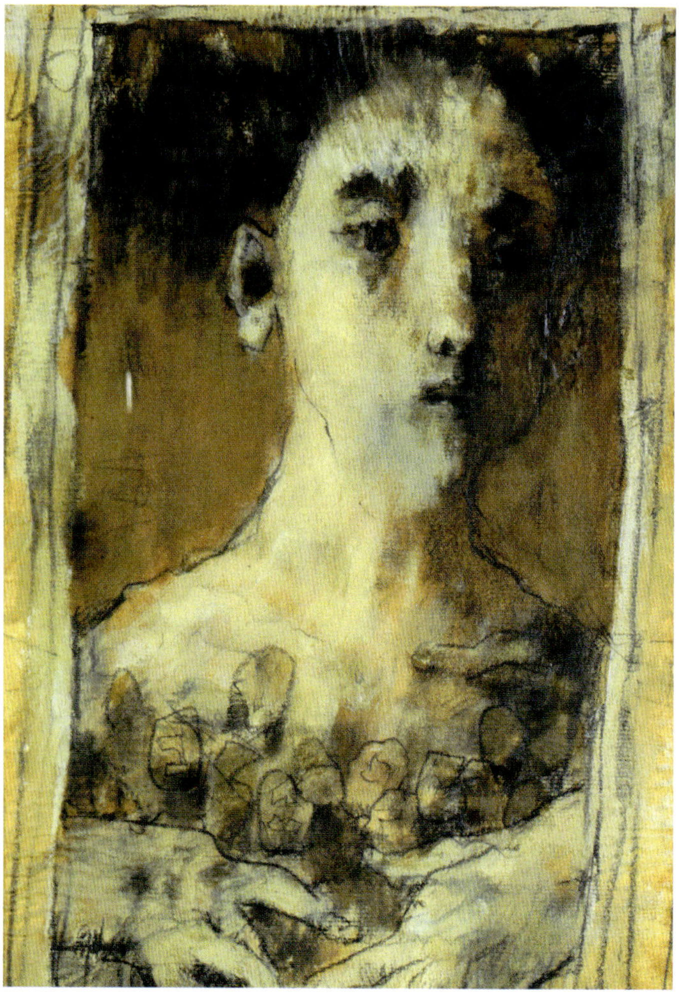

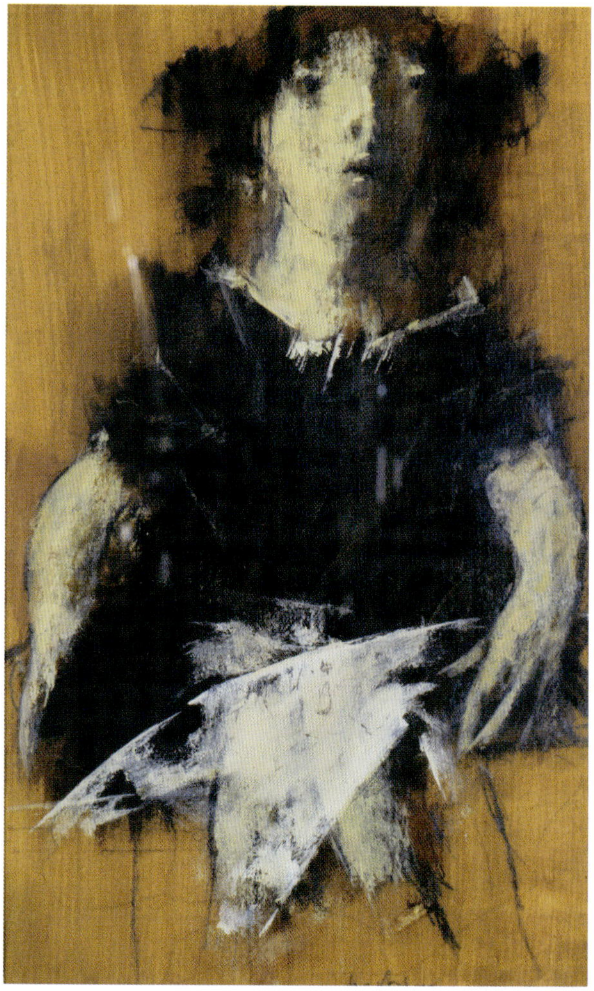

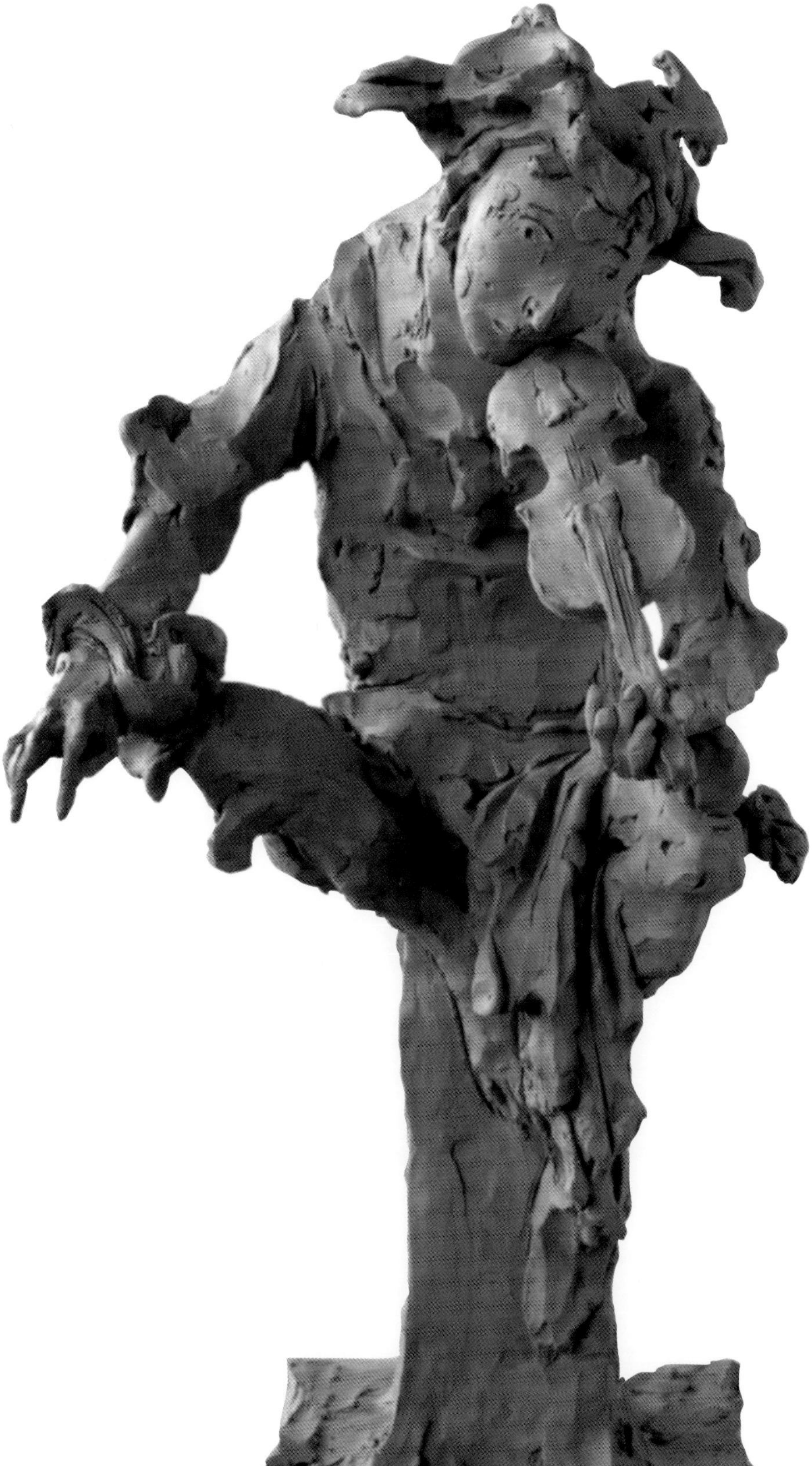

Fiddler, 1974-1976 (photographed in clay)
bronze 22¾ x 11¾ x 11"

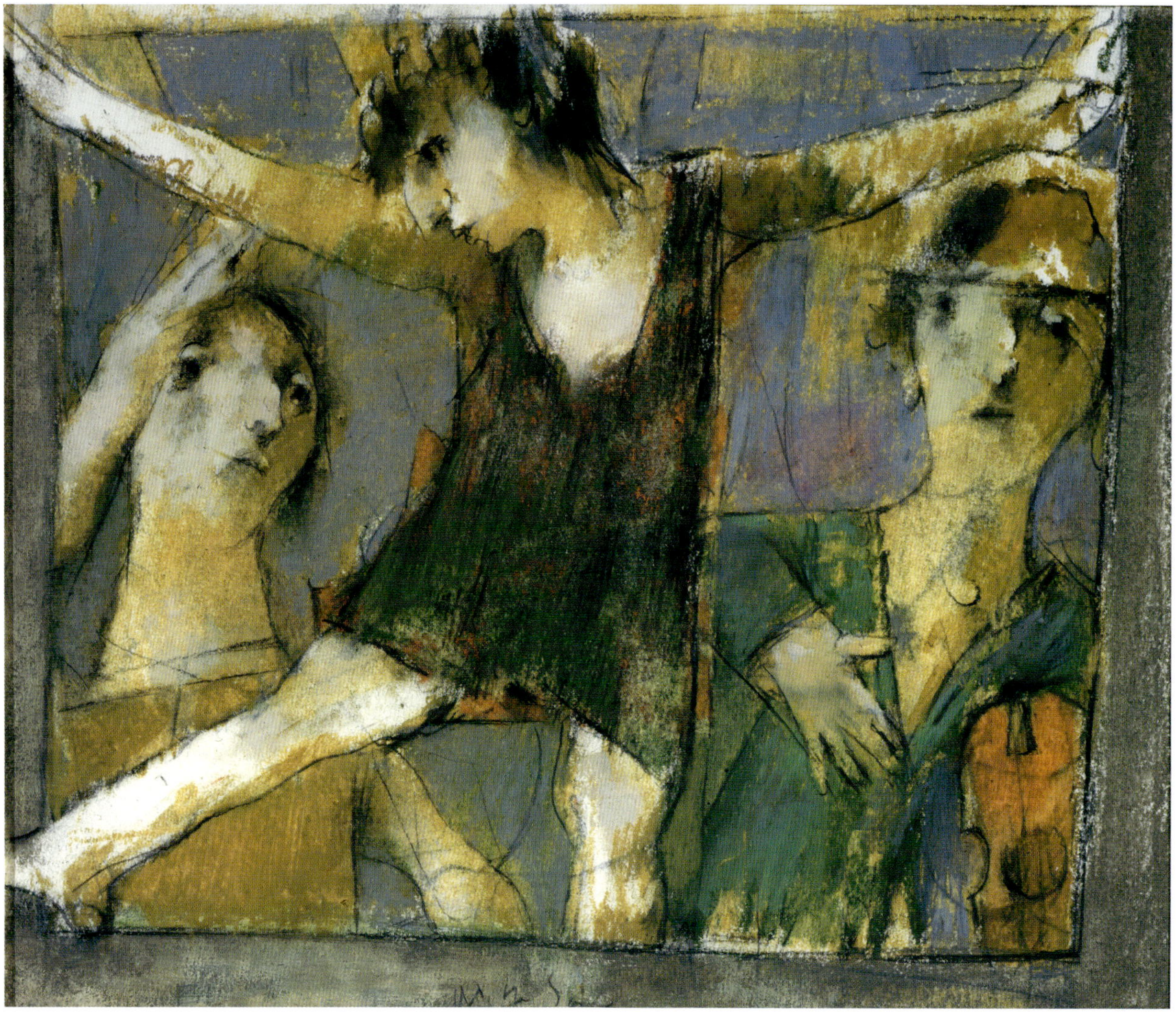

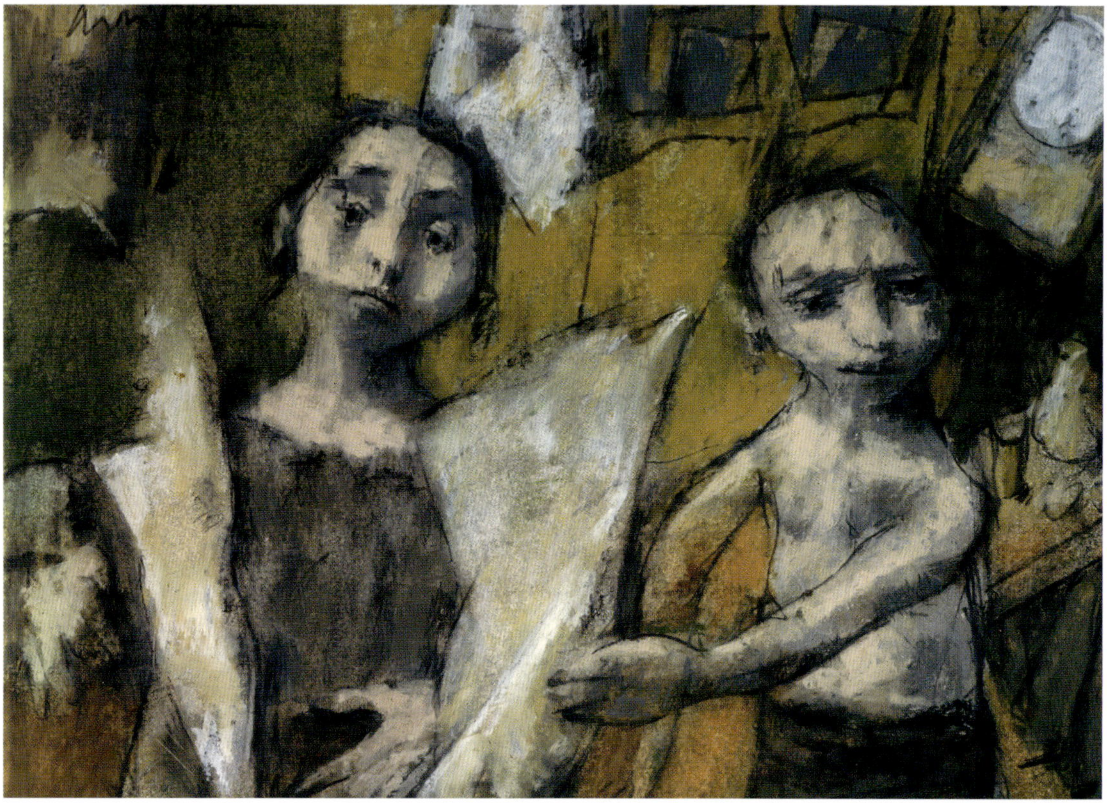

The Performers, 1980
oil pastel $9^3/_4$ x 12"
Private Collection

Scribe and Apprentice, 1980
oil pastel $6^1/_4$ x $8^3/_4$"
Private Collection

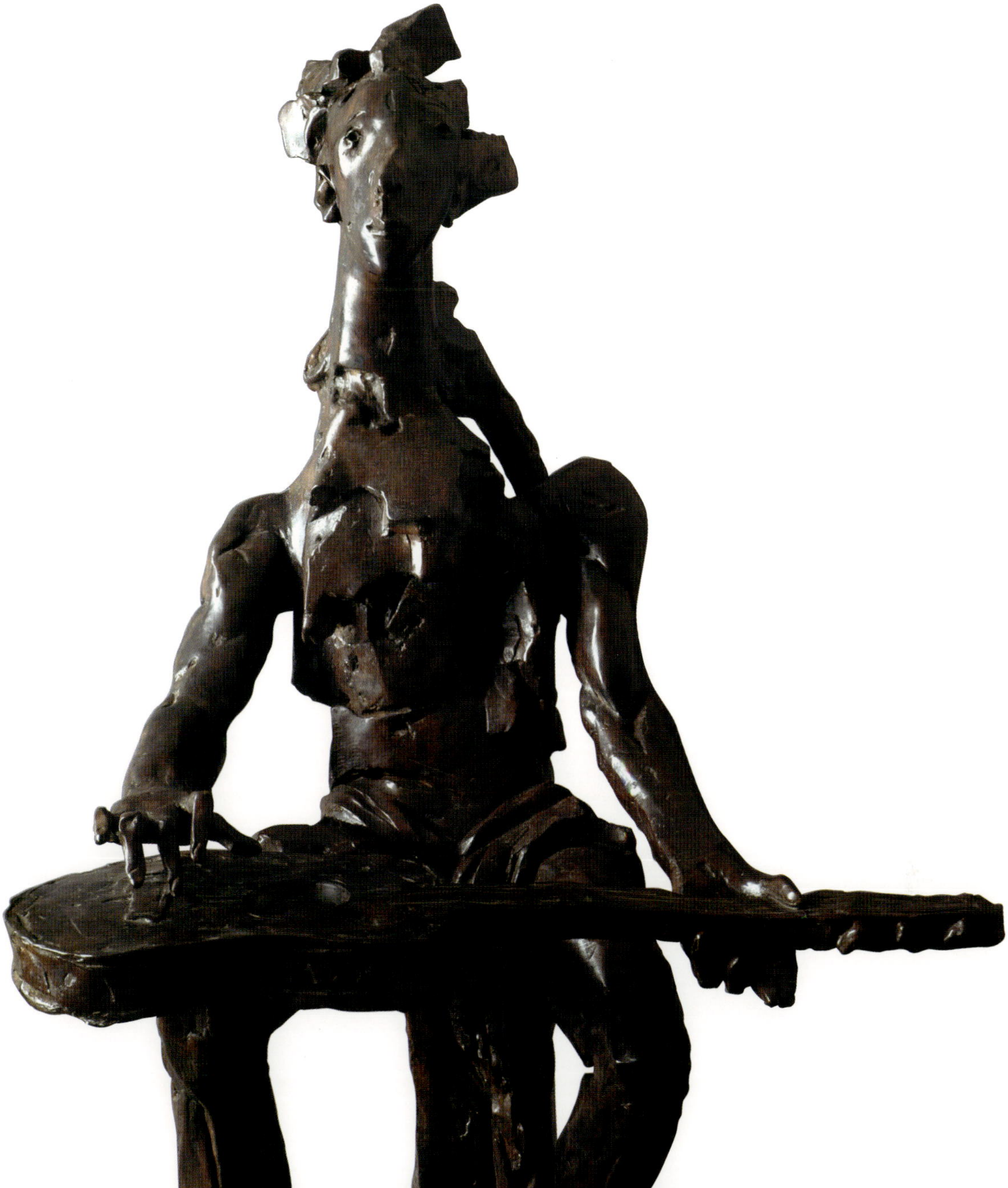

Seated Angel with Guitar, 1977-1978
bronze 32 x 21 x 18"

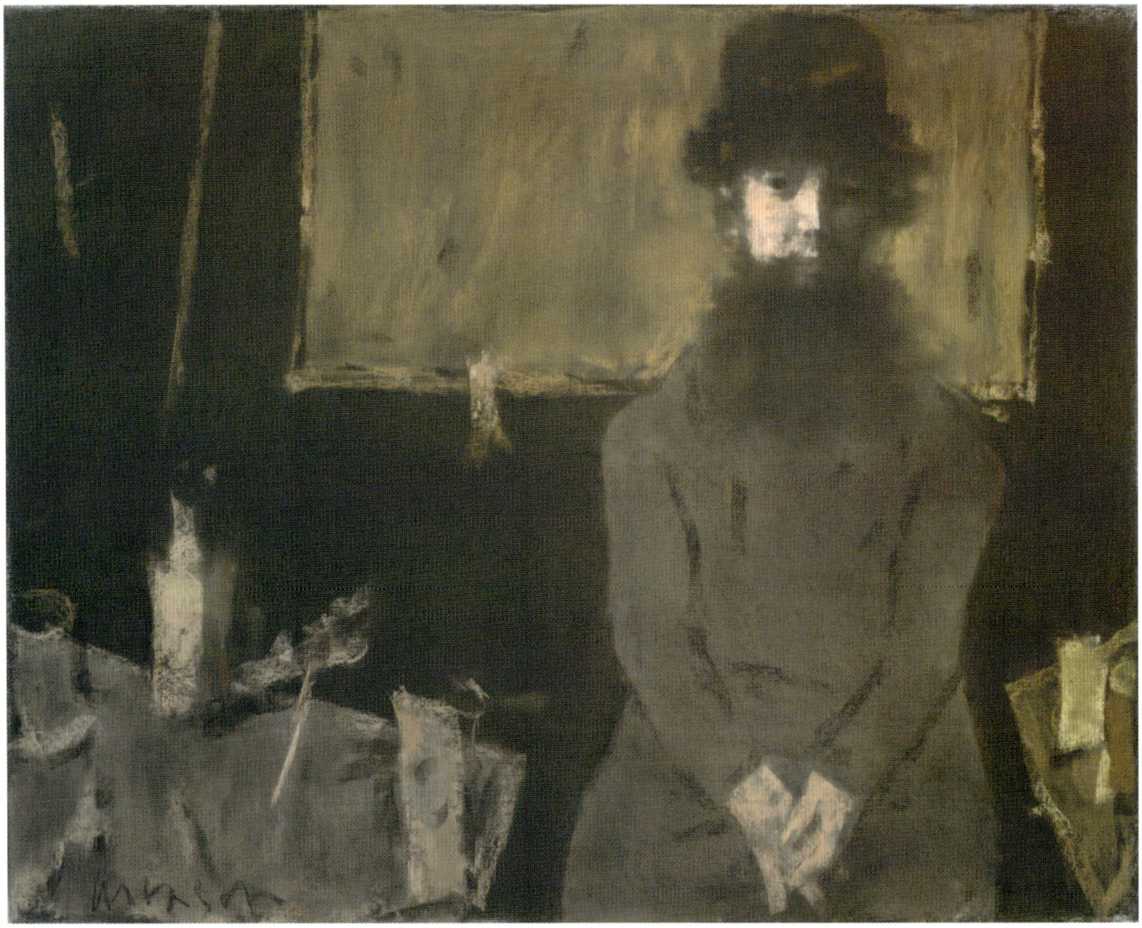

Bearded Man with Still Life, 1983
pastel 32 x 40"
Private Collection

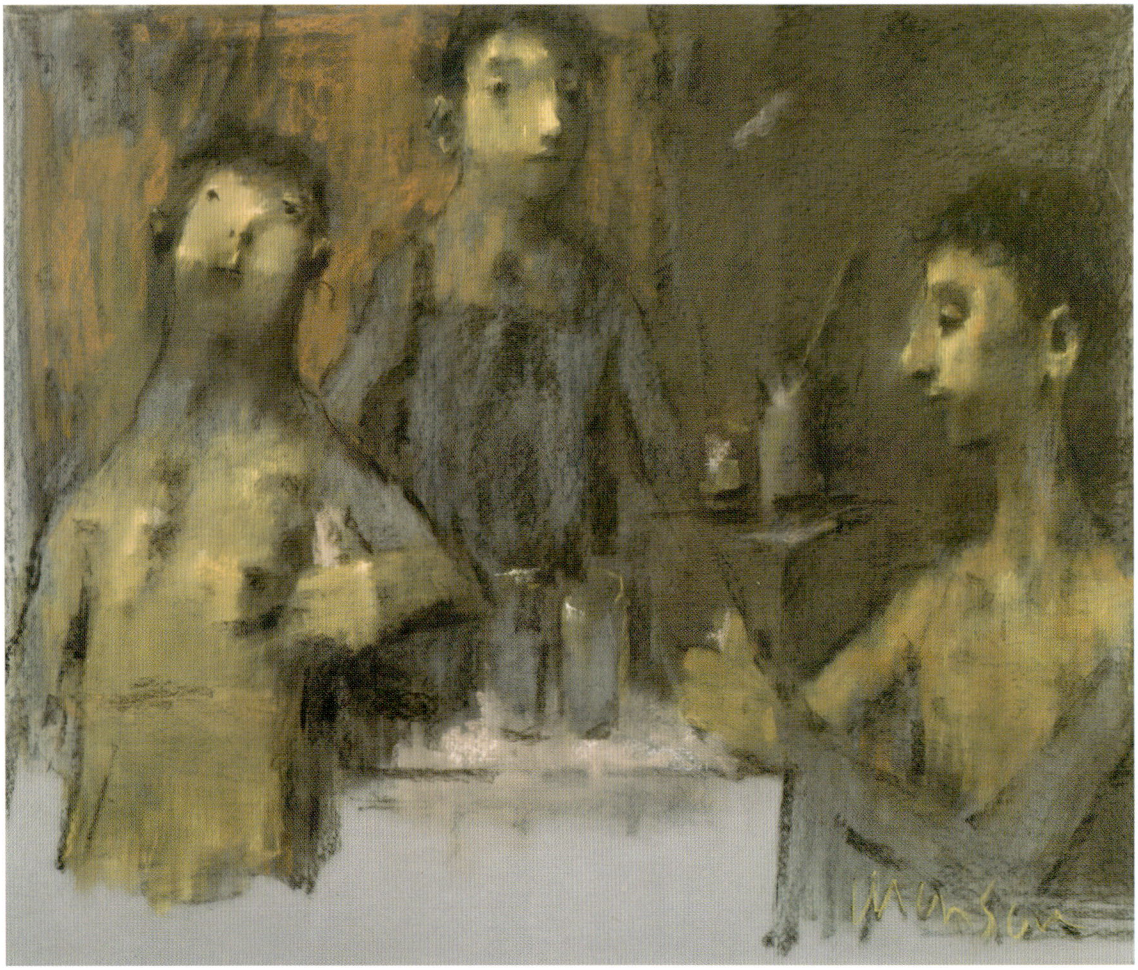

Three Men at Table
1983
pastel 32 x 40"
Private Collection

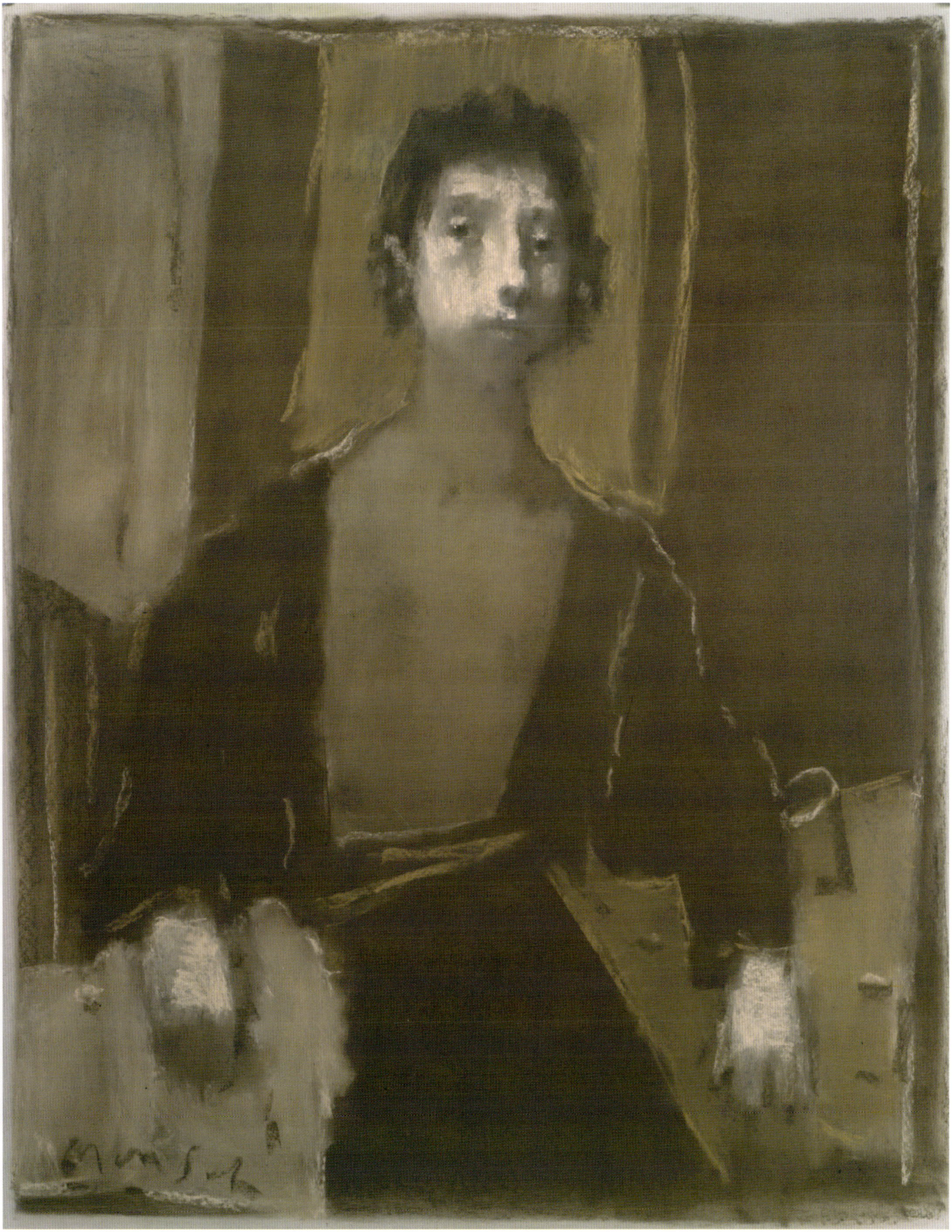

Seated Figure, 1983
pastel 40 x 32"
Private Collection

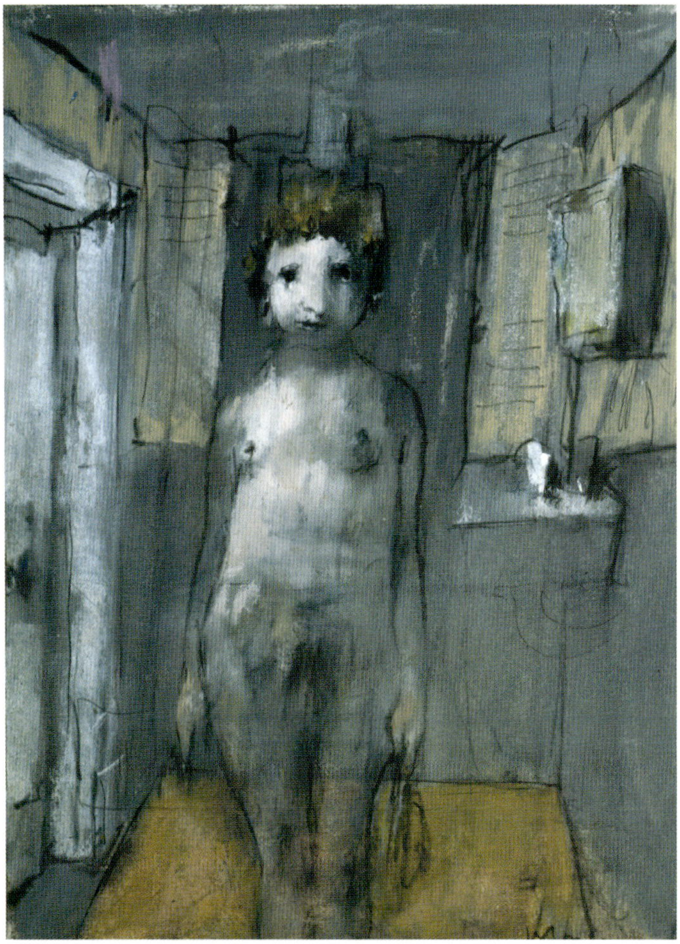

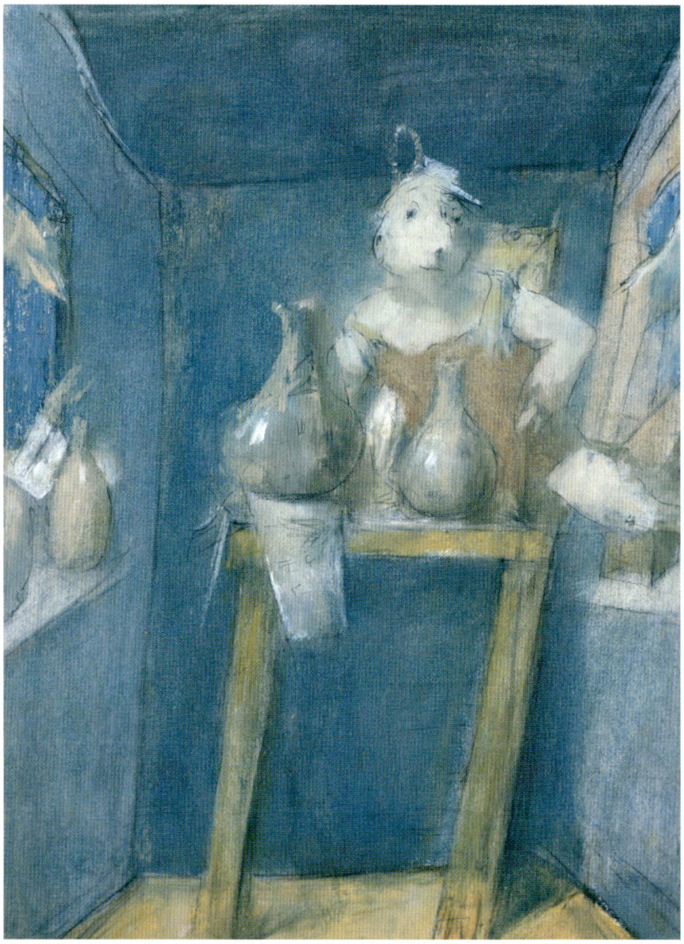

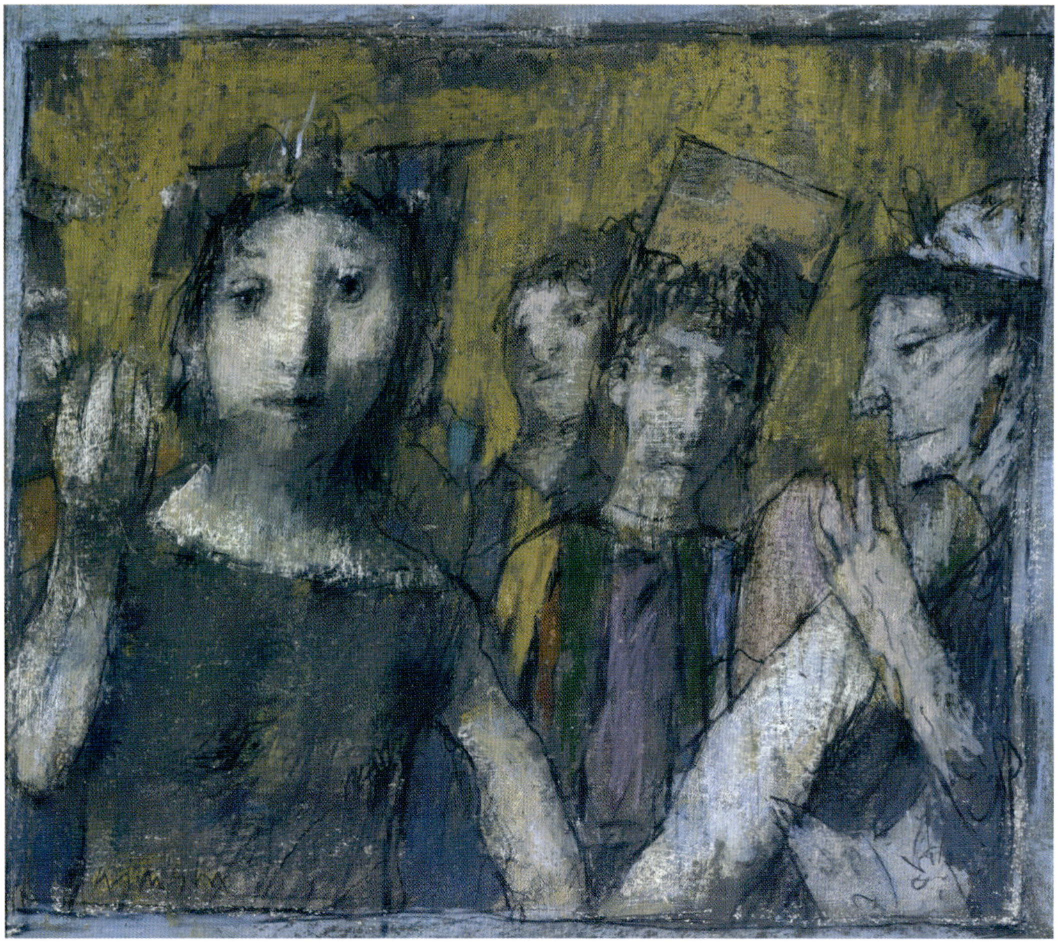

Figure in Interior 1984
oil pastel 15½ x 11½"
Private Collection

Angel with Still Life, 1986
oil pastel 14½ x 10"
Private Collection

The Procession, 1980
oil pastel 8½ x 9 ¾"
Private Collection

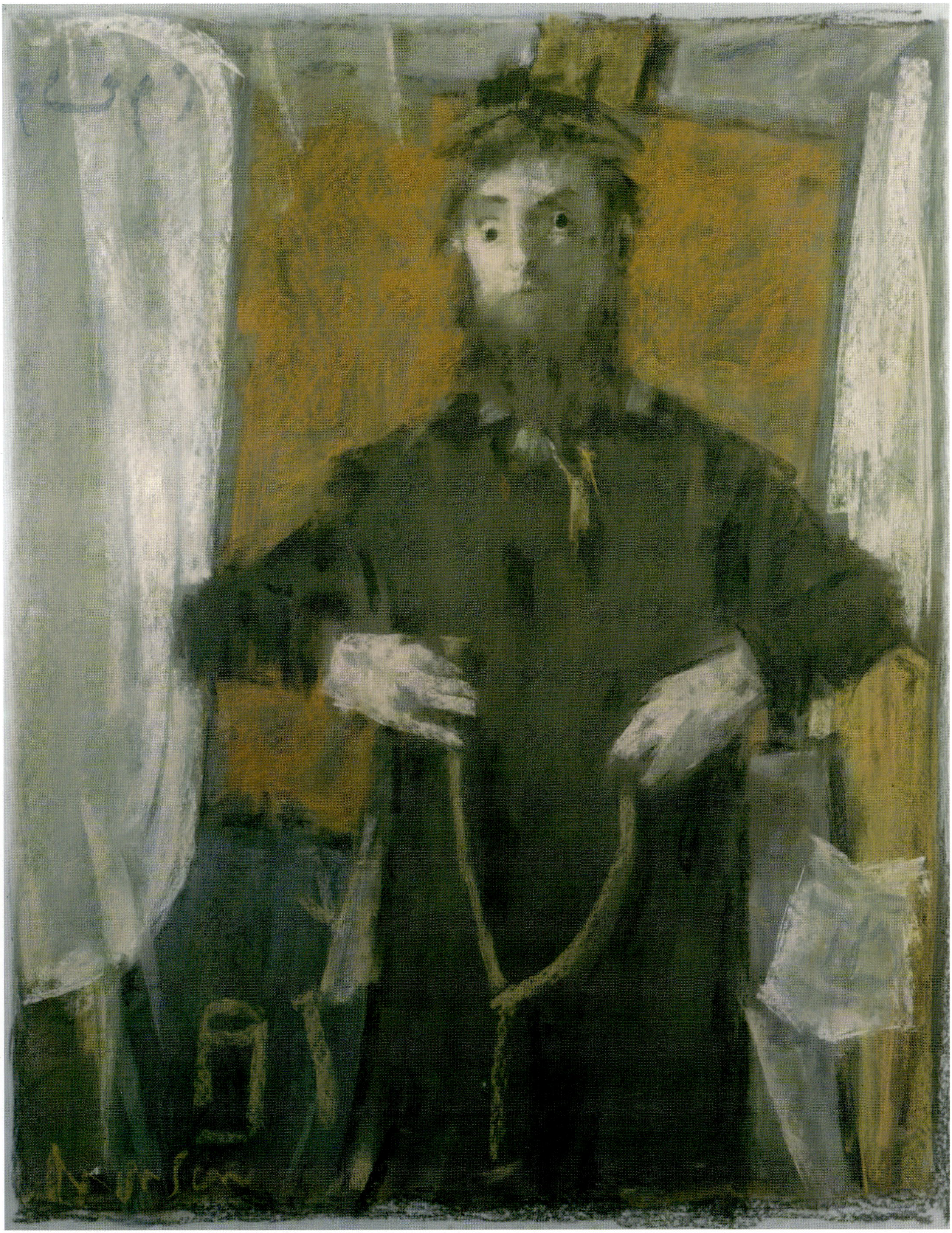

Maimonides, 1983
pastel 40 x 32"
Collection of the Museo Sefardi, Toledo, Spain

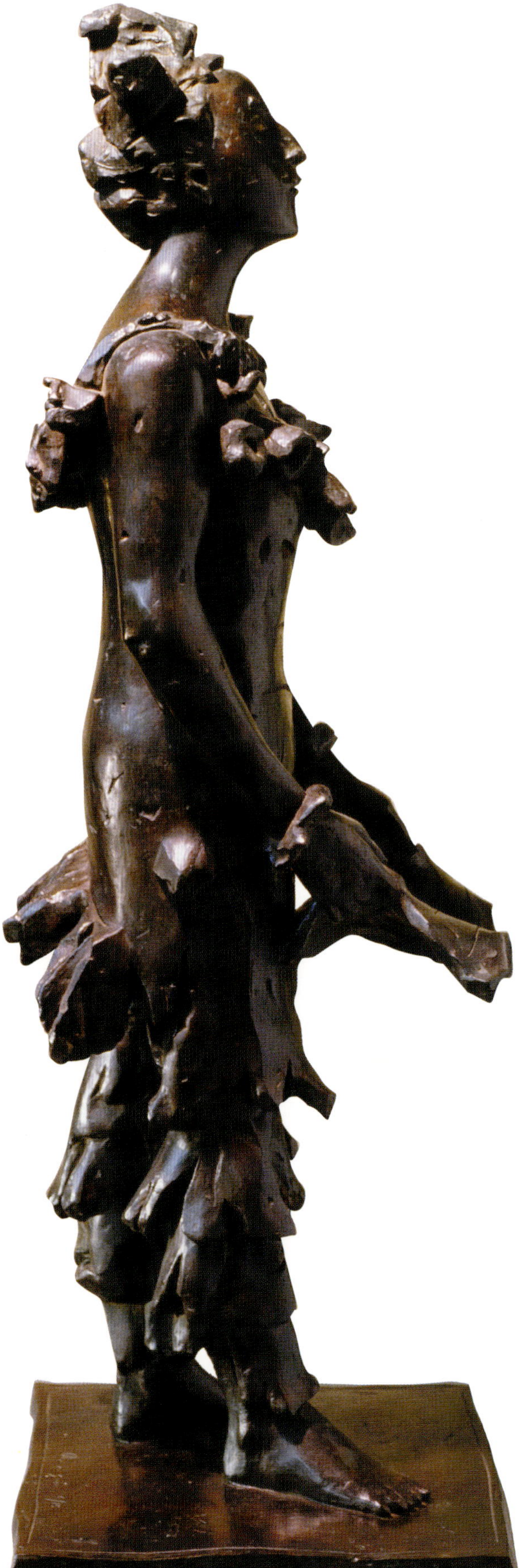

Harlequin, (Side View) 1986
bronze   39 3/4 x 12 3/4 x 14"

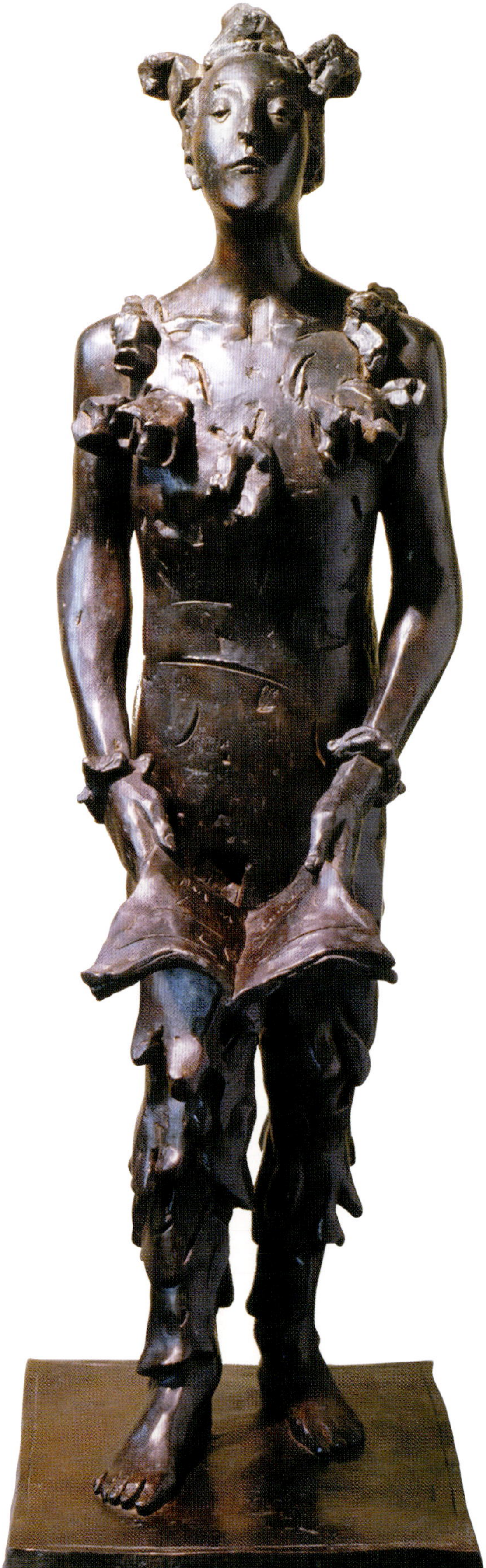

Harlequin, (Front View) 1986
bronze   39 3/4 x 12 3/4 x 14"

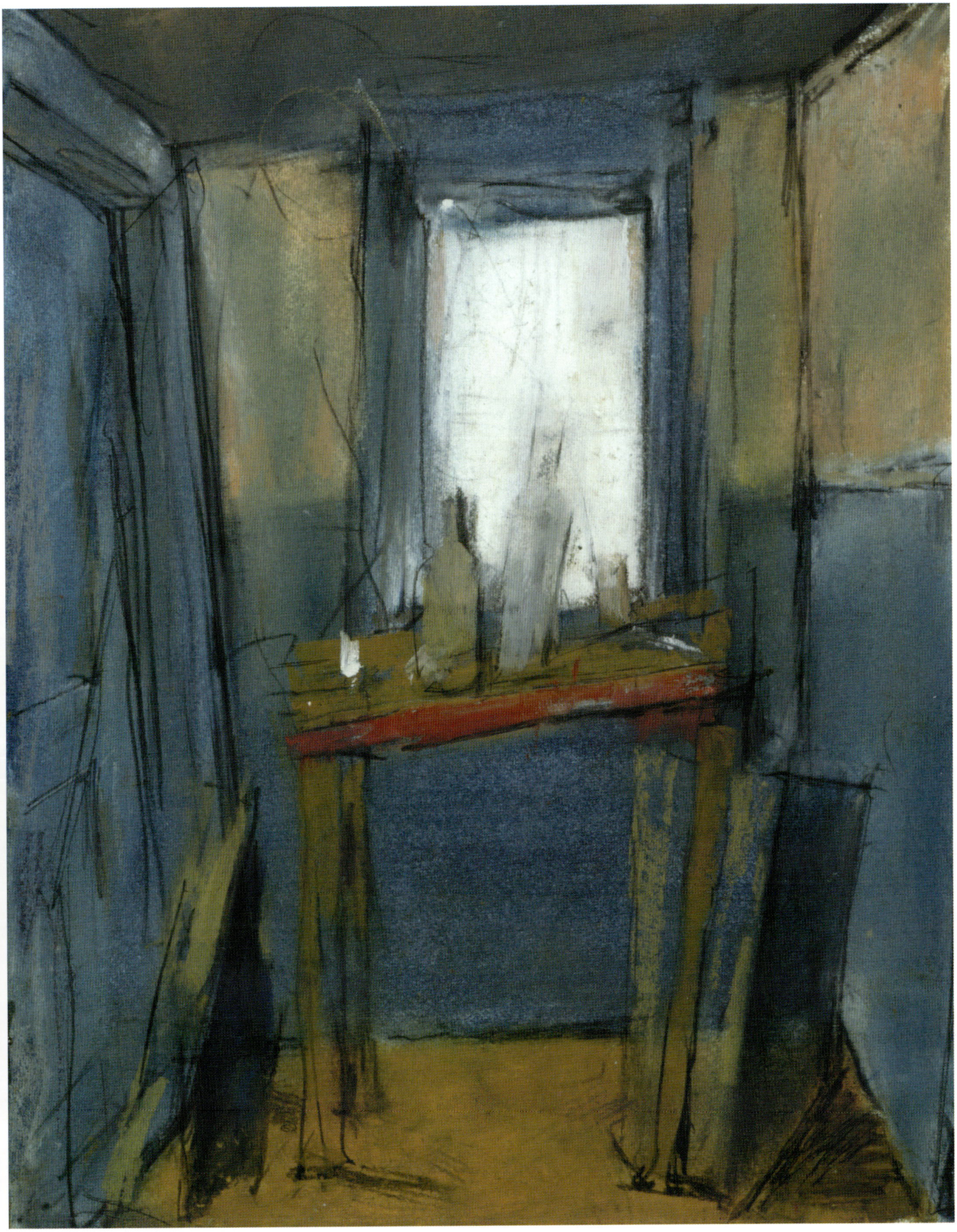

Interior with Still Life, 1984
oil pastel 15 x 10"
Private Collection

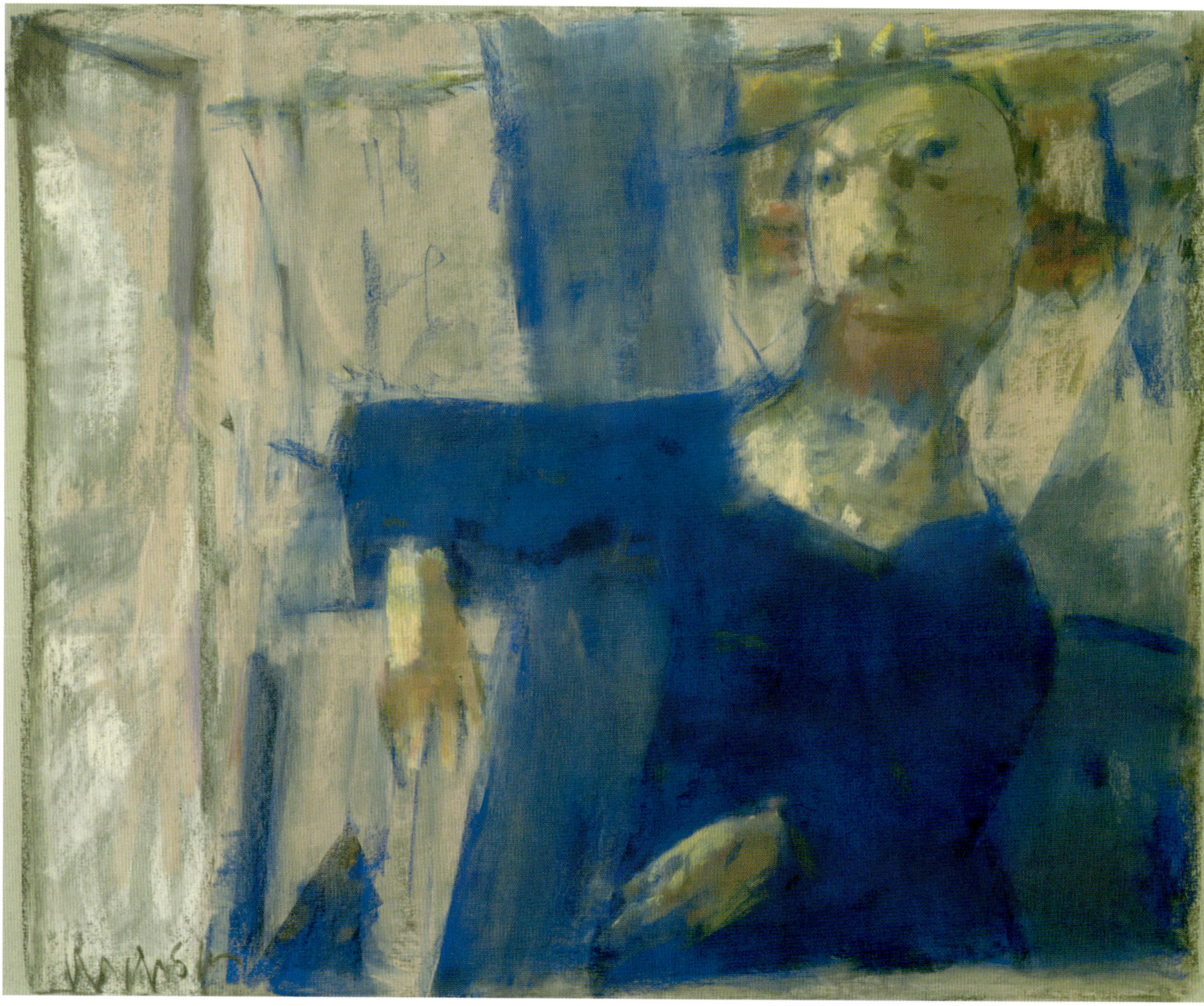

The King, 1989
pastel 32 x 40"
Private Collection

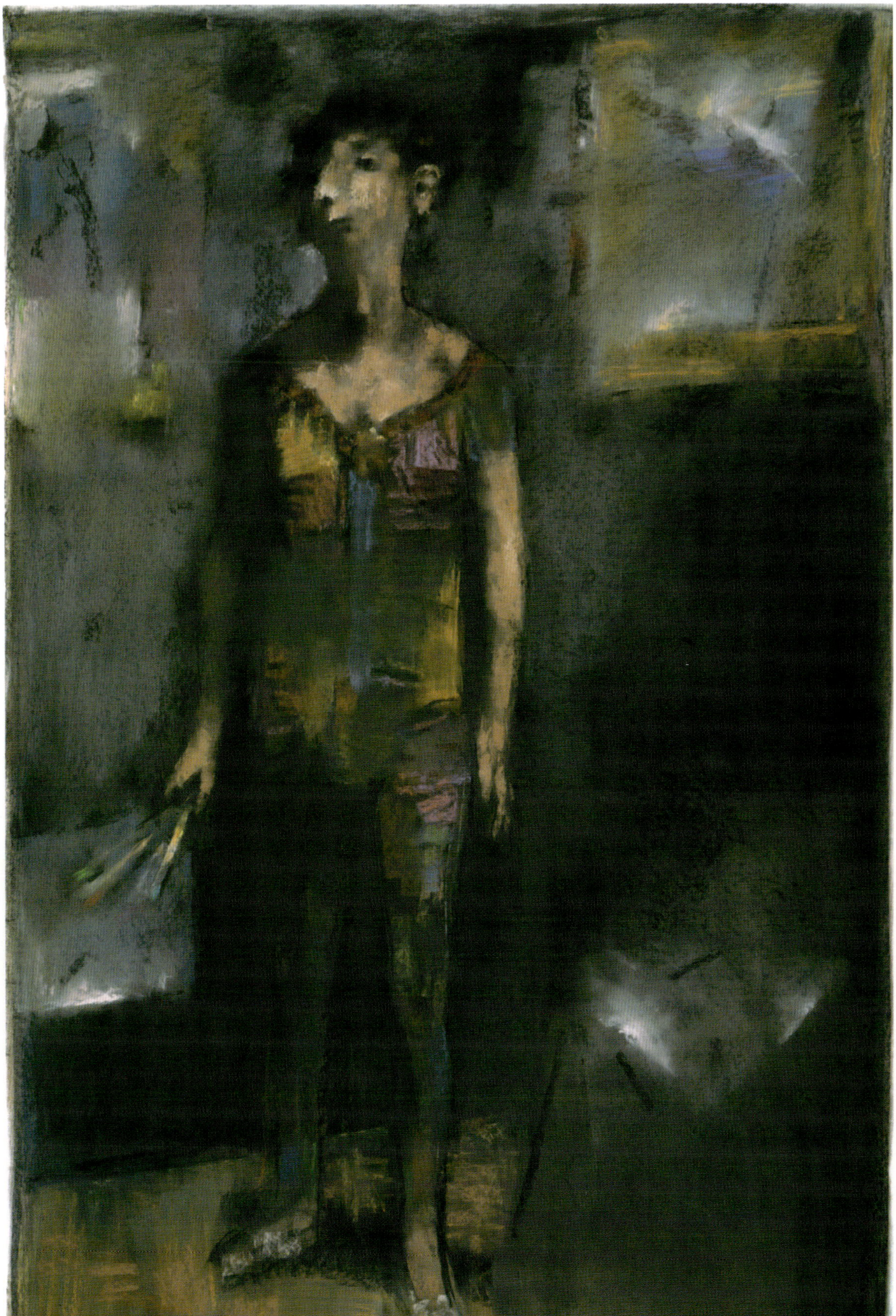

Harlequin, 1986
pastel   60 x 40"
Private Collection

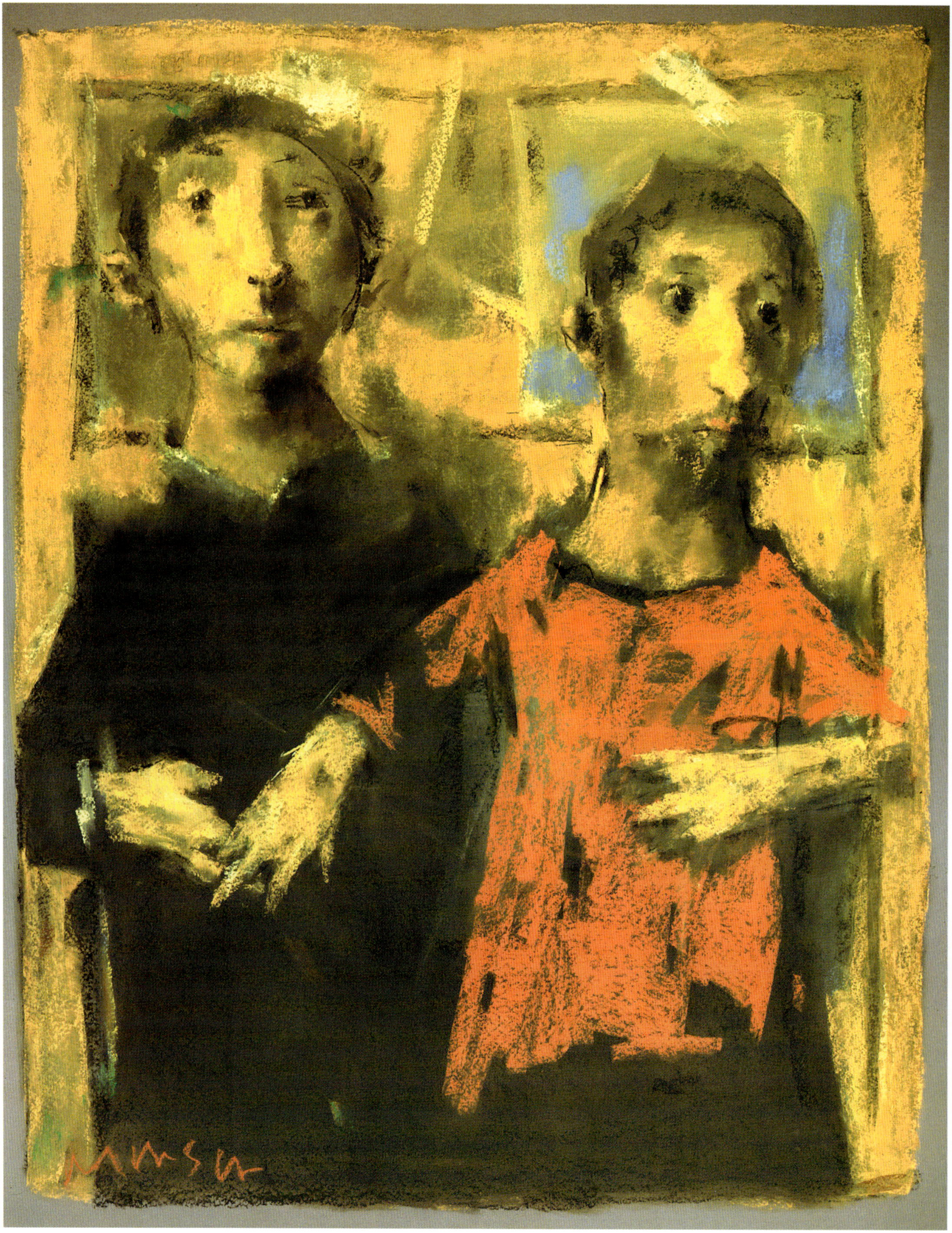

The Brothers, 1989
pastel 40 x 32"
Private Collection

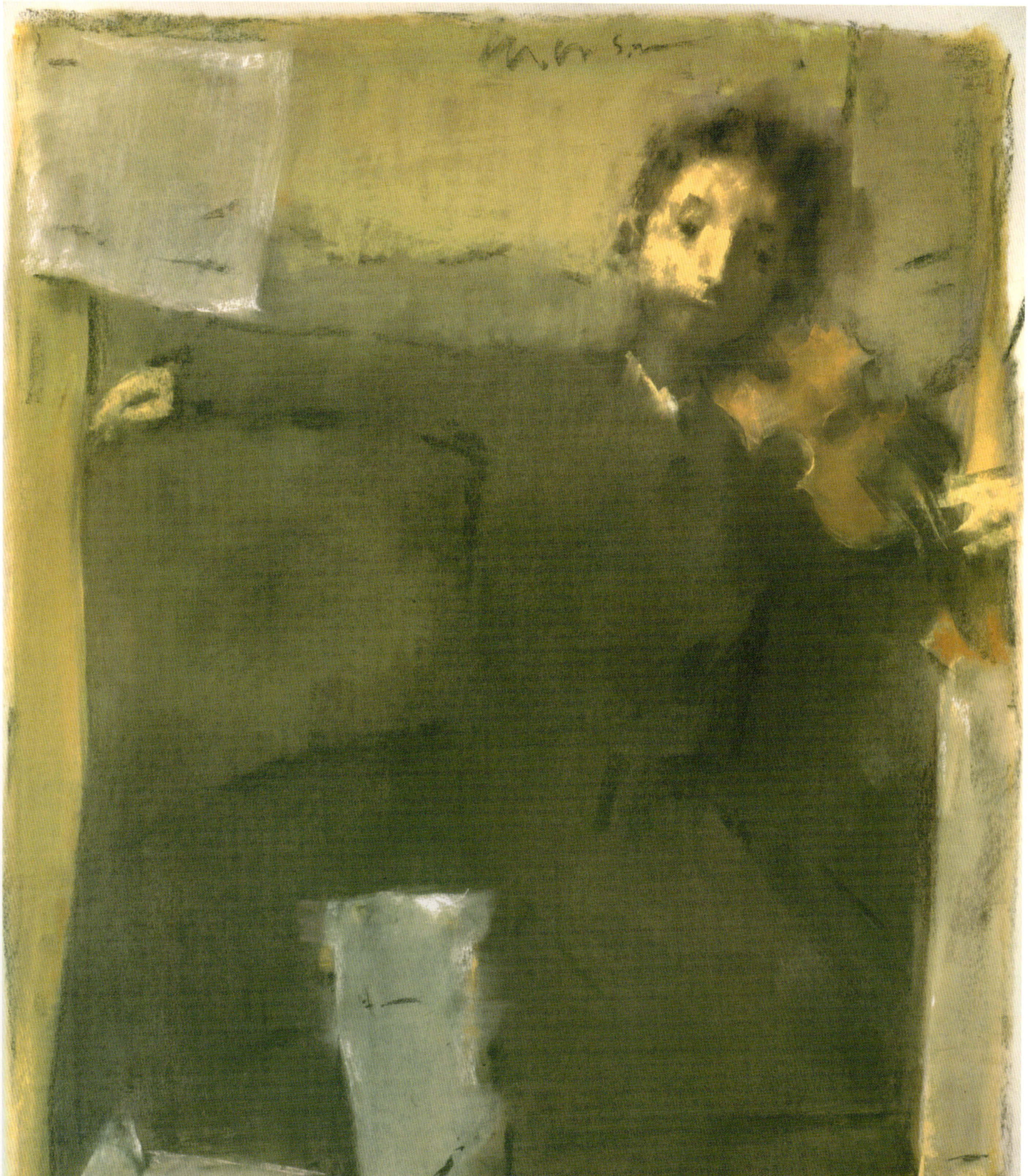

Green Violinist, 1990
pastel 40 x 32"
Private Collection

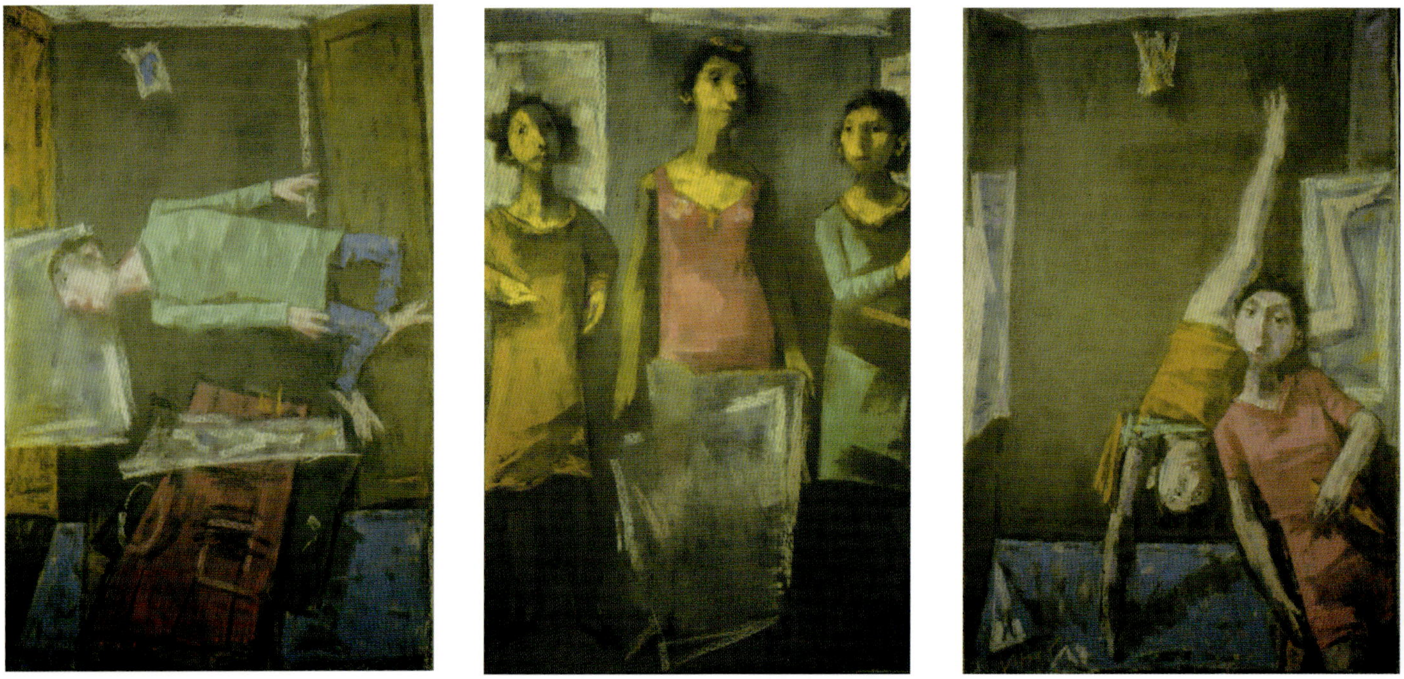

Performance, Triptych, 1986
pastel 59$\frac{1}{4}$ x 39$\frac{1}{2}$" each
Private Collection

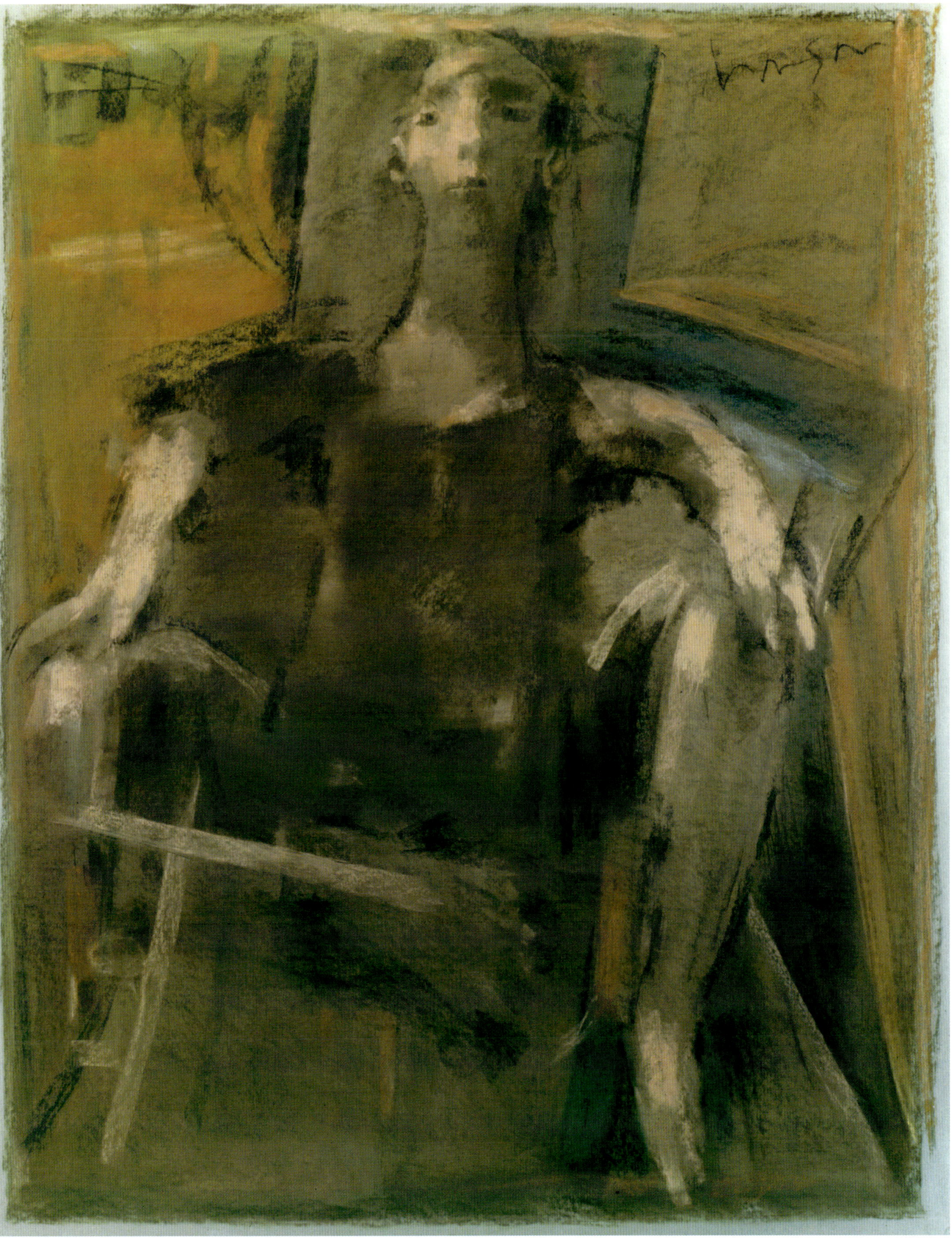

Reclining Figure, 1989
pastel   40 x 32"
Private Collection

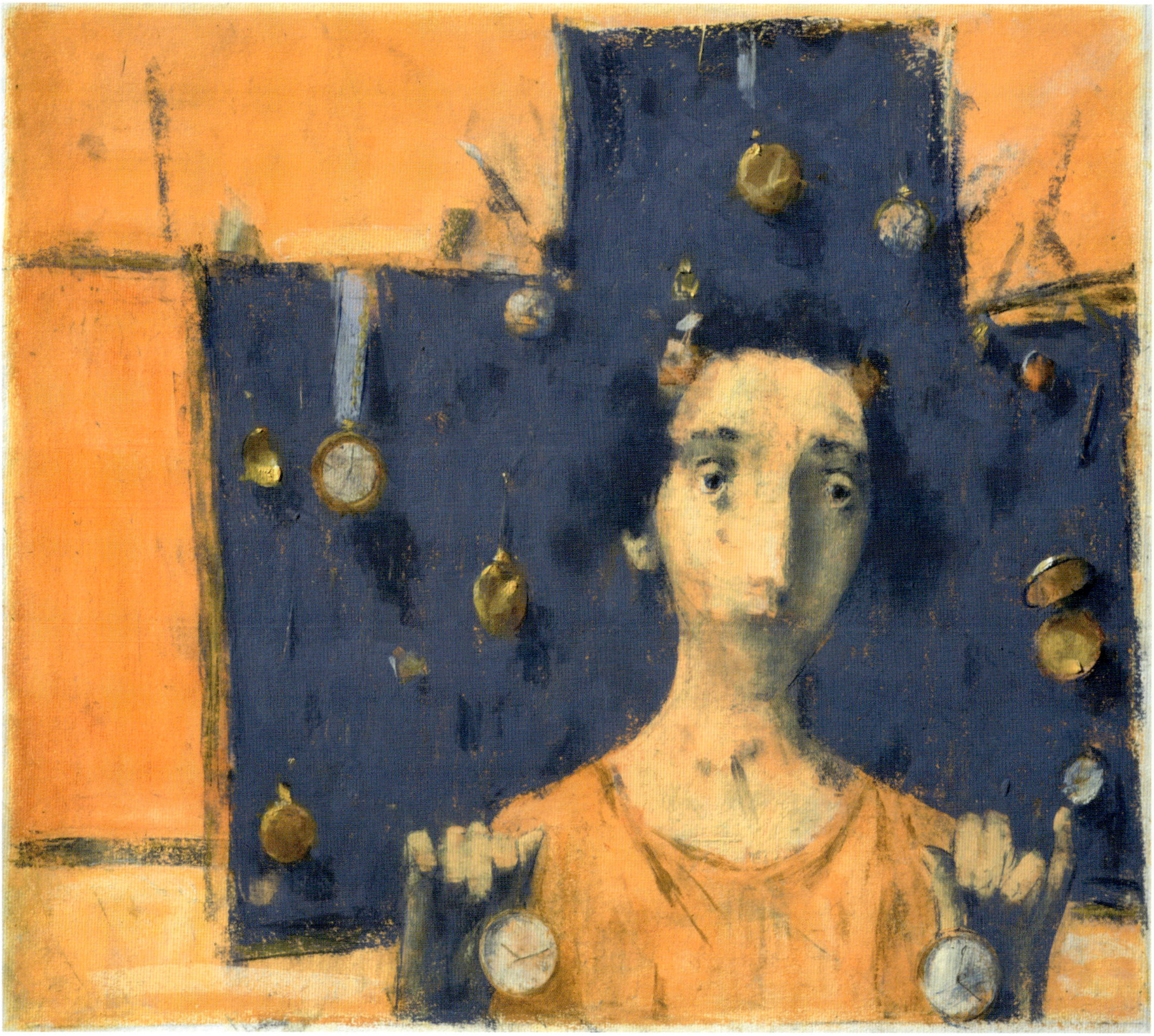

Woman with Watches, 1990
oil pastel 12 1/2 x 16"
Private Collection

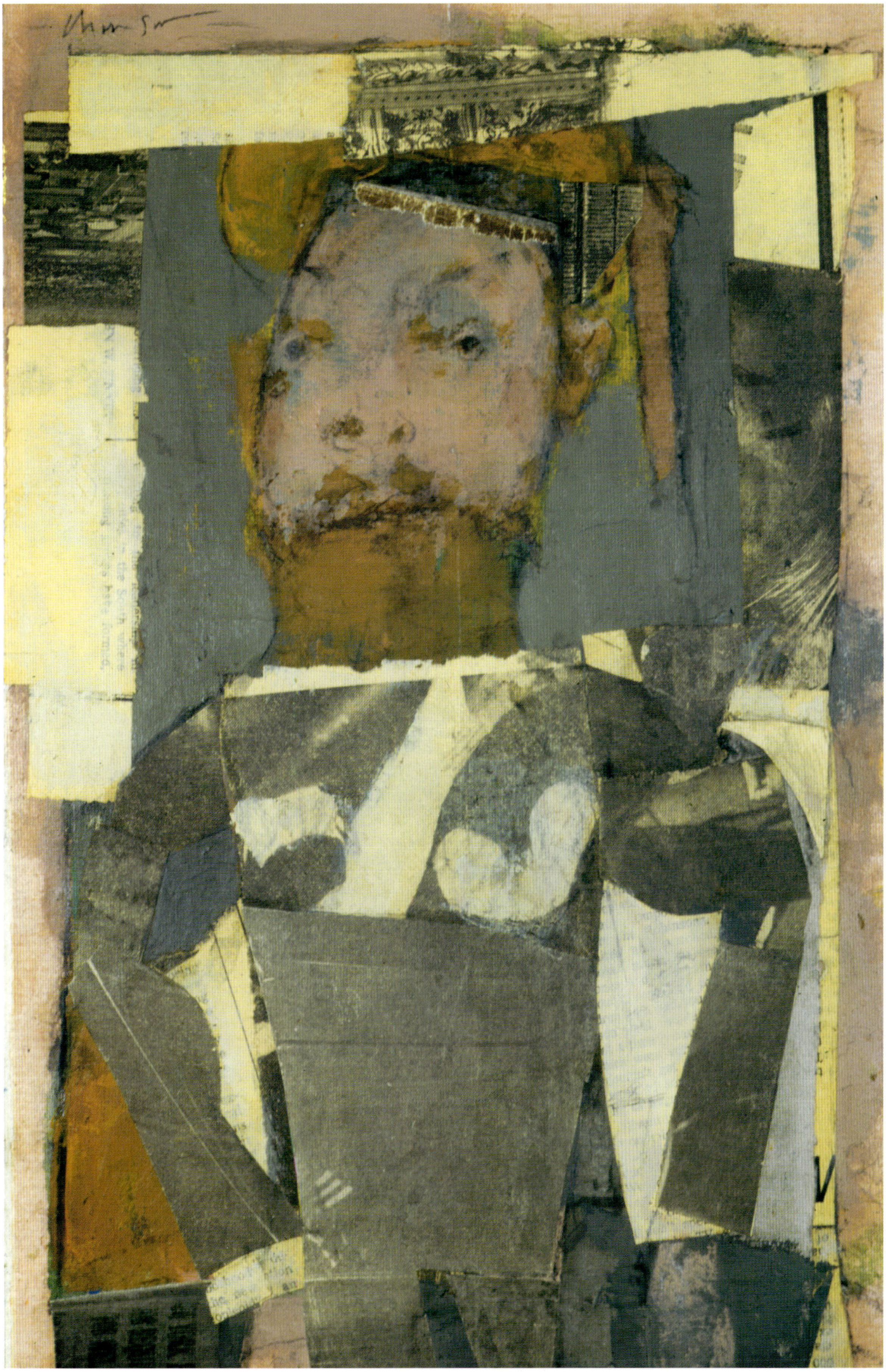

King II, 1990
oil pastel with collage 11¼ x 8"
Private Collection

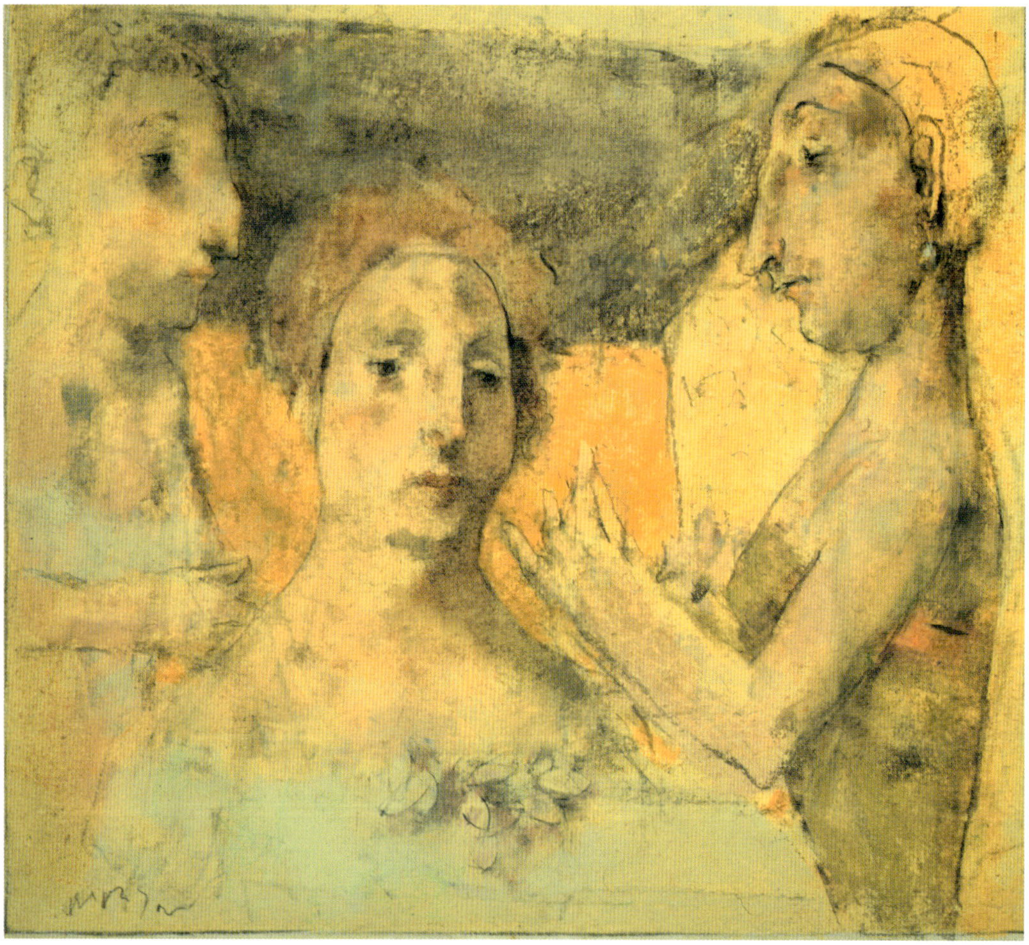

Ladies in Waiting, 1999
oil pastel 7 5/8 x 8 6/16"
Private Collection

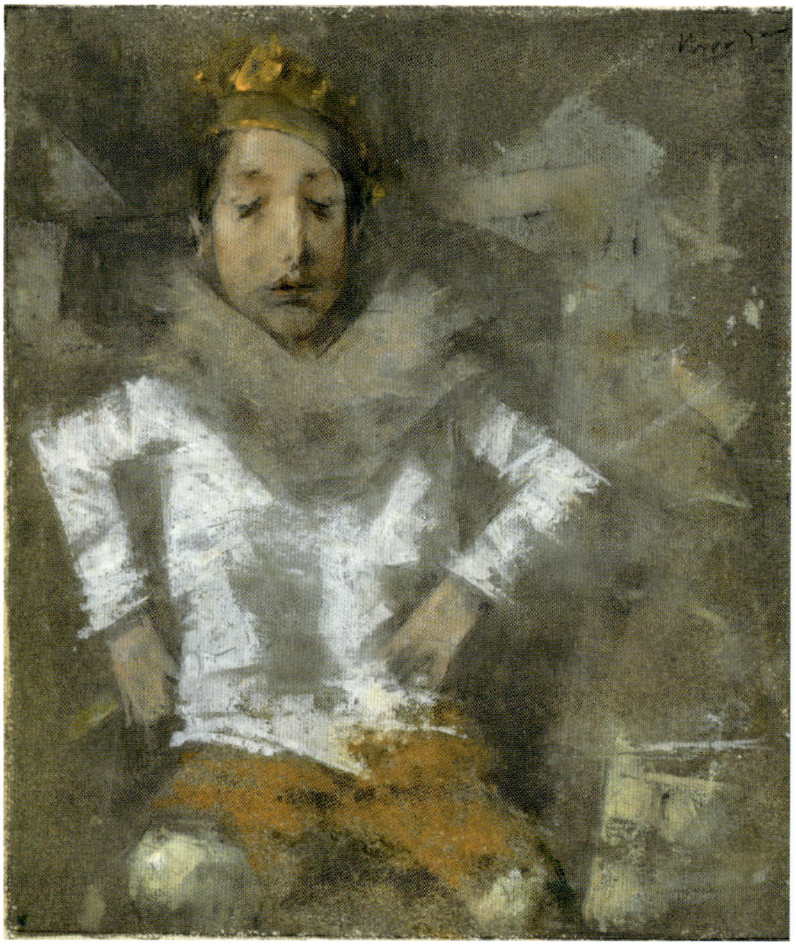

Young King, 1997
oil pastel 8 1/8 x 7 1/8"
Private Collection

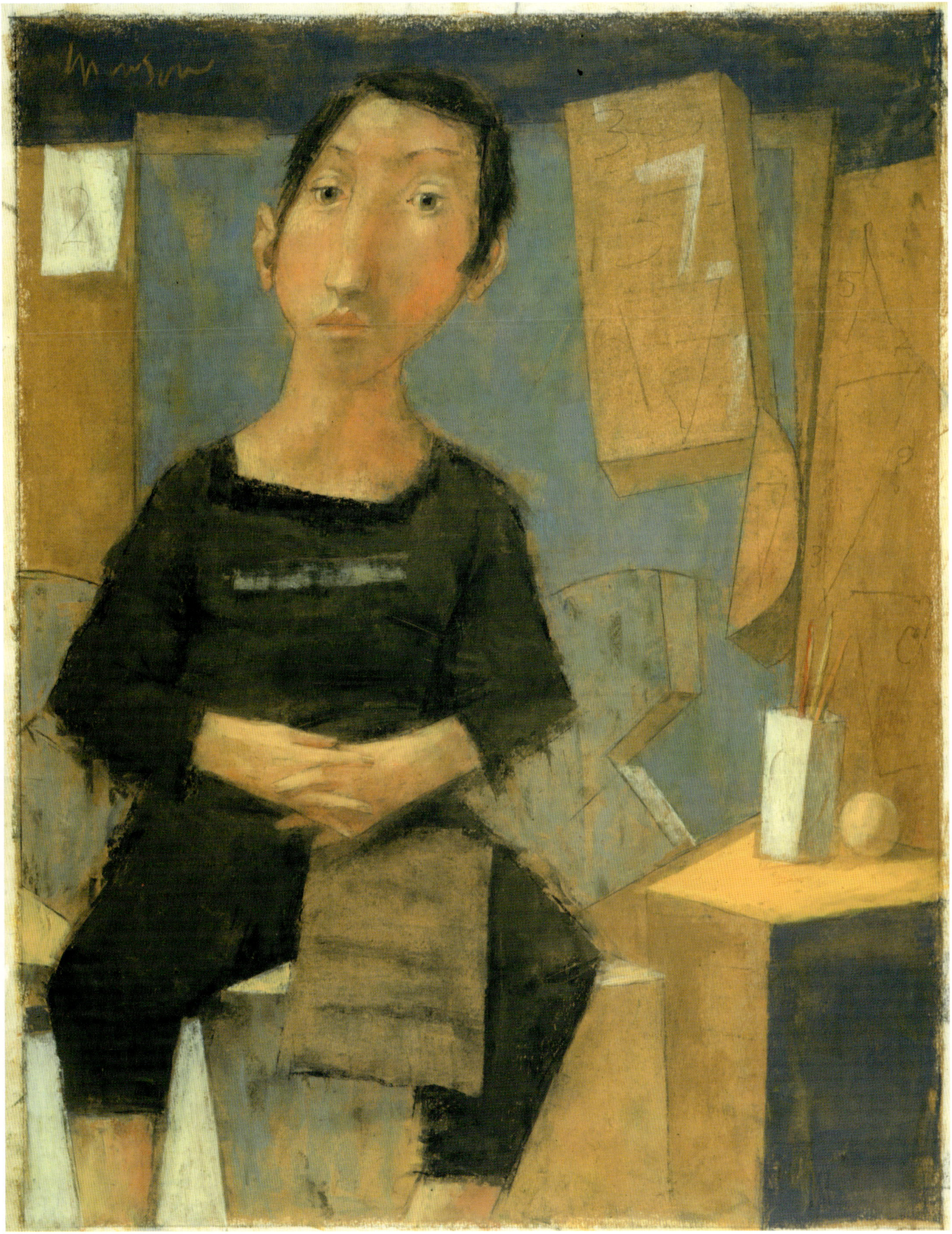

Mathematician, 1993
oil pastel 20⅝ × 16"
Private Collection

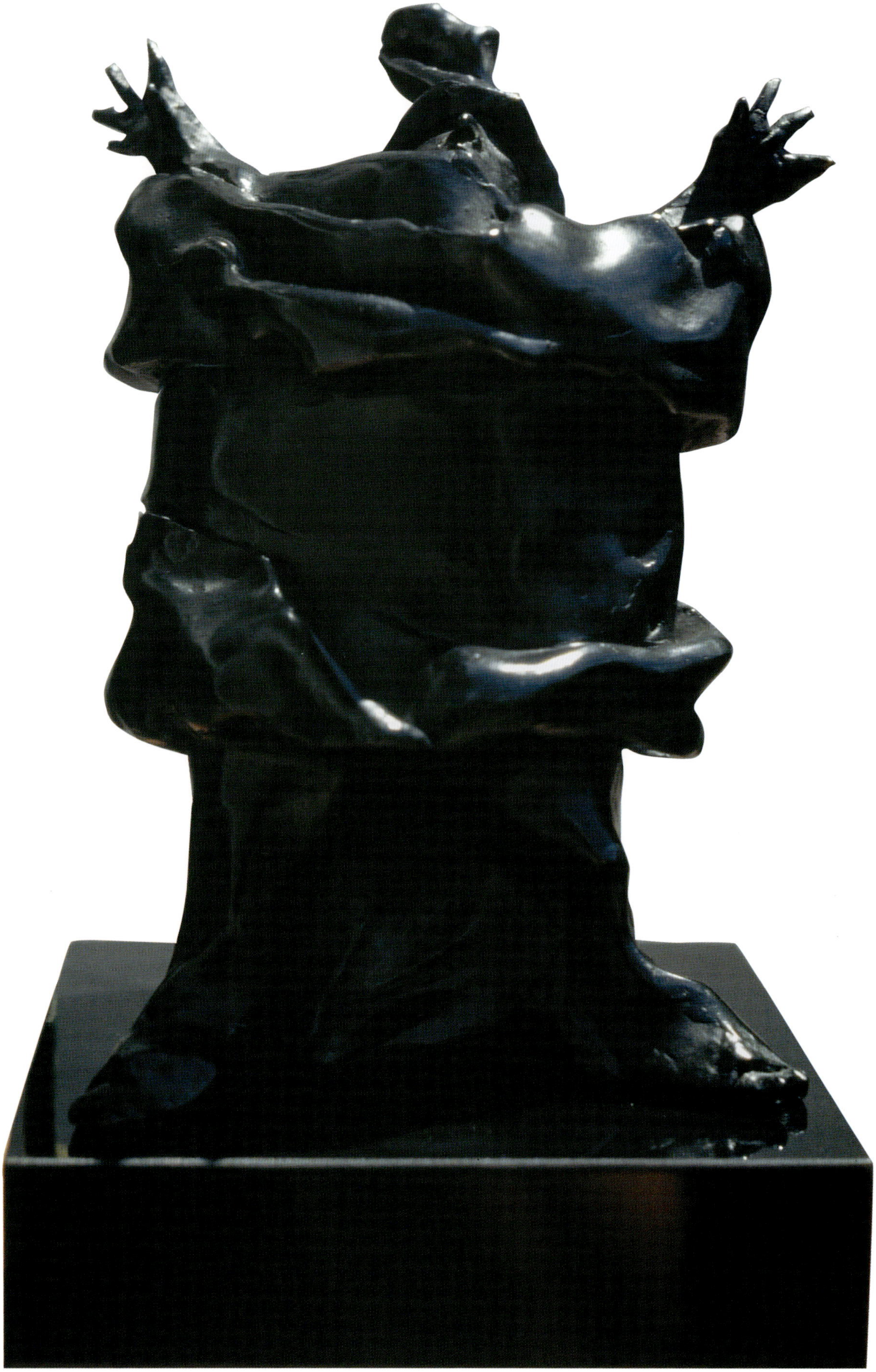

The Prophet, 1969
bronze 7 x 5 1/4 x 5 1/2"

The Bride, 1996
oil pastel $8^1/_4 \times 7^3/_{16}$"
Private Collection

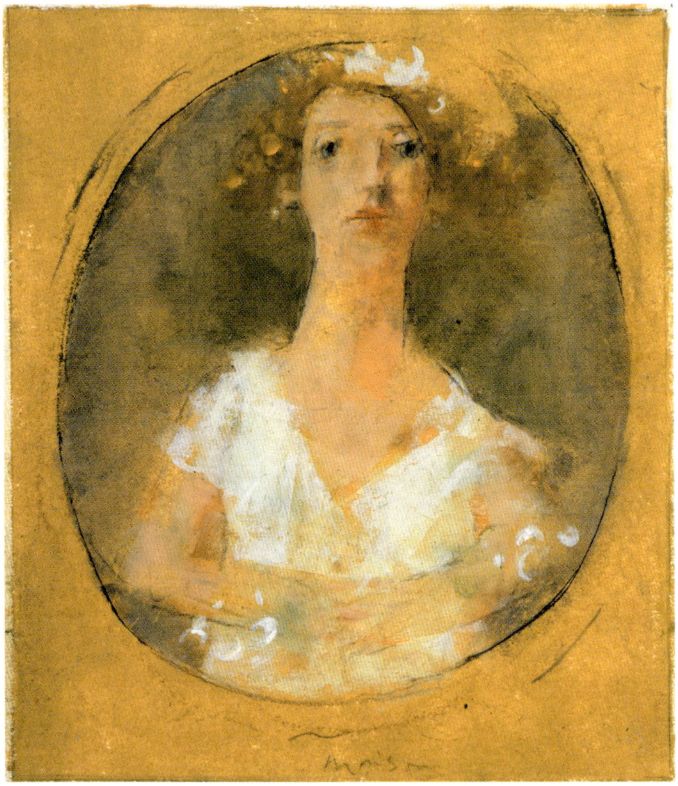

Adam and Eve, 1999
oil pastel $6^7/_8 \times 7^7/_{16}$"
Private Collection

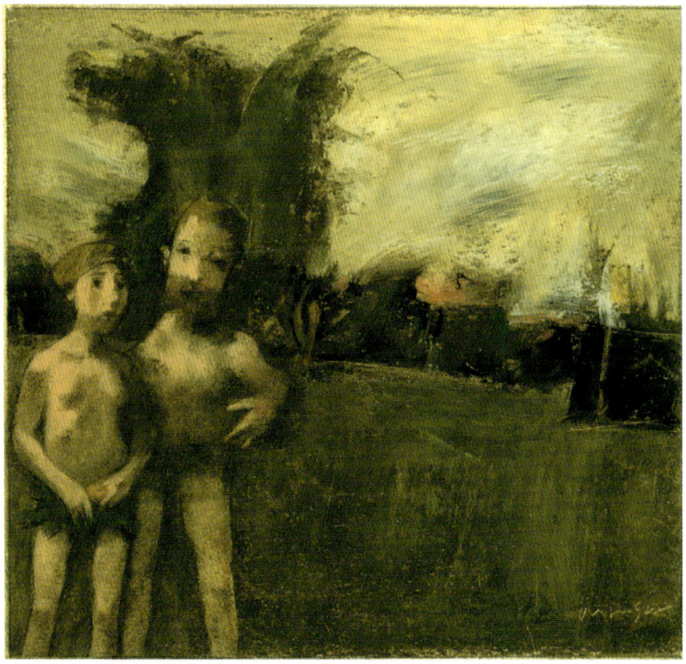

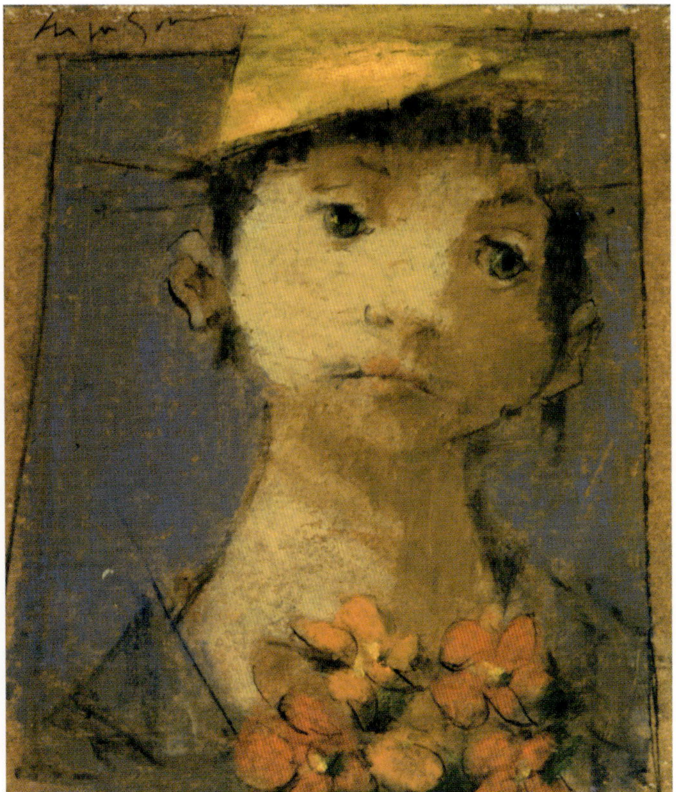

Flower Vendor I, 1993
oil pastel $5 \times 4^1/_8$"
Private Collection

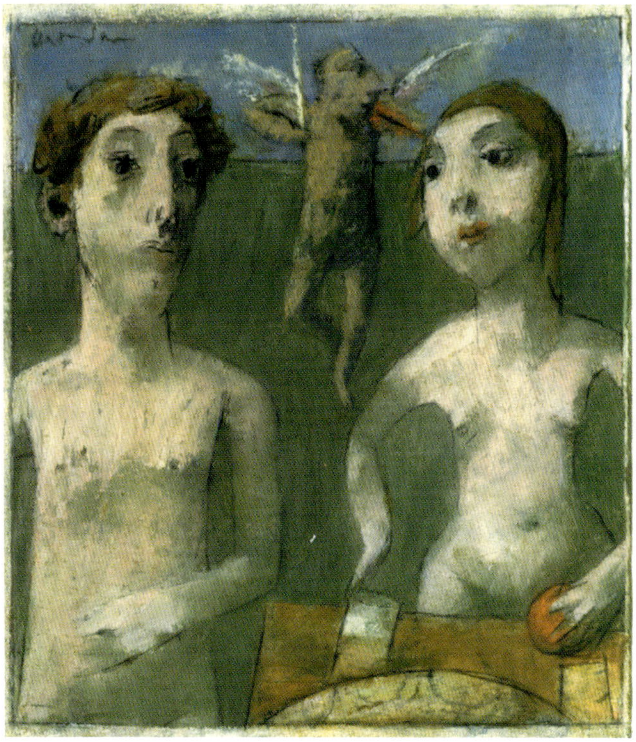

Adam and Eve, 1993
oil pastel $5 \times 4^1/_2$"
Private Collection

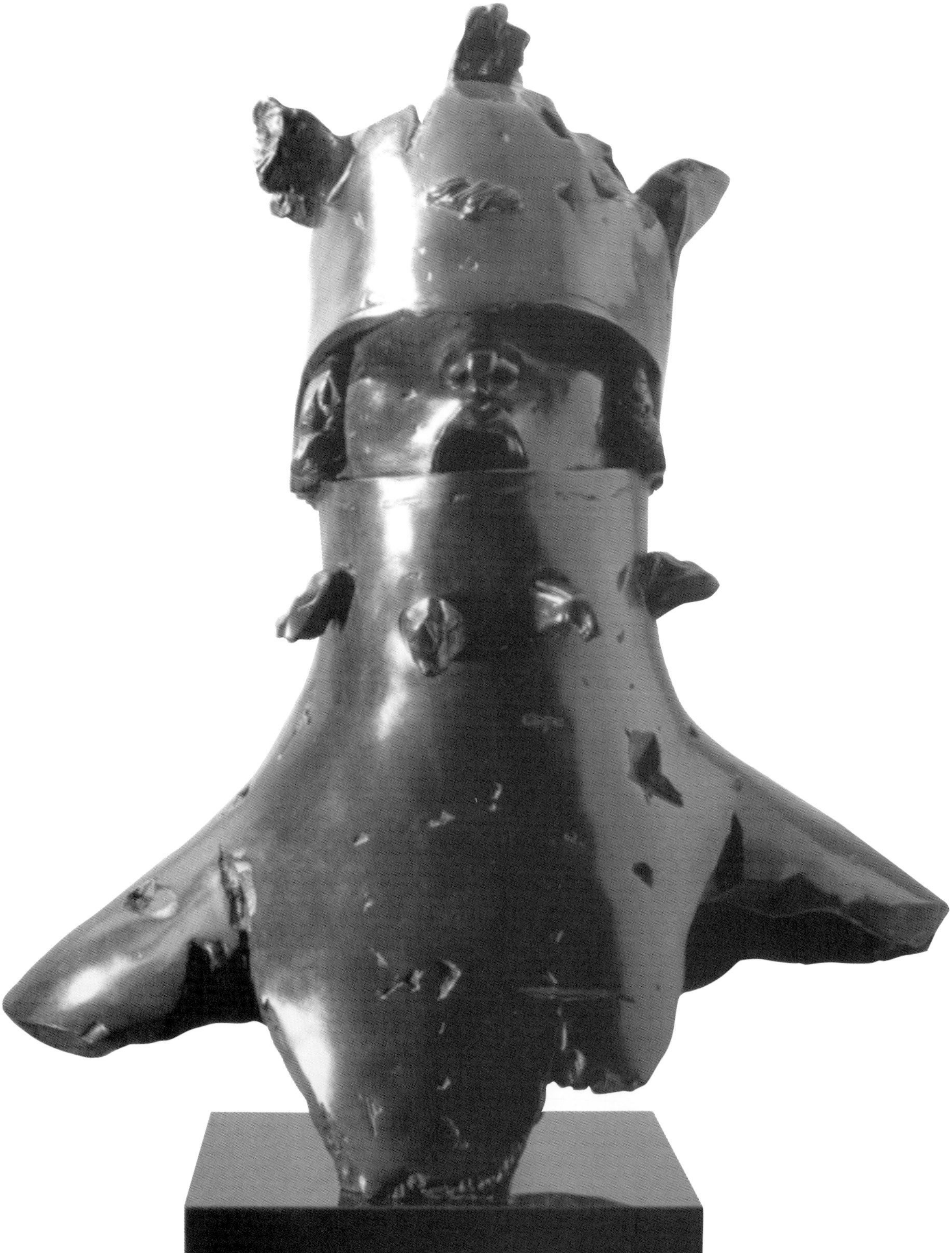

Warrior II, 1995
bronze 30 x 24 x 20"

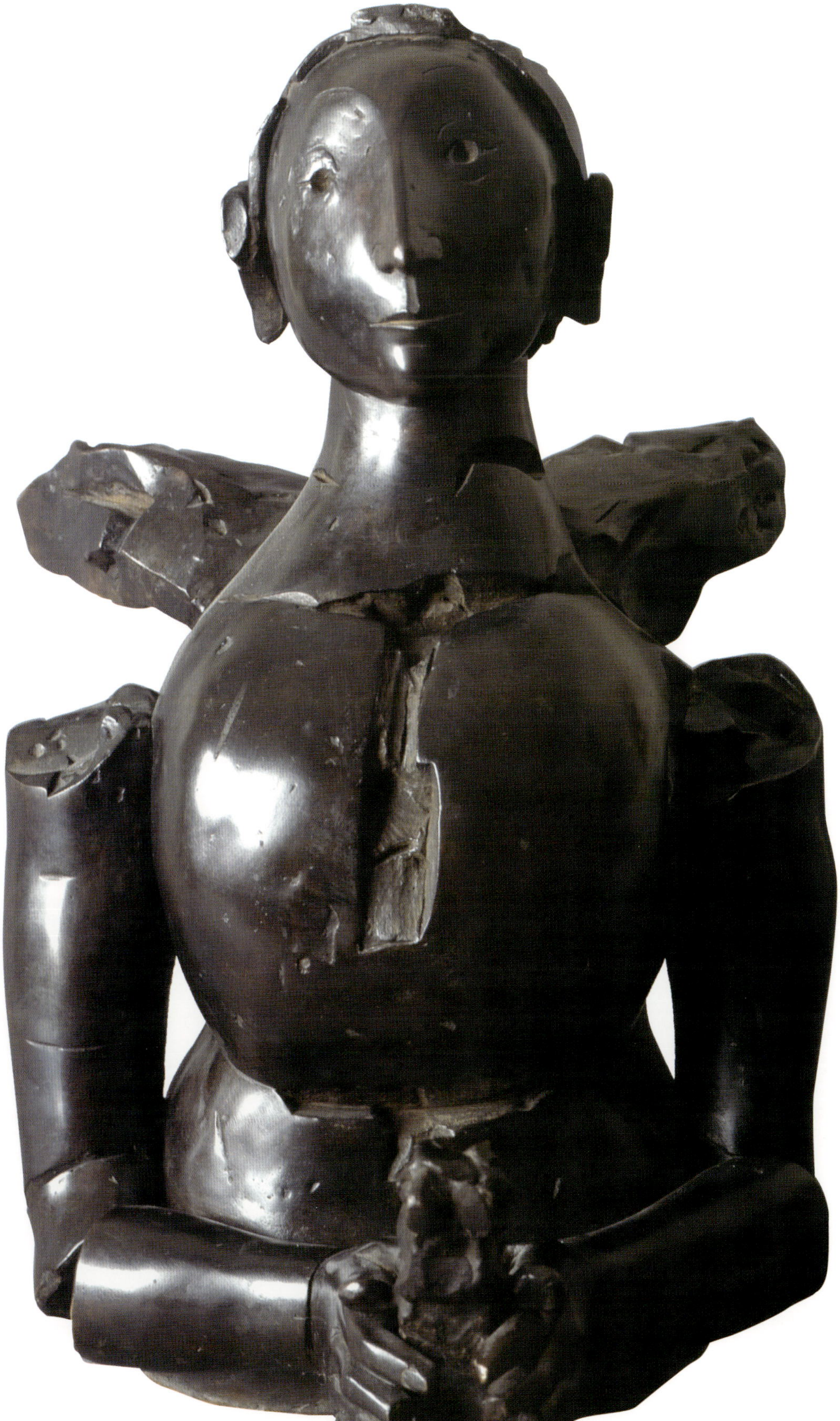

Violinist II, 1987
bronze 20¼ x 13½ x 17"

Lute Player, 1999
oil pastel $7\frac{1}{2} \times 6\frac{15}{16}$"
Private Collection

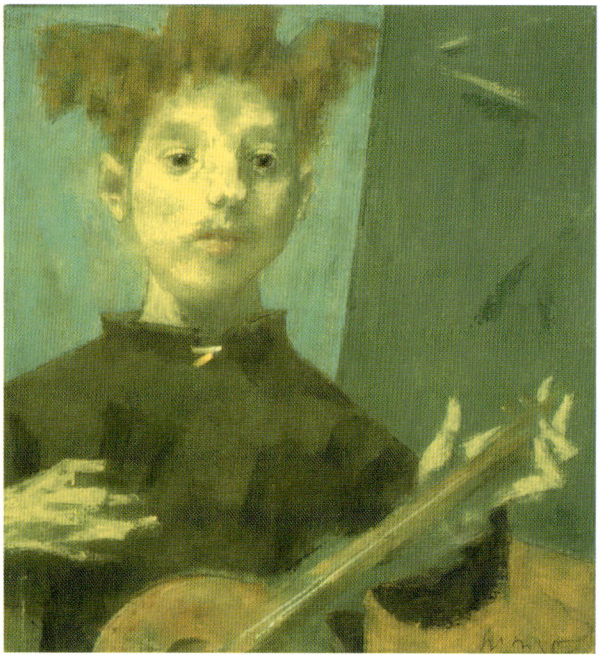

Flute Player, 1999
oil pastel $7\frac{5}{16} \times 7\frac{11}{16}$"
Private Collection

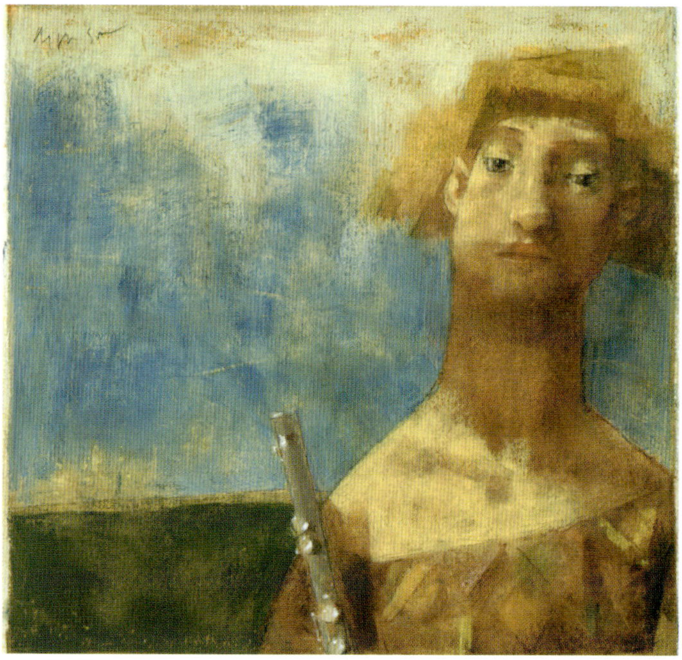

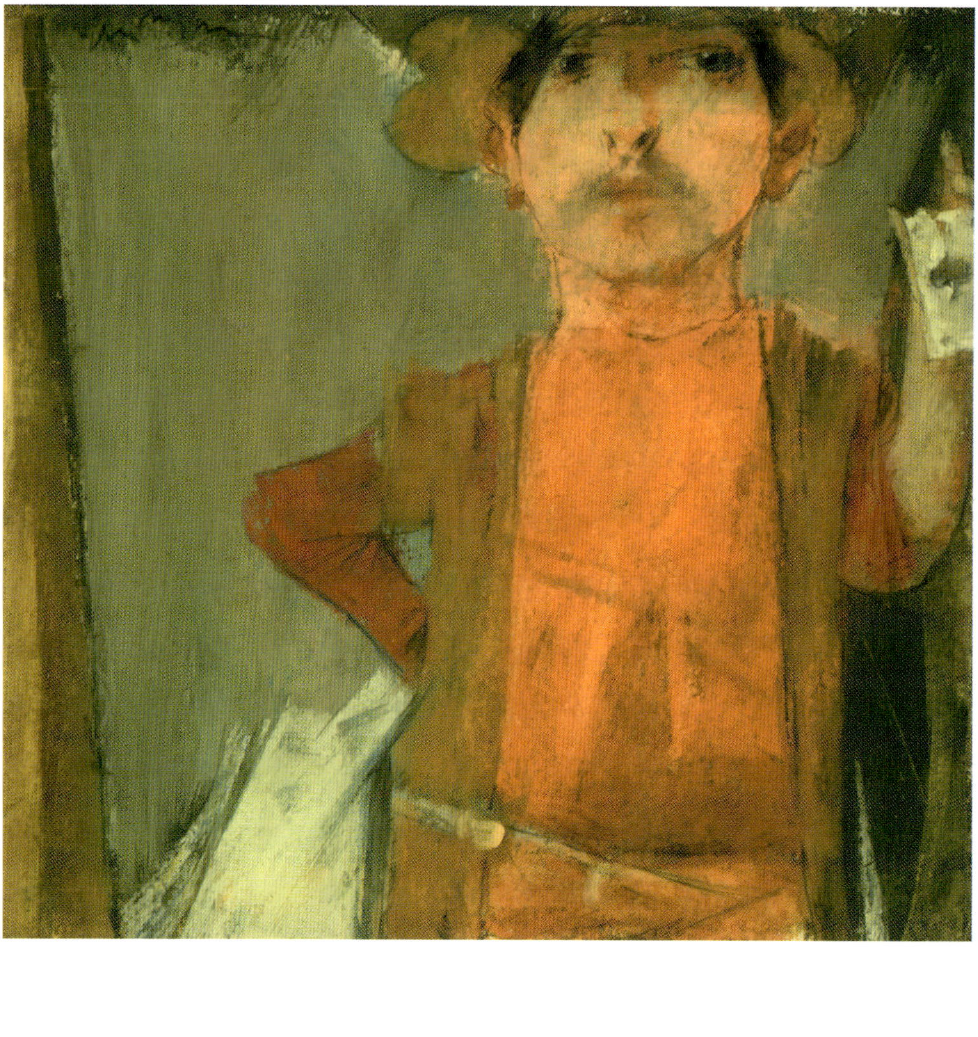

The Gambler
1993
oil pastel
$6\frac{5}{8} \times 7\frac{1}{4}$"
Private
Collection

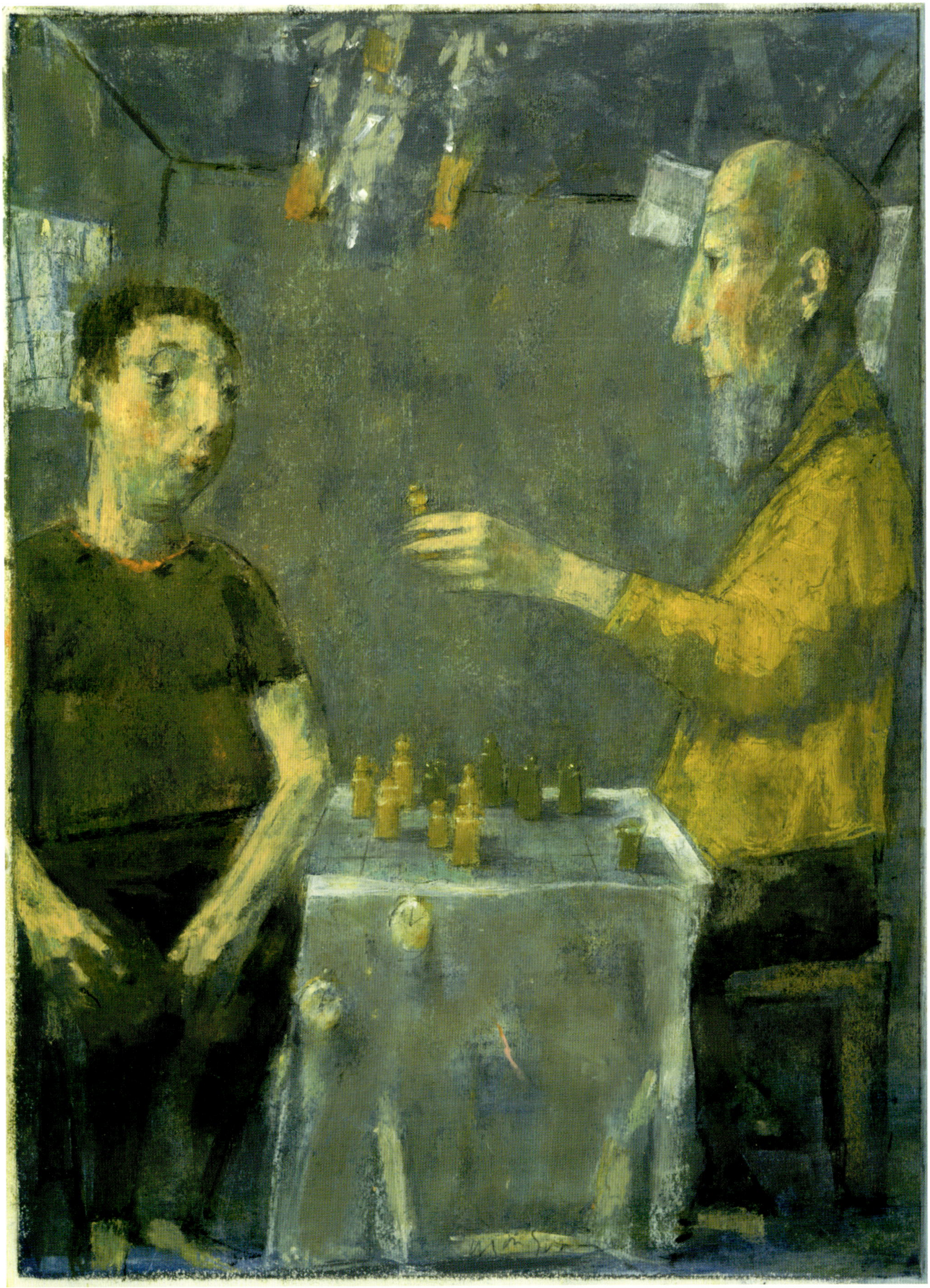

Teacher and Student, 1999
oil pastel 16 x 12"
Private Collection

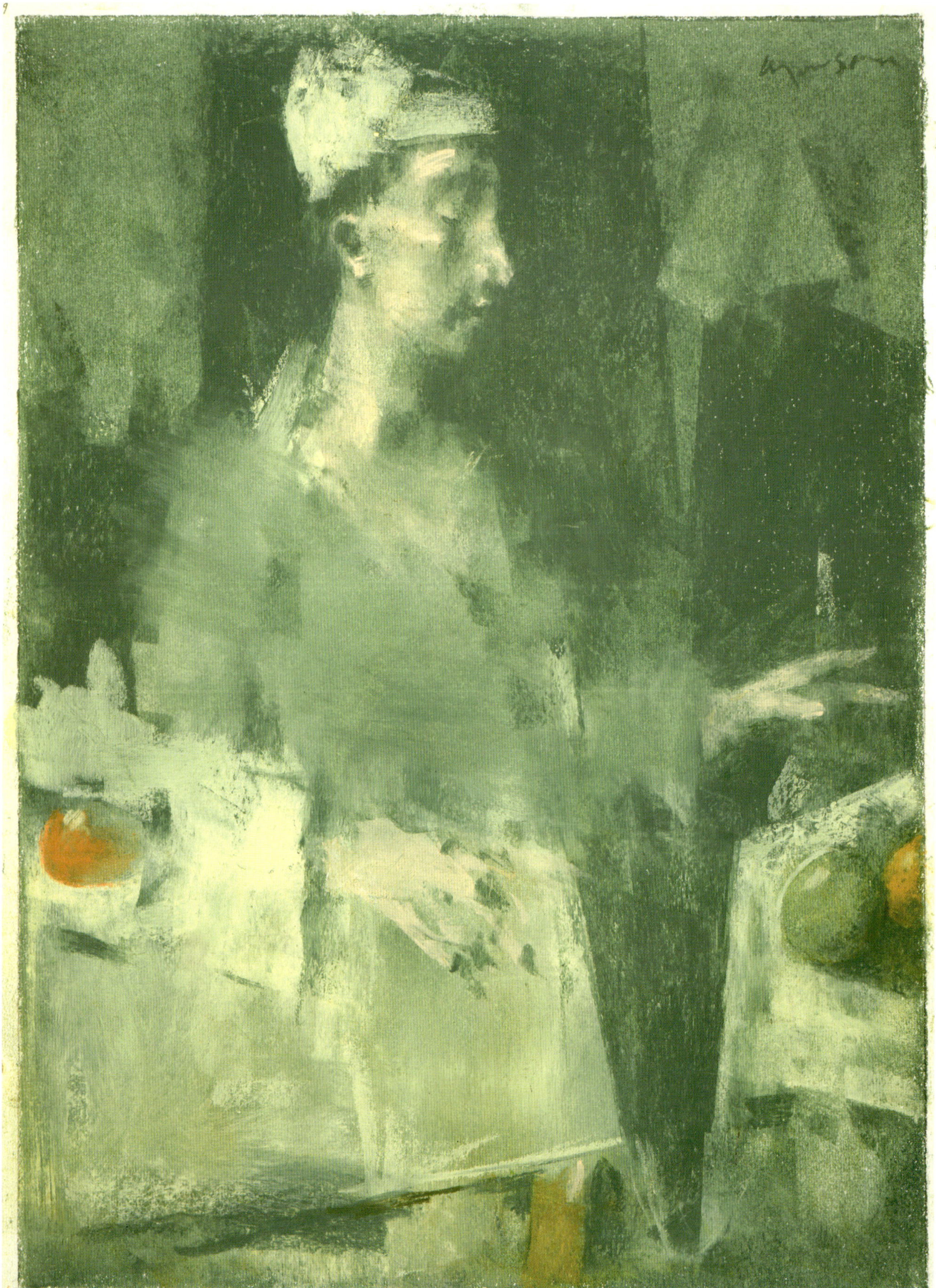

Man with Fruit, 1999
oil pastel 15 x 11"
Private Collection

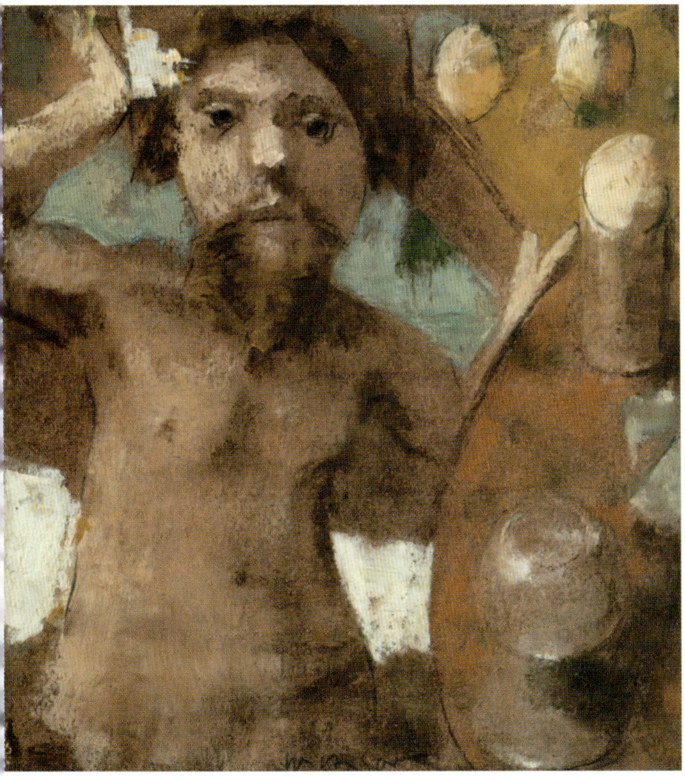

Figure with Still Life, 1993
oil pastel 9 x 8½"
Private Collection

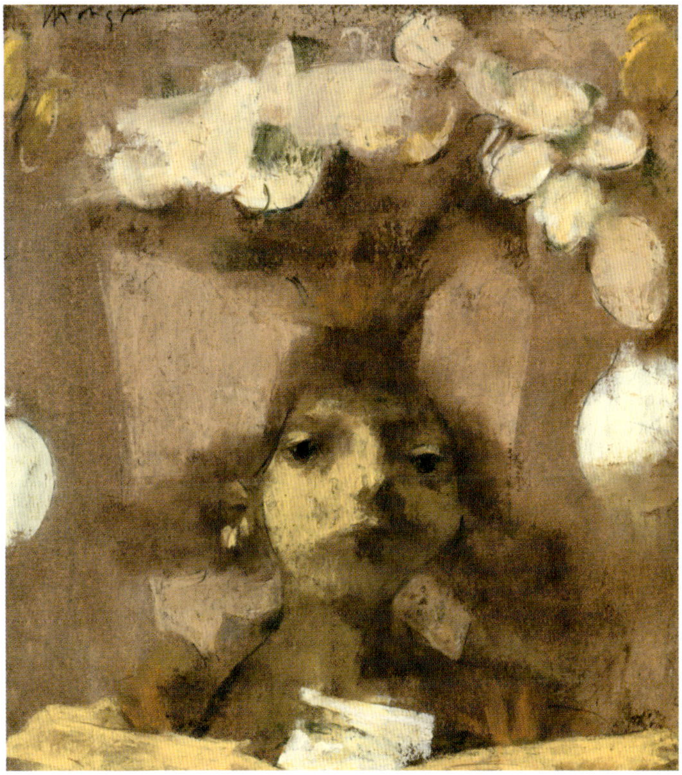

Figure with Ornaments, 1993
oil pastel 6⅞ x 7¼"
Private Collection

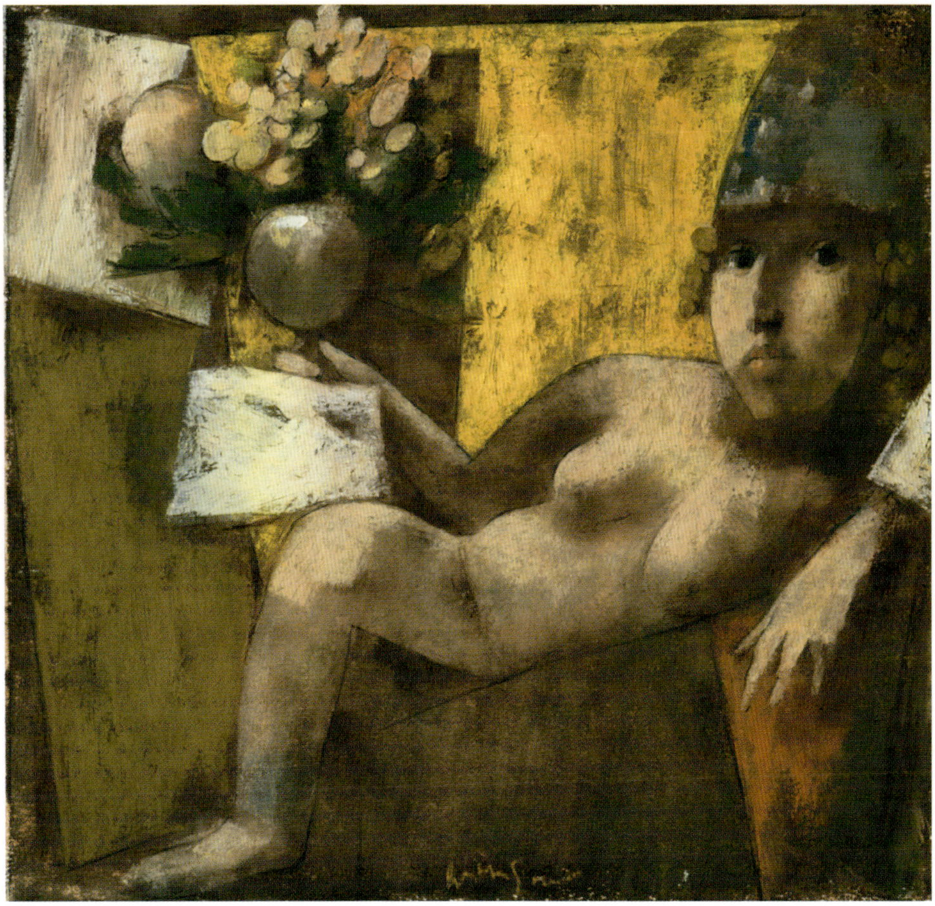

The Bouquet, 1993
oil pastel 8½ x 9"
Private Collection

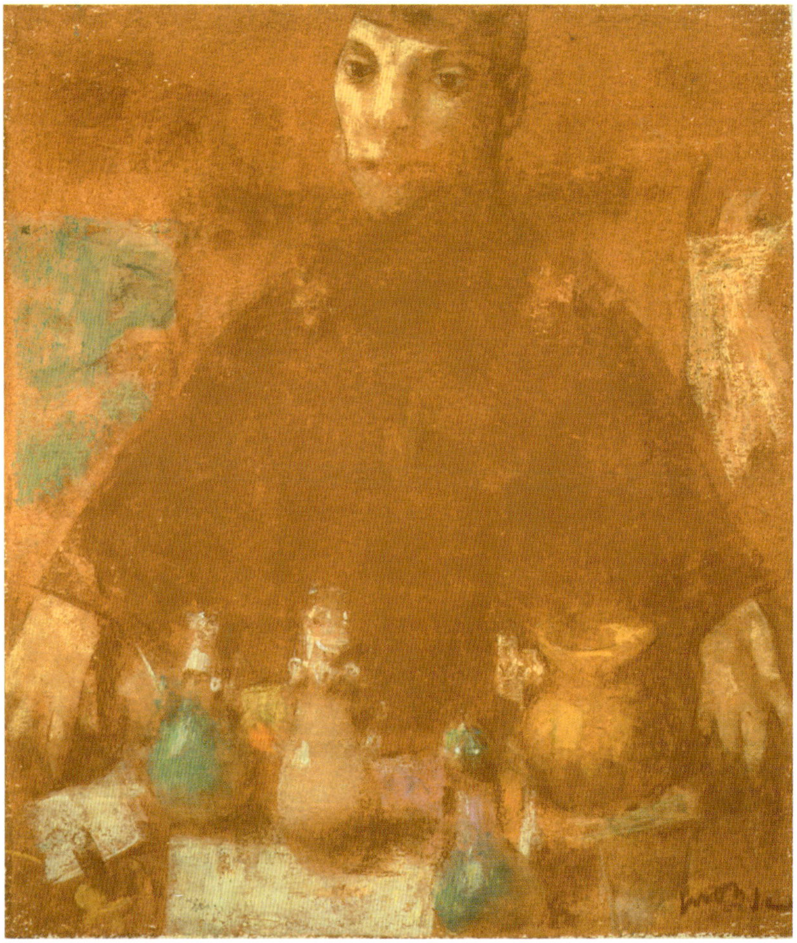

The Alchemist, 1998
oil pastel 11 9/16 x 10 1/8"
Private Collection

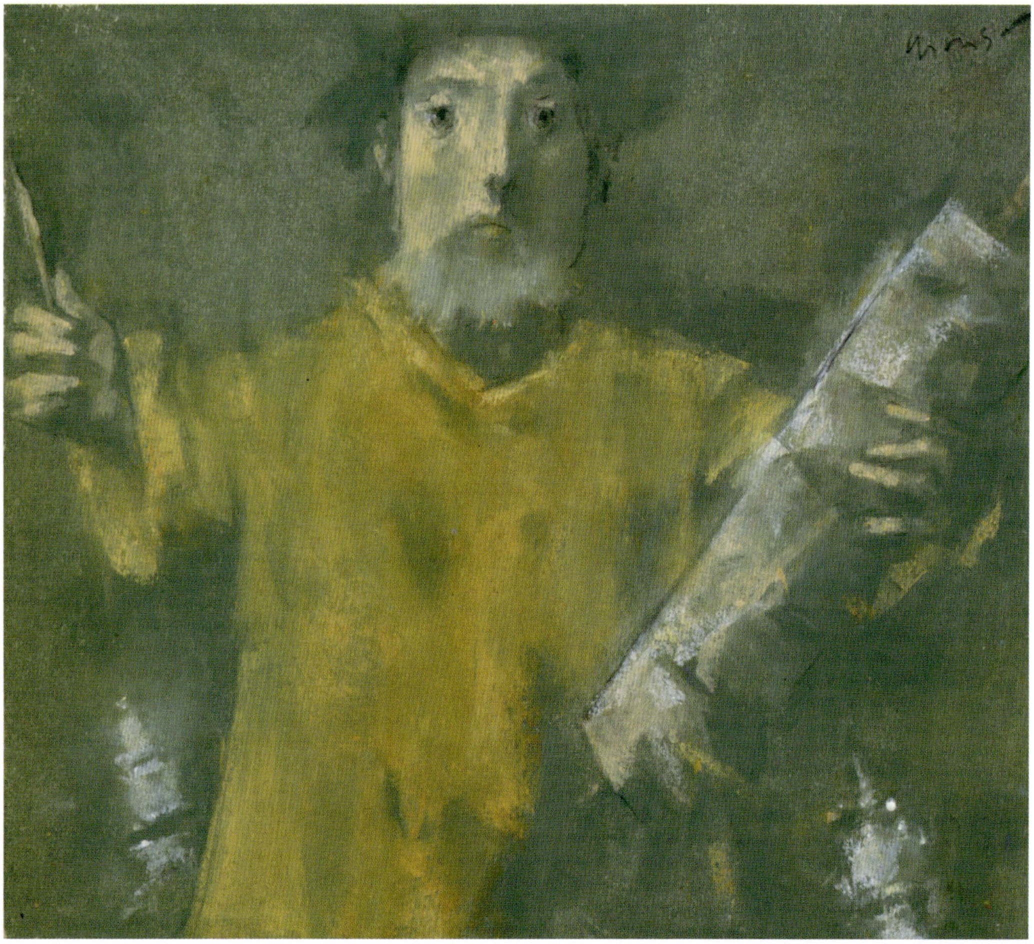

The Scribe, 1996
oil pastel 7 x 8 1/4"
Private Collection

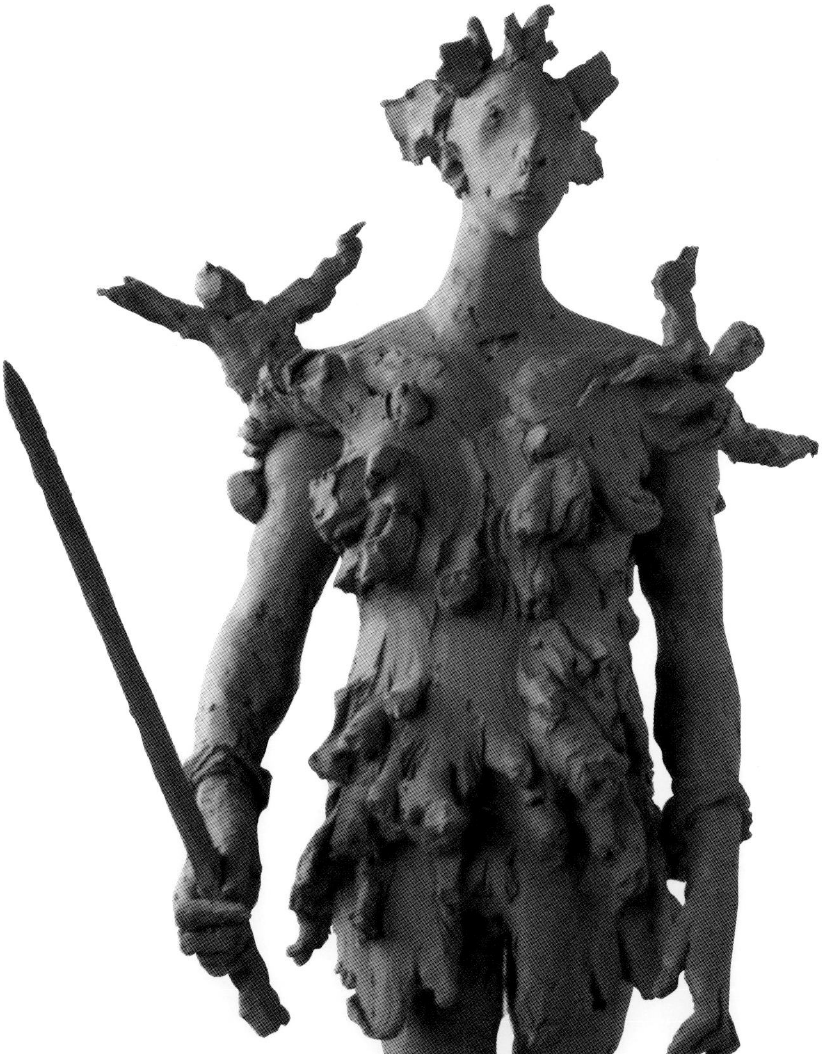

Avenging Angel, 1973-1976 (photographed in clay)
bronze 43 x 18 x 23"

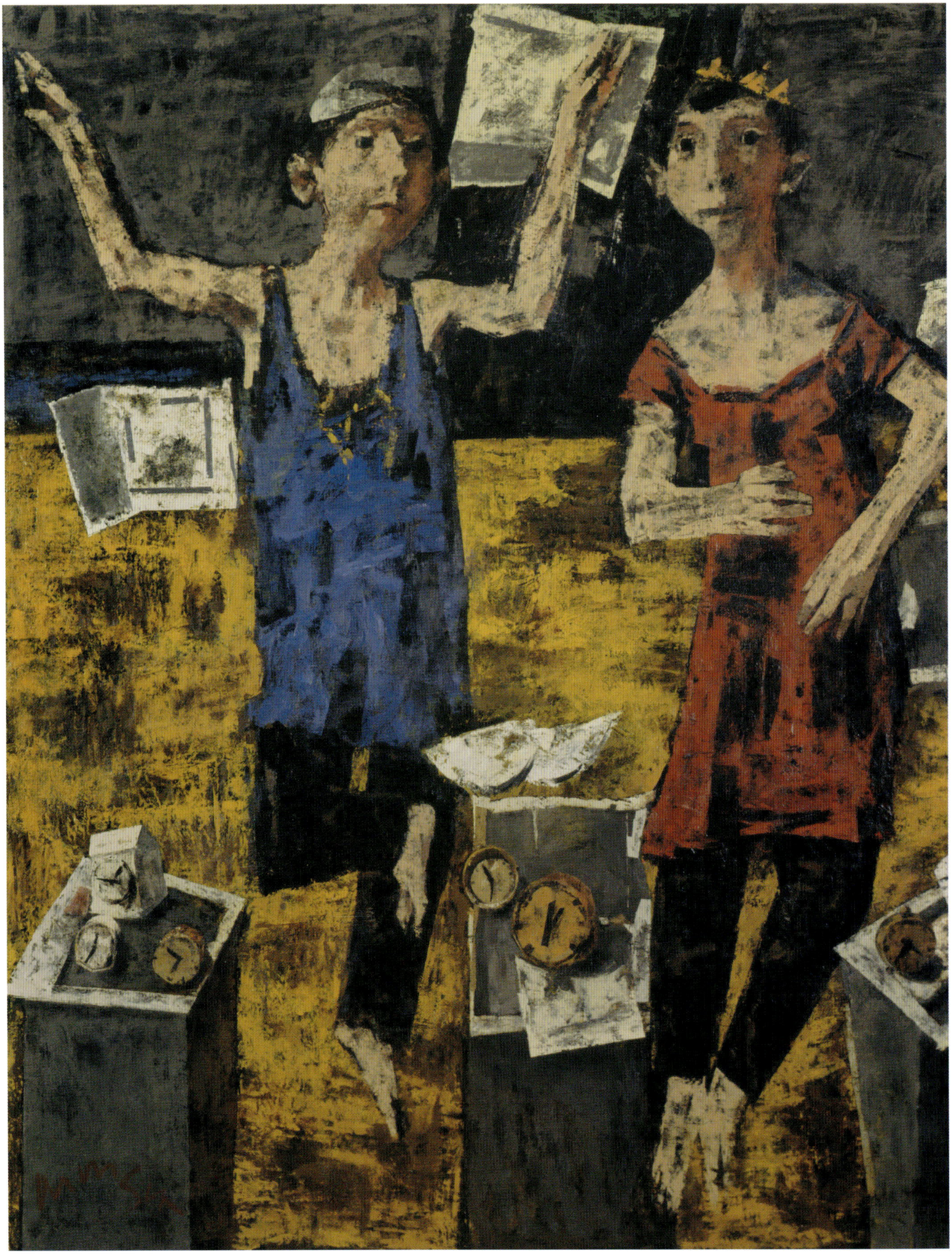

Angels with Clocks, 1993
encaustic on panel 60 x 48"
Private Collection

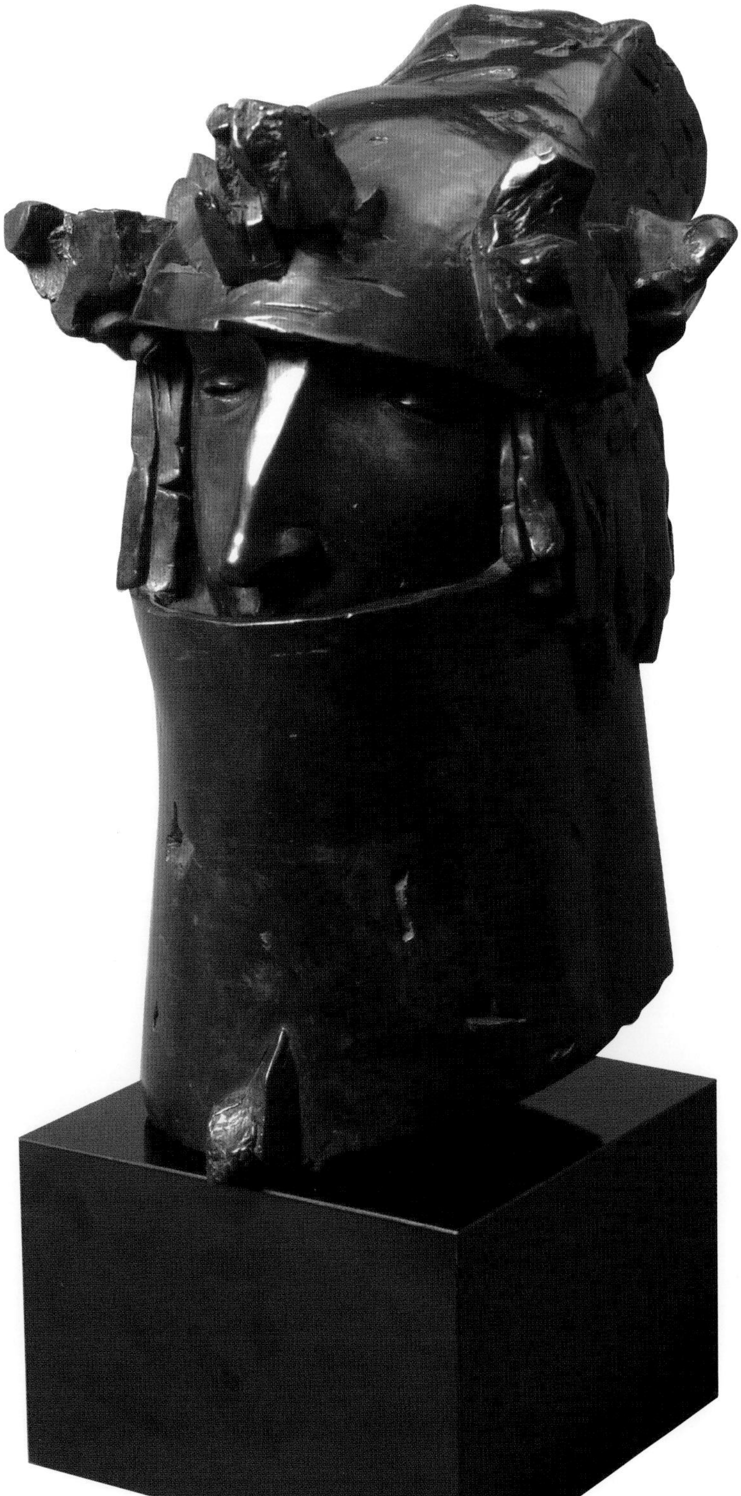

Warrior III, 1995
bronze 14 x 9 x 10¾"

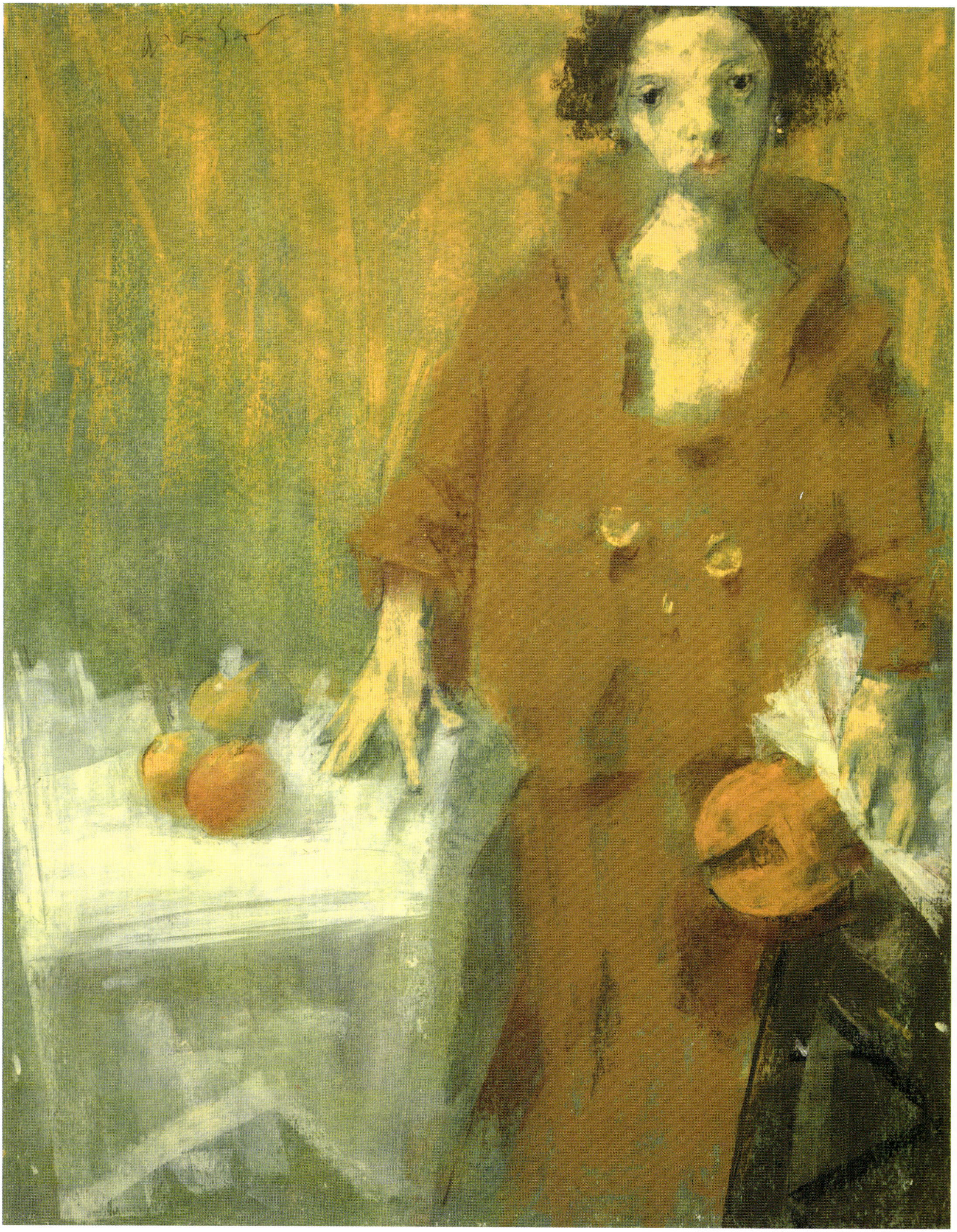

Entertainer, 1998
oil pastel 16 x 13"
Private Collection

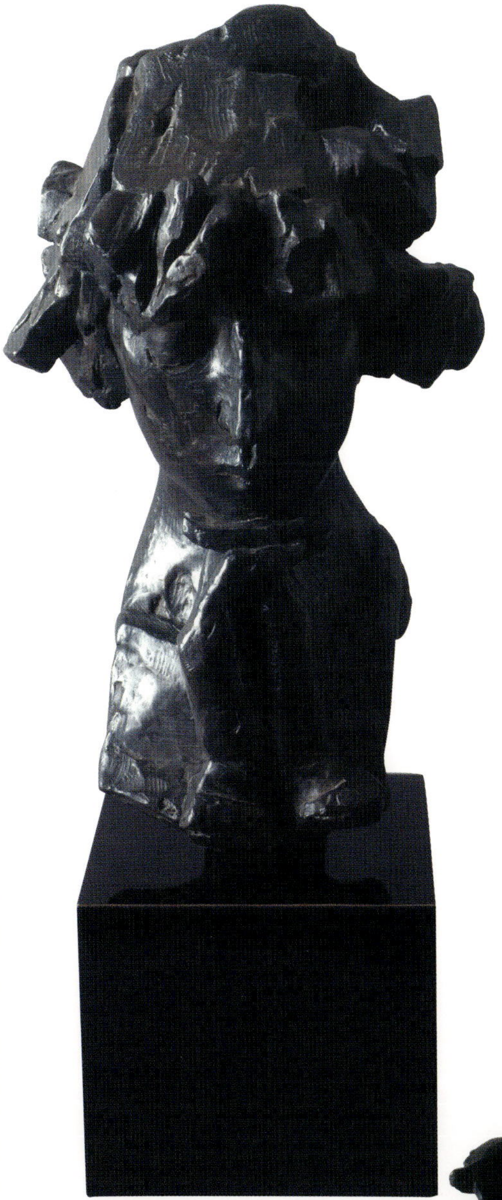

Thinker II, 1983
bronze 14 x 9 x 10¾"

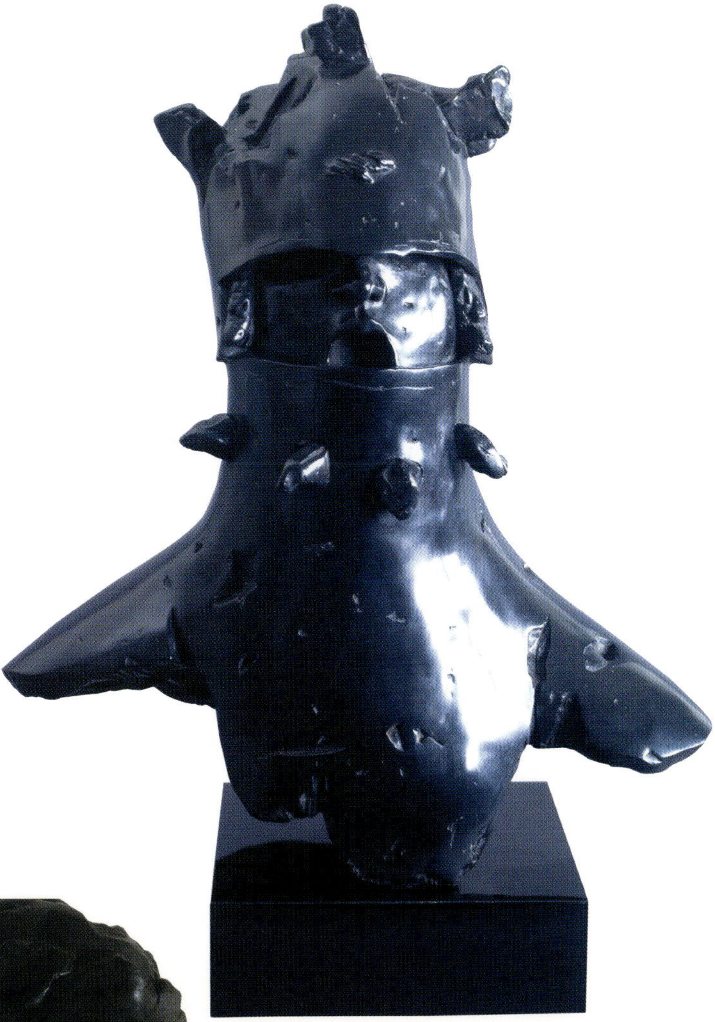

Warrior II, 1995
bronze 30 x 24 x 20"

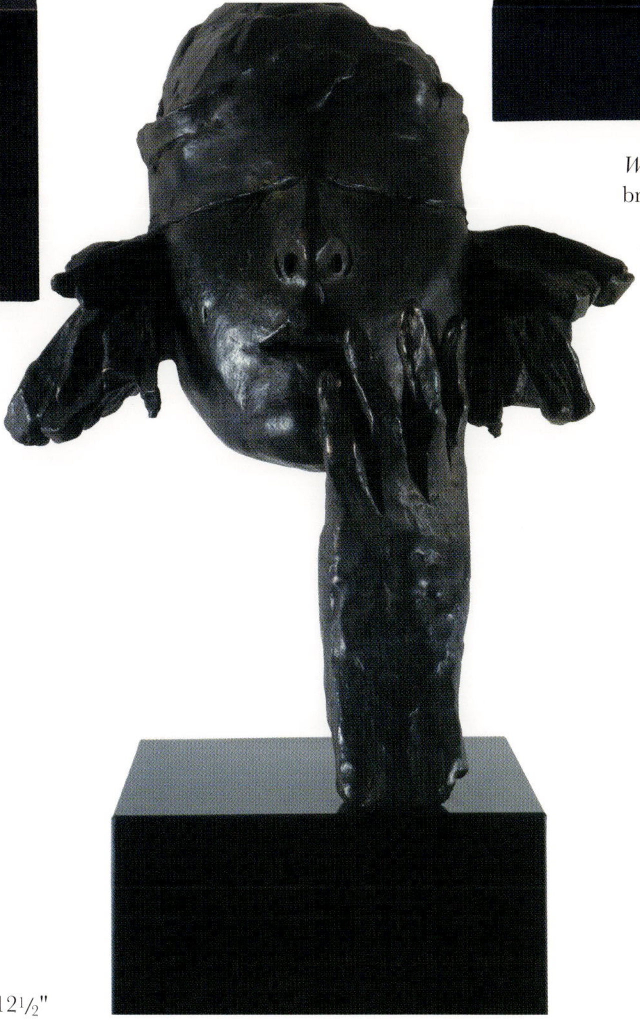

The Medium, 1983
bronze 15 x 13 x 12½"

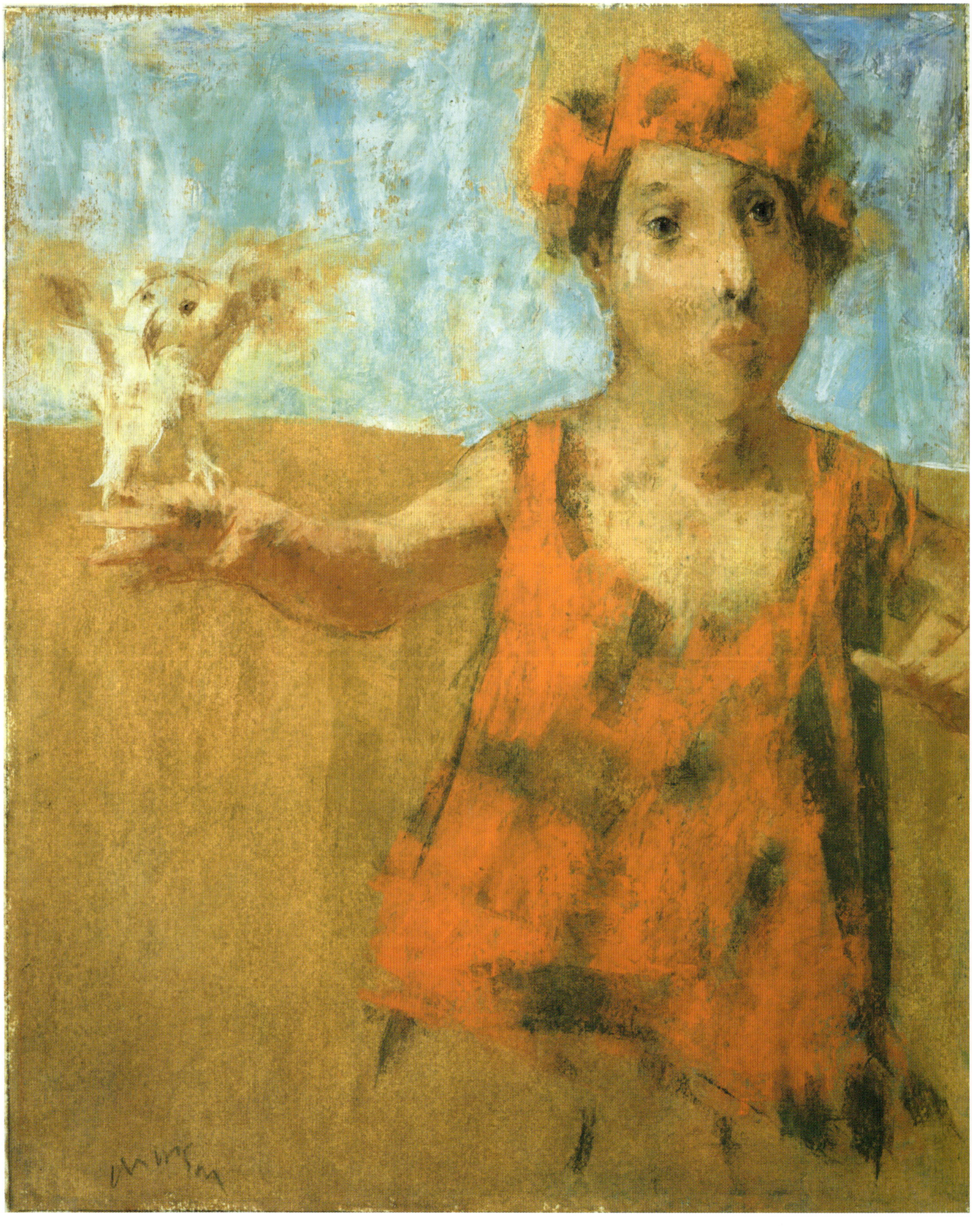

Figure with Bird, 1998
oil pastel $15^3/_8$ x $13^1/_{16}$"
Private Collection

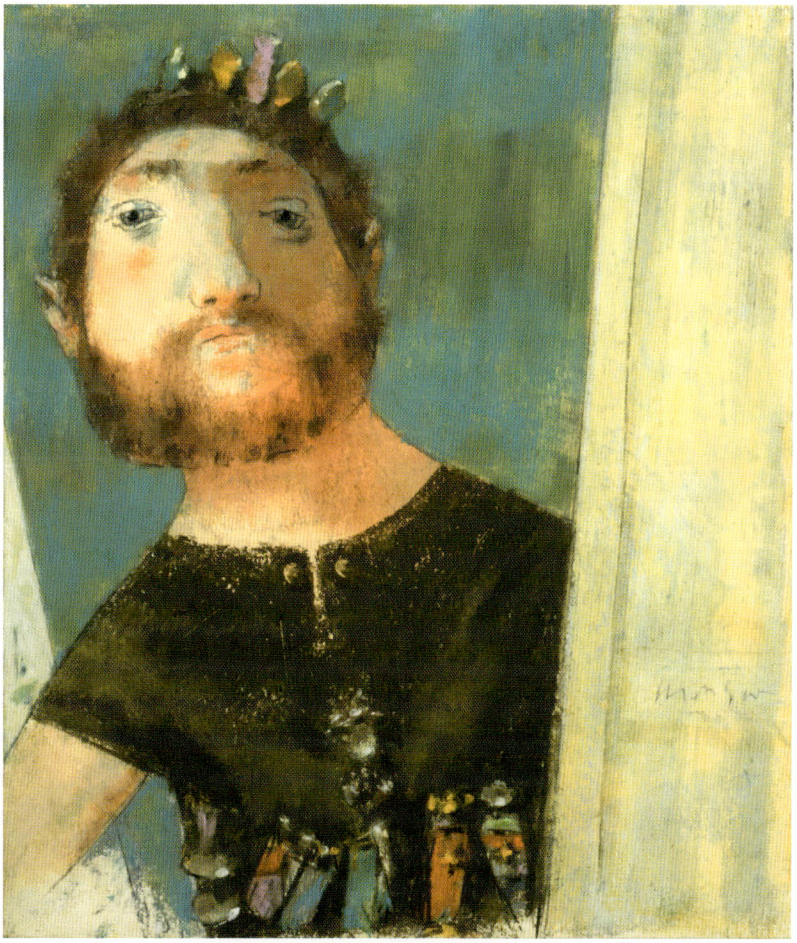

The General, 1999
oil pastel 8¾ x 7⁹⁄₁₆"
Private Collection

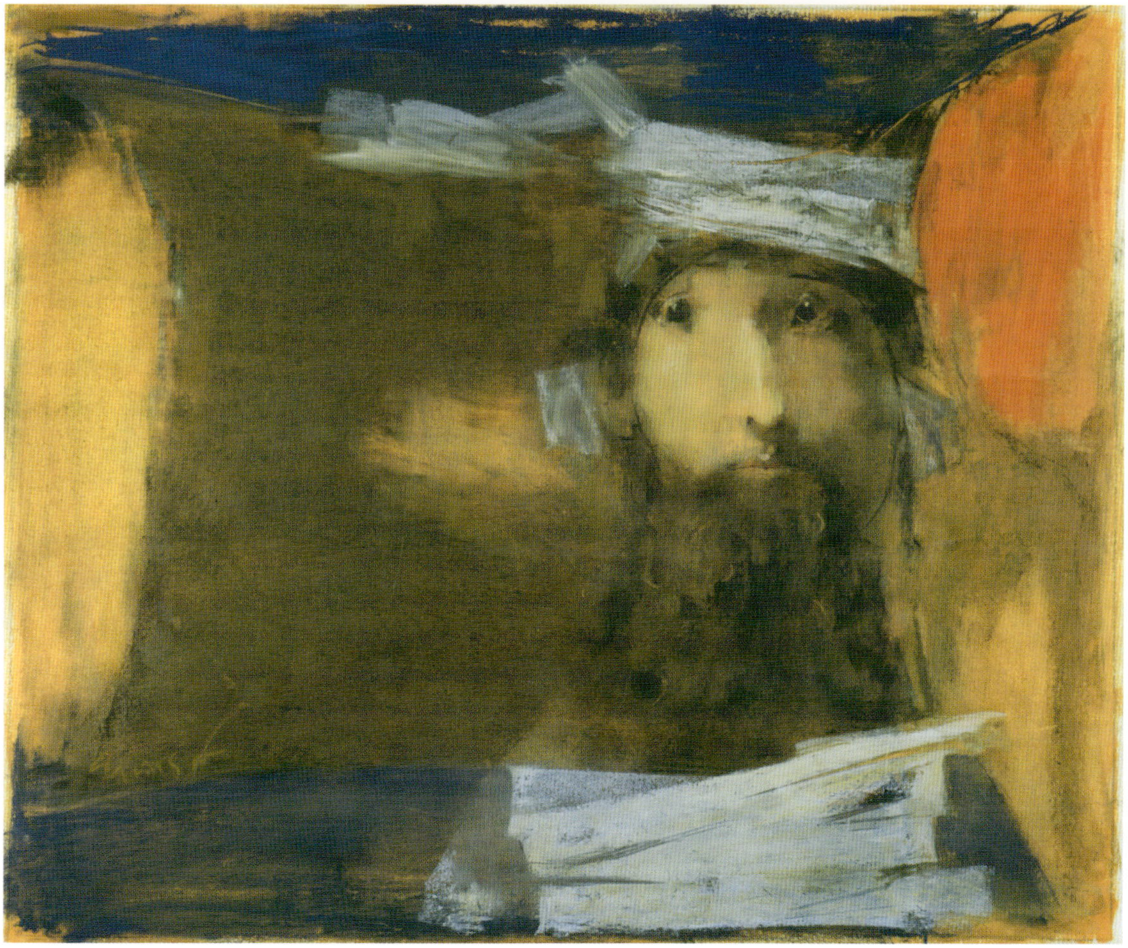

Man in White, 1990
oil pastel
12½ x 15"
Private Collection

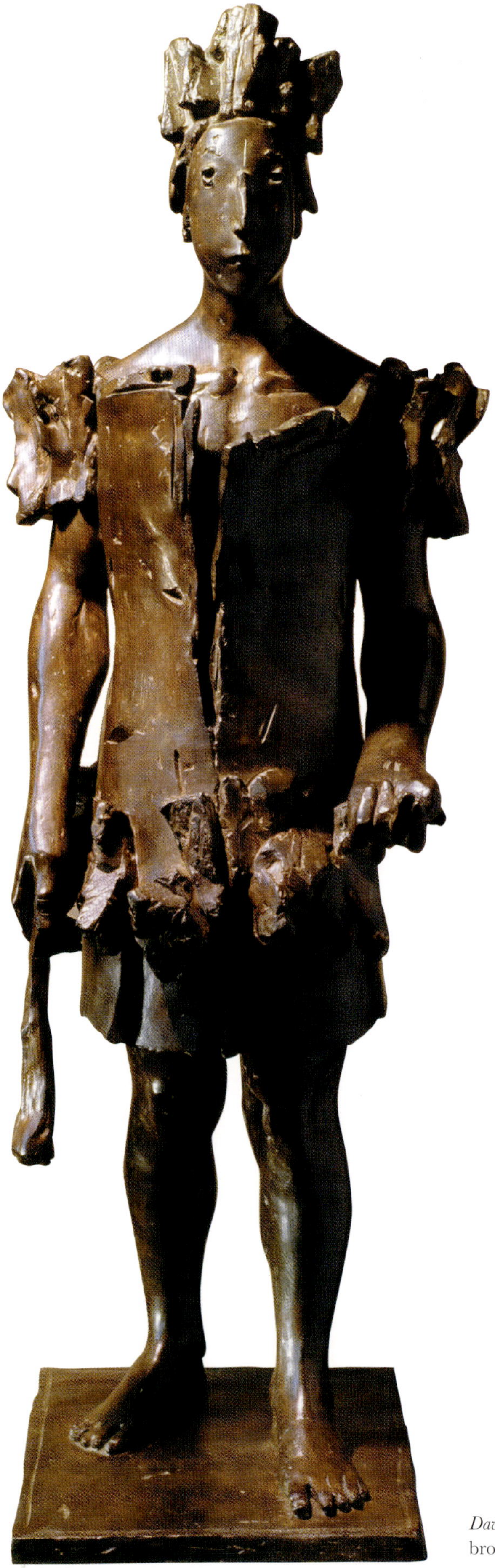

David, 1987
bronze 41 x 13 x 12$^{5}/_{8}$"

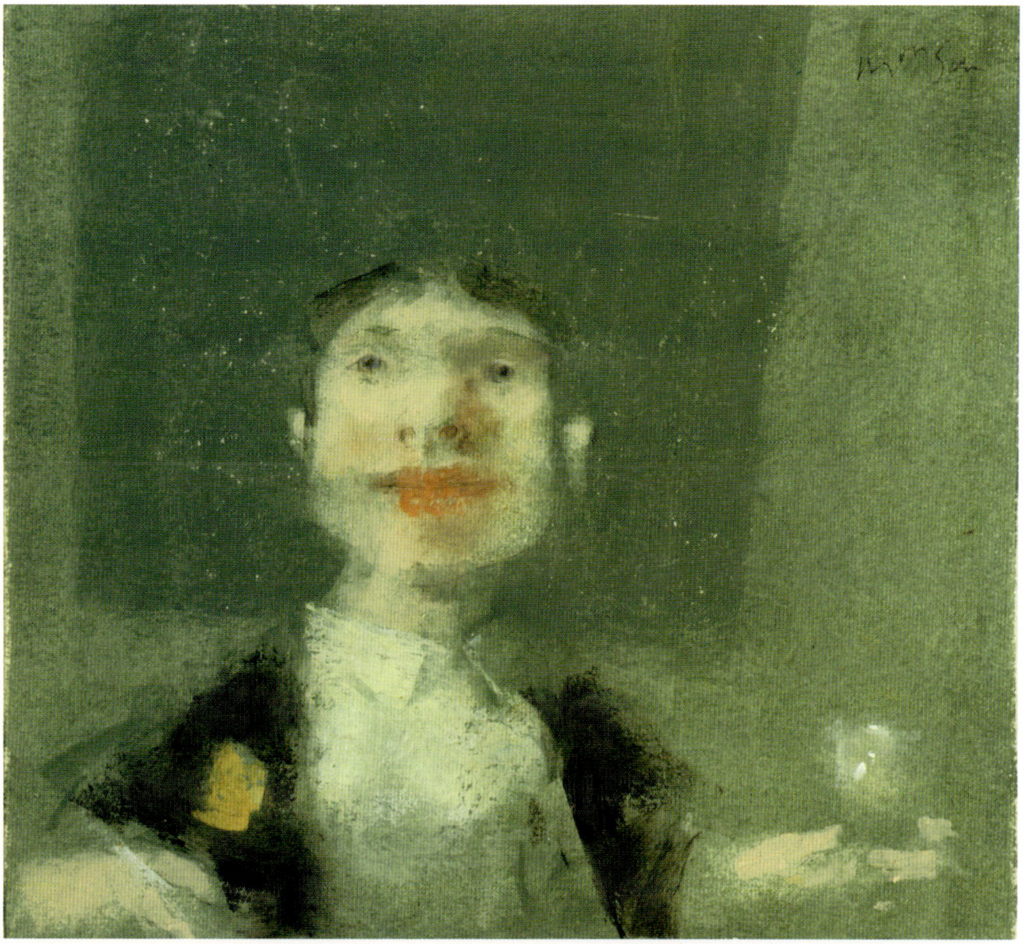

The Hedonist, 1999
oil pastel 7 3/8 x 7 3/8"
Private Collection

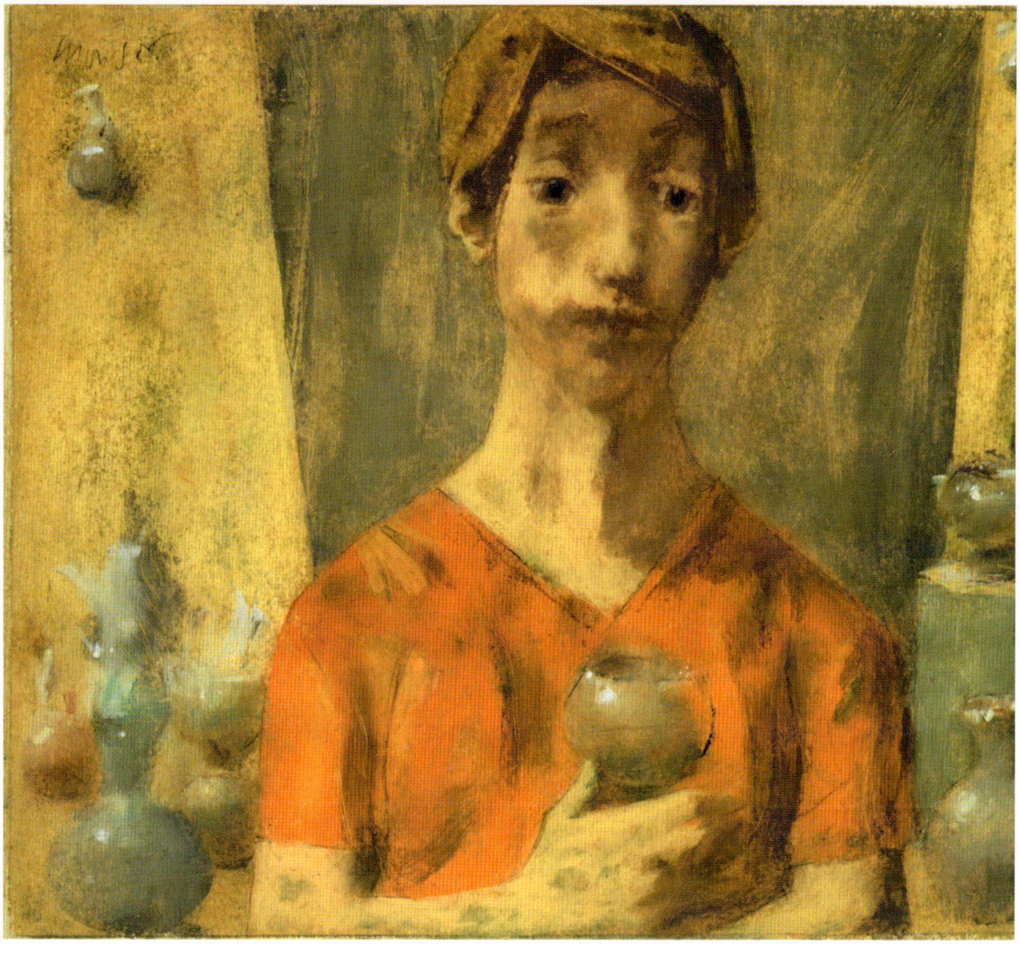

The Collector II, 1999
oil pastel 10 1/8 x 11 5/8"
Private Collection

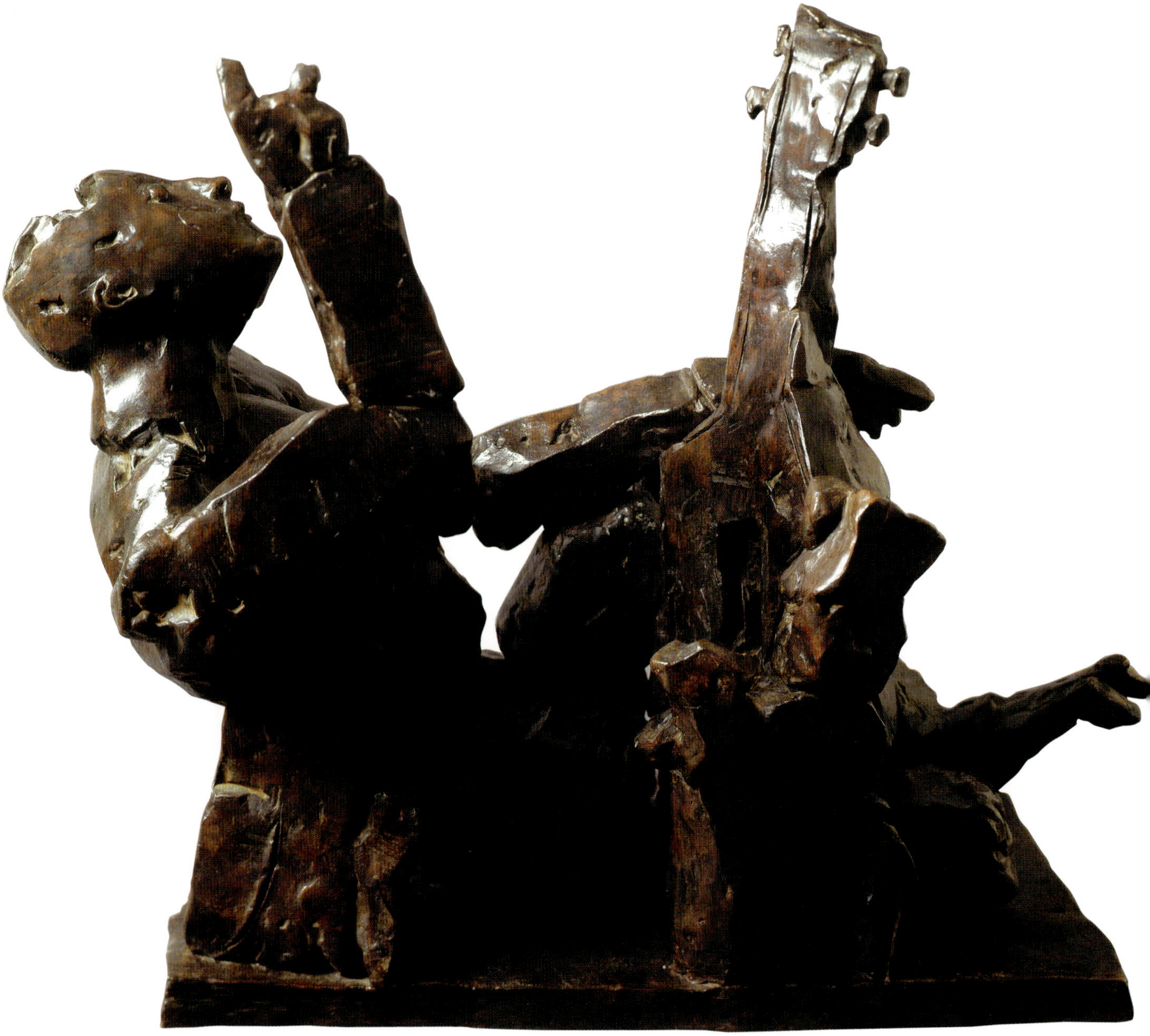

Fallen Angel, 1987
bronze 21 1/2 x 25 1/2 x 16 1/2"

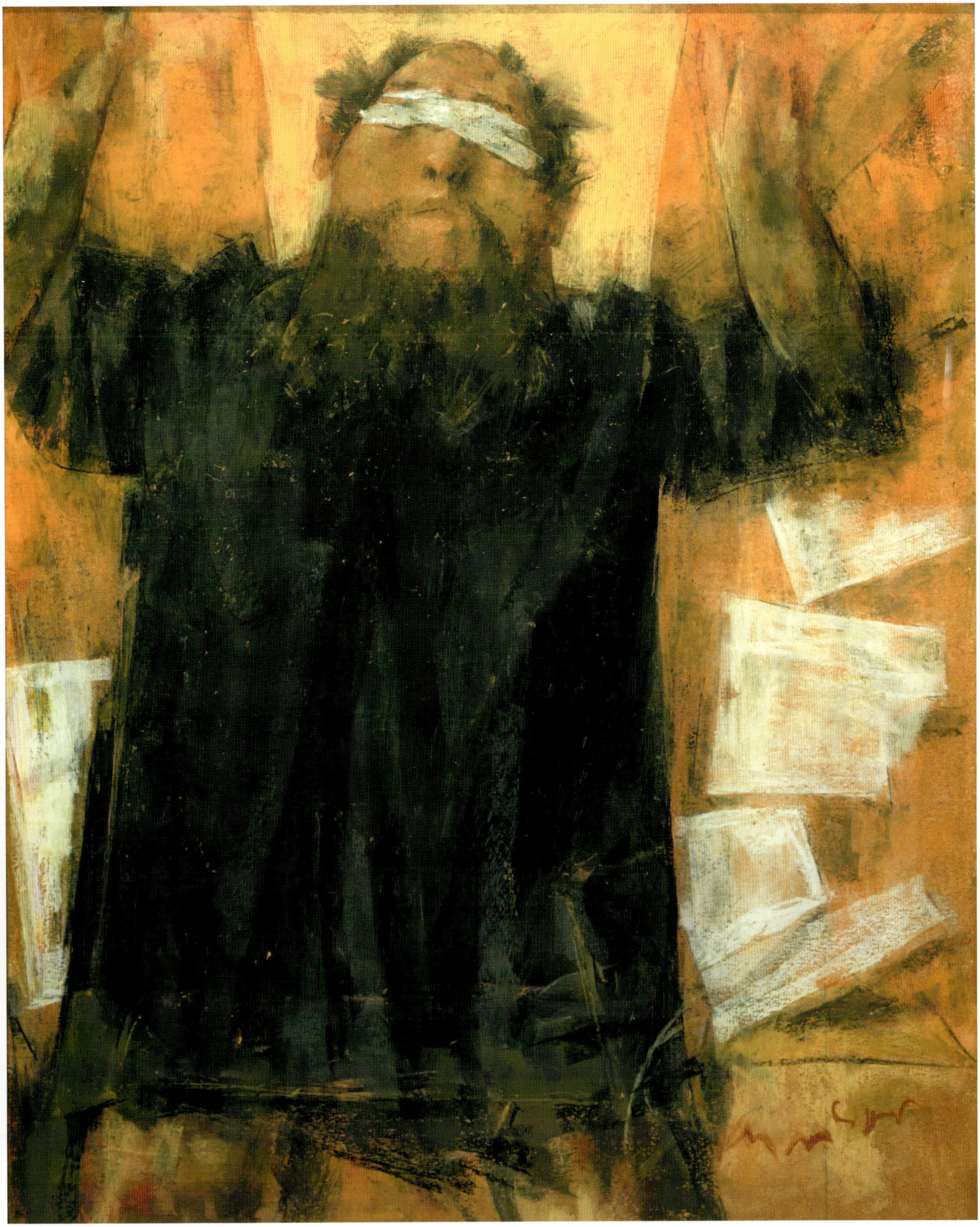

Samson, 1997
oil pastel 22½ x 18½"
Private Collection

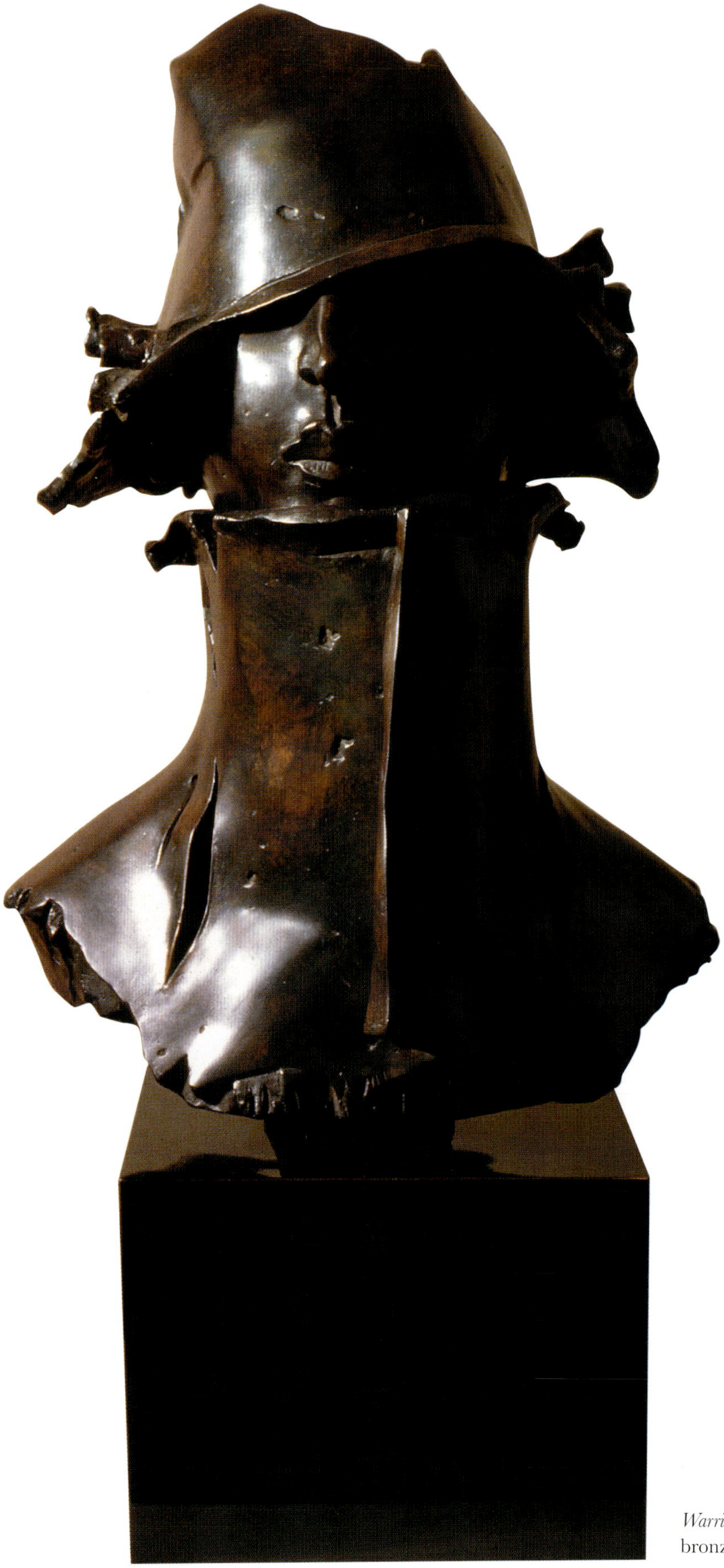

Warrior, 1989
bronze 17 x 12 x 10$\frac{1}{4}$"

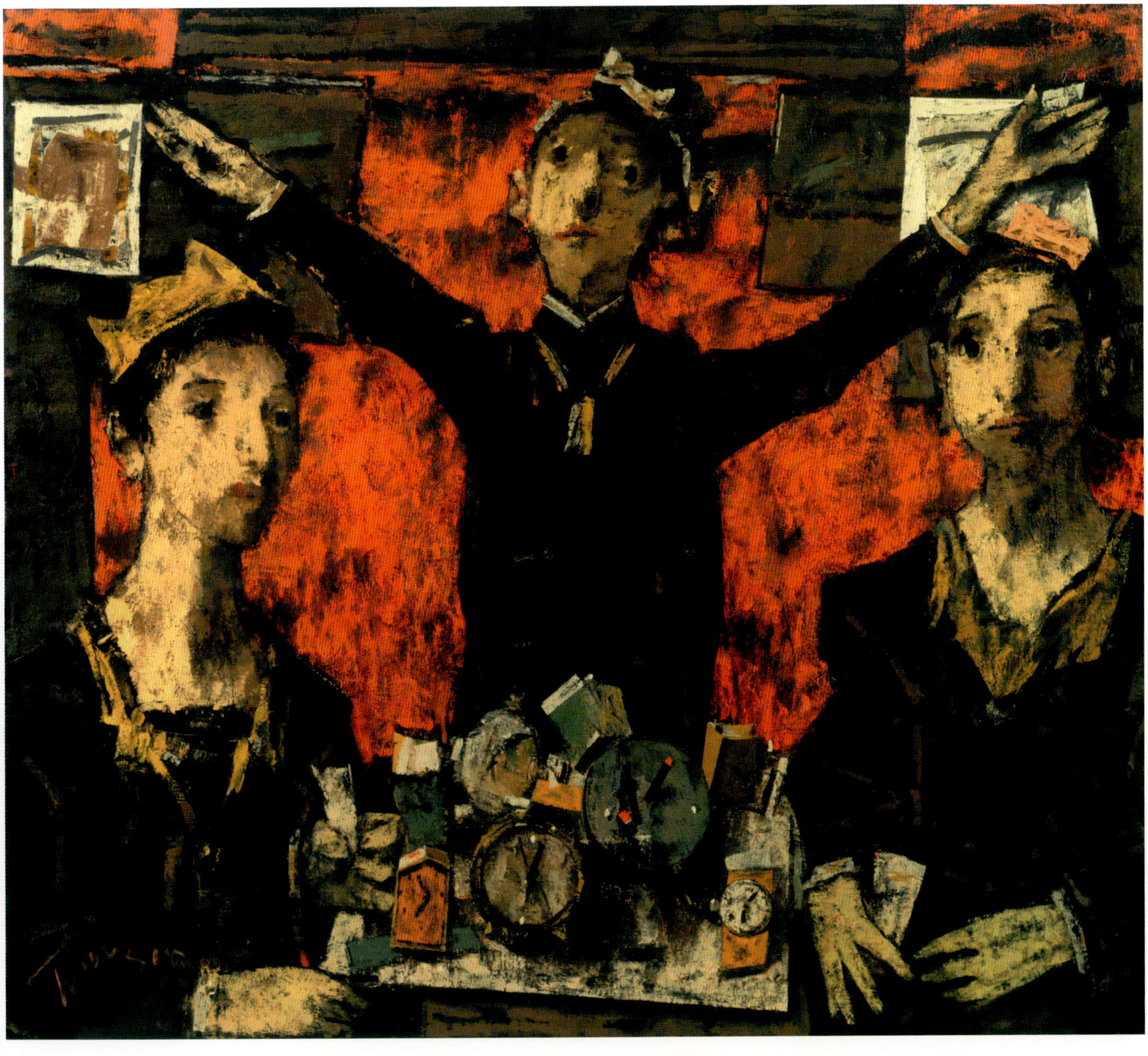

The Timekeepers, 1994
encaustic on board   42 x 48"
Private Collection

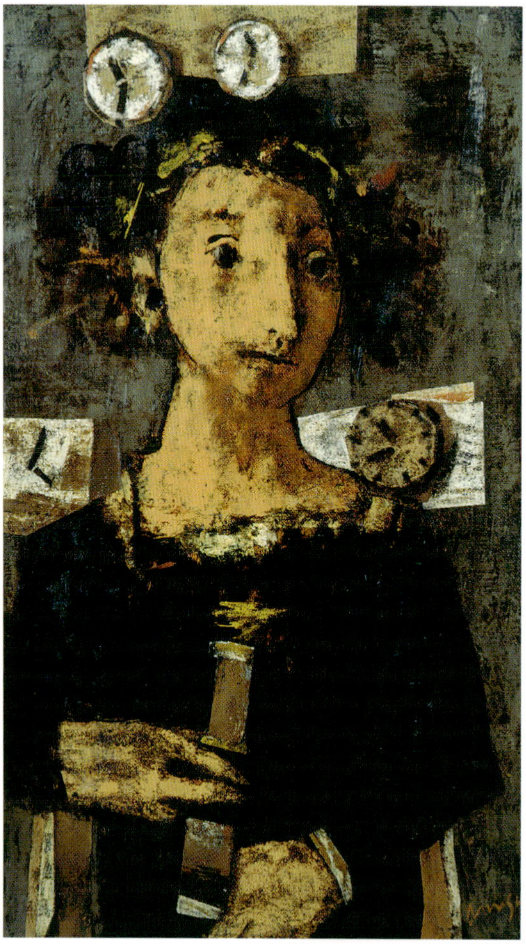

Timekeeper I, 1994
encaustic on board
24 x 14"
Private Collection

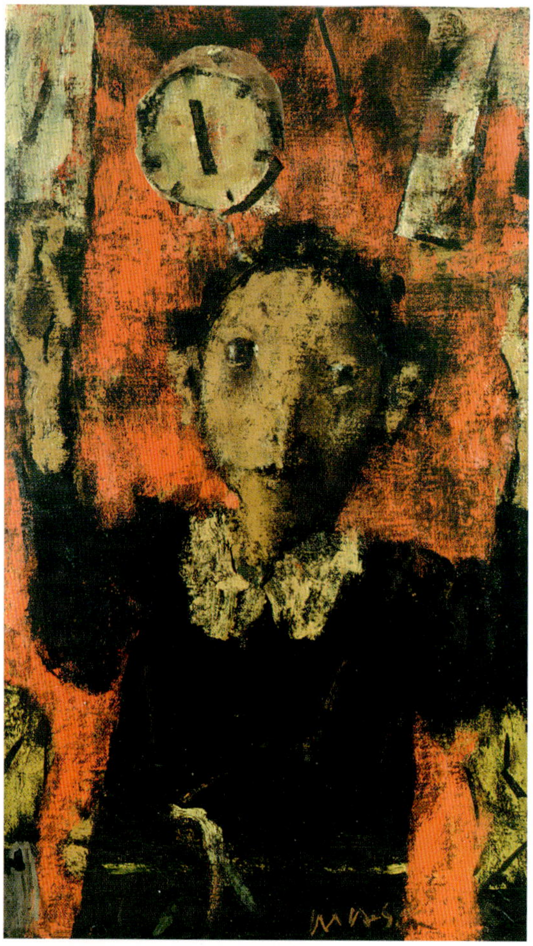

Timekeeper II, 1994
encaustic on board
24 x 14"
Private Collection

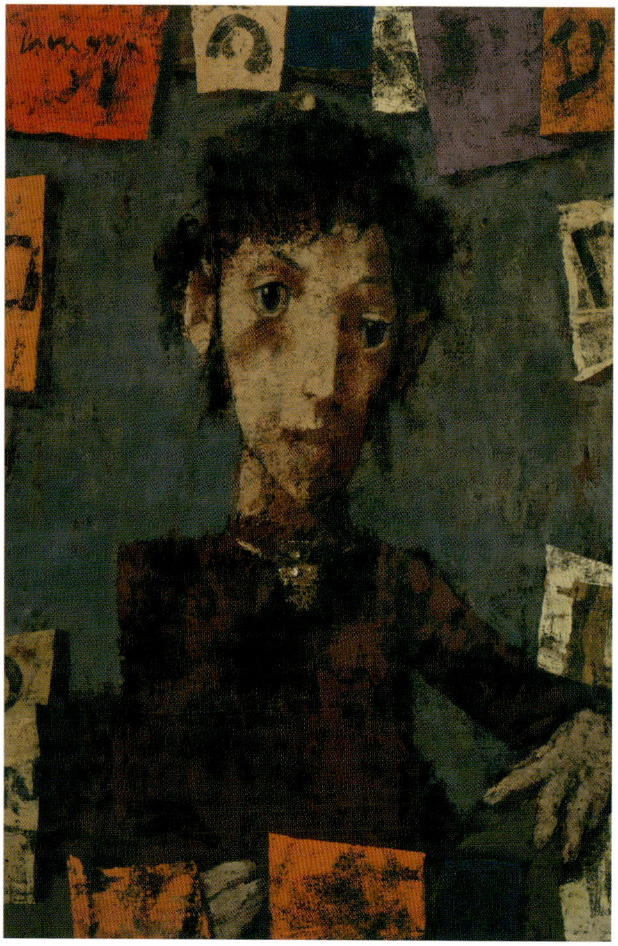

Boy with Amulets, 2000
encaustic on board
$23\frac{3}{8} \times 15\frac{7}{8}$"
Private Collection

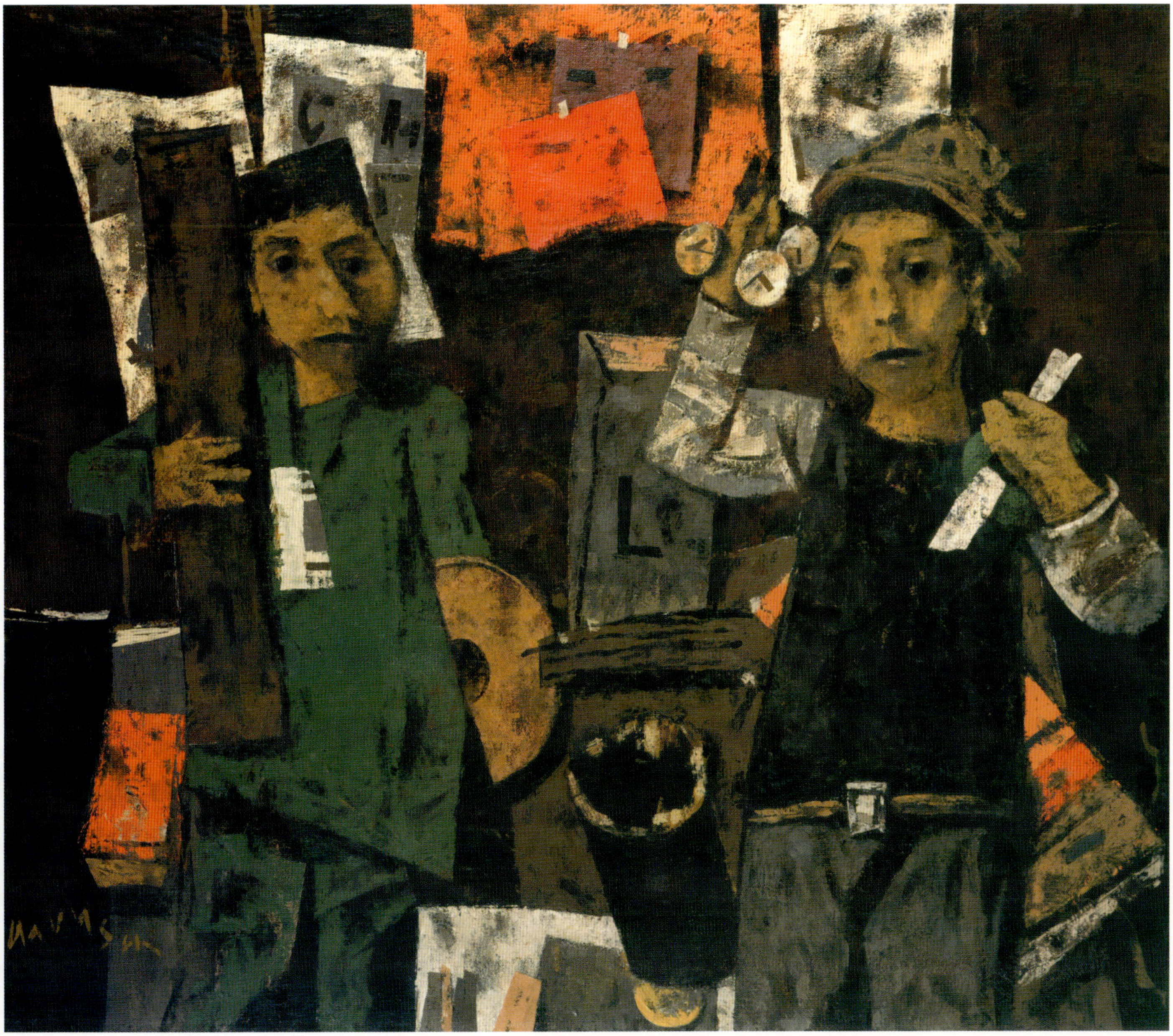

The Pawnbrokers, 2000
encaustic on board 36 x 42"

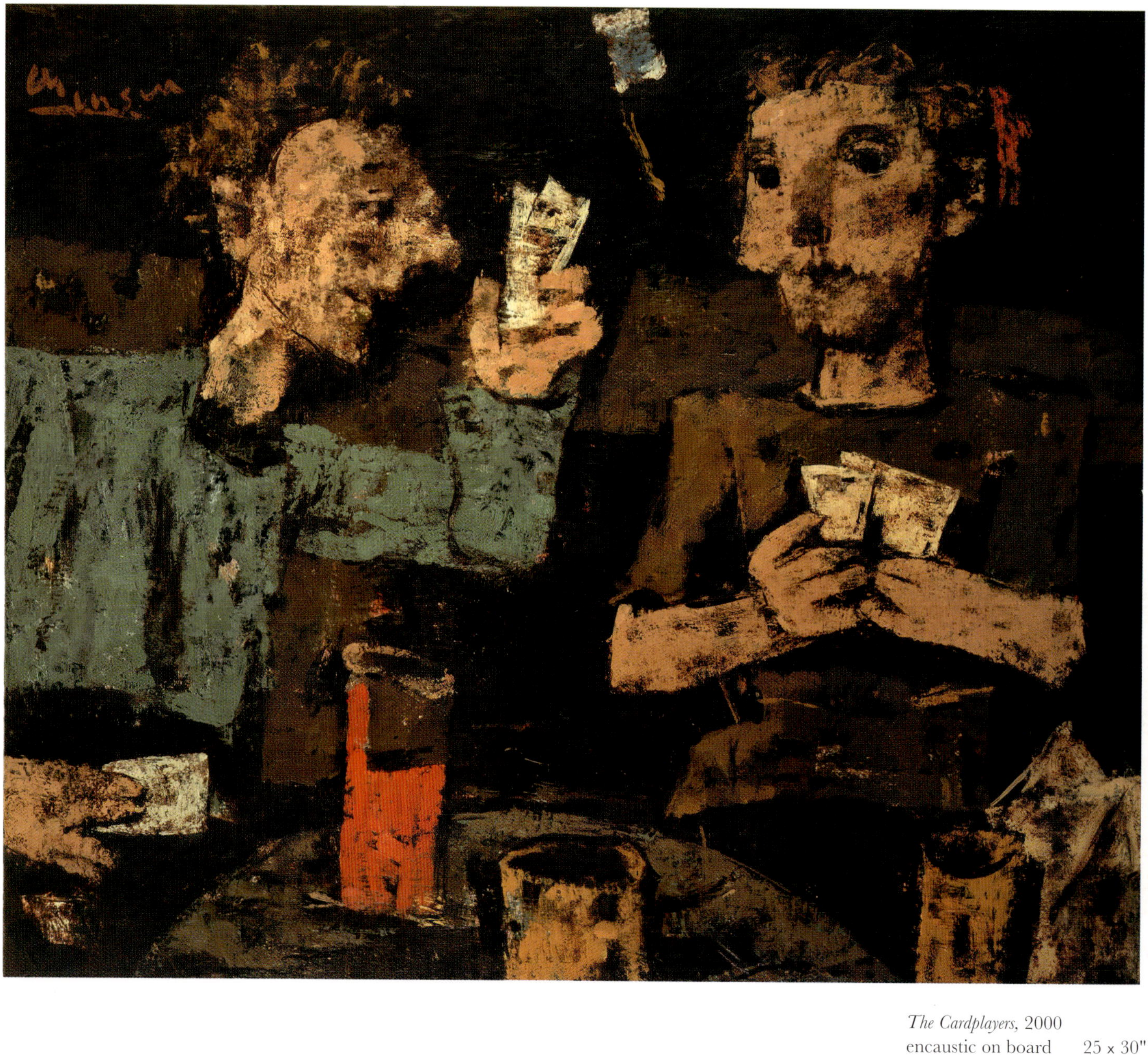

The Cardplayers, 2000
encaustic on board 25 x 30"
Private Collection

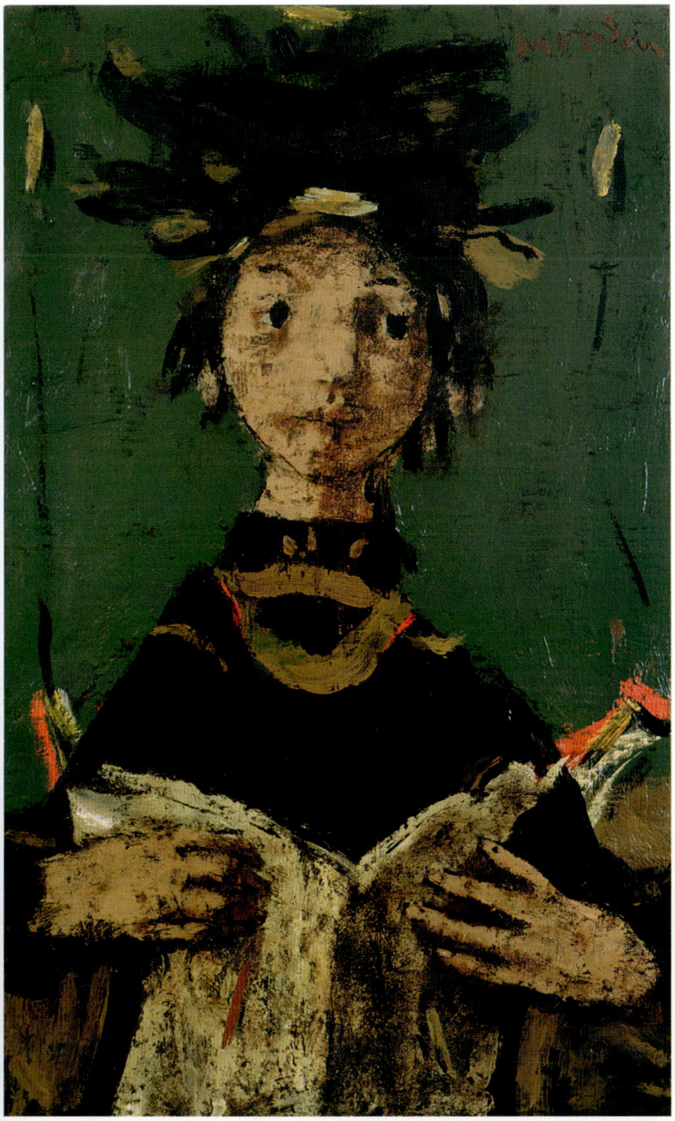

Boy with Feathered Headdress, 1994
encaustic on board $23\frac{1}{2}$ x 26"
Private Collection

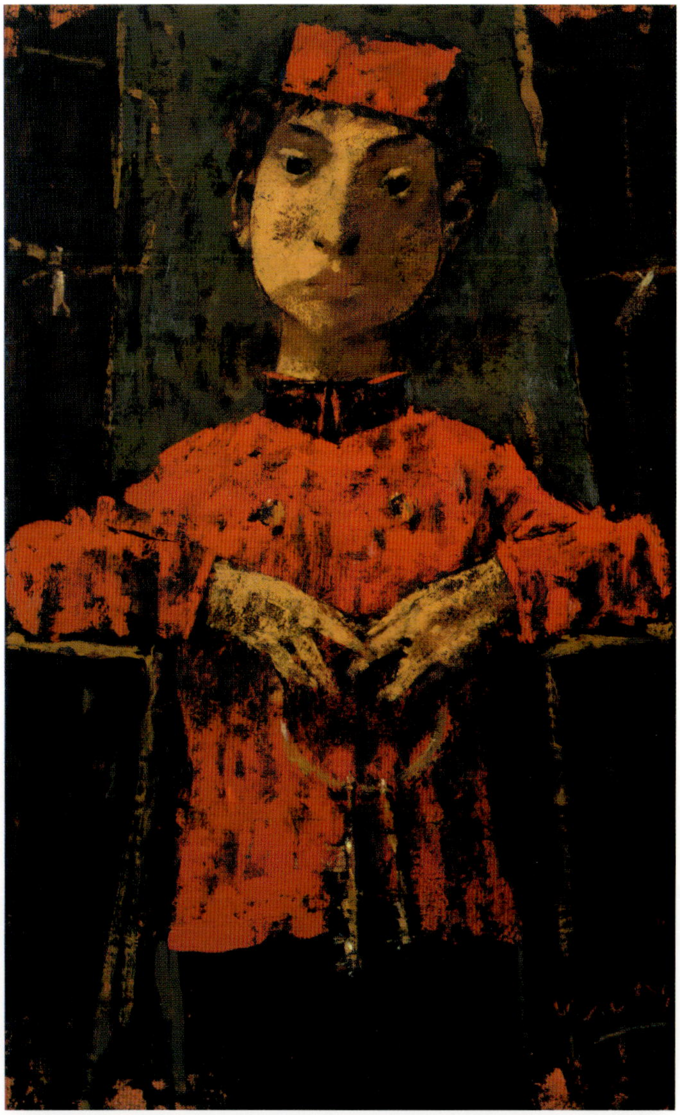

Bell-boy, 2000
encaustic on board 28 x 18"
Private Collection

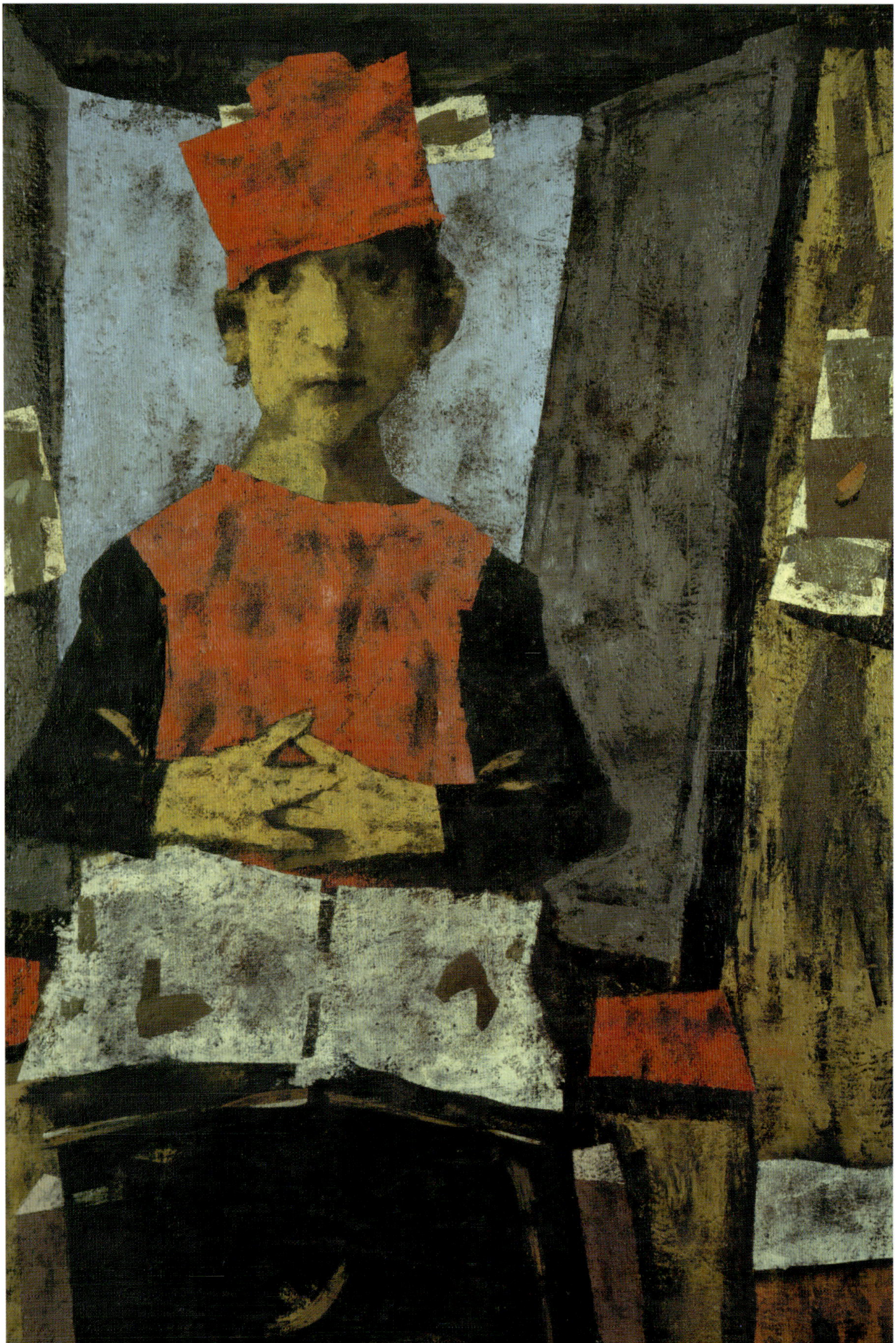

Young Cabbalist, 2001
encaustic on board 30 x 20"
Private Collection

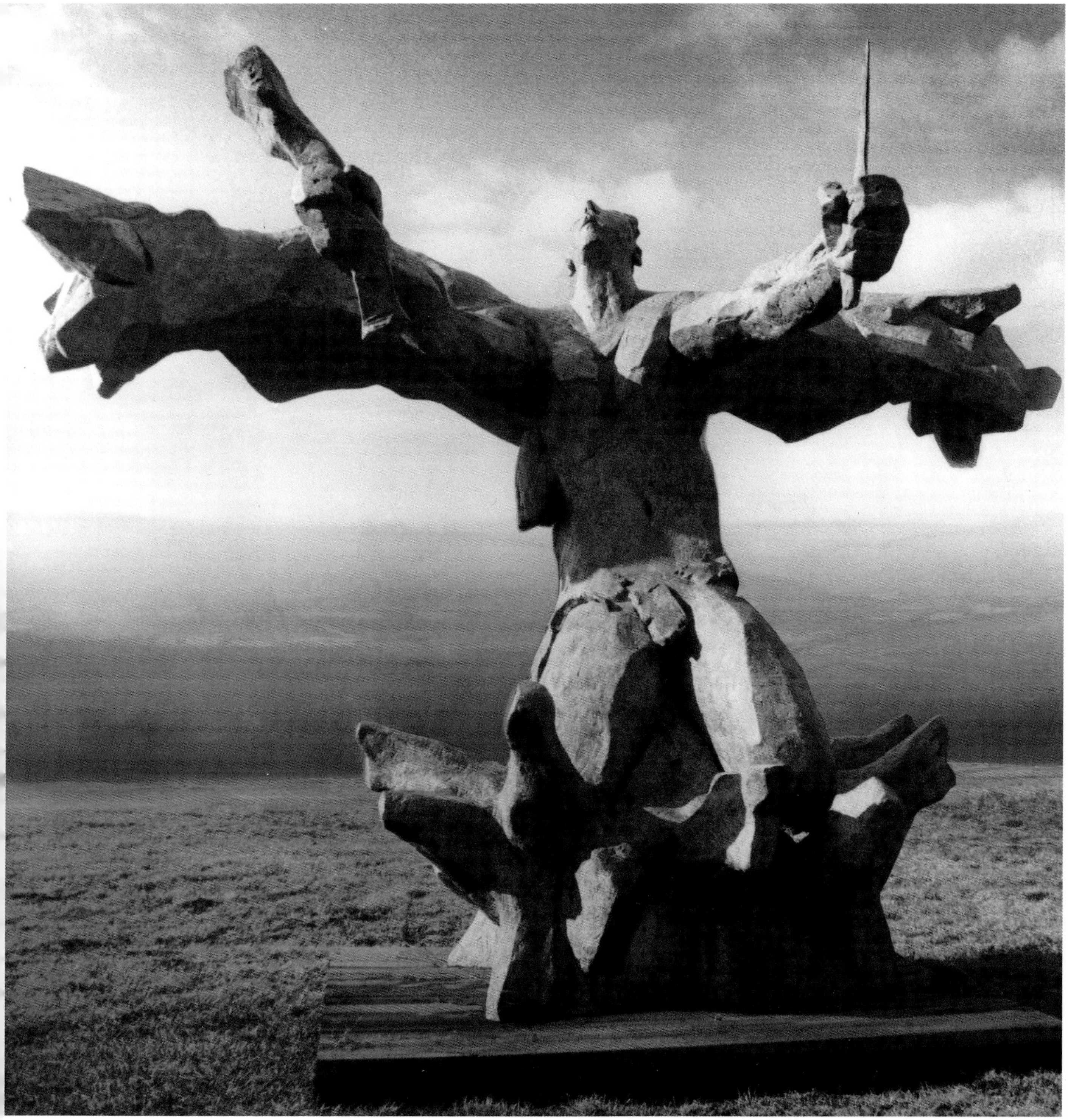

Spirit of Israel, 1986
bronze 108 x 168 x 84"
Collection of Brandeis University, Waltham, MA

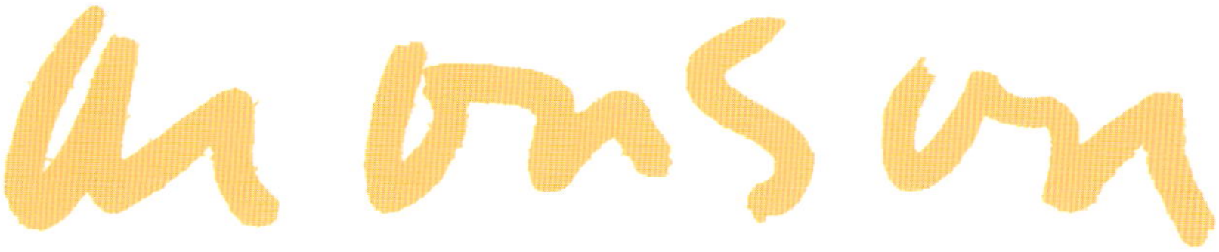

REAL AND UNREAL: THE DOUBLE NATURE OF ART

REAL AND UNREAL:
The Double Nature of Art

by David Aronson

Lecture given at Boston University
upon his appointment in 1967 as University Lecturer

THE ARTIST'S ISOLATION AND alienation have a long history. In Plato's Apology, Socrates went to the poets and artisans and asked them to explain some of their more elaborate works. He confessed in embarrassment that there was hardly a bystander who could not have talked better than the artists themselves about these works. Wisdom, he said, was in no way involved, but rather "a sort of genius and inspiration: they are diviners or soothsayers who say many fine things but do not understand the meaning of them." The artist is seen as something between a dexterous visionary and an idiot savant who, during the trance-like state of artistic creation, is the helpless vision of the uprush of the super-conscious. His body, though subject to the earthiest of appetites, mysteriously becomes the instrument through which pass the purest and most sublime of divine forces. His works, no matter how great, are beyond his control and apprehension and are produced by an emotional disturbance called "Inspiration." It has come to be believed that any use of knowledge would hinder his imagination, that exercise of reason would impede cosmic receptivity, and that reflective decision making on his part would contaminate the creative product. One has only to go to the writings of artists like Cennini and Cellini, Rubens and Reynolds, Da Vinci and Delacroix to find that such romantic notions have no basis in fact. That artists have been verbal and sensitively articulate is demonstrated in the letters Michelangelo, Van Gogh and Pissaro and so many others. This does not mean the artist is always able or willing to transpose essentially non-verbal conceptions and activities into expository phrases or methodical systems. He may find it unworthwhile and even pointless to present for public display matters which are of a most personal or private nature. And, furthermore, the creation of a work of art is not always a very orderly or systematic business. Delacroix remarked, "The pen is not my tool; I am conscious of my thought, but the need for order to which I am obliged to submit I find quite terrifying. Would you believe, but the thought of writing a page gives me a sick headache." Yet he went on to write in his Journal many pages of richly illuminating material which provide extraordinary insights into his creating process.

It might be useful to give here some historical perspective to the early 1940s, the years during which my artistic beliefs took root and grew into a body of work which expressed publicly through a personal imagery my private convictions. The preceding decade had seen the economic depression, and several art movements which grew from it. The socially conscious painters William Groper, Ben Shahn, Robert Gwathmey, Philip Evergood, Raphael Soyer and others recorded the American scene, the people, the poverty and the politics with great fervor. Their work took on the qualities of nationalistic art which was in part a revolt against the international modernism – particularly the French aesthetic. At the same time there was the militant regionalism of painters like Thomas Hart Benton, John Stuart Curry and Grant Wood with their principle spokesperson Thomas Craven who ranted against the "emasculated tradition of the French modernists" and proclaimed the end of American subservience to foreign cultural fashions. Yet alongside this provincialism an American expressionism directly traceable to European forebears spread widely thought this country's art in the works of men like Max Weber, Franklin Watkins, John Marin, Marsden Hartley, Yasuo Kuniyoshi, George Grosz and Abraham Rattner. In the mid 1930s and early 1940s Boston was the center of an Expressionistic style of painting which was influenced by such diverse sources as Rouault and Soutine in France, Kokoschka in Central Europe and Orozco and Siquieiros in Mexico. This came about as a result of the presence in Boston of three influential teachers, Harold Zimmerman, Denman Ross and Karl Zerbe along with the coincidental emigration to Boston of the families of three Jewish painters of Baltic origin, those of Jack Levine, Hyman Bloom and myself. Zimmerman, a Boston high school teacher, and Ross, a Harvard professor and color theorist with a wide knowledge of art, helped Levine and Bloom develop their own styles. Years later, Karl Zerbe, a fine teacher, accomplished painter and technician, encouraged me in my preoccupation with humanistic expressionism and its deep involvement in spiritual and psychological values. By the mid 1930s Levine and Bloom, though very young, were making mature artistic statements. I did not begin to produce pictures till a decade later. The early works of all three show a great debt to Rouault and Soutine. Beyond that, each moved in his own direction.

My own choice of religious subjects stemmed largely from my proximity to them during the formative years. I grew up in a setting still redolent in the atmosphere of the Eastern European Jewish village. The New World made only slight inroads into a closely ordered family hierarchy and pattern of living centered around breadwinning, the synagogue and religion-related scholarship. These were people for whom religion was the main purpose for survival and for whom figurative art was denied by Scriptural precept. The male child was prepared from the earliest age by means of a rigorous religious education for entrance into the adult religious community through the ceremony of confirmation at the age of thirteen. During my own period of preparation for this ritual, I found that the ceremonial trapping had lost contact with the real meaning of the event. My father was a rabbi, and I was destined to be the same and might yet have been except for the fact that I committed the combined profanations of refusing confirmation and choosing as my life's work that which is prohibited in the second commandment – the making of graven images.

About 25 years ago, while studying to become a painter at the Boston Museum School, I painted a picture of a group of characters passing the time in a café. Against the back wall rose two Gothic church windows, and on the right, serving to support one of the figure's arms was a 2 x 3 inch panel upon which was hung a motley collection of jewel-like junk. Here, in my first painting which I called *The Paradox*, I expressed with the carefree enthusiasm of a second year art student, the bravura desire to produce, with a two-haired brush, minuscule objects with a heightened sense of realism, against the setting of my orthodox religious background and a passing interest in Jazz. To ascribe to this curious combination of objects and ideas anything more than a flippant observation on society would under no stretch of the imagination have occurred to me. With a persisting levity, I felt attracted to works that tweaked the nose of a morally deficient society such as Goya's painting of Charles the Fourth and the royal family – a magnificent painting of idiots, sadists and perjurers, resplendent in silks, jewels, and medals where the Queen, licentious and haggard, stands beside the good-natured boor of a King. I marveled at these splendid characterizations not the least of which was the remarkable resemblance between her son and her lover on the extreme right. Or I would look with pleasure at Veronese's *Christ in the House of Simon* where, during an event destined for the immortality of the ages, Peter, who sits at the table to the right of Christ, is nonchalantly picking his teeth with his fork. And while I reveled in anything that punctured convention, I recoiled in the face of a great art tradition from dignifying my own work with significance. Yet it was the confrontation with the religious subject of seeming incompatibilities and incongruities such as I presented quite unconsciously in my first painting that became the recurring theme in my work as a professional artist.

My earliest interests in painting centered around the illusionistic *trompe l'oeil* or fool-the-eye paintings of the 17th century Haarlem painters and the magic realism of painters like Harnett, Dali and Albright. It was as though I could make plausible the improbabilities of mysterious and vague themes through insistence on an exact technique and a meticulously detailed rendering. A decorative detail from a

Fontainbleau carving, photographed in sharp focus suggested to me the backdrop for a painting called *Trinity*. Here, I visualized my forms, the large ones and the profusion of small ones, in raking light to dazzle the vision, and along with the heightened focus increase the picture's impact. And my concern with the illusionistic properties of light and dark went hand in hand with what was for me a great discovery, one I had made many years back which allowed for the materialization of my fantasies. I learned later, of course, that all artists are aware that exciting images may be found in cloud formations, wallpaper designs, frost on a window, etc. *Leonardo in his treatise on painting wrote on The Method of Awakening in the Mind a Variety of Inventions,* "I will not omit to introduce among these precepts a new kind of speculative invention, which though apparently trifling, and almost laughable, is nevertheless of great utility in assisting the genius to find variety for composition. By looking attentively at old and smeared wall or stones and veined marbles of various colors you may fancy that you see in them several compositions, landscapes, battles, figures in quick motion, strange countenances and dresses with an infinity of other objects. By these confused lines, the creative genius is excited to new exertions." Odilon Redon also spoke of provoking the imagination by looking long enough at veins of marble, misted windows, wallpaper and cloud formations. The fact that I discovered this for myself is important, for the phenomenon had that much more meaning. It is worth mentioning too, that the timely accident and unexpected development do not require scientific substantiation to justify their place as part of a valid artistic discipline. Reyonlds said in his *Discourses,* "Accident in the hands of an artist who knows how to take advantage of its hints will often produce bold and capricious beauties of handling and facility such as he would not have thought of or ventured under the regular restraint of his hand." And Stravinsky in his *Poetics of Music,* said, "If his finger slips, he will notice it; on occasion he may draw profit from something unforeseen that a momentary lapse reveals to him." Such occurrences in the right place, at the right time and recognized immediately, may propel the work toward new and exciting involvements.

Though the title I gave to this early painting did not have specific reference to the Holy Trinity, I would not deny its religious implications, since I was then in the midst of my own perhaps immature but necessary rebellion against an authoritarian, orthodox environment chafed by its claims of exclusive salvation. As an antidote I explored the subjects of the New rather than the Old Testament, feeling comfort in their midst both in regard to the common patrimony and in the fact that they had supplied rich material for the greatly admired Old Masters. And yet, as much as I rejected the authoritarian ethos from my own past, I did moralize and presented what I felt to be universal biblical truths against a background of a self-righteous Christianity contained in its bureaucratic institutional shell. Though the grotesque characterizations mirrored to an extent such concerns, they represented even more my abiding wish to work with the human figure in expressing my artistic beliefs and with the human face and hands in particular. I can recollect that as a child I would draw a variety of facial types and would become fascinated by the limitless variations in the features. Leonardo spoke of ten different sorts of noses in profile: "Straight, hunched, concave, some raised above, some below the middle, aquiline, flat, round and sharp. In the front view," he continued, "there are eleven different sorts: Even, thick in the middle, thin in the middle, thick at the tip, thin at the beginning. Broad, narrow, high and low nostrils; some with large opening and some more shut toward the tip." To these I added a few of my own, doing the same with eyes, mouths, chins, ears, foreheads, necks, cheeks and skull shapes. While a very young art student, I would take my drawing pad into the subway and ride for hours while studying and drawing the passengers. Each car had its own dramatis personae. With such experiences began a continuing interest in characterization through endless reassembling of seen and imagined facial features.

We each pass our days carrying on simultaneously two different lives – the personal, private one and the communal, public one. For the duration of our earthly existence we are unalterably entombed in a prison of flesh along with our savage appetites, our natural virtues, our secret vices, our hidden thoughts and all that is base and lofty within us. Most often we are able to conceal this existence as we look out upon other prisoners similarly confined and conduct our communal lives. These two lives seriously affect one another; they interact and pose perpetual problems in adjustment. It is only after our public lives are protected by the appropriate inscrutability that we submit ourselves to public view. Only when we are alone do we allow ourselves to remain unguarded and incautious, but in the company of others our manners do change. They change in differing ways when we are among our friends, our families, strangers, recent acquaintances or even someone very close. And as these manners change so do our faces. Raymond Mortimer said, "If we really had modesty, it is our faces that we should conceal. By comparison our legs are anonymous, our bellies uneventful." Rodin, in his sculptural portraits of the great personalities of his time, left us some of the most intensely revealing characterizations to be found in the history of art. An enthusiastic student of physiognomy, he confidently believed that from the shape and configuration of the head and face, the formation and proportion of the features and the set of head on the neck, he was able to read inner character and that the artist "has only to look into a human face in order to read there the soul within – not a feature deceives him." He further believed that in addition to discovering a subject's psychology and personal character traits, he could, when doing a portrait bust, reveal his ethnic, geographical, historical, professional and cultural background. Before Carlyle would proceed at a biographical study, he would first obtain a contemporary picture of the person he was to deal with. This, he felt, gave him more information than historical facts and documents. As he put it, "all that a man does is physiognomical of him."

In my earlier work I used distortions freely, for they served the dual purpose of registering my youthful rebellion and also heightening the characterizations of the biblical personages into symbols of human emotions and behavior. Goethe described a favorite project, "To work away at a canon of masculine and feminine proportions to seek the variations out of which character arises." I was not interested as much in the transient distortions produced in the face by an ephemeral emotion or a mood. I was fascinated more by the modification of the physical appearance with maturity after repeated recurrences of such moods and emotions. That internal disorders and diseases will manifest themselves in the face is well known, but that states of mind and traits of personality and character affect our external flesh appears to be harder to accept. Medical science in its studies of "constitutional psychology" sanctions a physical approach to the understanding of individuality. It considers the way in which the head, neck, trunk, arms, legs and extremities are structured to be the first and most important clues to what the human being is and will be. Based on bodily measurements, this science covers every aspect of human behavior, and tendencies to behave in certain ways are largely predetermined. Most of us fall predominantly in one or another of three psychical components, endomorphy, mesomorphy and ectomorphy and, we are told, behave and react in preordained ways to every life situation. Hands speak to me as persuasively as heads. Their attitudes can express effectively all manner of moods or feelings, actions or emotional states of being. And yet more can be seen in the hand. Its shape and markings, according to the criminologists, are permanent signs of a person's uniqueness and individuality. Researchers in the burgeoning field of medical genetics tell us that certain medical conditions are predetermined in the chromosomal structure of the cell to the point where the swirls of the finger and the lines of the palm take on certain identifiable configurations. At the least this recalls the words from the Book of Job, "God causes signs and seals on the hands of every man, that all men might know his works." And at the most it corresponds to what the palmists have been saying all along. We are generally outraged by application of the deterministic and pseudo sciences such as astrology, phrenology, physiognomy, chirography and chiromancy. Yet in the hand of a creative artist, through strange and abstruse transformations and permutations, such interests may result in significant works. At this point it ceases to be important or relevant whether or not such systems are true or false, right or wrong, scientific or unverifiable. Bur more of this later.

I painted Resurrections, Coronations of the Virgin, Crownings with Thorns, and pondered the inevitable questions of good and evil, whether they are absolute values or relative ones, whether one can be known without the contrast of the other. I admired the work of the pessimistic moralist Hieronymous Bosch who saw the world as inhabited by hordes of delusive phantoms where no borderline exists between good and evil or fantasy and reality. He mistrusted both God and man and revealed, against a setting of false security and empty dogma, an unholy alliance between man and the devil. Though convinced about the ideal I feared that extravagant moralizing in art had something comical, pedantic and even platitudinous about it. My confusion was not lessened by the knowledge that it had been and could be done well, but the real question remained "Was it for me?" Berenson applauded this function in art and wrote, "No matter how little the artist means to influence character and conduct, he yet does influence them." While on the other hand Thomas Mann, in speaking about art as a moral force said, "Art is the last to cherish illusions about her influence on the fate of men. Intent on endowing life with reason and dignity she has never been able to put a stop to the most arrant nonsense. She is not a force, not a power, she is only a comfort. Playing a game of the profoundest seriousness, she symbolizes man's eternal striving after perfection. Art has been granted to him as his companion from the very beginning of time. And from her unclouded innocence man will never be able to turn away his guilt-darkened eye."

My dilemma really centered around the relationship and conflict between the saint and the organized church, the priest and the prophet. The burden of the church's power and its hierarchical nature would provide perpetual tension between it and its "prophetic" member. This is, I am sure, an extension of the artist's essential concern between himself and his society. I was able to accept the rationale that every few centuries religion, and the society in which it exists, undergo a cataclysmic transformation, most often under great pain and with the benefit of the "new vision" reshapes its structure to withstand better the hard, cold light of the present. Beyond this I was content to leave such speculations to the theologians and philosophers. My interests ranged from the moral concerns of good and evil to the aesthetic ones of beauty and ugliness. (Our conceptions of these overlap and usually good is associated with beauty and evil with ugliness and this certainly is not always true). Thomas Mann speaks of the artists' striving after perfection. Yet I am sure that this is not limited to the perfection of a simple, symmetrical order. I believe there is a "hierarchy of perfections" not at the bottom of which is the one that may appear as a result of skillfully controlled departures from the obvious and the familiar. My distortions, heretofore called up by intense emotional demands, could now be introduced more for aesthetic considerations. With less need to rebel, the images became less grotesque as I sought more to discover the physical and spiritual aspects of the religious subject and the essential beauty of the painting itself.

I was attracted to the mystical and physical splendor of Catholic ritual and pomp with its processionals and pageantry, magnificent ceremonial objects, pontifical miters, ecclesiastical vestments and precious embroideries. I marveled at the displays of sheer physical brilliance which were hypnotically beautiful and served as a proper background to a Liturgy that abounded in unfathomable mysteries and converted to it such highly creative minds as Werfel, Mahler, Berenson, Max Jacob, etc. All the while my preoccupations with New Testament texts was neither devotional nor anecdotal; it did not burlesque nor mock. Yet my paintings were bitterly attacked by the Jewish press as the blatant apostasy of a rabbi's son, and by the secular and institutional Christian press as the heretical work of a religious renegade who was heaping profanation and sacrilege upon sacred soil. I experienced for a while, at least, the condition of the artist-outcast flavored with added distinction of being a Jew among Christians and a Christian among Jews. My painting *The Last Supper* when first shown in this city drew the following critique from one of the leading Boston critics: "This oil is an abomination of cartoon portraiture...(It) might make a footboard for the devil's bed." I had apparently transgressed and paid no heed to the Anglo-Saxon maxim "Thou shalt not commit irony." Ten years later, after the painting had been purchased by the Art Institute of Chicago and after my work had received recognition in New York, the following was written about the same painting when shown in Boston for the second time: "It has tremendous religious fervor, not entirely in unorthodox ways but in shining ways of the Soul and Spirit." I could take neither offense nor comfort from these evaluations for both, alas, were written by the same man. And there were the times when I would have wished deliverance from my supporters as well. I received an award from the National Society of Arts and Letters where my work was honored for its "humor".

To inquire a bit further into an art already fraught with conflicts and contradictions there is the matter of my choice of techniques. I have long marveled at the highly developed methods used by artists of the past in producing works of superior artistry which set standards for artistic and technical perfection. So many of these works of art still remain mysteriously fashioned with a high degree of beauty and physical permanence and provided great incentive, as they did for Dürer, "to learn the secrets of the golden ages," to unearth what is to be found in the "books of the ancients." I read Vasari, Laurie and Doerner avidly and made experiments with the techniques they described. Tantalizing references to the *gesso alla putrida* (the Renaissance material which became better the more foul it smelled) and Maroger's black oil of the Flemings, (which involved the boiling of lead white in linseed oil – a potentially explosive mixture) – would set me off on binges of medieval cookery. This inevitably resulted in a series of paintings using the "new" material. In this age of plastic paints and materials of the future, I settled on the ancient technique of encaustic, the mixing of dry pigments in hot wax used 2000 years ago by the Greeks, as the method which expressed most effectively what I had to say. The colors had the luminosity of stained glass and lent themselves effectively to the religious subjects. They did not yellow, fade or darken though the years as did oil ground colors. They dried immediately on application to the painting surface as the hot wax cooled and could thereupon be painted over and glazed. It allowed me to indulge myself in beautifully textured surfaces and richly pigmented colors. The painting could be reheated, its surface melted once again, allowing colors in lower layers to reappear. I sought the brush stroke and surface which had at the same time an Expressionist crudeness and directness and a Flemish finish and patina.

Such an emphasis on technique is a characteristic of the Boston School of Painting. Karl Zerbe, from whom I learned much about the use of encaustic, brought with him from Germany a great interest in the methods and materials of the artist and taught his valuable courses in techniques, beginning in 1937. Jack Levine, very much in touch with the European tradition, gave careful attention to the techniques of the great artists of the past and worked to discover their secrets. At that time and even more emphatically now, such a fixed concern with the past is considered by many to indicate nothing more than a fear of the present. Yet we must realize, though change is an inevitable part of the opening of new frontiers, that the force of tradition is very strong, and provides that ingredient of continuity without which the new art form would exist *in vacuo.* In each era creative artists inherit a body of procedures and techniques which it enriches by its own productions and passes on to those who follow. The new derives from the old and retains certain of its characteristic features – though at first what is new may appear to destroy the past, the dust will soon settle and there will stand the inevitable continuation.

I wished to amass strong technical equipment toward another purpose. I wanted my paintings to have so high a degree of finish that each square inch would be brought to the summit of technical perfection; that the painting become a beautifully fashioned object in itself. For me, the Masters passed on a tradition of making things of beauty, perfect objects. The artist presented his ideas through his craft and when the manner was weak the matter suffered.

During the years of the early 1940s through the present my interest in subject matter and content with the human figure as the central image continued to express itself in my works; this against a background of prevailing contemporary styles and criticisms which sought increasingly to reject such concerns as unsuitable for the artist of today. The worship of formal manipulation became the convention and all else was rejected. The earlier preoccupation with slavish imitation and sentiment to the exclusion of form was now turned upside down. No serious artist would deny the importance of formal qualities in a work of art, and certainly no great work is without formal excellence. Composition, pattern, color and texture have been traditional implements of the artist's trade with which he expressed and embodied meanings. The meanings have now been carefully filtered out and the tools alone are left to be admired. A mystique has been woven around this aspect of art, by legion of spellbinding apologists speaking in strange and unknown tongues like the disciples at Pentecost when the Holy Ghost descended upon them. And as art became either increasingly obvious or unintelligible, they chronicled the changing scene using a secret language accepted eagerly by the initiates without comprehension. The critics, art historians and museum officials became the self-appointed, indispensable middlemen between the artist and the public. They transformed aesthetic liabilities into bitter-sweet assets. As one artist shoots bullets of paint in the direction of the easel, another spends a lifetime paying homage to the square. One immortalizes the coke bottle and the beer can while another casts excrement into bronze. The music gets madder, the wine stronger. From the Bauhaus maxim of "less is more", by extension bad became good – as long as it had style. "Camp" came to the rescue of absurdity crowning Berenson's "originality of incompetence" as a leading aesthetic doctrine in the land. The art public, in the throes of a cultural explosion, accepted art under almost any conditions, displaying an unparalleled appetite which according to Edgar Wind is "matched only by an increasing atrophy of the receptive organs." The cultural lag had become a thing of the past, and the time gap between the *avant-garde* and the general public dropped to an all time low. To keep pace, an artist's one-man show was expected to be a radical departure from his previous one of the year before, and so many artists were quick and happy to oblige. New became True.

It was fairly easy for me to realize that my artistic salvation did not lie in the tension between two different kinds of red on opposite sides of a canvas or that a plastic hamburger had little relevance to my existence. It was also clear to me that by and large the universities had accepted these activities into their midst with enthusiasm, and though they had no meaning for me as an artist they did involve me as a teacher. Nature, which offers to the artist the most numerous and varied images, lost its traditional importance as the fundamental source for the young artist's education. He was no longer being trained to use his eye; the visual world becoming invisible. Instead the paint itself became both the object and the subject, and the act of painting took on the function of a ritual. The production of optical effects, painted puns and a variety of visual seductions, offered the universities entertainingly teachable systems where the demanding discipline of a traditional art training was unnecessary. The university art program became so concerned with concepts of style that the student was encouraged to embrace a current mode as the major part of his training. This commitment to manner before a period of exploration denied the young artist the very essence of a meaningful and profound self-discovery. Instead, however, the university continued in the time-honored academic tradition of exposition through highly developed verbal systems and these recent developments in art lent themselves excellently to verbal transposition. Then, too, this art being non-committal and impersonal was really a threat to no one.

My colleagues and I see the work of hundreds of such students, each of whom has spent at least four crucial years and thousands of dollars learning to paint pictures in pastiches of currently popular styles, without foundation and ill prepared to meet the conditions of a demanding profession. As the university continues to produce them in ever increasing numbers, in what Veblen called "trained incapacity," it must accept a great portion of the responsibility for the students' eventual disillusionment. The setting up of even more efficient job clearing houses only compounds the problem. W. McNeil Lowry has for a number of years as director of the Ford Foundation Program in the Humanities and the Arts spoken of the college's and university's lowering of standards of excellence in professional art training. He takes the rather extreme view of advising university deans that "under present conditions the best service you can perform for the potential artist is to throw him out." His feeling is that the universities "in the main" sacrificed professionalism and "drifted along with society in the perpetuation of the amateur and the imitator." The price we might be paying for our cultural explosion may well be the dilution of the quality and standard of artistic production. In this context, Tocqueville's assertion is most illuminating – that "in aristocracies, a few great pictures are produced; in democratic countries, a vast number of insignificant ones."

My own work during this time remained independent of these developments. In 1954 I read Thomas Mann's *Joseph and His Brothers,* and this had a serious effect on my work. Though my paintings never relied strictly upon biblical texts, and I took liberties as I felt they were necessary to give emphasis to the idea I had in mind at the time, Mann made much freer departures as he allegorized the bible story. Though the essential story was there, he allowed himself to luxuriate in his fantasies with complete latitude. He strayed with abandon into the remote reaches of his imagination, weaving a web of allegorical exposition which illuminated and spiritualized the text. I painted a picture called *Joseph and the Ishmaelites,* in which I characterized Joseph as a precocious, insufferable young prattler in the center of a booth where some traveling Midianite merchants display their wares. Chronometers co-exist with ancient coins and parchments, lockets containing miniature unknown portraits hang alongside a Venetial picture postcard and the *Jewish Daily Forward* contrasts with fragments of Aramaic hieroglyphs. I preferred this curious collocation of heretofore unrelated artifacts and assorted bric-a-brac along with their allusion to miscellaneous historical and archeological facts and hypotheses over those which were chronologically accurate and categorically correct. I could allow my imagination to roam freely through time and to shuffle its sequences like the medieval metaphysical conjurers. Aesthetic relevancies were set up and empathetic relationships established. And with all this, I found myself working for the first time with subjects from the Old Testament – subjects with which I could not until now become involved without sufficient detachment from the highly charged emotional overtones of the early religious background.

I did a number of paintings of the "Joseph" subject and other Old Testament themes all the while making preliminary sketches for them. The drawings themselves began to interest me more and more to the point where I put paintings aside and concentrated completely on the drawing. Heretofore, very much in the Renaissance tradition, my drawings served as preparatory sketches for paintings, as blueprints of the total composition or studies of its individual parts. I devoted a great deal of time toward making drawings which were in no way preparations for other works – drawings which would exist as ends in themselves. They pursued in a more specific way my preoccupation with light and shade, the *chiarascuro* of Leonardo, Raphael, Caravaggio and Rembrandt, and I sought out the works of these painters during my European trips.

A painting like Leonardo's *Adoration of the Magi* in the Uffizi Gallery in Florence was very instructive to me. The artist had executed a complete underpainting in varying tones of warm umber and the painting was left in this unfinished state. It was thus limited to a monochromatic rendering whose forms were released in bold contrasts and glowed with stunning impact due to this very limitation of color. It was at the same time a painting without color and a drawing with color. I was convinced that a drawing approached in this manner – not as a study, sketch or trial but as highly developed painterly effort – could be as serious, as impressive and as authoritative as a painting. So many other paintings which I knew so well from reproductions in books and magazines had proved however to be somewhat disappointing in the flesh. Having first seen them small and in black and white, my mental image of them was very different from what they were really like. I had read into them conceptions of color and scale in a highly personal way. I envisioned the black and white print in a color scheme that was entirely my own, or solely in value as in the Leonardo painting. In this and other ways paintings which I admired had an effect on my work – I took what I could use, and what I used was modified and amplified to conform to my own image. I realized then that it was not possible for me to look at works of art (or anything else for that matter) with complete innocence and without design. I worked on many drawings rather large in size (some six and seven feet in height) in pastel crayons of varying shades of brown and in charcoal on toned paper.

In my search for a more speculative approach to Scripture, I considered the place of the Talmud with its parochial definitions, rigid disputations and rational systems. This certainly had little relation to what I was doing nor did it suggest the pantheistic tendencies of religion with which I wished my work to identify. I did find such a source in the Cabbala, an esoteric doctrine concerning God and the universe which branched out as an extensive literature from the 13th century onward, alongside and in opposition to the Talmud. It contained a symbolic commentary on the Bible around the Zohar, its holy book. The Cabbala, meaning the received or traditional lore, is asserted to have come down as a revelation to elect saints from a remote past and is preserved today by a privileged few members of the Hasidic Sect. It is a complex poetic interpretation of the universe diagrammed as a cosmic chain consisting of ten spheres with the essence of pure Divinity at the top. Descending spheres of values in gradual transition from the infinite to the finite join with the sphere of the Kingdom at the bottom containing man and all forms of matter. The pious, in proportion to the degree to which they carry out the teachings of the Torah, bring that much closer the ultimate union of man and God. Piety became joyous, ritual became spiritualistic instead of formalistic. Cabbala taught that man is not a spoke in a wheel, a small insignificant fragment of the universe, but the center around which everything moves. Its philosophy stood out in sharp contrast against Christian and Hindu doctrines of self-renunciation. I was overwhelmed with the artistic possibilities and highly subtlized ideas and ideals mingled. Sparkling displays of logic steeped in Neoplatonic philosophy blended with Persian beliefs in superstition and magic, and focused themselves on the Bible. There were the Cabbalists who believed that Jewish saints could become masters of holy combinations of letters and numbers and could by their manipulation effect miracles in the upper spheres. This numerological jugglery along with the writing of amulets, trust in the efficacy of charms, conjuration of devils, frenzied rituals, and sublime levitations provoked dazzling images and provided a wealth of visual material for my work.

Against such a background, the belief arose in the possibility of infusing life into a clay or wooden figure of a human being. This figure was called a *golem* meaning an embryo, a thing not fully formed, or in a state of incompletion. It would be created by a wonder-working rabbi or saint called a *Ba'al Shem* or master of The Name. He would insert into the mouth or forehead of the golem a piece of paper inscribed with a combination of letters forming a *Shem* which signifies any one of the names of God. This golem would obey mechanically any order of the master, and as a benevolent Frankenstein he could be the instrument to alleviate the oppressive situations of medieval Jews. I painted a large picture of Rabbi Judah Loew of 16th Century Prague in the process of creating a golem. All the props were there. While the apprentices properly adorned with amulets and charms chant magical incantations, the sorcerer in a state of ecstatic levitation, hovers over the figure of the emerging golem. Solomon ibn Gabirol, the 11th Century poet-philosopher-Cabbalist, while still fairly young, is said to have created a maid-servant in this manner. But the king quickly put as stop to that, forcing Solomon to restore everyone of the creature's parts to its original form. This Cabbala raised to the rank of dogma the doctrine of metempsychosis – the transmigration of souls. It explains that the soul, after being freed from bodily trammels, passes into the region of the dead and remains there till it is sent back into this world to inhabit some other body, human or animal. When it is in a sufficiently purified state, having undergone various trials and purgations, it returns to the eternal source from which it first proceeded. This explained for the Cabbalists the otherwise unanswerable question of why God often permits the wicked to lead a happy life while many of the righteous live in misery. It also described the cruel infliction of pain on children as imposed in punishment for a crime committed by the soul in a previous state. There was widespread belief in the theory of impregnation of souls and legends of the *Dybbuk'im* (meaning literally things which cleave unto something else). Here are souls which are condemned to wander in this world for a time, and they are everywhere watched and tormented by evil spirits. To escape the tormenting demons, these souls take refuge in the bodies of pious men and women over whom the evil spirits have no power. Interestingly enough, it was made clear that the souls of men transmigrate into the bodies of men, and those of women into the bodies of women with rare exceptions being made only as punishment for the commission of the most heinous sins. A person to whom such a soul clings loses his individuality and suffers the tortures of the damned. Only the *Ba'al Shem,* the miracle-working rabbi can expel this devil by exorcism and amulets, forcing him to leave through the small toe in order that the least possible damage be done to the afflicted body.

The Cabbala exhibits a thorough knowledge of astrology which was practiced by Jews throughout the Middle Ages both as a professional art and science. Coming from the East they were looked upon as the heirs of the Chaldeans, the ancient casters of horoscopes. Throughout the period multitudes were filled with awe and fear at the supposed power of the position of the planets at birth to influence the destiny of man. In the canon of the *Brethren of Purity* of Arabia in the 9th and 10th Centuries there was developed a schematic method for rendering pictorially the human figure for the purpose of revealing a vast harmonious cosmology unified by numerical and musical correspondences. The Italian Renaissance fused astrological doctrine with theories of human proportions – less for technical purposes than for purposes of metaphysical speculation (on the existence of God) – a predestined harmonistic relationship between the universe and man.

It is this search for basic qualitative patterns that commonly underlie every unit of whatever entity that is irresistible to the philosopher, the theist, the scientist and the artist. He will superimpose the features of one phenomenon upon those of another and will often indulge his thoughts in the most irrational, subjective peregrinations in the hope that some gears will mesh or that something will click. Such a superimposition of astrological doctrines and symbols on the Bible offers some fascinating correspondences. The Zodiacal signs seem to fall into places as descriptive of the character, psychology, and chronology of Biblical figures and events. Each of the twelve signs offers revelations through its own emblem and is also symbolic of one of the four elements of Genesis (fire, water, air or earth). The sign to be observed is seen not only by itself but also in relation to the sign at the opposite end of that particular diameter of the Zodiacal circle. We can take as a random example Libra, which might represent Moses, and in direct relation on the other side of the circle is Aires, the sign of the Lamb. Libra with its scales would symbolize the Law which was given to Moses. The Aries lamb would signify the blood of the lamb on the lintels and the side-posts of the last plague prior to the exodus. Aries is also a fire sign which calls to mind the burning bush out of the midst of which God revealed himself to Moses. There is also the pillar of innumerable references to sacrificial offerings "made by fire unto the Lord," and Aaron's remark to Moses of the golden earrings of the Hebrews which he "cast into the fire and there came out this calf." And God told Moses that a "perpetual fire shall be burning upon the altar; it shall not go out." One is hard put to find other references to fire in the entire Pentateuch outside of Moses' lifetime. Aries with its lamb would also symbolize Jesus and is iconographic of him whose birth was preceded by the appearance in the heavens of a cataclysmic supernova which guided the three wise men who, incidentally, were astrologers. Whereas in Libra Moses received the Law and gives it to the people, Jesus co-exists in Aries, having stated that he was the fulfillment of the Law. This is but one of the curious correspondences, cosmic preordinations, or common coincidences (call them what you will) to be found within the vast complex of astrological systems. As an artist I find such speculation rich in productive fantasy and provocative of image-forming possibilities. It discloses a meaningful iconography to be found within interdependent worlds. Creative artists have often concerned themselves with these outer limits of man's perception from Mozart's *Magic Flute* to Yeats' *Vision*, from Michelangelo's Neoplatonic sibyls and prophets to Rembrandt's Faust.

A number of years ago Oskar Kokoschka talked to a group of painting students in Boston and he referred constantly to the fact that his prophetic visions and second sight played an important part in the conception and painting of his pictures. He showed color slides of many of his portraits including a number of well known European personalities and told that all the sitters met their death shortly after completion of the paintings. One would ordinarily dismiss apocalyptic statements of this sort except for the fact that this was made by one of the great painters of our time – one whose substantial contribution included some of the finest psychological portraits ever painted. I talked with Kokoschka later. He said he knew my work and liked it – a remark which meant a great deal to me coming from one of the giants of art whom I admired greatly. I was at the point of asking him where he had seen my work but I didn't allow the conversation to continue for as I looked into those eyes that clearly had in them the wisdom of the ages, I couldn't help but get the unsettling feeling that he was going to ask me to sit for a portrait.

My drawings continued to picture sages, scholars, saints, Bible students, moonworshipers, visionaries and false messiahs. The intention, as in my early paintings, was not so much the imposition of a three dimensional effect upon a two dimensional surface but an intense effort to pull the forms physically away from this surface and with the help of highly contrasting values achieve an actual presence. Benvenuto Cellini wrote of this in his *Treatise on Sculpture* and said, "To say of a certain painting that it detaches itself in such a way that it seems to be in relief – is not that the greatest praise?" Though the drawing and painting illustrated my subjects satisfactorily I felt a sense of failure in the realization of a more substantial space. And the only answer was to draw with a material that had more substance to it – such as clay. Now I had often resorted to making clay studies of figures, their parts and drapery, since I rarely used living models. I would lay a light on them to materialize an imaginary lighting situation and I would study their perspectives for the purpose of solving painting problems. But the thought of doing sculpture as an end in itself stunned me. The artistic and emotional ramifications were enormous. Would there by stylistic changes, formal readjustments and even more important a complete upheaval of artistic sensibilities with the involvement of another dimension? There were of course painters who were excellent sculptors – Degas for example. Yet he neither dared nor cared to cast his waxes or even show them in his lifetime. I saw it clearly; I would be producing magnificent monuments to artistic pretense – preserved forever in living bronze! As I worked on the first pieces I saw myself as a defector from the ranks of painters, an interloper among sculptors, producing works which exist in some artistically questionable no-man's land that is nether painting nor sculpture, like the works in the Cemetery of the Stalieno in Genoa. Yet I could see visual logic in a reciprocal relationship between the graphic and plastic arts, particularly in regard to my own problems. The Egyptian wall paintings are as much sculpture reliefs as they are paintings. The Greek pediment reliefs and the doors of Ghiberti, Filarete and Manzu are as much paintings as they are sculpture. At the proper viewing distance they are divested of their inherent weight and take on the appearance of pictures. The artists of the Renaissance were well aware that draftsmanship is the underpinning of all visual arts, and so many of these artists practiced several simultaneously. Rodin spoke often of the primacy of the contours in sculpture. I approached sculpture much as I did drawing and painting and the transition was natural and developmental. The possibilities were exciting and I began to feel reasonably secure in the results. I was unwilling, as the work developed, to accept the Gospel of the Monolithic Form spawned by Michelangelo's highly favored dictum that in order for a sculpture to be good it must be able to roll down a hill. This would not have applied too well to the Laocoön group which Michelangelo himself called "a miracle of art." So great was his respect and admiration for this sculpture, which was excavated in 1506, that he declined modestly to restore the work and its missing arms which apparently were broken off on the way down a hill. I looked back to my early painting *Trinity* and its particular conception made more sense to me as I worked on the relief called *The Judges*. I enjoyed combining elaborate bas-reliefs with sculpture in the round as on the cuirass worn by the Emperor Augustus in that fine sculpture at the Braccio Novo of the Vatican. Benin bronzes, magnificently sculptural and at the same time painterly in their calligraphic decoration and rich patinas also provided stimulating sources

As I produced reliefs and pieces in the round of moonworshipers, troubadours, scribes and Biblical figures I was well aware that it was primarily against such images, the three-dimensional ones, that the popular interpretation of the Biblical prohibition was directed. Though there have been occasional examples of representational art in Jewish history, rarely was it seen in the synagogue. As far as statues are concerned, however, their production has been considered a direct affront to the basic monotheistic code of Judaism in that they represent through scriptural reference the substitution of other Gods for the Divinity. And under the recurrent spectre of the golden calf their inclusion within the synagogue proper had been and still is anathema. I prefer, however, to read the second commandment's restriction against he making of graven images in conjunction with the following verse, "Thou shalt not bow down to them and shalt not serve them." I have always imagined that significant figurative art can intensify spiritual awareness in the temple and synagogue and can heighten the religious atmosphere. If this be sacrilege then let such profanity enrich what is sacred as was the case with the highly organized Christianity of the Renaissance where the sacred and profane blended to produce an art of unparalleled magnificence. At fairly regular intervals, I am asked as an artist with a certain reputation for working with religious subjects, to discuss with temple and synagogue groups the possibility of creating works of art for their places of worship. Usually the businessmen – board members – outline their art needs in relation to the tightest of budgets and I can usually understand these problems. A sketch, always figurative, is prepared which I present at the next meeting and in march the shock troops: the art committee of the Ladies' Auxiliary, seasoned veterans of five years of temple art festivals, all experts in the latest art fashions. It doesn't take them long to convince me of the errors of my figurative ways and to convince themselves that I really wasn't what they wanted in the first place. I retreat, beaten and bleeding into the vestibule, convinced that I would sooner have faced the legendary wrath of Pope Julius II or hordes of Biblical Philistines than a handful of aesthetic ones. The rabbi, an acknowledged liberal in matters of art and religion and truly catholic in his tastes, privately and somewhat apologetically explains to me that the congregation is not yet ready to accept figuration in its sanctuary while he can scarcely hide his own revulsion at such a thought. The temple, in profound relief, thereupon settles happily on the safe and well known religious-abstract clichés, each passed upon and often improved upon by the ladies. The archeologists of the future will unearth a vast cache of noncommittal burning bushes and geometric ceramic tile murals of modern design. I shall label in advance this period of ecclesiastical art, created half way through the twentieth century as Mid-Atrocean, and be content to stay forever out of this sphere of art activity.

At least in this regard the pattern of my career appears to have been fairly consistent. Having grown up in a religion that rejected the figurative image, I have found it necessary to fashion graven forms. And having developed as an artist in a period of time when the figurative image was no longer taken seriously, I have found it necessary to use it as the essential focus of my work. I continue to make paintings and sculpture with hope that my work will be judged not for how it satisfies the pre-determined demands of any philosophy or religion but rather for its value as objects made of visions perceived.

At this point I would expect to be asked whether I personally believe in astrology, God, or any other of the transcendental systems I refer to. I would say that to ask such a question would be to miss the point of this talk. But I will go a step beyond and (if I am assured that it will not go further than this room) I will answer the question. Certainly I believe in astrology (I am always impressed with personality correspondences between dates of birth, and characteristics of the Zodiacal signs). I believe in religion – as a matter of fact I believe in a number of religions with their prophesies and their miracles. I believe in chirognomy, chiromancy (I've never known the hand to lie) and in pre-existence. I believe in phrenology, physiognomy, in extra-sensory communication and intuitive cognition. I believe in ritual and pagan myths. I even believe in science. As an artist I believe in any thing that will set my imagination in motion toward the purpose of creating meaningful fantasies. For art is not a reflection of experienced reality. It exists in a world of illusions. And as Stravinsky says in his *Poetics*, "a living illusion is more valuable in such matters than a dead reality." Baudelaire writes that "The artist is an artist only on the condition that he is double and that he neglects no aspect of his double nature." His split being allows him to live in two different worlds simultaneously, one which is illusory and another which is real. With his artistry he can make real the illusion – he can reconcile the opposites and incongruities which confound us. And with an instinct that is infallible he creates with his phantoms and his fictions a new existence, one that becomes increasingly transparent and plausible as we periodically reassess our values. Edgar Wind said, "The aim of any artist is to produce a persuasive figment, and if he succeeds, why call that his failure?" ■

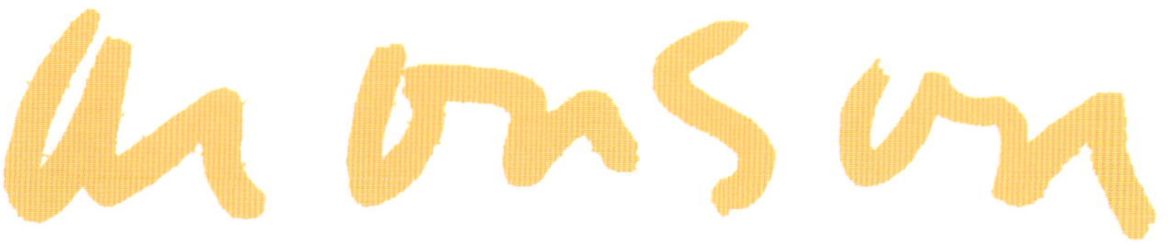

CATALOGUE RAISONNÉ OF SCULPTURE

SMALL EDITIONS

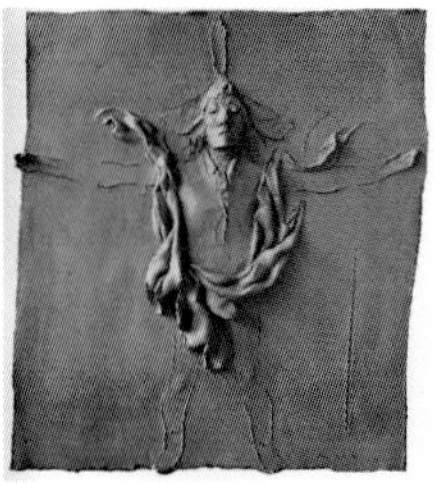

Angel (relief), 1983
Edition of 12
26 x 24 x 2"

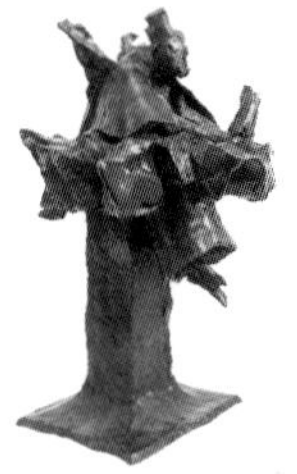

Angel with Book, 1973-1976
Edition of 12
20 x 12 x 12"

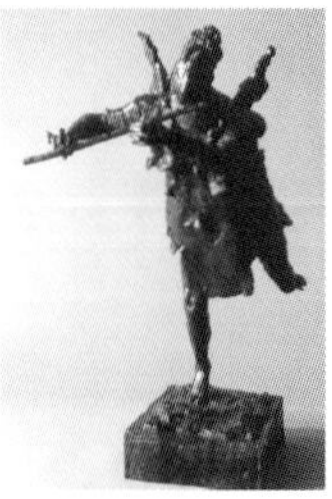

Angel with Flute, 1978
Edition of 15
24 1/8 x 8 x 20"

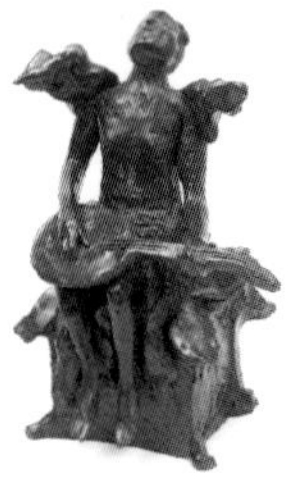

Angel with Lute, 1974-1976
Edition of 12
12 x 8 x 7"

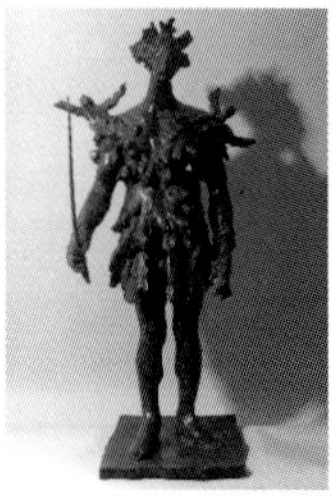

Avenging Angel, 1973-1976
Edition of 12
43 x 18 x 23"

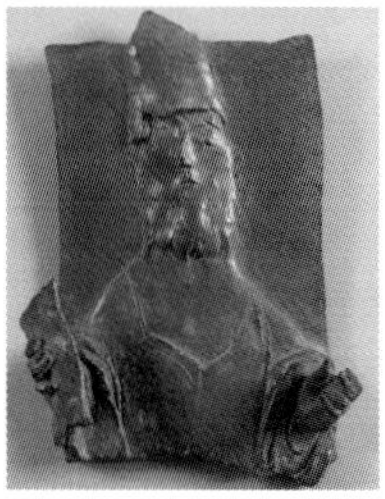

Beadle (relief), 1985
Edition of 25
9 x 5 3/4 x 2"

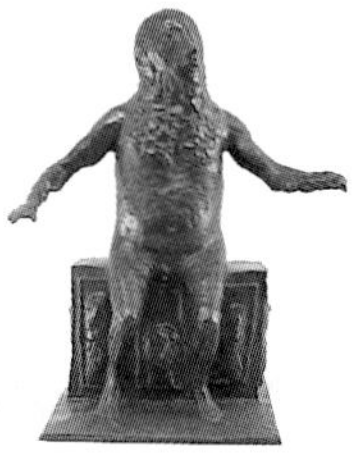

Blind Samson, 1961
Edition of 12
27 x 18 x 13"

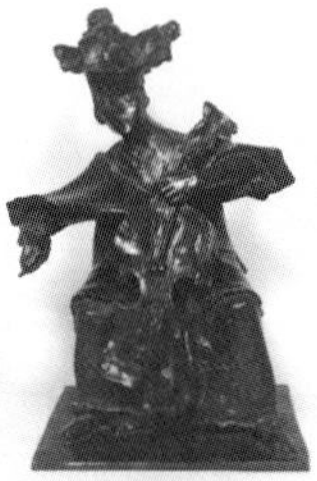

Cellist, 1974-1976
Edition of 12
20 x 14 x 11"

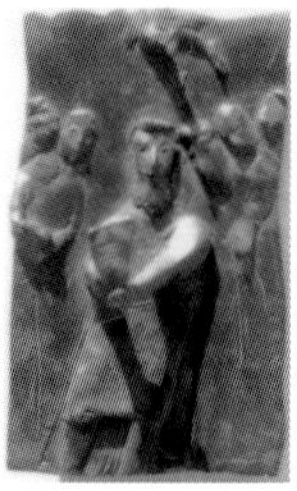

Chorus (relief), 1983
Edition of 25
9 x 5 x 2"

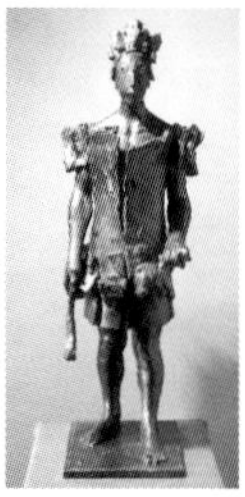

David, 1987
Edition of 15
41 x 13 x 12 5/8"

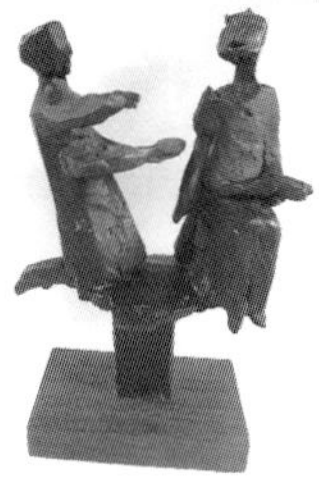

David and Saul, 1980
Edition of 25
10 x 7 x 4 3/4"

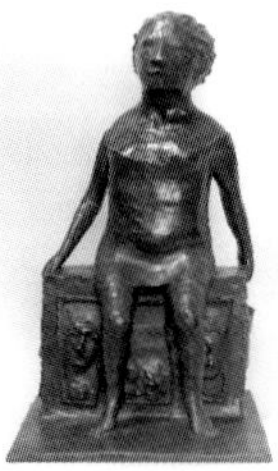

Delilah, 1961
Edition of 12
26 x 12 x 13"

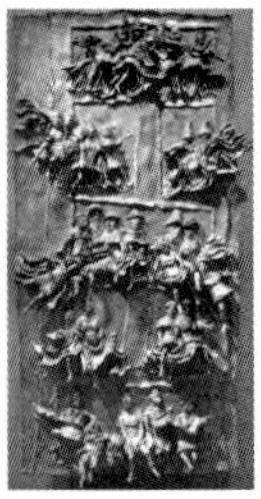

The Door, 1963-1969
Edition of 8
94 x 50 x 12"

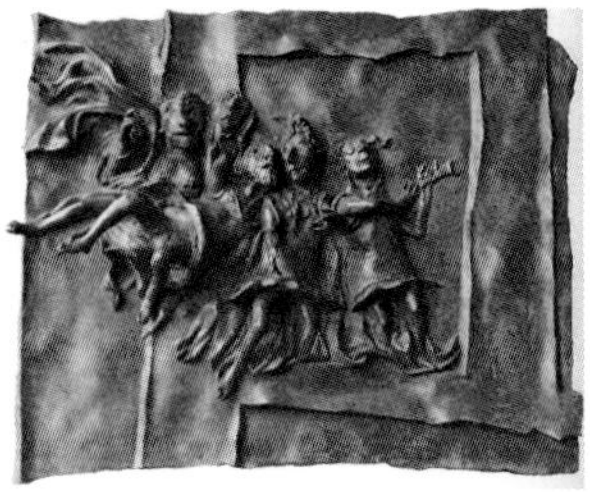

Panel from *The Door:*
Angel Choir, 1963-1969
Edition of 12
31 x 27 x 6"

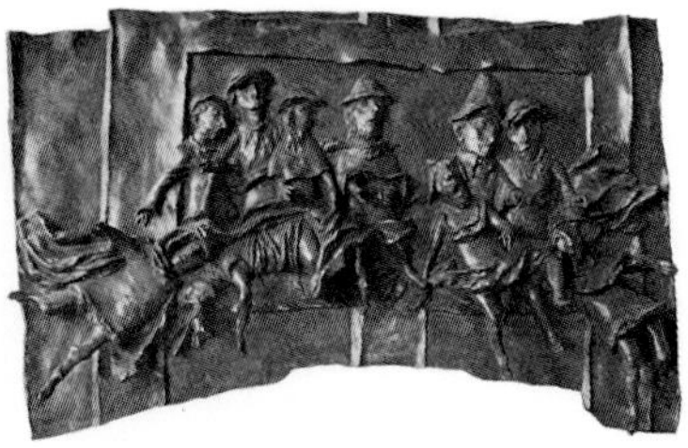

Panel from *The Door:*
The Doctors, 1963-1969
Edition of 12
29 x 46 x 7"

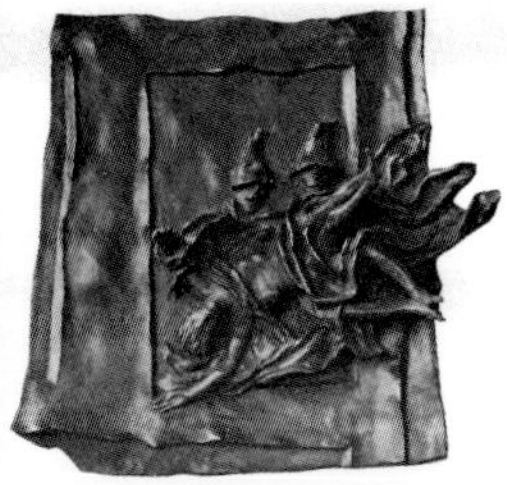

Panel from *The Door:*
The Golem, 1963-1969
Edition of 12
26 x 25 x 7"

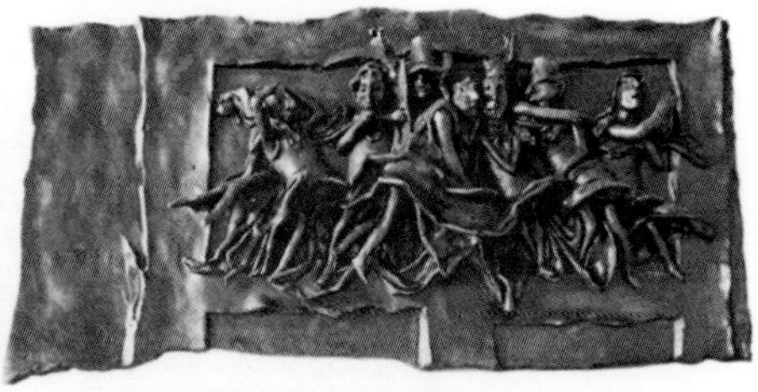

Panel from
The Door:
Moonworshipers,
1963-1969
Edition of 12
22 x 46 x 4"

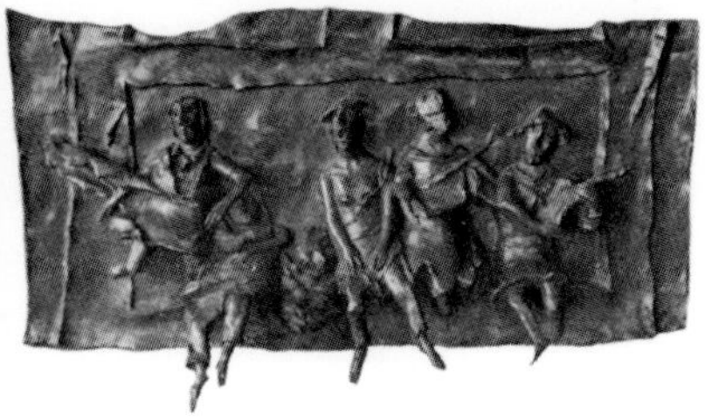

Panel from *The Door:*
Musicians in Ecstasy,
1963-1969
Edition of 12
21 1/2 x 45 x 12"

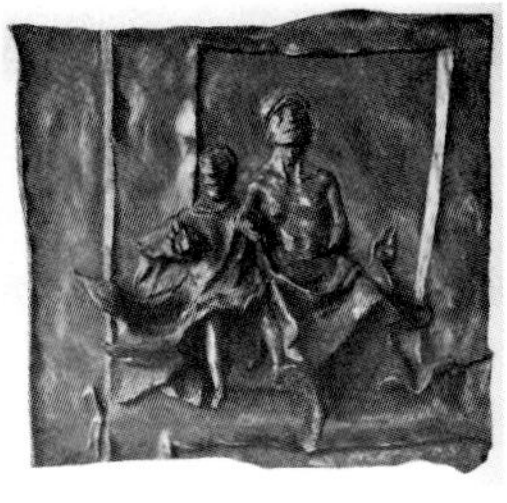

Panel from *The Door:*
Two Apprentices, 1963-1969
Edition of 12
24 x 21 x 2 3/4"

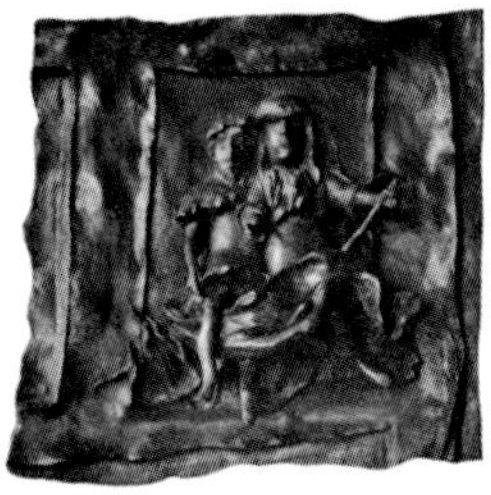

Panel from *The Door*
Two Musicians, 1963-1969
Edition of 12
23 x 25 x 6"

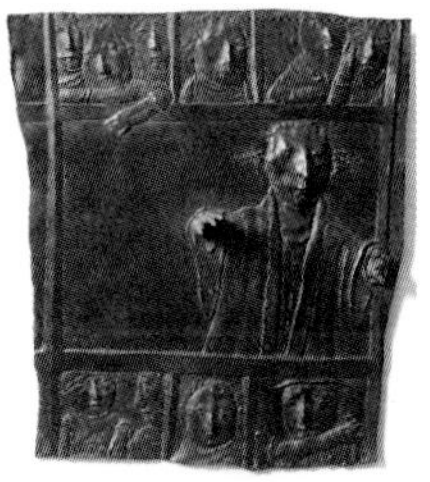

Edmund Burke (relief), 1963-1969
Edition of 12
24 x 21 x 2 3/4"

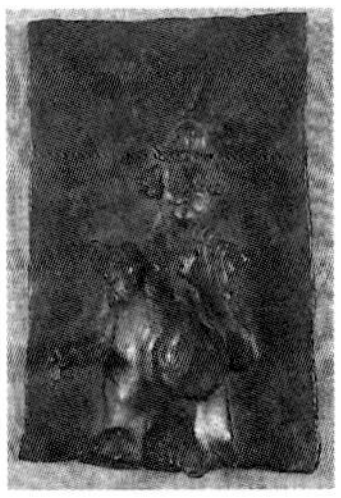

Entertainer (relief), 1983
Edition of 25
10 x 6 3/4 x 2"

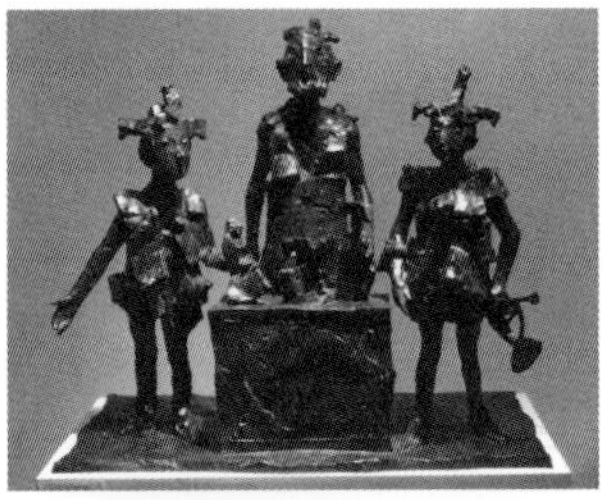

The Entertainers, 1976-1978
Edition of 12
39 x 42 1/2 x 22"

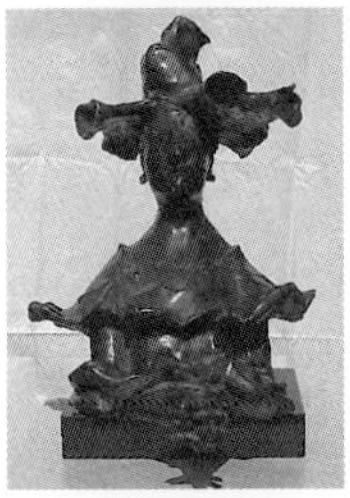

The Entertainer, 1968
Edition of 12
14 1/2 x 12 x 14 1/2"

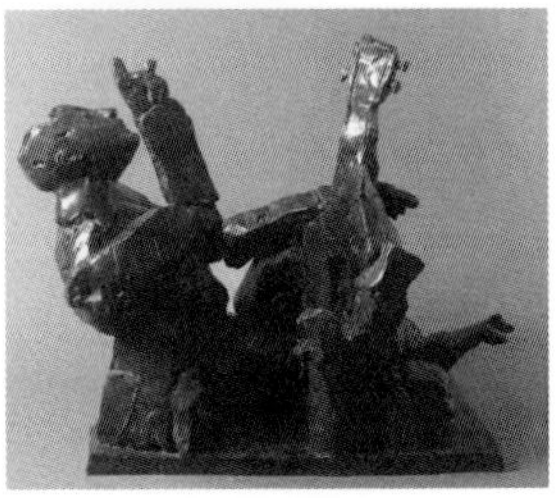

Fallen Angel, 1987
Edition of 15
21 1/2 x 25 1/2 x 16 1/2"

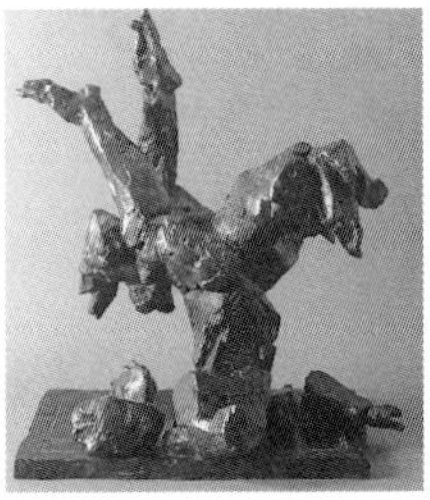

Fallen Angel II, 1987
Edition of 12
26 1/2 x 22 1/2 x 17 3/4"

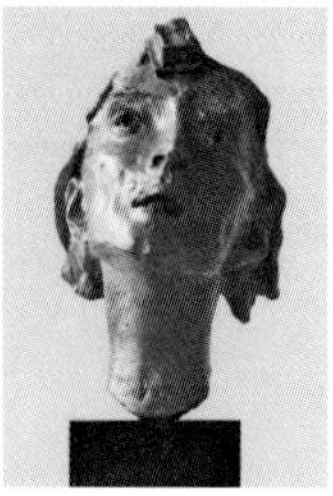

False Messiah, 1964-1968
Edition of 12
13 x 8½ x 10½"

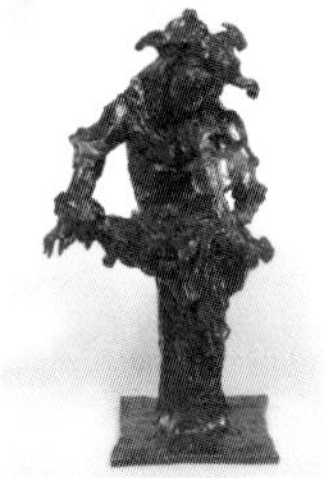

Fiddler, 1974-1976
Edition of 12
22¾ x 11¾ x 11"

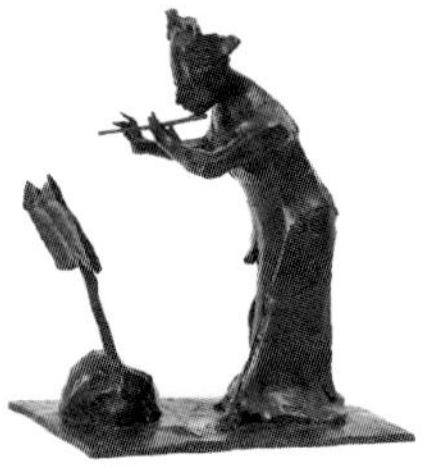

Flute Player, 1979
Edition of 15
14 x 12 x 9½"

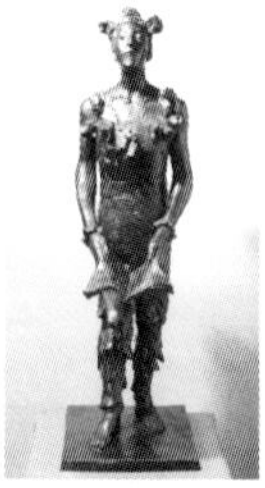

Harlequin, 1986
Edition of 15
39¾ x 12¾ x 14"

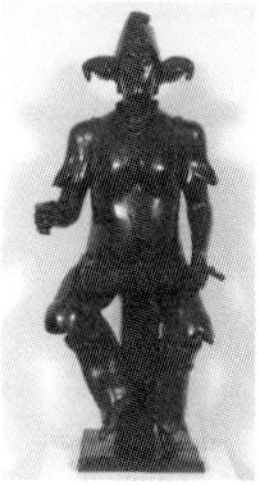

Harlequin II, 1999
Edition of 12
40 x 17½ x 13¼"

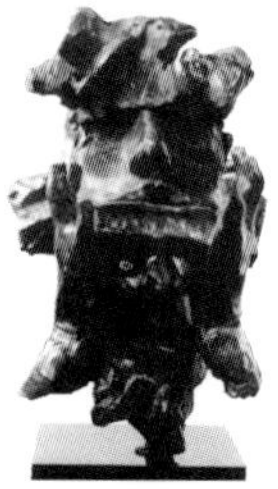

Harmonica Player, 1987
Edition of 12
14 x 10 x 12"

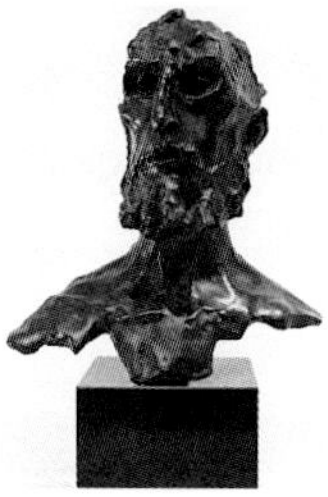

The Hermit, 1967
Edition of 12
10½x 10 x 6½"

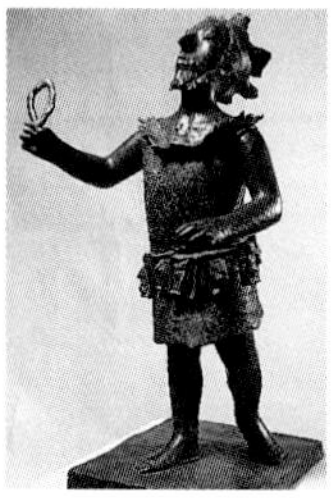

High Priest, 1964
Edition of 12
27 x 13½ x 15"

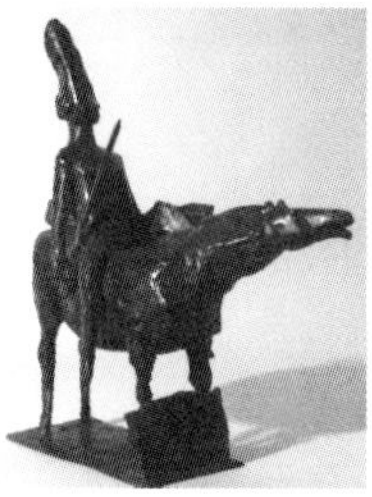

Horse and Warrior, 1976-1978
Edition of 15
16 x 6 ½ x 13½"

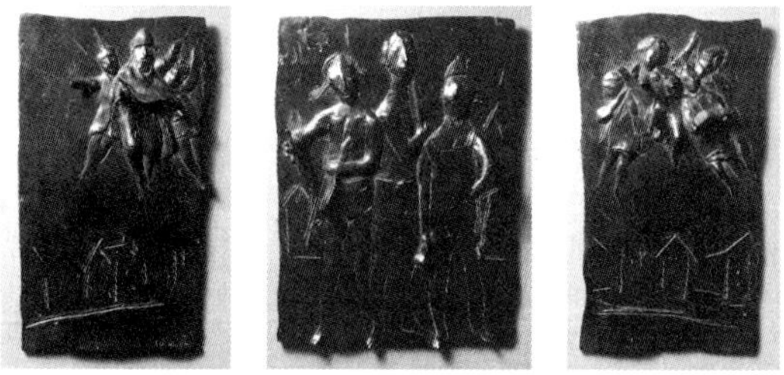

Itinerant Musicians (relief), 1983
Edition of 12
10 x 19 x 1½"

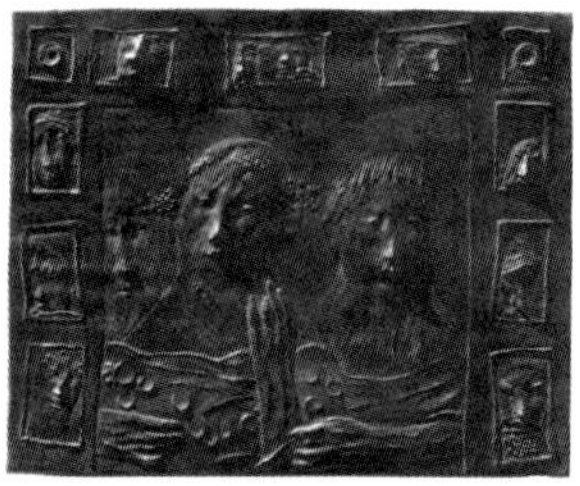

Judges (relief), 1961
Edition of 12
19½ x 23¾ x ¾"

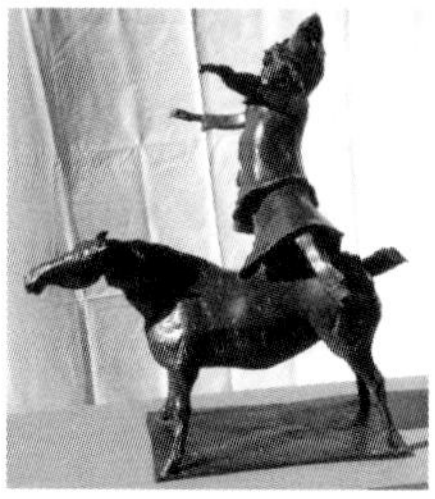

Kneeling Rider with Violin, 1977-1978
Edition of 15
20½ x 17 x 18"

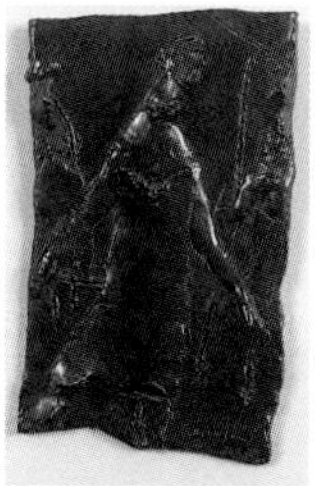

Levitation (relief), 1983
Edition of 25
7¾ x 4¾ x ½"

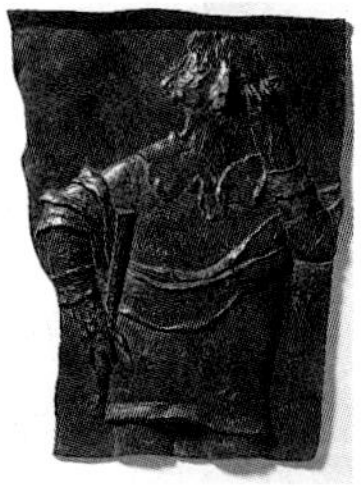

Man with Flute (relief), 1963
Edition of 12
15¾ x 12 ¼ x ⅝"

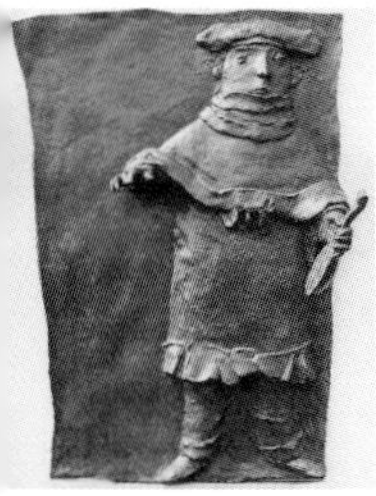

Man with Mandolin (relief), 1963
Edition of 12
$16\frac{5}{8} \times 12 \times 2\frac{3}{4}$"

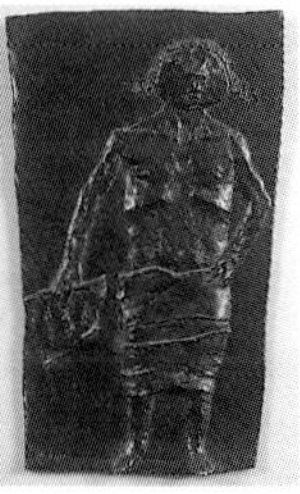

Man with Music (relief), 1963
Edition of 12
$17 \times 10\frac{3}{8} \times 1\frac{1}{8}$"

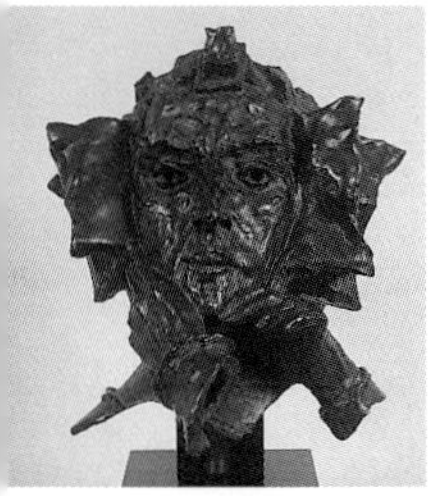

Man with Phylacteries, 1964-1968
Edition of 12
$16\frac{1}{2} \times 12 \times 15$"

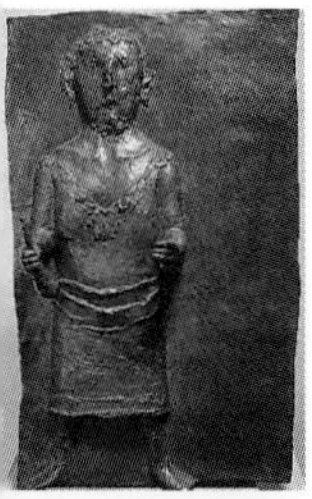

Man with Ram's Horn, (relief),1963
Edition of 12
$17\frac{1}{2} \times 11 \times 3\frac{5}{8}$"

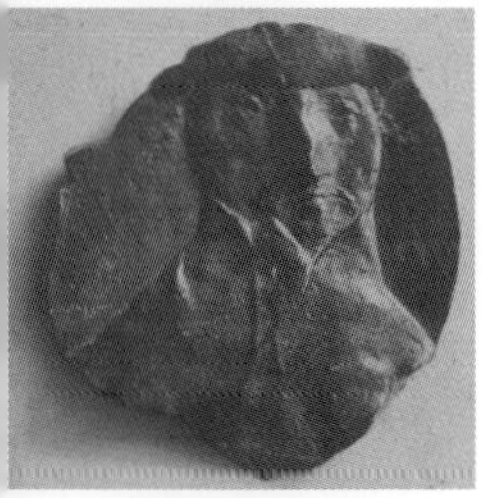

Medieval Man (relief), 1964
Edition of 20
$5 \times 4\frac{1}{2} \times \frac{3}{4}$"

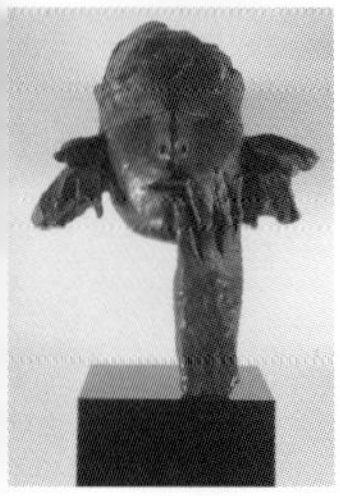

The Medium, 1983
Edition of 15
$15 \times 13 \times 12\frac{1}{2}$"

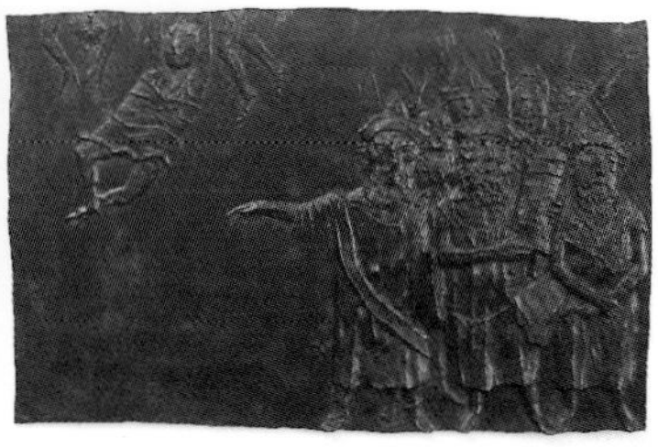

Moonworshipers (relief), 1963
Edition of 12
$22 \times 34 \times 1\frac{1}{2}$"

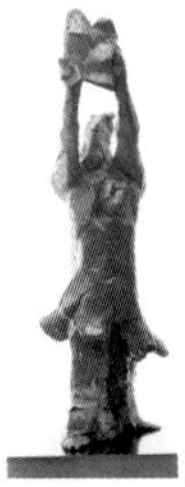

Moses, 1981
Edition of 15
$29 \times 8\frac{1}{4} \times 9\frac{1}{4}$"

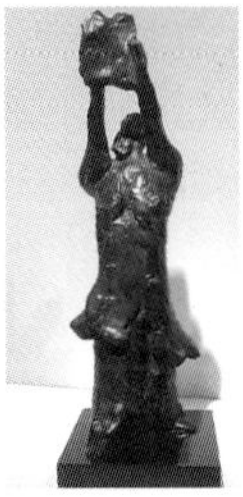

Moses, 1981
Edition of 25
$17 \times 5 \times 5\frac{1}{4}$"

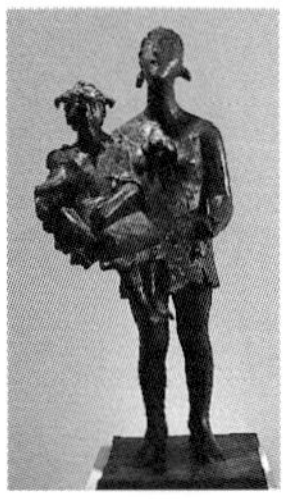

Mother & Child, 1973-1976
Edition of 12
$44 \times 19\frac{1}{4} \times 17\frac{1}{2}$"

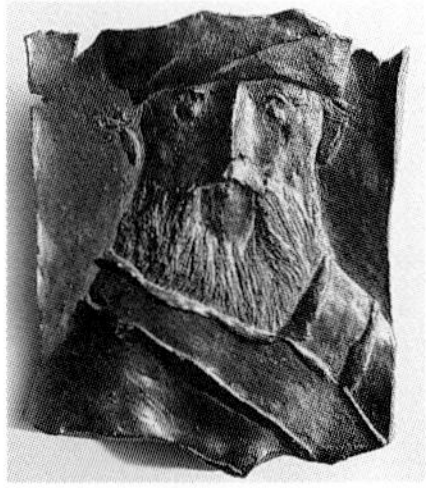

The Patriarch, (relief), 1964
Edition of 12
$7 \times 5\frac{3}{4} \times 1$"

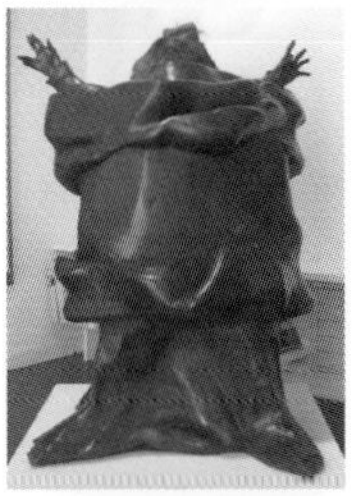

Prophet II, 2002
Edition of 8
$50 \times 36 \times 36\frac{1}{2}$"

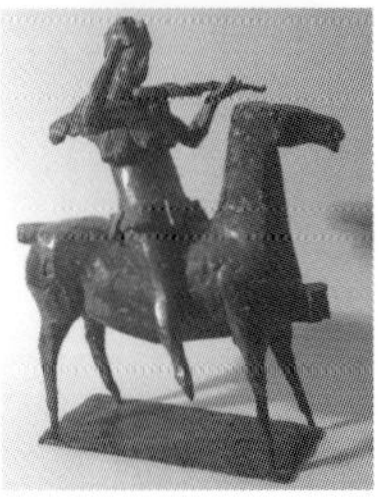

Rider with Amulets, 1977-1978
Edition of 12
$21 \times 7 \times 13$"

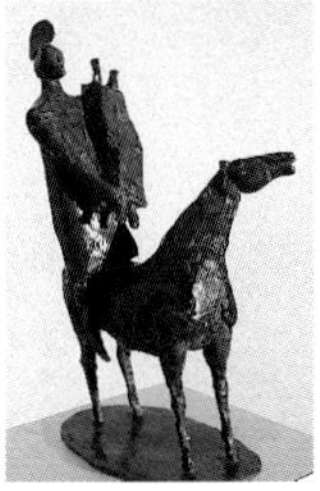

Rider with Torah, 1977-1978
Edition of 15
$15\frac{1}{2} \times 9 \times 8\frac{1}{4}$"

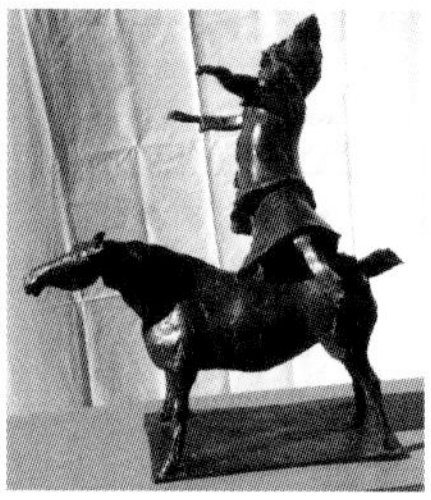

Rider with Violin, 1976-1978
Edition of 15
18 x 13 x 17"

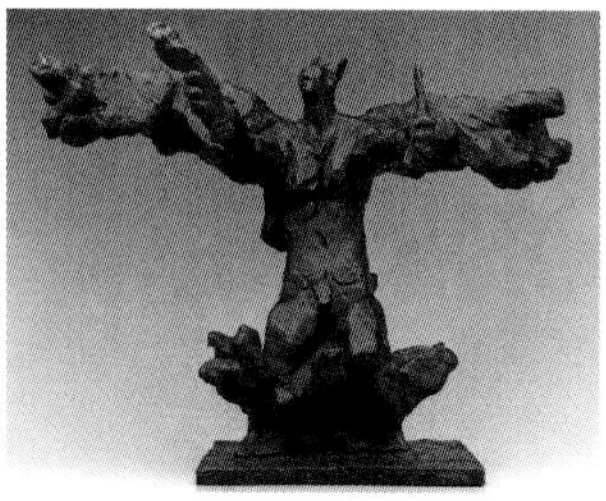

Spirit of Israel, 1986
Edition of 36
$9\frac{3}{4}$ x $14\frac{1}{2}$ x $8\frac{1}{2}$"

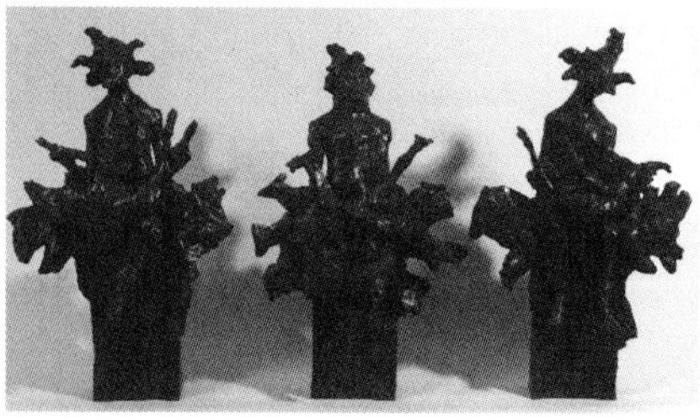

Sacrifices (3), 1973-1976
Edition of 12
$23\frac{1}{2}$ x $12\frac{1}{2}$ x 13"

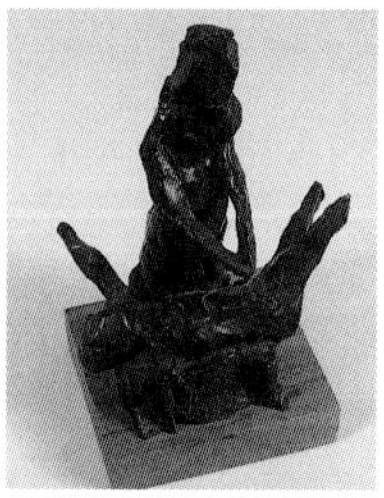

Sacrifice of Isaac I, 1980
Edition of 25
$7\frac{5}{8}$ x $6\frac{1}{2}$ x $\frac{1}{4}$"

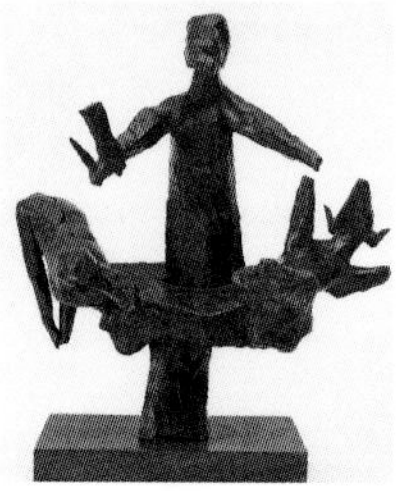

Sacrifice of Isaac II, 1980
Edition of 25
$11\frac{1}{8}$ x $10\frac{1}{2}$ x 8"

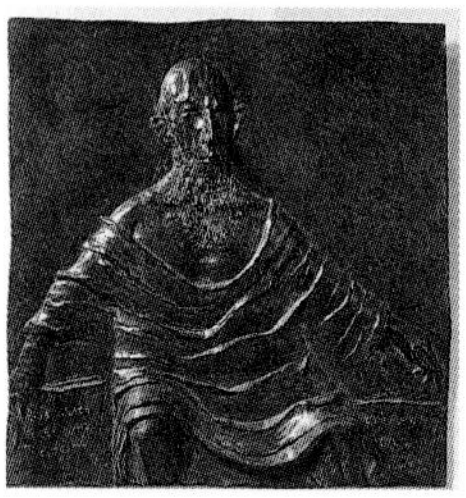

The Sage (relief), 1963
Edition of 8
$14\frac{3}{8}$ x 14 x 1"

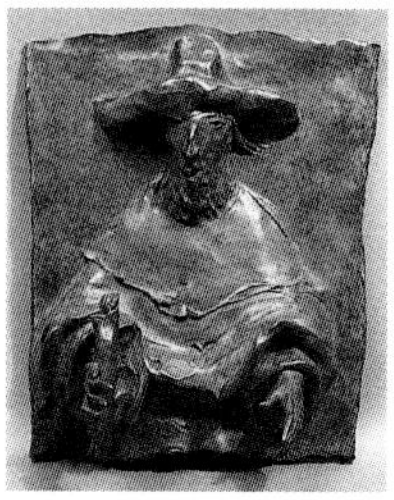

The Sage II (relief), 1967
Edition of 12
14 x 11 x $2\frac{3}{4}$"

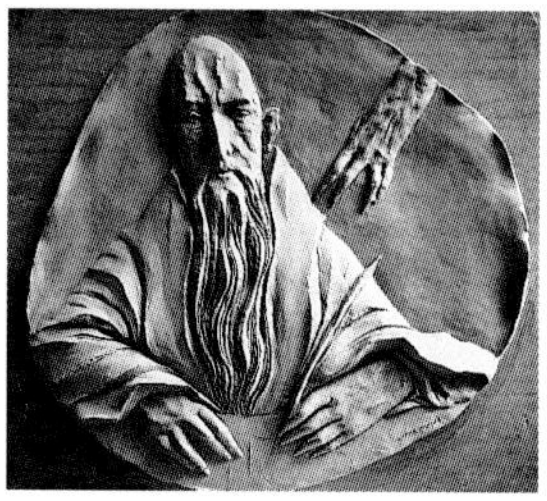

The Scribe (relief), 1965
Unique
11 x 12 x $2\frac{3}{4}$"

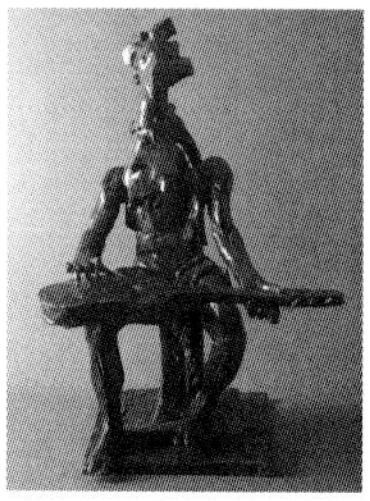

Seated Angel With Guitar, 1977-1978
Edition of 12
32 x 21 x 18"

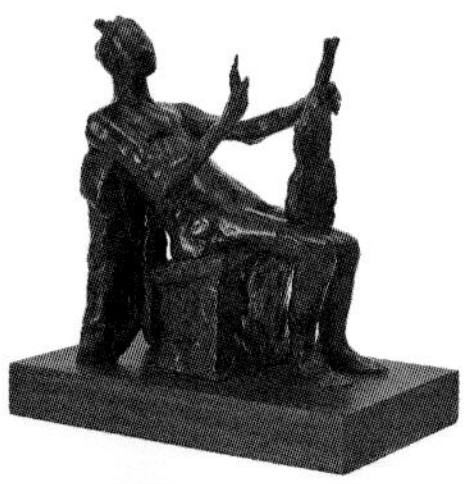

Seated Angel With Violin, 1978
Edition of 25
$7\frac{1}{2}$ x $3\frac{3}{4}$ x $6\frac{3}{8}$"

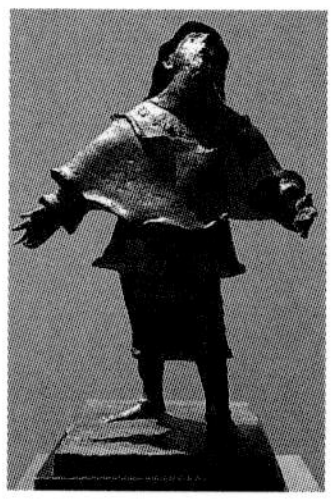

The Singer, 1963-1969
Edition of 12
$15\frac{1}{2}$ x 11 x $9\frac{1}{4}$"

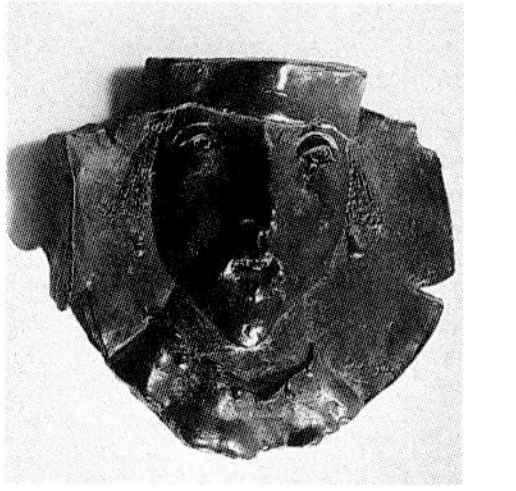

The Singer (relief), 1965
Edition of 25
4 x 4 x 1"

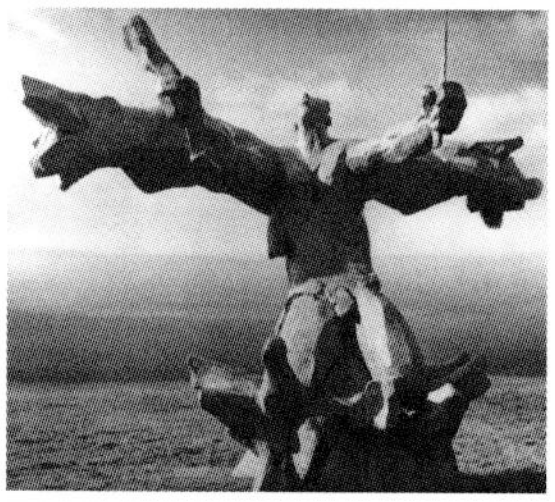

Spirit of Israel, 1986
Edition of 3
108 x 168 x 84"

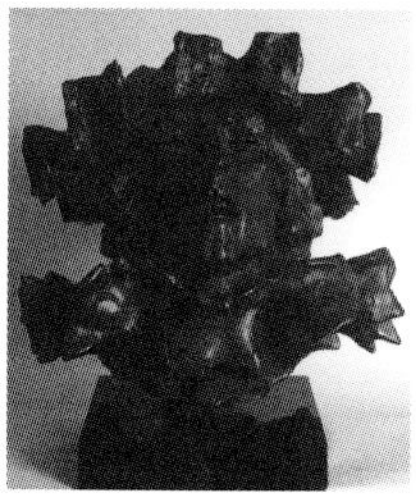

Spinoza, 1965-1969
Edition of 12
19 x $18\frac{1}{2}$ x 19"

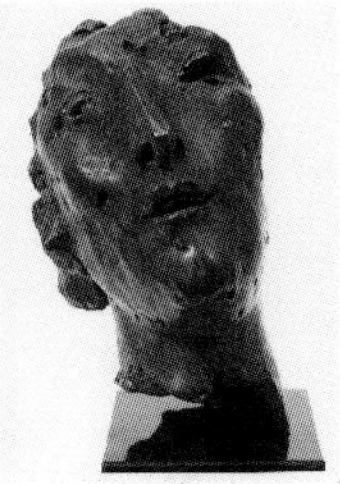

Student I, 1965-1969
Edition of 12
10 x 6 x 8 1/2"

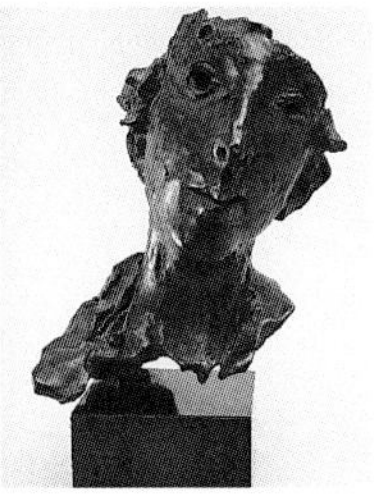

Student II, 1965-1969
Edition of 12
12 x 8 1/2 x 8 1/2"

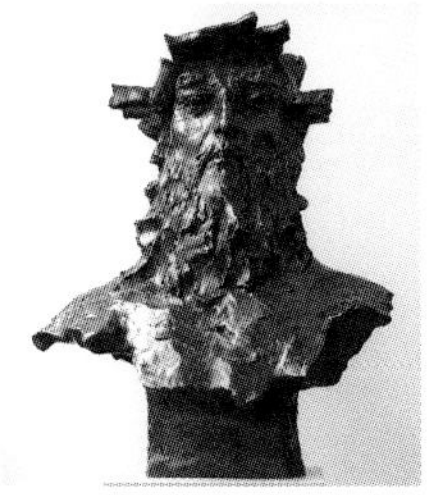

The Teacher, 1965-1969
Edition of 12
27 x 24 x 13 1/2"

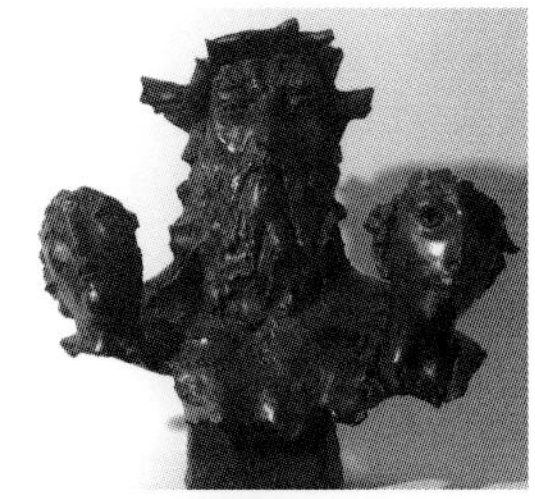

Teacher and Students, 1965-1969
Edition of 12
36 1/2 x 25 1/2 x 20 1/2"

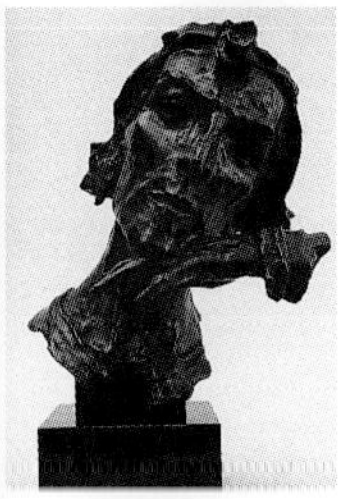

The Thinker, 1964-1968
Edition of 12
15 3/4 x 12 x 11 1/2"

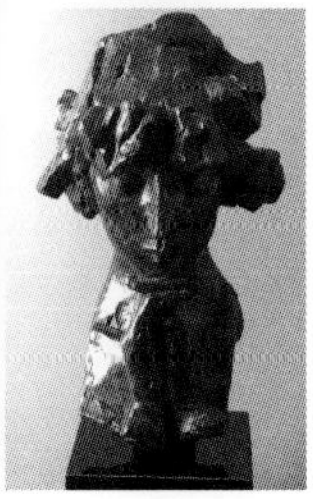

Thinker II, 1983
Edition of 15
17 x 7 x 17"

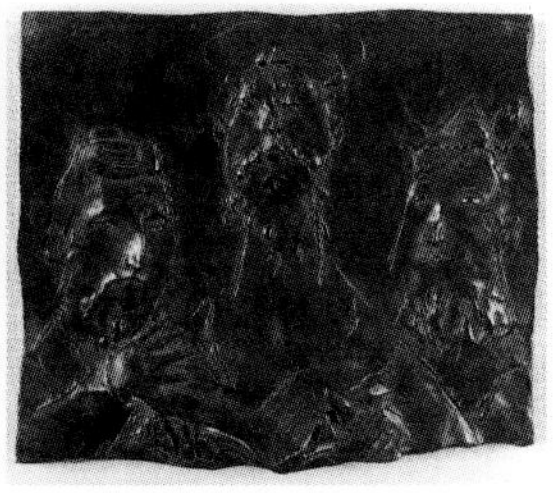

Three Scholars, (relief) 1983
Edition of 25
9 1/4 x 11 x 2 1/2"

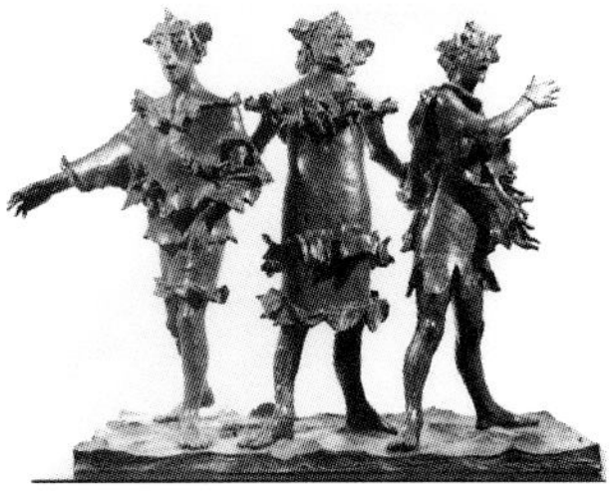

Three Singers, 1963-1969
Edition of 8
58 x 68 x 30"

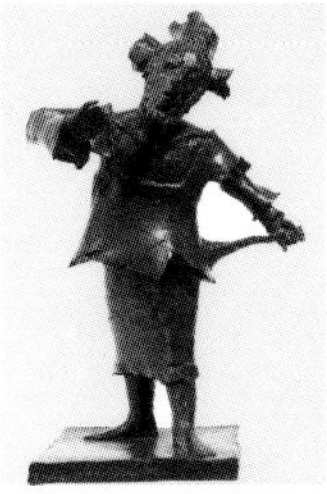

Troubadour, 1964
Edition of 12
21 1/2 x 13 x 11"

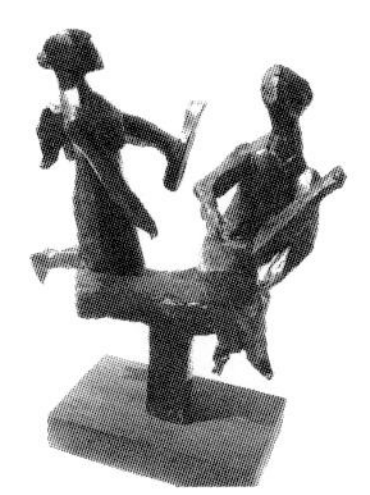

Two Musicians, 1980
Edition of 25
10 1/4 x 8 5/8 x 5 1/8"

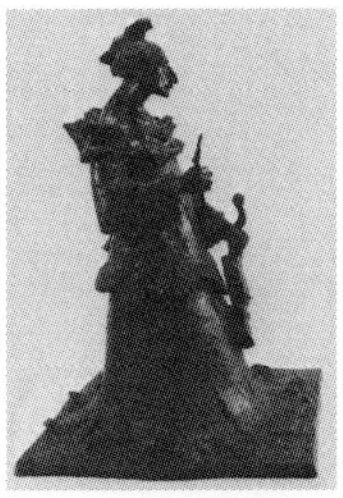

The Violist, 1973-1976
Edition of 12
44 x 19 1/4 x 17"

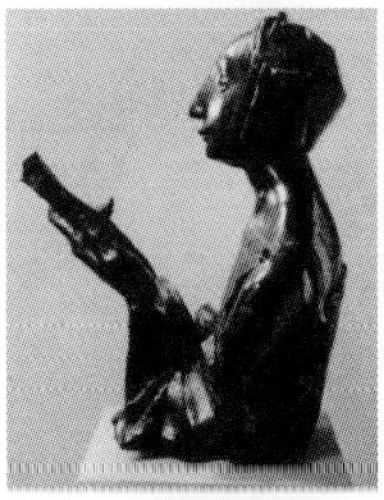

Violinist, 1987
Edition of 15
19 x 13 1/2 x 15"

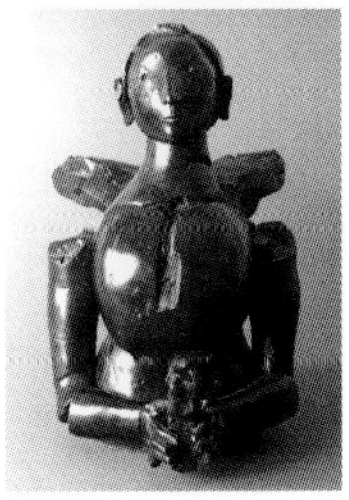

Violinist II, 19
Edition of 12
20 3/4 x 13 1/2 x 17"

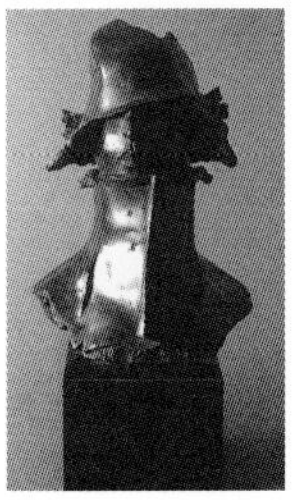

Warrior, 1989
Edition of 12
17 x 12 x 10 1/4"

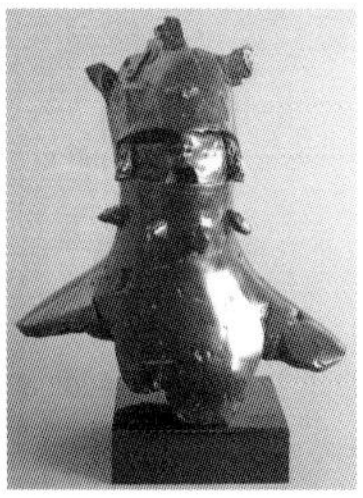

Warrior II, 1995
Edition of 12
30 x 24 x 20"

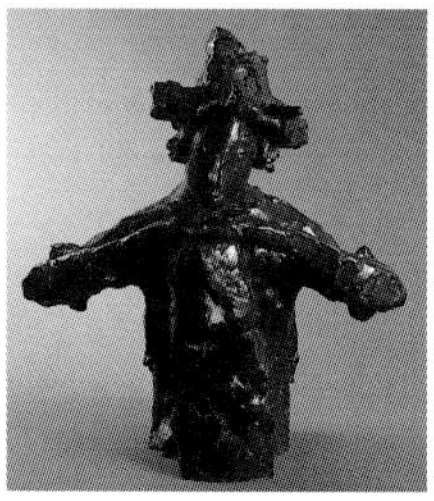

Young Man Contemplating Torah, 1988
Edition of 15
27 3/4 x 22 x 14"

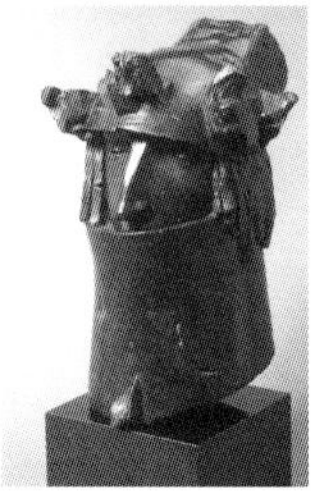

Warrior III, 1995
Edition of 12
14 x 9 x 10 3/4"

Not Pictured: *The Singer II*, 2002
Edition of 12
23 x 16 1/2 x 14 1/2"

MULTIPLES

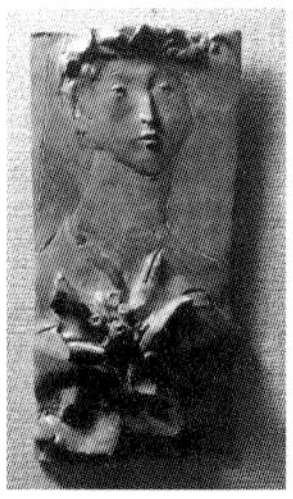

Boy with Flowers (relief), 1980
Edition of 100
9 3/4 x 4 3/4 x 1 1/2"

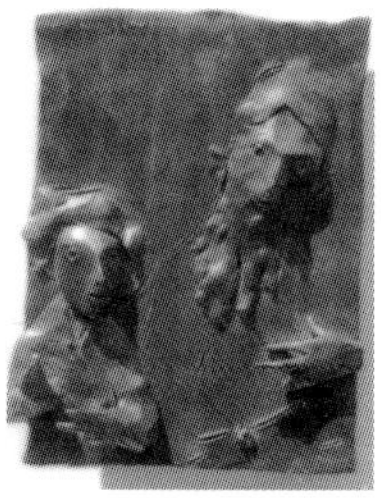

Generation to Generation (relief), 1980
Edition of 100
8 1/8 x 6 1/2 x 5 3/4"

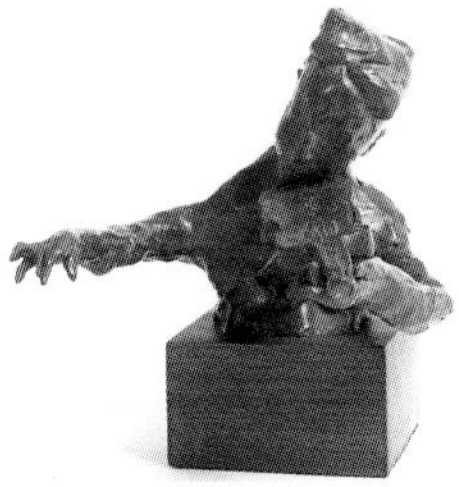

Boy with Violin, 1978
Edition of 250
6 x 6 3/4 x 7 1/2"

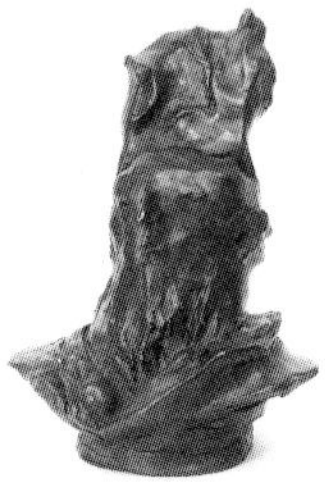

Isaiah, 1969
Edition of 250
7 1/4 x 6 x 5 1/4"

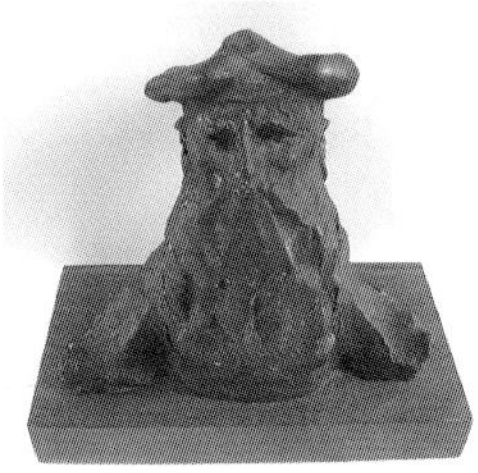

Daniel, 1974
Edition of 250
6 3/8 x 7 1/2 x 4"

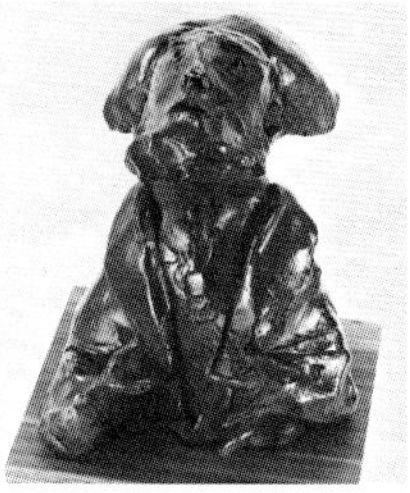

Job, 1969
Edition of 250
6 1/4 x 5 3/4 x 6"

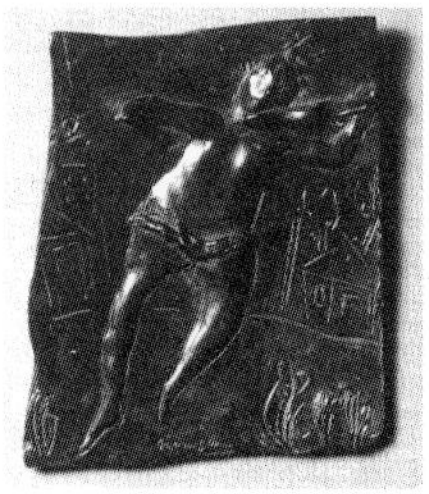

Flying Violinist (relief),1980
Edition of 100
5 1/2 x 4 5/8 x 5/8"

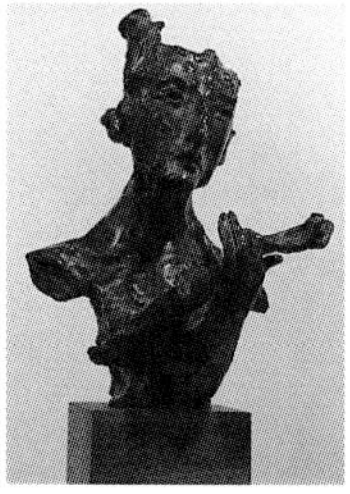

Man with Violin, 1969
Edition of 250
10 1/4 x 6 1/2 x 7 1/4"

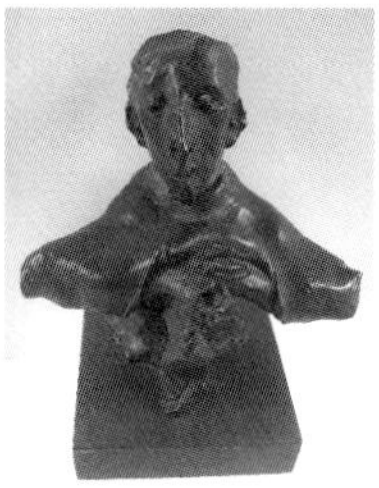

Man Praying, 1974
Edition of 250
$7 \times 7\frac{1}{2} \times 5\frac{1}{2}$"

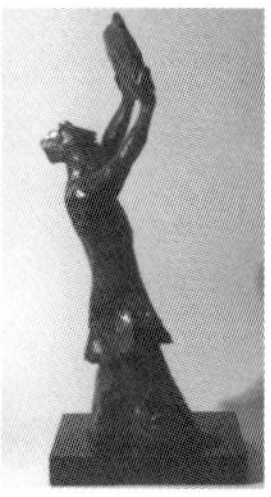

Moses, 1980
Edition of 100
$8\frac{1}{4} \times 2\frac{1}{2} \times 2\frac{3}{4}$"

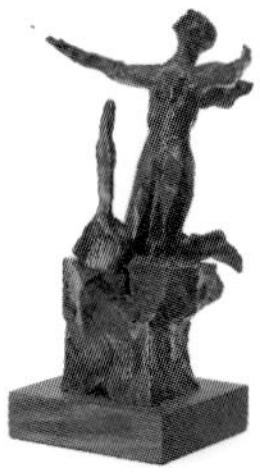

Praying Angel, 1978
Edition of 100
$9\frac{1}{2} \times 6\frac{3}{4} \times 5\frac{1}{4}$"

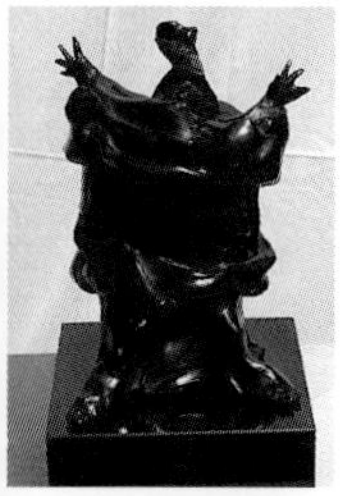

The Prophet, 1969
Edition of 250
$7 \times 5\frac{1}{4} \times 5\frac{1}{2}$"

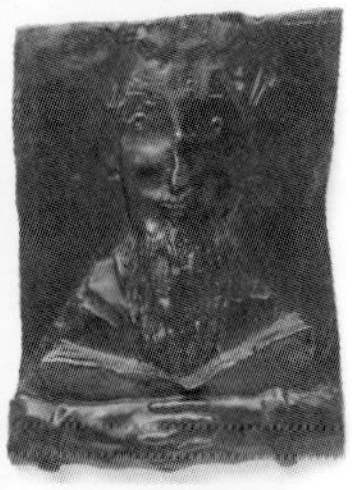

Scholar I (relief), 1977
Edition of 100
$7\frac{1}{2} \times 5\frac{3}{4} \times 1\frac{1}{4}$"

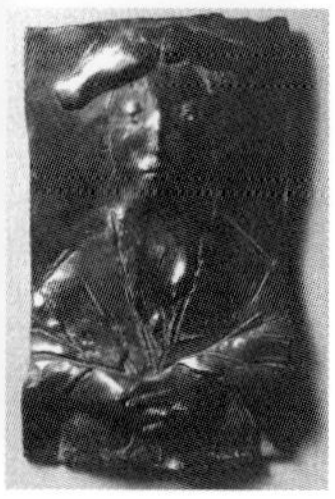

Scholar II (relief), 1978
Edition of 100
$9 \times 5\frac{3}{4} \times 1\frac{1}{2}$"

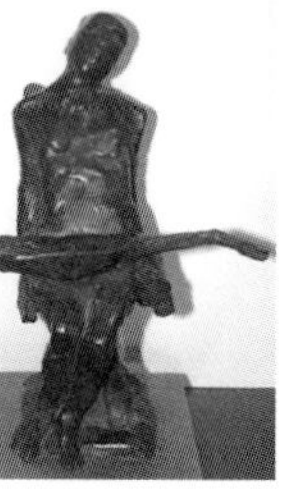

Sleeping Angel, 1978
Edition of 250
$9 \times 5\frac{3}{4} \times 5\frac{1}{4}$"

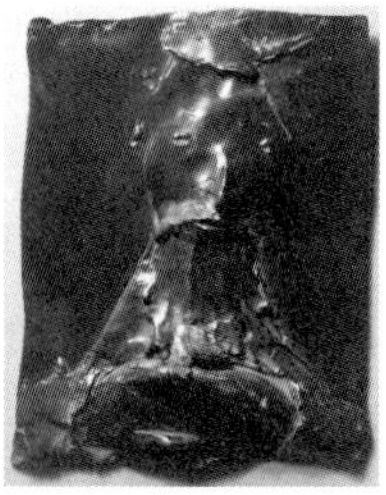

The Teacher (relief), 1977
Edition of 100
$8\frac{1}{2} \times 6\frac{1}{2} \times 1\frac{1}{2}$"

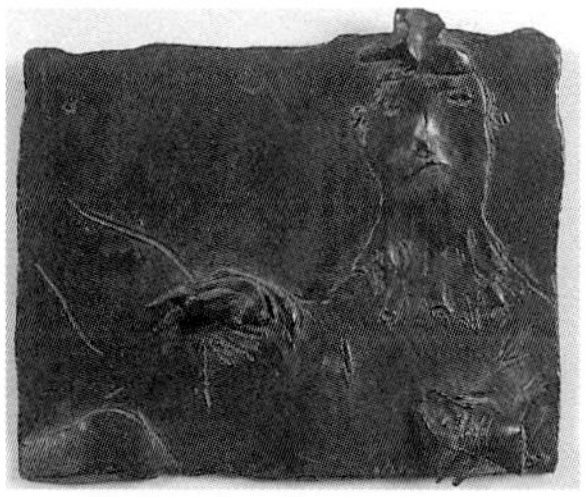

Teacher II (relief),1980
Edition of 100
$5\frac{3}{4} \times 6\frac{3}{4} \times 1\frac{1}{4}$"

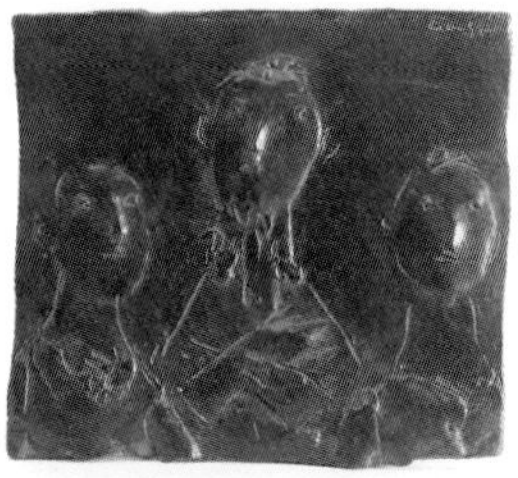

Teacher and Students (relief), 1980
Edition of 100
$6\frac{1}{4} \times 5\frac{1}{4} \times \frac{3}{8}$"

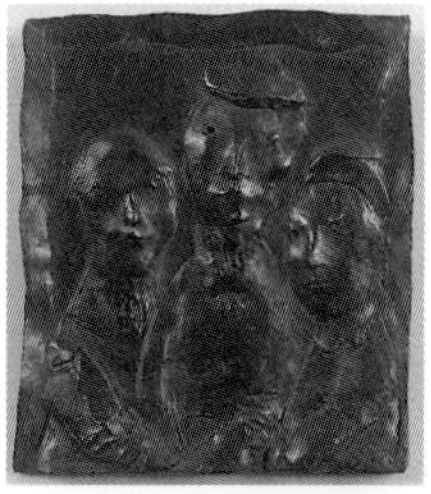

Three Judges (relief), 1980
Edition of 100
$4\frac{3}{4} \times 3\frac{7}{8} \times \frac{1}{4}$"

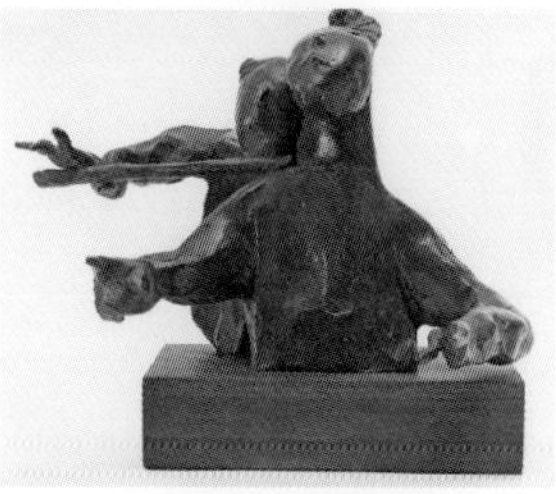

Two Musicians II, 1980
Edition of 100
$4\frac{3}{4} \times 6\frac{3}{4} \times 5\frac{3}{8}$"

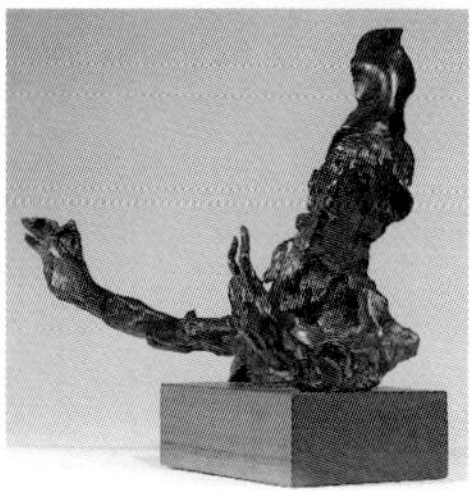

Virtuoso, 1969
Edition of 250
$10\frac{1}{4} \times 11\frac{1}{2} \times 8\frac{1}{2}$"

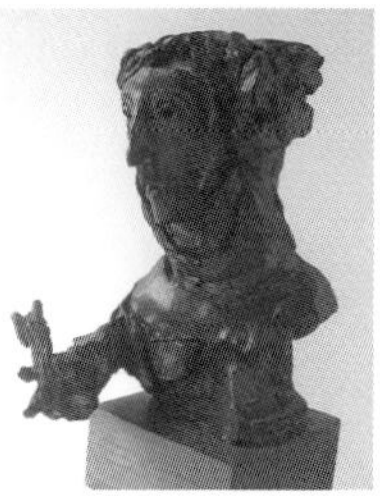

Woman with Violin, 1969
Edition of 250
$8\frac{3}{4} \times 7\frac{1}{4} \times 5\frac{1}{2}$"

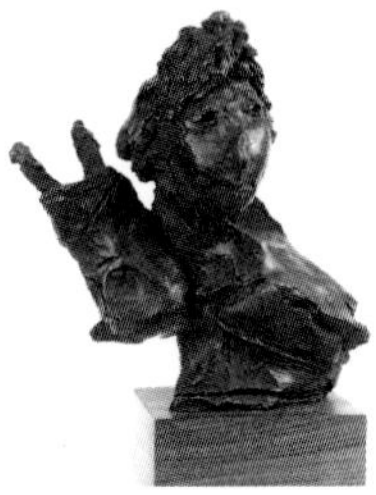

Young Man with Torah, 1969
Edition of 250
8 1/2 x 7 1/4 x 5 1/2"

Not Pictured: *Boy with Flute* (relief), 1978
Edition of 250
5 1/4 x 7 x 6 1/2"

Not Pictured: *Reclining Musician,* 1978
Edition of 250
8 3/8 x 9 3/4 x 9 3/4"

JUDAICA

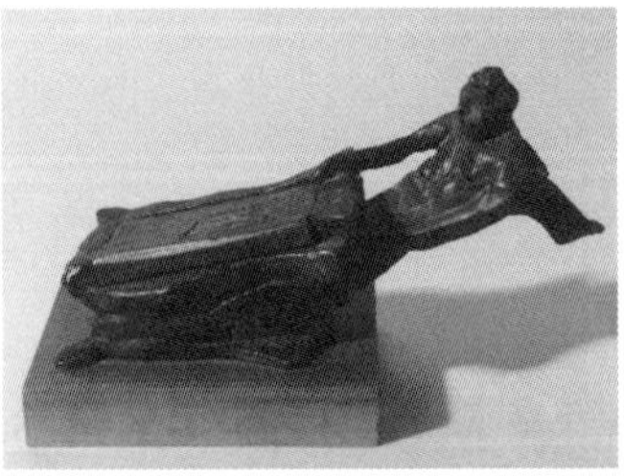

Mezzuzah with Angel, 1980
Edition of 100
8 1/2 x 4 1/2 x 4"

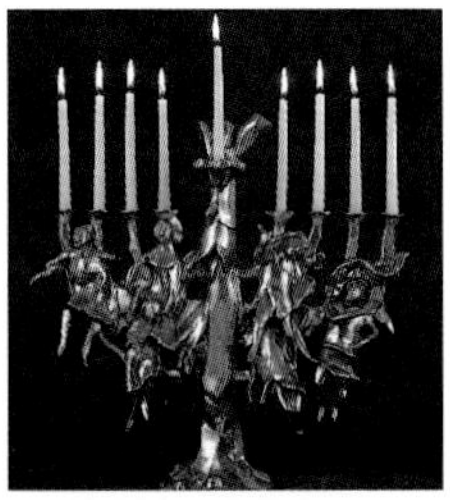

HANNUKKAH MENOROT
Angels of Light
Polished Bronze (edition of 200)
Patinated Bronze (edition of 200)
Gold Plate (edition of 200)
Silver Plate (edition of 200)
Sterling Plate (edition of 50)
17"

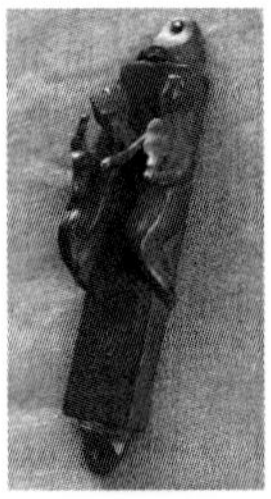

MEZZUZOT
Bronze (edition of 500)
Silver Plate (edition of 100)
Gold Plate (edition of 100)
Sterling Silver (edition of 100)
Gold (edition of 25)
6 1/4"

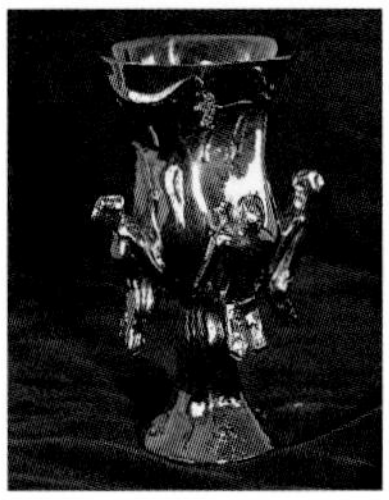

KIDDUSH CUP
Polished Bronze (edition of 250)
Silver Plate (edition of 250)
7"

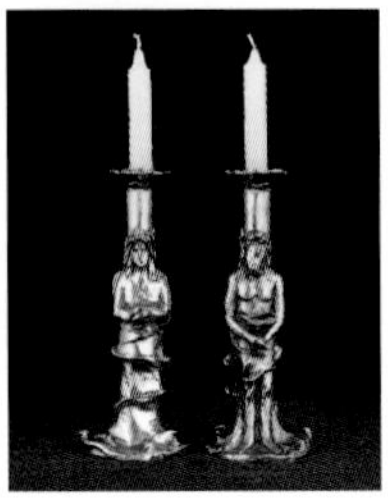

SHABBAT CANDLESTICKS
Polished Bronze (edition of 200)
Silver Plate (edition of 200)
9 1/4"

ARTIST BIOGRAPHY

BORN:

Shilova, Lithuania, October 28, 1923.

EDUCATION:

School of Boston Museum of Fine Arts,
Hebrew Teachers College.

TEACHING:

School of Boston Museum of Fine Arts, 1942-1955
Boston University College of Fine Arts
Associate Professor of Art, 1955-1962
Professor of Art, 1962-1989
Professor Emeritus, 1989-present

AWARDS:

First Judges' Prize, Institute of Contemporary Art, Boston, 1944.
First Popular Prize, Institute of Contemporary Art, Boston, 1944.
Choice of Friends of Art Institute of Chicago, 1946.
Purchase Prize, Virginia Museum of Finc Arts, 1946.
Traveling Fellowship, School of the Museum of Fine Arts, Boston, 1946.
Grand Prize, First Annual Boston Arts F estival, 1952.
Second Prize, Second Annual Boston Arts Festival, 1953.
Grand Prize, Third Annual Boston Arts Festival, 1954.
First Prize, Tupperware Annual Art Fund Award, 1954.
Grant in Art, National Society of Arts and Letters, 1958.
John Simon Guggenheim Fellowship, 1960.
Purchase Prize, National Society of Arts and Letters, 1961, 1962, 1963.
Gold Medal, Art's Directors' Club Philadelphia, 1963.
Adolph & Clara Obrig Prize, National Academy of Design, 1967.
Purchase Prize, Pennsylvania Academy of Fine Arts, 1967.
Samuel F.B. Morse Gold Medal, National Academy of Design, NY, 1973.
Isaac N. Maynard Prize for Painting, National Acad. of Design, NY, 1975.
Purchase Prize in Drawing, Albrecht Art Museum, St.Joseph, MO, 1976.
Joseph Isador Gold Medal for Painting, National Academy of Design,1976.
Purchase Prize, National Academy of Design, Henry Ward Ranger Fund, New York, 1976.
Certificate of Merit, National Academy of Design, 1990.

RETROSPECTIVE EXHIBITIONS:

Rose Art Museum, Brandeis University, Waltham, MA, 1979.
Jewish Museum, New York together with The National Academy of Design, New York, NY, 1979.
American Museum of Jewish History, Philadelphia, PA, 1979.
Mickelson Gallery, Washington, DC, 1985.
Boston University Art Gallery, Boston, MA, 2005.

SOLO EXHIBITIONS:

Niveau Gallery, New York, 1945, 1956.
Museum of Modern Art, New York, 1946.
Boris Mirski Gallery, Boston, 1951, 1959, 1969.
The Downtown Gallery, New York, 1953.
Nordness Gallery, New York, 1960, 1963, 1969.

Rex Evans Gallery, Los Angeles, 1961.
Westhampton Gallery, New York, 1961.
Hunter Gallery, Chattanooga, 1965.
Zora Gallery, Los Angeles, 1965.
Kovler Gallery, Chicago, 1966.
J. Thomas Gallery, Provincetown, 1964.
Verle Gallery, West Hartford, 1967.
Bernard Danenberg Galleries, New York, 1969, 1972.
Towne Gallery, Lenox, MA, 1982.
SaidyE Bronfman Art Center, Montreal, 1982.
Pucker Gallery, Boston, 1976, 1978, 1984, 1986, 1990, 1994, 1999, 2005.
Louis Newman Galleries, Beverly Hills, 1977, 1982, 1984, 1986, 1989, 1992.
Horwitah Newman Gallery, Scottsdale, 1996.
Alter Gil Gallery, Beverly Hills, 1999.
Galerie Yoram Gil, Beverly Hills, 2004.

OTHER EXHIBITIONS: [PARTIAL]

Art Institute of Chicago, IL
Bridgestone Gallery, Tokyo, Japan
Charlotteborg, Copenhagen, Denmark
Congresse Halle, Berlin, Germany
Institute of Contemporary Art, Boston, MA
Metropolitan Museum of Art, New York, NY
Museum of Fine Arts, Boston, MA
Museum of Modern Art, Paris, France
New York World's Fair, 1965
Palais des Beaux Arts, Brussels, Belgium
Palazzo Venezia, Rome, Italy
Royal Academy of Art, London, England
University of Illinois, Champaign, IL
Virginia Museum of Fine Arts, Richmond, VA
Whitney Museum of American Art, New York, NY

PUBLIC COLLECTIONS:

Albrecht University Museum of Art, St. Joseph, MO
Art Institute of Chicago, IL
Atlanta Art Association, Atlanta University, Atlanta, GA
Bezalel National Museum, Jerusalem, Israel
Boston College, Chestnut Hill, MA
Boston University, Boston, MA
Brandeis University, Waltham, MA
Bryn Mawr College, Bryn Mawr, PA
Chico State College, Chico, CA
Colby College, Waterville, ME
Container Corporation of America, St. Louis, MO
Corcoran Gallery of Art, Washington, DC
Cornell University, Herbert F. Johnson Museum of Art, Ithaca, NY
Danforth Museum of Art, Framingham, MA
David and Alfred Smart Museum, Chicago, IL
DeCordova Museum, Lincoln, MA
Fine Arts Center, Cheekville, TN
Hebrew College, Newton, MA
Hunter Art Gallery, Chattanooga, TN
The Jewish Museum, New York, NY
The Johnson Foundation, Racine, WI
Krannert Art Museum, University of Illinois, Champaign, IL
Milwaukee Art Institute, Milwaukee, WI
Munson Williams Proctor Institute, Utica, NY
Museo Sefardi, Toledo, Spain
Museum of Fine Arts, Boston, MA
Museum of Modern Art, New York, NY
Pennsylvania State University Museum of Art, Altoona, PA
Pennsylvania Academy of Fine Arts, Philadelphia, PA
Portland Art Museum, Portland, ME
Skirball Museum, Los Angeles, CA
Smithsonian Institution, Washington, DC
Stone Foundation, Newton, MA
Syracuse University, Syracuse, NY
Temple Beth El, Hartford, CT
Temple Beth Elohim, Wellesley, MA
Temple Emanuel, Dallas, TX
Temple Israel, Brookline, MA
Tupper Museum, Orlando, FL
University of Judaism, Los Angeles, CA
University of Michigan, Ann Arbor, MI
University of Nebraska, Lincoln, NE
University of New Hampshire, Durham, NH
Virginia Museum of Fine Arts, Richmond, VA
Whitney Museum of American Art, New York, NY
William Lane Foundation, Leominster, MA
Witherspoon Art Gallery, University of North Carolina, Chapel Hill, NC
Worcester Art Museum, Worcester, MA

SELECTED BIBLIOGRAPHY

1945–2004

BOOKS AND EXHIBITION CATALOGUES

Adlow, Dorothy, "Introduction," *17 Jewish Artists in Boston* (Exhibition catalogue), Boston: Boston Young Men's Hebrew Association, 1945.

Adlow, Dorothy, "David Aronson," *David Aronson* (Exhibition catalogue) New York: Niveau Gallery, 1945.

Miller, Dorothy (ed.), *Fourteen Americans,* New York: The Museum of Modern Art, 1946. Reprint as *Americans 1942-1963: Six Group Exhibitions,* New York: Museum of Modern Art, 1972.

1946 Brittanica Book of the Year (Encyclopedia Brittanica, Supplement), Chicago: Encyclopedia Britannica, Inc., 1946, p. 533.

Genauer, Emily, *Best of Art,* Garden City, NY: Doubleday, 1948.

Pratt, Frances and **Fizell, Becca**, *Encaustic. Methods and Materials,* New York: Lear, 1949.

Baur, John, *Revolution and Tradition in Modern Art,* Cambridge, Mass.: Harvard University Press, 1951.

Pearson, Ralph, *Modern Renaissance in American Art,* New York: Harper & Row, 1954.

Puma, Fernando (ed.), *Seven Arts,* Garden City, NY: Permabooks, 1954.

Barr, Alfred H., Jr. (ed.), *Masters of Modern Art,* New York: The Museum of Modern Art, 1955.

Nordness, Lee and **Waller, Allen**, *Art: U.S.A. Now,* Lucerne: C. J. Bucher, 1962.

Taubes, Frederic, *Abracadabra in Modern Art,* New York: Dodd, Mead & Co., 1963.

Taubes, Frederic, *A Guide to Traditional and Modern Painting Methods,* New York: Viking Press, 1963.

Taubes, Frederic, *A Painter's History and Critique of Modern Art,* New York: Dodd, Mead & Co., 1963.

Aronson, David, *Real and Unreal: The Double Nature of Art* (University Lecture, Boston University, 1967), Boston: Boston University Press, 1967. Reprint, Boston: Pucker/Safrai Gallery, n.d.

Newman, Thelma, *Wax as Art Form,* Brunswick: Yoseloff, 1967.

Grossman, Emery, *Art and Tradition,* New York, Brunswick, London: Thomas Yoseloff, 1967.

Ablow, Joseph, [Introduction], *David Aronson: Sculpture* (Exhibition catalogue), New York and Boston: Lee Nordness and Boris Mirski Galleries, 1969, pp. 2-6.

Werner, Alfred, "Perception of the Beautiful," David Aronson. Sculpture (Exhibition catalogue), New York: Bernard Danenberg Galleries, 1969.

Cohen, George, *A History of American Art,* New York: Dell, 1971.

Taylor, Robert, "Foreword," *David Aronson. Recent Paintings* (Exhibition catalogue), New York: Bernard Danenberg Galleries, 1972.

Nagano, Paul T., "The Expressionism of David Aronson," *Aronson* (Exhibition catalogue), Boston: Pucker Safrai Gallery, 1976.

"Of Men, Music, Horses, and Angels," *Aronson* (Exhibition Catalogue), Boston: Pucker/Safrai Gallery, 1978.

Ablow, Joseph, "The Art of David Aronson," *David Aronson: A Retrospective* (Exhibition Catalogue), Waltham and New York: Rose Art Museum and The Jewish Museum, 1979, pp. 4-6.

Wolff, Theodore F., "The Persistence of the Expressionist Mode," *Expressionism in Boston: 1945-1985* (Exhibition catalogue), Lincoln, MA.: DeCordova Museum, 1986.

Tarlow, Lois, "An Interview with David Aronson, Reed Kay, and Sidney Hurwitz," S. Tatiana Spinari, *Jack Kramer: A Retrospective,* Boston: Boston University Art Gallery, 1988.

Fletcher, Pamela F., [Introduction], *Figures: Recent Paintings* (Exhibition catalogue), Boston: Pucker Gallery, 1994.

Bookbinder, Judith A., "Figurative Expressionism in Boston and its Germanic Cultural Affinities: An Alternative Modernist Discourse on Art and Identity," vols. I & II, Diss., Boston University, 1998.

Bookbinder, Judith, "David Aronson: The Artist as Warrior," *David Aronson: The Artist as Warrior* (Exhibition catalogue), Boston: Pucker Gallery, 2000.

Hitchings, Sinclair and **Mayer, Stephanie** (eds.), *The Visionary Decade: New Voices in Art in 1940s Boston* (Exhibition catalogue), Boston: Boston University Art Gallery, 2002.

Lafo, Rachel Rosenfield, Capasso, Nicholas, and **Uhrhane, Jennifer** (eds.), *Painting in Boston: 1950-2000* (Exhibition Catalogue), Lincoln and Amherst, Mass.: DeCordova Museum and University of Massachusetts Press, 2002.

PERIODICALS AND REVIEWS

Dame, Lawrence, "IMA Members' Show," *Boston Herald* (September 1944).

Carmichael, Gregory, "The Easel: Art in America--No. 1, Boston," *Tricolor,* vol. 3 (July-August 1945), pp. 52-59.

"Niveau Gallery Opening," *New York World Telegram* (November 17, 1945).

"New Testament Teacher," *Newsweek,* vol. XXVI (November 26, 1945), p. 114.

"Fifteen on a Limb," *Newsweek,* vol. XXVIII (September 23, 1946), pp. 96, 99.

"Coronation: Old and New," *Newsweek,* vol. XXVIII (September 30, 1946), pp. 6-7.

Driscoll, Edgar J. Jr., "Boston Museum Teacher Repeater for $ 500 Prize," *Boston Globe,* June 7, 1954.

"Culture Outdoors," *Newsweek,* vol. XLIII (June 28, 1954), p. 52.

Adlow, Dorothy, "Solo Exhibition by David Aronson," *The Christian Science Monitor,* September 28, 1959.

Adlow, Dorothy, "Aronson's Authentic Talent," *The Christian Science Monitor,* October 24, 1960.

Aronson, David, "Encaustic," *The Artist,* vol. 64 (December 1962), p. 78.

Time, vol. LXXXI (May 24, 1963), p. 74.

"Modern Testament of David Aronson," *Time,* vol. 82, no. 21 (November 22, 1963), pp. 72-73.

Audience, Pilot Issue, Spring 1968.

Taylor, Robert, "A Master reflects on the State of Art," *Boston Sunday Globe,* June 13, 1976.

Kur, Carol, "David Aronson's Art," *Moment,* vol. 4 (November 1978), pp. 25-37.

Taylor, Robert, "Aronson's Works at Brandeis," *Boston Sunday Globe,* February 11, 1979 (also idem, "David Aronson, a Retrospective at Rose Art

Museum, Brandeis," A.R.T. [February 11, 1979]).

Glueck, Grace, "Museum Drops 19 Aronson Paintings From Show Over Christian Themes," *New York Times,* May 25, 1979, p. C7.

"Exhibitors," *New York Times,* June 1, 1979.

Temin, Christine, "Perspectives," *Boston Globe,* October 23, 1986, p. 93.

D'Angelo, Gail, "The Fine Art of David Aronson," *Bostonia,* Spring 1992, pp. 44-47.

ARCHIVES

David Aronson Papers. Archives of American Art, Smithsonian Institution, Washington, D.C.

INDEX OF WORKS

INDEX OF NAMES

AFTERWARD

Just to be is a blessing.
Just to live is holy and yet being alive is no answer to the problems of living.
To be or not to be is not the question.
The vital question is: how to be and how not to be.

– ABRAHAM JOSHUA HESCHEL

FOR NEARLY THREE DECADES WE HAVE been privileged to share the art of David Aronson. Even before we were presenting his work in our Gallery, we admired it at Boris Mirski's Gallery.

We belived then and now that his art ranks among the most important figurative, humanist work of our era. The search for the meaning of life, the need to ask crucial questions whose answers can lead to a better universe, fill the 60-year journey of David Aronson.

His mastery of drawing, paintings and sculpture has allowed him to probe the meaning of life in our day with aesthetic energy and uniqueness. Art historical movements have nourished his artistic journey and his unique personal vision has enriched his creations.

As our society continues to struggle for a more humane and inclusive path, David Aronson's work calls out to each of us and our spirits to remain true to ourselves and to our responsibilities to all humankind. The work challenges and stimulates our moral direction while enriching our aesthetic hunger.

It is our hope that this monograph will serve to bring the reader into the complex world of David Aronson and his art. We could not have realized this dream without the superb essay by Asher Biemann. His remarkable discussion of the art of David Aronson has provided the necessary structure for the book. The centered, bright presence of Jeanne Koles as editor has provided a stable focus on the work. Ken Gray appeared at the right moment to help retrieve images from ancient slides and photographs.

The artist was crucial to the selection and organization of the book. His wife Georgianna and son, Ben, have been strong advocates for this publication.

In so many ways, the appearance of this volume is a blessing. We hope that the art of David Aronson, its power and magic will enable all who read and view it to be!

— *Bernard H. Pucker*